"Restaurant patrons looking for quality dining have Zagat to guide their cuisine needs. For the recruitment industry, the name is Weddle ... Peter Weddle that is."

American Staffing Association

Praise for Peter Weddle's Books & Guides

WEDDLE's Guide to Employment Sites on the Internet

"Restaurant patrons looking for quality dining have Zagat to guide their cuisine needs. For the recruitment industry, the name is Weddle … Peter Weddle that is."
—American Staffing Association

"I've known Peter Weddle for years. He is an immensely likeable guy. He is also extremely knowledgeable. Highly recommended!"
—Richard Nelson Bolles, *What Color is Your Parachute?*

"A wealth of updated and useful information."
—*Library Journal*

"WEDDLE's is a very useful tool that recruiters and HR professionals will find helpful."
—*Fortune Magazine*

"When in doubt, consider WEDDLE's … an industry standard."
—HR WIRE

"If you're looking for an objective guide to employment Web-sites, ExecuNet recommends WEDDLE's Guide."
—ExecuNet Center for Executive Careers

A Multitude of Hope: A Novel About Rediscovering the American Dream

"… engaging and thoughtful."
—Joyce Lain Kennedy, Syndicated Career Columnist

"… a provocative take on the job search … holds a lot of weight."
—Rathin Sinha, CEO America's Job Exchange

"… one of the bravest books I've read in a long time. Its depiction of today's unforgiving, anxiety-inducing world of work is accurate and honest."
—Christine Ramsey, President Boxwood Technology

"As a long-time consultant working with individuals exploring career opportunities, I highly recommend this book. ... by bringing the Horatio Alger story up-to-date, *A Multitude of Hope* lives up to its name."
—Joan Learn, Regional Manager The Ayers Group

"I am an author of a research guide for older Americans as well as founder of RetiredBrains.com, a website that includes information on finding employment and *A Multitude of Hope* is one of the best reads for Boomers who are seeking a job or interested in getting the inside story on what some very smart people have done and are doing with their lives."
—Art Koff, CEO RetiredBrains.com

Work Strong: Your Personal Career Fitness System

"Peter Weddle's *Career Fitness System* empowers you to take your job search to the next level and achieve lasting career success."
—Diana Miller, CEO Community Job Club

"There are few people in the world who are as passionate about our careers and our own unique talents as Peter Weddle. *Work Strong* changes the paradigms of career management books and is sure to give you a new perspective on how to Work Strong in your own career."
—Aaron Matos, CEO Jobing

"This book is a guide to finding yourself and to charting a new course for a 21st Century career. A must read!"
—Kevin Wheeler, CEO Global Learning Resources, Inc.

"A lifetime of career happiness in a single book!"
—Dan Honig, COO DiversityJobs.com

"In today's world, it's not enough to work hard. You also have to work strong and perform at your peak. That's the power and promise of this book."
—John Bell, CEO Boxwood Technology

Generalship: HR Leadership in a Time of War

"… a wake-up call for those of us in HR. We need to take on the accountability for effecting change. … This book provides a great strategy for doing just that."

—Regina DeTore, VP/HR Sepracor, Inc.

"… a must-read book for human resource professionals, especially those who seek to be true leaders in their corporation."

—Jerome N. Carter, SVP/HR International Paper

"Human Resources is now facing extra-ordinary challenges. This demanding time requires the kind of bold, thoughtful and thorough leadership suggested by this book."

—Guy Patton, EVP/HR Fidelity Investments

"Don't miss this book. It's Machiavelli's The Prince and Covey's 7 Habits of Highly Effective People all rolled into one for the HR profession."

—Donna Introcaso, VP/HR iVillage

"This book is a must-read on HR leadership, not only for HR practitioners, but for every CEO and Company Director, as well."

—Robert S. Nadel, President Nadel Consulting

Recognizing Richard Rabbit: A Fable About Being True to Yourself

"A magical way to explore the essence of you."

—Jennifer Floren, CEO Experience

"… a very intriguing and unique book."

—Patrick Erwin, The Work Buzz CareerBuilder.com

"… if you're thinking about making changes in your personal life or want a pep talk about being true to yourself, check out this book."

—Celeste Blackburn, Managing Editor, Resources for Humans

"The story inspires useful reflection and a practical rethinking of your own personal effectiveness in work and life."

—Jonathan Goodman, Review on Social Median

Career Fitness: How to Find, Win & Keep the Job You Want in the 1990s

"This book is phenomenal! It'll help you run the race of your life at work each day."

—Harvey McKay, *Swim With the Sharks Without Being Eaten Alive*

"… street-smart wisdom, coupled with practical career workout tools … sure to be useful to people at any point in their career."

—Madelyn Jennings, SVP/HR Gannett Company, Inc.

Also by Peter Weddle

The Career Fitness Workbook: How to Find, Win & Hang Onto the Job of Your Dreams

A Multitude of Hope: A Novel About Rediscovering the American Dream

The Success Matrix: Wisdom from the Web on How to Get Hired & Not Be Fired

Job Nation: The 100 Best Employment Sites on the Web

The Career Activist Republic

Work Strong: Your Personal Career Fitness System

Recognizing Richard Rabbit: A Fable About Being True to Yourself

The All Pro Career Pocket Planner: The Career Fitness Regimen

Generalship: HR Leadership in a Time of War

Career Fitness: How to Find, Win & Keep the Job You Want in the 1990's

Postcards from Space: Being the Best in Online Recruitment & HR Management (2001, 2005)

WEDDLE's Guide to Association Web Sites

WEDDLE'S Guide to Staffing Firms & Employment Agencies

WEDDLE's Directory of Employment-Related Internet Sites

Internet Resumes: Take the Net to Your Next Job

CliffsNotes: Finding a Job on the Web, Writing a Great Resume

WEDDLE's WIZNotes: Fast Facts Series on Job Boards

'Tis of Thee: A Son's Search for the Meaning of Patriotism

WEDDLE's

Guide

to

Employment Sites
on the Internet

Full page site profiles of
The Top 100

PLUS
A directory of 9,000+ sites for
The Best & the Rest

ISBN: 978-1-928734-80-2

The information that appears in this Guide was obtained directly from the Web-sites themselves. Most of the data provided in the Consumer Profiles were collected in late 2012 and early 2013. The Internet changes quickly, however, and we work continuously to keep our information current. If you find a discrepancy in a site's profile, please notify WEDDLE's by telephone at 203.964.1888 or on the Internet at corporate@weddles.com.

Special thanks to the WEDDLE's research and production team and to our friends at Adicio, Boxwood, JobTarget and VetJobs for their contribution to The Best & the Rest section of the book.

Special discounts on bulk quantities of WEDDLE's books are available for libraries, corporations, professional associations and other organizations. For details, please contact WEDDLE's at 203.964.1888.

The Guide is also available as an e-book through Amazon.com.

WEDDLE's
www.weddles.com
2052 Shippan Avenue
Stamford, CT 06902

Where People Matter Most.

Contents

Welcome to
WEDDLE's Guide!

Welcome to *WEDDLE's Guide to Employment Sites on the Internet*, the gold standard of consumer guides for job boards, social media sites, aggregators, career portals, employment-related search engines, job ad distribution companies, job search and recruitment blogs and other resources for employment success. This edition—our eleventh—has been completely updated to deliver the information you need to survive and prosper in the fast-paced world of work of the 21st Century.

Today's job market is a challenging environment for individuals and organizations alike. Job seekers are finding it extraordinarily difficult to find a new or better job. And, employers are struggling to find individuals with the talent they need to achieve their mission.

While there is no single solution to this problem, the Internet is an especially powerful resource that can assist both job seekers and employers. With over 100,000 job boards, social media sites and career portals now operating online, however, it's easy to waste your time on the wrong sites and overlook the right ones—the ones that will help you succeed.

That's why our *WEDDLE's Guide* has been specifically designed as a "consumer's aide." It is composed of two primary sections, each of which offers a one-of-a-kind reference for you to use.

- **The first section of the book—The Top 100—features our picks for the best job boards, social media sites and career portals on the Web.** This listing enables you to find the best sites quickly. Rather than lurching through thousands of search engine results, you can now "shop smart" and identify the right employment sites for you right away.

- **The second section of the book—The Best & the Rest— is the single most comprehensive listing of employment sites anywhere.** It enables you to conduct your own research and do so with precision. Instead of relying on the hit or miss experiences of friends and coworkers, you can explore the full range of sites that are likely to be helpful to you.

Taken together, these two sections provide you with the most complete reference to the Web's employment resources in print, e-book, online or any other medium. It continues WEDDLE's tradition of publishing timely, accurate and useful information that will help you achieve the success you deserve on the Internet.

We hope you put the Guide to work for you and will tell others about it.

Peter Weddle
Stamford, Connecticut

What is WEDDLE's?

WEDDLE's is a research, publishing and consulting firm specializing in organizational sourcing and recruiting and individual job search and career self-management.

▶ Since 1996, WEDDLE's has conducted groundbreaking surveys of:

- recruiters and job seekers,

  and

- Web-sites providing employment-related services.

Our research and findings have been cited in such publications as *The Wall Street Journal, The New York Times*, and in *Money, Fortune*, and *Inc.* magazines.

In addition, we have conducted employment-related research for commercial enterprises, global corporations and professional societies and trade associations on topics ranging from market, product and service evaluation to strategy formulation and brand positioning.

▶ WEDDLE's also publishes guides and other books that provide information and best practices for employers, staffing firms, job seekers, career activists, career counselors and coaches, reference librarians and academicians.

For a complete listing of WEDDLE's publications, please visit Weddles.com. WEDDLE's books are available on Amazon.com and in the secure bookstore on the WEDDLE's site.

▶ WEDDLE's also provides consultation to organizations in the areas of:

- Designing and operating corporate recruitment Web-sites and job boards,

- Optimizing the candidate experience

  and

- Talent acquisition and management.

Who is Peter Weddle?

Peter Weddle is a former recruiter and business CEO turned author and speaker. He is the author or editor of over two dozen books and has been a columnist for *The Wall Street Journal, National Business Employment Weekly* and CNN.com.

Weddle has been cited in *The New York Times, The Washington Post, The Boston Globe, U.S. News & World Report, The Wall Street Journal, USA Today* and numerous other publications and has spoken to trade and professional associations and corporate meetings all over the world.

WEDDLE's Guides are widely recognized for their accuracy and usefulness, leading the American Staffing Association to call Weddle the "Zagat" of employment sites on the Internet.

How Does WEDDLE's Guide Work for You?

As always, this Guide is a reference book that serves three important communities:

- **Those looking for talent**, including Employment Managers, in-house corporate recruiters and Human Resource practitioners, executive recruiters, staffing firm and agency recruiters, contract recruiters, and independent and consulting recruiters. If that's your job, this Guide will help you find and select the right job boards, social media sites and career portals to reach those individuals with the right skills for each of your recruiting requirements.

- **Those looking for employment opportunities**, including individuals actively searching for a new or better job, those setting the course for their career in the future, and those simply exploring the job market out of curiosity. Whether you're a first time job seeker or a mid-career professional, a senior executive or an hourly worker, whether you want a full time position or part time, contract, consulting or free agent work, this Guide will help you find the right job boards, social media sites and career portals to succeed at your employment objective.

- **Those who assist job seekers, career changers and individuals who seek greater fulfillment from their work,** including career counselors, coaches, reference librarians and career and employment center staff professionals. If that's what you do, this Guide will help you find and select the job boards, social media sites and career portals that will best serve your clients in their job search campaigns and/or quest for more meaningful and rewarding work.

Why do recruiters and HR professionals, job seekers and career activists, career counselors and coaches and reference librarians need such a guide?

By our estimate, there are now over 100,000 employment-related Web-sites. Given that huge array of options, it's very difficult to know which sites are available and how to pick the best for a specific recruiting requirement or employment objective.

This Guide solves those problems. It introduces a wide range of the employment sites now operating online—in the United States and around the world—and provides the accurate, unbiased information that recruiters, job seekers, career counselors and librarians need to make smart choices among those sites.

How is the Guide Organized?

WEDDLE's Guide is composed of two sections:

The Top 100

This section lists our pick for the 100 best job boards, social media sites and career portals on the Internet today and provides detailed information about their services, features and fees for both recruiters and job seekers. There are, of course, other helpful employment destinations on the Web, but these sites are the elite.

To be considered for inclusion in The Top 100, a site must have completed an extensive questionnaire and:

· been selected to appear in a previous edition of WEDDLE's Guide,

 and/or

· be a Member of the International Association of Employment Web Sites (Please see page 21 for a description of this organization.).

We use all of this information—plus the unique insight and experience Peter Weddle has accumulated during his 15+ years of observing the online employment services industry—to evaluate and select The Top 100 job boards, social media sites and career portals on the Internet today. But we don't stop there. We also provide this same information to you, so you can evaluate the sites for yourself and select the best of the best for you.

Each of The Top 100 sites is described in the Guide's full-page Consumer Profiles. These profiles look much like the descriptions that appear in popular travel guides. Each profile offers a detailed set of information carefully tailored to the needs of recruiters, job seekers, career counselors and librarians.

In addition, this section also provides a Cross Reference Index of the profiled sites that organizes them according to the career fields, industries and employment situations (e.g., free lance work) they cover.

The Best & the Rest

This section provides the most comprehensive directory of online employment destinations in the world. It lists over 9,000 sites and organizes them according to their occupational, geographic, industry or other specialty.

What are "online employment destinations?" They include:

- job boards,
- career portals,
- labor exchanges,
- resume databases,
- resume development and distribution sites,
- search engines that specialize in employment,
- professional and social networking sites,
- work or employment-related blogs, and
- any other site that provides employment services to individuals or employers over the Internet.

What are "employment services?" They include:

- Job postings and other employment advertisements,
- Resume and profile databases,
- Professional networking platforms,
- Career counseling information and services,
- Job search information and services, and
- Recruitment information and services.

Each site in The Best & the Rest is listed by its name and URL or Internet address.

So, whether you're looking for a job or for a talented new employee, whether you counsel those seeking a more meaningful occupation or you're working to advance your own career, this Guide can help you succeed. It provides the accurate, up-to-date and complete information you need to make smart choices among employment sites on the Internet. Said another way, *WEDDLE's Guide to Employment Sites* is a handy and reliable reference that can help you tap the extraordinary advantages of the Internet and put them to work for you.

Be a Smart Consumer of Employment Web Sites

The number of job boards, social media sites and other employment-related web-sites is growing by leaps and bounds. By our count at WEDDLE's, there are now over 100,000 such sites operating around the world, and that figure will likely double in the next three-to-five years.

Most of these sites are operated in accordance with generally accepted business practices. Some, however, are not. These unscrupulous organizations misrepresent the services and capabilities they provide to employers and recruiters and abuse the trust of job seekers. When you use them, therefore, they undermine your ability to succeed.

How can you protect yourself and/or the organization you represent?

Use job boards, social media sites and career portals that are members of the **International Association of Employment Web Sites (IAEWS)**.

International Association of Employment Web Sites
The Sources of Success™

It's the trade association for the global online employment services industry. Its members include job boards, career portals, aggregators, social media sites, job ad distribution companies, applicant tracking system companies, technology companies, content providers, recruitment advertising agencies and the vendors which support them.

Every member of the IAEWS has agreed to abide by the only **Code of Ethics** published for the online employment services industry. That code ensures that you will receive accurate information about a site's capabilities and that its services will be delivered as they are represented to you.

Who are the Members of the IAEWS? You'll find a complete membership list at the association's site: **www. EmploymentWebSites.org**. They range from some of the most famous job board and networking brands in the world to highly regarded niche sites that specialize in a career field, industry or geographic region. They include sites that are stand-alone enterprises and those that are operated by newspapers, professional publications, radio and TV stations, professional societies and associations, college and university alumni organizations and affinity groups.

So, what should you do? Shop smart when selecting an employment site. Use one you can trust. Use a site operated by an IAEWS Member:

❑ Look for the IAEWS Member icon on the site.

    or

❑ Visit the IAEWS site and check the Member Roster.

They are *The Sources of Success*™.

WEDDLE's

Guide

to

Employment Sites
on the Internet

The
Top 100

Key to Career Field Abbreviations Used in the Web Site Profiles

In some cases, abbreviations have been used to denote the kinds of jobs currently being posted on a site. These abbreviations are presented in the Table below.

AD   Administrative
CM   Computer-related
CN   Communications
CS   Customer Service
DP   Data Processing
EC   Electronic Commerce
EN   Engineering
FA   Finance/Accounting
HR   Human Resources
IS   Info Systems/Technology
MG   Management
OP   Operations
PG   Programming
SM   Sales/Marketing

Index

Academic

Biospace

HigherEdJobs

Inside Higher Ed

Administration

BrokerHunter.com

DiversityJobs.com

HealtheCareers Network (multiple associations)

HIMSS JobMine (Healthcare Information & Management Systems Society)

Job.com

Net-Temps

Agriculture/Farming

AgCareers.com

Associations/Societies

AHACareerCenter.org (American Hospital Association)

ALA JobLIST (American Library Association)

APA Job Central (American Psychiatric Association)

ASAE Career Headquarters (American Society of Association Executives)

ASME Career Center + Job Board (American Society of Mechanical Engineers)

ASTD Career Center and Job Bank (American Society for Training & Development)

HealtheCareers Network (multiple associations)

HIMSS JobMine (Healthcare Information & Management Systems Society)

IEEE Job Site (Institute of Electrical & Electronics Engineers)

JAMA Career Center (American Medical Association)

JobsinBenefits.com (International Federation of Employee Benefit Plans)

NCAA Market (National Collegiate Athletic Association)

National Healthcare Career Network (multiple associations)

Physics Today Jobs (American Institute of Physics)

PRSA Jobcenter (Public Relations Society of America)

PsycCareers (American Psychological Association)

SHRM HR Jobs (Society for Human Resource Management)

SPIE Career Center (The International Society for Optics & Photonics)

Biotechnology/Life Sciences
AfterCollege
Biospace
PharmaDiversity Job Board

Building Management
ApartmentCareers.com
SeniorHousingJobs.com

College – Students, Recent Graduates
AfterCollege
CollegeRecruiter.com

Communications – Corporate, PR
MediaBistro
PRSA Jobcenter (Public Relations Society of America)

Construction
ConstructionJobs.com
MEP Jobs

Customer Service
AllRetailJobs.com
BrokerHunter.com
LatPro
RetirementJobs.com

Data – Computation & Analysis
Actuary.com
icrunchdata

Defense
ClearanceJobs.com
ClearedJobs.Net
MilitaryConnection.com
MilitaryHire.com
VetJobs

Diversity

disABLEDperson.com
DiversityJobs.com
LatPro
PharmaDiversity Job Board
RetirementJobs.com
WorkplaceDiversity.com

Engineering

AfterCollege
ASME Career Center + Job Board (American Society of Mechanical Engineers)
CollegeRecruiter.com
Dice.com
IEEE Job Site (Institute of Electrical & Electronics Engineers)
LatPro
MEP Jobs
Physics Today Jobs (American Institute of Physics)
SPIE Career Center (The International Society for Optics & Photonics)

Environmental

EHSCareers.com

Finance/Accounting

BrokerHunter.com
CA Source
eFinancialCareers.com
Job.com
JobWings.com
LatPro
Net-Temps
WallStJobs.com

General

AllCountyJobs.com
America's Job Exchange
Beyond.com
Bright.com
CareerBuilder.com

CareerCast.com
ChicagoJobs.com
disABLEDperson.com
EmploymentGuide.com
iHire.com
Indeed
Job.com
Jobing
Jobs2Careers.com
JobServe
JobsintheUS.com
JobsRadar
Juju
LinkedIn
LiveCareer
Matchpoint Careers
Monster.com
NationJob.com
RegionalHelpWanted.com
Simply Hired
TopUSAJobs.com
Workopolis
WorkplaceDiversity.com
ZipRecruiter.com

Geo-Specific

USA

AllCountyJobs.com (East Coast USA)
CareerCast.com (Local markets)
ChicagoJobs.com (Chicago, IL)
Jobing (Local markets)
JobsintheUS.com (Northeast USA)
NationJob.com (Local markets)
RegionalHelpWanted.com (Local markets)
TopUSAjobs.com
WorkplaceDiversity.com

Canada
CA Source
JobWings.com
Workopolis

Healthcare/Medical – All Fields
Absolutely Health Care
AfterCollege
AHACareerCenter.org (American Hospital Association)
APA Job Central (American Psychiatric Association)
DiversityJobs.com
Health Callings
HealtheCareers Network (multiple associations)
HealthJobsNationwide.com
HIMSS JobMine (Healthcare Information & Management Systems Society)
Hospital Dream Jobs
Hospital Jobs Online
JAMA Career Center (American Medical Association)
LocumTenens.com
MedReps
National Healthcare Career Network (multiple associations)
PharmaDiversity Job Board
PracticeLink.com
PsycCareers (American Psychological Association)
Simply Hired
SnagAJob.com

Hospitality
Casino Careers
Cool Works
Hcareers
JobMonkey

Hourly
EmploymentGuide.com
JobMonkey
SnagAJob.com

Human Resources

ASTD Career Center and Job Bank (American Society for Training & Development)
DiversityJobs.com
EHSCareers.com
EmployeeBenefitsJobs.com
ExecuNet
JobsinBenefits.com (International Federation of Employee Benefit Plans)
Openreq
SHRM HR Jobs (Society for Human Resource Management)

Information Systems/Technology

AfterCollege
ALA JobLIST (American Library Association)
BrokerHunter.com
Dice.com
ExecuNet
HIMSS JobMine (Healthcare Information & Management Systems Society)
IEEE Job Site (Institute of Electrical & Electronics Engineers)
Job.com
MilitaryHire.com
Net-Temps
Simply Hired

Insurance

Actuary.com
Great Insurance Jobs

Job Search Resources - Resume

LiveCareer

Logistics & Transportation

JobsinLogistics.com
JobsinTrucks.com

Management/Executive

AllRetailJobs.com
ASAE Career Headquarters (American Society of Association Executives)

Cool Works
ExecuNet
Hcareers
IEEE Job Site (Institute of Electrical & Electronics Engineers)
JobWings.com
Net-Temps

Military Transition into the Private Sector

ClearanceJobs.com
ClearedJobs.Net
MilitaryConnection.com
MilitaryHire.com
VetJobs

Operations

BrokerHunter.com
Hcareers

Pharmaceutical

Biospace
MedReps
PharmaDiversity Job Board

Retail

AllRetailJobs.com
JobMonkey
Net-Temps

Sales/Marketing

ASAE Career Headquarters (American Society of Association Executives)
BrokerHunter.com
CollegeRecruiter.com
DiversityJobs.com
ExecuNet
Job.com
JobMonkey
LatPro
MedReps
RetirementJobs.com

Science

IEEE Job Site (Institute of Electrical & Electronics Engineers)
Physics Today Jobs (American Institute of Physics)
SPIE Career Center (The International Society for Optics & Photonics)

Search Engines – Employment

Indeed
Jobs2Careers.com
JobsRadar
Juju
Simply Hired
TopUSAJobs.com

Sports/Recreation

NCAA Market (National Collegiate Athletic Association)
Work in Sports

Security – Corporate & Individual

Security Jobs Network

Staffing Firms

Net-Temps
Openreq

Telecommuting

FlexJobs.com

Absolutely Health Care

SITE'S SELF-DESCRIPTION

Absolutely Health Care specializes in U.S. healthcare and medical positions. We offer single job postings and programs that allow unlimited postings and resume database access. Jobs posted by our clients are also cross-posted to 4,800+ affiliate sites at no extra charge. Unlimited postings and resume database access average $333 per month for annual subscribers.

GENERAL INFORMATION

URL: www.healthjobsusa.com

Date the site was activated online: 1999

Parent organization of the site: Healthcare Staffing Innovations, LLC

What field, industry or location does the site cover: Healthcare, Medical

Is the site an IAEWS Member: Yes

Employment Opportunities

Are full time jobs posted on the site: Yes

Are part time jobs posted on the site: Yes

Are contract jobs posted on the site: Yes

Are consulting jobs posted on the site: Yes

Resume Services

Are resumes or profiles stored on the site: Yes

Recruiters

Is there an automated resume agent: Yes

Is banner advertising available: Yes

Other Employment Services

Is a discussion forum or blog offered on the site: Yes

Are assessment instruments offered on the site: Yes

Job Seekers

Is there an automated job agent: Yes

Is career info provided: Yes

Actuary.com

SITE'S SELF-DESCRIPTION

Actuary.com is the leading career and professional resource for actuaries on the Internet. Actuary.com offers single job postings from $225 or job posting packs at a significant price reduction. Top name actuarial companies have posted on Actuary.com for years.

GENERAL INFORMATION

URL: www.actuary.com

Date the site was activated online: 1999

Parent organization of the site: RSG, Inc.

What field, industry or location does the site cover: Actuarial, Insurance, Mathematics

Is the site an IAEWS Member: Yes

Employment Opportunities

Are full time jobs posted on the site: Yes

Are part time jobs posted on the site: Yes

Are contract jobs posted on the site: Yes

Are consulting jobs posted on the site: Yes

Resume Services

Are resumes or profiles stored on the site: Yes

Recruiters

Is there an automated resume agent: No

Is banner advertising available: Yes

Other Employment Services

Is a discussion forum or blog offered on the site: Yes

Are assessment instruments offered on the site: Yes

Job Seekers

Is there an automated job agent: Yes

Is career info provided: Yes

AfterCollege

SITE'S SELF-DESCRIPTION

AfterCollege is the largest career network specializing in college recruitment, helping over 2,250,000 college students and alumni connect with employers. AfterCollege reaches students and alumni through 1,300 partner academic departments and student groups as well as through a network of 17,500+ faculty and group contacts.

GENERAL INFORMATION

URL: www.aftercollege.com

Date the site was activated online: 2000

Parent organization of the site: AfterCollege, Inc.

What field, industry or location does the site cover: EN, IS, Business, Life Sciences, Nursing

Is the site an IAEWS Member: Yes

Employment Opportunities

Are full time jobs posted on the site: Yes

Are part time jobs posted on the site: Yes

Are contract jobs posted on the site: No

Are consulting jobs posted on the site: No

Resume Services

Are resumes or profiles stored on the site: Yes

Recruiters

Is there an automated resume agent: No

Is banner advertising available: Yes

Other Employment Services

Is a discussion forum or blog offered on the site: No

Are assessment instruments offered on the site: Yes

Job Seekers

Is there an automated job agent: Yes

Is career info provided: Yes

AgCareers.com

SITE'S SELF-DESCRIPTION

A member of the Farms.com family, AgCareers.com is the leading online job board and human resource provider for the agriculture, food, natural resources and biotechnology fields.

GENERAL INFORMATION

URL: www.agcareers.com

Date the site was activated online: 2001

Parent organization of the site: Farms.com

What field, industry or location does the site cover: Agriculture

Is the site an IAEWS Member: Yes

Employment Opportunities

Are full time jobs posted on the site: Yes

Are part time jobs posted on the site: Yes

Are contract jobs posted on the site: Yes

Are consulting jobs posted on the site: Yes

Resume Services

Are resumes or profiles stored on the site: Yes

Recruiters

Is there an automated resume agent: Yes

Is banner advertising available: Yes

Other Employment Services

Is a discussion forum or blog offered on the site: Yes

Are assessment instruments offered on the site: No

Job Seekers

Is there an automated job agent: Yes

Is career info provided: Yes

AHACareerCenter.org

SITE'S SELF-DESCRIPTION

The American Hospital Association's Career Center is the site for hospitals and healthcare employers seeking highly qualified applicants (from entry level to CEO), as well as job seekers looking to land the right job within healthcare. AHACareerCenter.org is part of the National Healthcare Career Network — the fastest growing healthcare association job network.

GENERAL INFORMATION

URL: www.ahacareercenter.org

Date the site was activated online: 2007

Parent organization of the site: AHA Solutions, Inc. (American Hospital Association)

What field, industry or location does the site cover: Healthcare

Is the site an IAEWS Member: Yes

Employment Opportunities

Are full time jobs posted on the site: Yes

Are part time jobs posted on the site: Yes

Are contract jobs posted on the site: Yes

Are consulting jobs posted on the site: Yes

Resume Services

Are resumes or profiles stored on the site: Yes

Other Employment Services

Is a discussion forum or blog offered on the site: No

Are assessment instruments offered on the site: No

Recruiters

Is there an automated resume agent: Yes

Is banner advertising available: No

Job Seekers

Is there an automated job agent: Yes

Is career info provided: Yes

ALA JobLIST

SITE'S SELF-DESCRIPTION

The leading international source for library and information science and technology jobs, ALA JobLIST hosts ads for *American Libraries* and *C&RL News* magazines. JobLIST's highly-qualified audience of MLIS job seekers have research, data curation, and metadata creation skills perfect for today's data-driven information positions in companies of all types, as well as positions in academic, public, school, and special libraries.

GENERAL INFORMATION

URL: http://joblist.ala.org

Date the site was activated online: 2006

Parent organization of the site: American Library Association/Association of College & Research Libraries

What field, industry or location does the site cover: Library & Information Science & Technology

Is the site an IAEWS Member: Yes

Employment Opportunities

Are full time jobs posted on the site: Yes

Are part time jobs posted on the site: Yes

Are contract jobs posted on the site: Yes

Are consulting jobs posted on the site: Yes

Resume Services

Are resumes or profiles stored on the site: Yes

Other Employment Services

Is a discussion forum or blog offered on the site: No

Are assessment instruments offered on the site: No

Recruiters

Is there an automated resume agent: No

Is banner advertising available: Yes

Job Seekers

Is there an automated job agent: Yes

Is career info provided: Yes

AllCountyJobs.com

SITE'S SELF-DESCRIPTION

We are a network of local online job boards. Since our start, we have always strived for one goal: connect employers with quality, targeted, local applicants. Our local job boards will let you search/post jobs from Washington, D.C. to Vermont and everywhere in between. Each site links to the others to form a network of thousands of job listings along the East Coast.

GENERAL INFORMATION

URL: www.allcountyjobs.com

Date the site was activated online: 1999

Parent organization of the site: OperationsInc.

What field, industry or location does the site cover: East Coast USA

Is the site an IAEWS Member: Yes

Employment Opportunities

Are full time jobs posted on the site: Yes

Are part time jobs posted on the site: Yes

Are contract jobs posted on the site: Yes

Are consulting jobs posted on the site: Yes

Resume Services

Are resumes or profiles stored on the site: Yes

Other Employment Services

Is a discussion forum or blog offered on the site: No

Are assessment instruments offered on the site: No

Recruiters

Is there an automated resume agent: No

Is banner advertising available: No

Job Seekers

Is there an automated job agent: No

Is career info provided: No

AllRetailJobs.com

SITE'S SELF-DESCRIPTION

AllRetailJobs.com is the largest recruiting job board for the retail industry. The site specializes in target marketing campaigns that attract retail executives, regional managers, store and assistant store managers, category managers/buyers, retail logistics managers, merchandisers and department managers as well as sales and hourly associates.

GENERAL INFORMATION

URL: www.allretailjobs.com

Date the site was activated online: 2001

Parent organization of the site: JobsInLogistics.com, Inc.

What field, industry or location does the site cover: CS, MG, SM

Is the site an IAEWS Member: Yes

Employment Opportunities

Are full time jobs posted on the site: Yes

Are part time jobs posted on the site: Yes

Are contract jobs posted on the site: Yes

Are consulting jobs posted on the site: Yes

Resume Services

Are resumes or profiles stored on the site: Yes

Other Employment Services

Is a discussion forum or blog offered on the site: No

Are assessment instruments offered on the site: No

Recruiters

Is there an automated resume agent: No

Is banner advertising available: Yes

Job Seekers

Is there an automated job agent: Yes

Is career info provided: Yes

America's Job Exchange

SITE'S SELF-DESCRIPTION

America's Job Exchange (AJE) provides search, job listings and career tools to help job seekers be successful in their job hunting and career growth. In addition, the AJE network offers specialized Web-sites for niche communities, such as veterans, seniors, disabled, minorities and many more to make the job search experience more personalized and effective.

GENERAL INFORMATION

URL: www.americasjobexchange.com

Date the site was activated online: 2007

Parent organization of the site: Time Warner Cable

What field, industry or location does the site cover: Wide variety

Is the site an IAEWS Member: Yes

Employment Opportunities

Are full time jobs posted on the site: Yes

Are part time jobs posted on the site: No

Are contract jobs posted on the site: No

Are consulting jobs posted on the site: No

Resume Services

Are resumes or profiles stored on the site: Yes

Other Employment Services

Is a discussion forum or blog offered on the site: Yes

Are assessment instruments offered on the site: Yes

Recruiters

Is there an automated resume agent: Yes

Is banner advertising available: Yes

Job Seekers

Is there an automated job agent: Yes

Is career info provided: Yes

APA JobCentral

SITE'S SELF-DESCRIPTION

The American Psychiatric Association (APA), founded in 1844, is the world's largest psychiatric organization. It is a medical specialty society representing more than 29,000 psychiatric physicians from the United States and around the world. APA is the voice and conscience of modern psychiatry.

GENERAL INFORMATION

URL: http://jobs.psychiatry.org

Date the site was activated online: 2012

Parent organization of the site: American Psychiatric Association

What field, industry or location does the site cover: Psychiatry

Is the site an IAEWS Member: No

Employment Opportunities

Are full time jobs posted on the site: Yes

Are part time jobs posted on the site: Yes

Are contract jobs posted on the site: Yes

Are consulting jobs posted on the site: No

Resume Services

Are resumes or profiles stored on the site: Yes

Recruiters

Is there an automated resume agent: No

Is banner advertising available: Yes

Other Employment Services

Is a discussion forum or blog offered on the site: No

Are assessment instruments offered on the site: Yes

Job Seekers

Is there an automated job agent: Yes

Is career info provided: Yes

ApartmentCareers.com

SITE'S SELF-DESCRIPTION

ApartmentCareers.com is the largest career site dedicated to advertising the staffing needs of the apartment industry. The National Apartment Association (NAA), the largest rental housing association in the U.S., selected ApartmentCareers.com to host the NAA Career Center and develop a nationwide network of association career sites to meet the needs of its 50,000 members.

GENERAL INFORMATION

URL: www.apartmentcareers.com

Date the site was activated online: 2000

Parent organization of the site: Realestatecareers, LLC

What field, industry or location does the site cover: On-site apartment staff

Is the site an IAEWS Member: Yes

Employment Opportunities

Are full time jobs posted on the site: Yes

Are part time jobs posted on the site: Yes

Are contract jobs posted on the site: Yes

Are consulting jobs posted on the site: Yes

Resume Services

Are resumes or profiles stored on the site: Yes

Recruiters

Is there an automated resume agent: Yes

Is banner advertising available: Yes

Other Employment Services

Is a discussion forum or blog offered on the site: Yes

Are assessment instruments offered on the site: Yes

Job Seekers

Is there an automated job agent: Yes

Is career info provided: Yes

ASAE Career Headquarters

SITE'S SELF-DESCRIPTION

The American Society of Association Executive's CareerHQ.org is the largest source of association industry jobs and resumes. It's where job seekers go to land the right job, and where employers go to find highly qualified applicants. CareerHQ.org also offers career development services, a mentoring program, and salary tables to help job seekers increase their competitive advantage.

GENERAL INFORMATION

URL: www.careerhq.org

Date the site was activated online: 2000

Parent organization of the site: American Society of Association Executives (ASAE)

What field, industry or location does the site cover: MG, SM, Association Executive/Manager

Is the site an IAEWS Member: Yes

Employment Opportunities

Are full time jobs posted on the site: Yes

Are part time jobs posted on the site: Yes

Are contract jobs posted on the site: Yes

Are consulting jobs posted on the site: Yes

Resume Services

Are resumes or profiles stored on the site: Yes

Other Employment Services

Is a discussion forum or blog offered on the site: No

Are assessment instruments offered on the site: No

Recruiters

Is there an automated resume agent: Yes

Is banner advertising available: Yes

Job Seekers

Is there an automated job agent: Yes

Is career info provided: Yes

ASME Career Center + Job Board

SITE'S SELF-DESCRIPTION

ASME (founded as the American Society of Mechanical Engineers) promotes the art, science and practice of multidisciplinary engineering and allied sciences around the globe. The ASME Career Center is the premier e-recruitment resource for mechanical engineering and related industries.

GENERAL INFORMATION

URL: http://jobboard.asme.org

Date the site was activated online: 2003

Parent organization of the site: American Society of Mechanical Engineers

What field, industry or location does the site cover: Engineers

Is the site an IAEWS Member: No

Employment Opportunities

Are full time jobs posted on the site: Yes

Are part time jobs posted on the site: Yes

Are contract jobs posted on the site: Yes

Are consulting jobs posted on the site: No

Resume Services

Are resumes or profiles stored on the site: Yes

Other Employment Services

Is a discussion forum or blog offered on the site: No

Are assessment instruments offered on the site: No

Recruiters

Is there an automated resume agent: Yes

Is banner advertising available: Yes

Job Seekers

Is there an automated job agent: Yes

Is career info provided: Yes

ASTD Career Center and Job Bank

SITE'S SELF-DESCRIPTION

ASTD is the largest professional association dedicated to the training and development field. The ASTD Job Bank is the leading employment source for training professionals.

GENERAL INFORMATION

URL: http://jobs.astd.org

Date the site was activated online: 2001

Parent organization of the site: American Society for Training & Development (ASTD)

What field, industry or location does the site cover: Training & Development

Is the site an IAEWS Member: No

Employment Opportunities

Are full time jobs posted on the site: Yes

Are part time jobs posted on the site: Yes

Are contract jobs posted on the site: Yes

Are consulting jobs posted on the site: No

Resume Services

Are resumes or profiles stored on the site: Yes

Other Employment Services

Is a discussion forum or blog offered on the site: No

Are assessment instruments offered on the site: No

Recruiters

Is there an automated resume agent: Yes

Is banner advertising available: Yes

Job Seekers

Is there an automated job agent: Yes

Is career info provided: Yes

Beyond.com

SITE'S SELF-DESCRIPTION

Reach over 25 million professionals on Beyond.com, The Career Network. With over 2,000 geographic and industry-based career sites and 500+ talent communities, our powerful niche network attracts focused professionals and helps you connect with the very best ones. Using precise targeting abilities, we deliver quality results through recruitment advertising, email marketing, mobile and social channels, and other highly effective tactics.

GENERAL INFORMATION

URL: www.beyond.com

Date the site was activated online: 1998

Parent organization of the site: Beyond.com, Inc.

What field, industry or location does the site cover: Niche industry and geo-focused sites and talent communities in the US and Canada

Is the site an IAEWS Member: Yes

Employment Opportunities

Are full time jobs posted on the site: Yes

Are part time jobs posted on the site: Yes

Are contract jobs posted on the site: Yes

Are consulting jobs posted on the site: Yes

Resume Services

Are resumes or profiles stored on the site: Yes

Other Employment Services

Is a discussion forum or blog offered on the site: Yes

Are assessment instruments offered on the site: Yes

Recruiters

Is there an automated resume agent: Yes

Is banner advertising available: Yes

Job Seekers

Is there an automated job agent: Yes

Is career info provided: Yes

BioSpace

SITE'S SELF-DESCRIPTION

BioSpace provides employment and career resources that span the life sciences. Unlike general job boards, our leading partnerships allow us to reach niche audiences within clinical research, academia, medical device sectors, government markets and other areas. More than 75% of BioSpace.com visitors return within a week, and another 90% don't visit other industry sites.

GENERAL INFORMATION

URL: www.biospace.com

Date the site was activated online: 1985

Parent organization of the site: onTargetjobs, Inc.

What field, industry or location does the site cover: Biotech, Pharma, Med Device, Academic

Is the site an IAEWS Member: Yes

Employment Opportunities

Are full time jobs posted on the site: Yes

Are part time jobs posted on the site: Yes

Are contract jobs posted on the site: Yes

Are consulting jobs posted on the site: Yes

Resume Services

Are resumes or profiles stored on the site: Yes

Other Employment Services

Is a discussion forum or blog offered on the site: Yes

Are assessment instruments offered on the site: No

Recruiters

Is there an automated resume agent: Yes

Is banner advertising available: Yes

Job Seekers

Is there an automated job agent: Yes

Is career info provided: Yes

Bright.com

GENERAL INFORMATION

URL: www.bright.com

Date the site was activated online: 2011

Parent organization of the site: Bright Media Corporation

What field, industry or location does the site cover: Wide variety

Is the site an IAEWS Member: Yes

Employment Opportunities

Are full time jobs posted on the site: Yes

Are part time jobs posted on the site: Yes

Are contract jobs posted on the site: Yes

Are consulting jobs posted on the site: Yes

Resume Services

Are resumes or profiles stored on the site: Yes

Recruiters

Is there an automated resume agent: Yes

Is banner advertising available: No

Other Employment Services

Is a discussion forum or blog offered on the site: Yes

Are assessment instruments offered on the site: Yes

Job Seekers

Is there an automated job agent: Yes

Is career info provided: No

BrokerHunter.com

SITE'S SELF-DESCRIPTION

BrokerHunter.com is the leading securities industry employment Web-site in the nation with over 145,000 candidates and over 8,000 job postings from hundreds of branches and firms. The company's area of expertise is in the gathering and presentation of highly tailored data related to securities industry job seekers and to financial services employers and recruiters.

GENERAL INFORMATION

URL: www.brokerhunter.com

Date the site was activated online: 2000

Parent organization of the site: BrokerHunter.com, LLC

What field, industry or location does the site cover: AD, CS, FA, IS, OP, SM

Is the site an IAEWS Member: Yes

Employment Opportunities

Are full time jobs posted on the site: Yes

Are part time jobs posted on the site: Yes

Are contract jobs posted on the site: Yes

Are consulting jobs posted on the site: Yes

Resume Services

Are resumes or profiles stored on the site: Yes

Other Employment Services

Is a discussion forum or blog offered on the site: Yes

Are assessment instruments offered on the site: No

Recruiters

Is there an automated resume agent: Yes

Is banner advertising available: Yes

Job Seekers

Is there an automated job agent: Yes

Is career info provided: Yes

CA Source

SITE'S SELF-DESCRIPTION

CA Source is the Canadian Institute of Chartered Accountants' national career site exclusively for Canada's 83,000 Chartered Accountants and CA Students. CAs can upload resumes, create email alerts, apply for jobs and access career information. Employers and recruiters can post positions and access matching qualified resumes allowing for a highly targeted search of Canada's leading financial professionals.

GENERAL INFORMATION

URL: www.casource.com

Date the site was activated online: 2001

Parent organization of the site: Canadian Institute of Chartered Accountants

What field, industry or location does the site cover: Chartered Accountants, Canada

Is the site an IAEWS Member: Yes

Employment Opportunities

Are full time jobs posted on the site: Yes

Are part time jobs posted on the site: Yes

Are contract jobs posted on the site: Yes

Are consulting jobs posted on the site: Yes

Resume Services

Are resumes or profiles stored on the site: Yes

Recruiters

Is there an automated resume agent: Yes

Is banner advertising available: Yes

Other Employment Services

Is a discussion forum or blog offered on the site: No

Are assessment instruments offered on the site: No

Job Seekers

Is there an automated job agent: Yes

Is career info provided: Yes

CareerBuilder.com

SITE'S SELF-DESCRIPTION

CareerBuilder.com is the nation's largest online job site with more than 25 million unique visitors and over one million jobs. Owned by Gannett Co., Inc. (NYSE:GCI), Tribune Company, and The McClatchy Company (NYSE:MNI), CareerBuilder offers a vast online and print network to help job seekers connect with employers.

GENERAL INFORMATION

URL: www.careerbuilder.com

Date the site was activated online: 1998

Parent organization of the site: CareerBuilder, LLC

What field, industry or location does the site cover: Wide variety

Is the site an IAEWS Member: Yes

Employment Opportunities

Are full time jobs posted on the site: Yes

Are part time jobs posted on the site: Yes

Are contract jobs posted on the site: Yes

Are consulting jobs posted on the site: Yes

Resume Services

Are resumes or profiles stored on the site: Yes

Recruiters

Is there an automated resume agent: No

Is banner advertising available: Yes

Other Employment Services

Is a discussion forum or blog offered on the site: Yes

Are assessment instruments offered on the site: Yes

Job Seekers

Is there an automated job agent: Yes

Is career info provided: Yes

CareerCast.com

SITE'S SELF-DESCRIPTION

CareerCast.com, created by Adicio, is a job-search portal that offers extensive local, niche and national job listings from across North America, as well as editorial content, videos and blogs on all aspects of job-hunting, career-management and corporate recruiting. CareerCast also provides recruiters with the ability to post jobs directly to more than 800 career sites and niche networks powered by Adicio. The Jobs Rated Report is the site's most popular feature and ranks 200 jobs across North America based on detailed analysis of specific careers factors.

GENERAL INFORMATION

URL: www.careercast.com, www.jobsrated.com

Date the site was activated online: 2009

Parent organization of the site: Adicio

What field, industry or location does the site cover: Wide variety

Is the site an IAEWS Member: Yes

Employment Opportunities

Are full time jobs posted on the site: Yes

Are part time jobs posted on the site: Yes

Are contract jobs posted on the site: Yes

Are consulting jobs posted on the site: Yes

Resume Services

Are resumes or profiles stored on the site: Yes

Recruiters

Is there an automated resume agent: Yes

Is banner advertising available: No

Other Employment Services

Is a discussion forum or blog offered on the site: Yes

Are assessment instruments offered on the site: Yes

Job Seekers

Is there an automated job agent: Yes

Is career info provided: Yes

Casino Careers

SITE'S SELF-DESCRIPTION

Casino Careers, LLC is the leading talent acquisition company to the gaming-hospitality/technology industry - serving land and sea-based casino-resorts, tribal enterprises, regulatory agencies, vendors/suppliers, iGaming, etc. Thousands of employees have been placed worldwide in entry-level to executive positions in every discipline. Job seekers can post a resume for free in open access or confidential format. They can also subscribe for fee-based resume enhancement or resume rewrite services.

GENERAL INFORMATION

URL: www.casinocareers.com

Date the site was activated online: 1998

Parent organization of the site: Casino Careers, LLC

What field, industry or location does the site cover: Gaming hospitality, Technology, Manufacturing and regulatory, Agencies and Native American Tribal Enterprises

Is the site an IAEWS Member: No

Employment Opportunities

Are full time jobs posted on the site: Yes

Are part time jobs posted on the site: Yes

Are contract jobs posted on the site: Yes

Are consulting jobs posted on the site: No

Resume Services

Are resumes or profiles stored on the site: Yes

Recruiters

Is there an automated resume agent: Yes

Is banner advertising available: Yes

Other Employment Services

Is a discussion forum or blog offered on the site: No

Are assessment instruments offered on the site: Yes

Job Seekers

Is there an automated job agent: Yes

Is career info provided: Yes

Chicagojobs.com

SITE'S SELF-DESCRIPTION

Exclusively focused on Chicagoland's 11 county area including the city, suburbs and beyond, ChicagoJobs.com's award-winning layout and enhanced services maximize exposure for both local employers and job seekers. Launched in 2004, we average 150,000 unique monthly visitors and more than 4.5 million page views each month.

GENERAL INFORMATION

URL: www.chicagojobs.com

Date the site was activated online: 2004

Parent organization of the site: Shaker Recruitment Advertising and Communications

What field, industry or location does the site cover: Wide variety

Is the site an IAEWS Member: Yes

Employment Opportunities

Are full time jobs posted on the site: Yes

Are part time jobs posted on the site: Yes

Are contract jobs posted on the site: Yes

Are consulting jobs posted on the site: Yes

Resume Services

Are resumes or profiles stored on the site: Yes

Recruiters

Is there an automated resume agent: Yes

Is banner advertising available: Yes

Other Employment Services

Is a discussion forum or blog offered on the site: No

Are assessment instruments offered on the site: No

Job Seekers

Is there an automated job agent: Yes

Is career info provided: Yes

ClearanceJobs.com

SITE'S SELF-DESCRIPTION

ClearanceJobs.com, a Dice Holdings, Inc. company, is a secure Web-site dedicated to matching job seekers who hold active U.S. Government security clearances to the best hiring companies searching for new and cleared employees.

GENERAL INFORMATION

URL: www.clearancejobs.com

Date the site was activated online: 2002

Parent organization of the site: Dice Holdings, Inc.

What field, industry or location does the site cover: Wide variety with U.S. Government security clearance

Is the site an IAEWS Member: Yes

Employment Opportunities

Are full time jobs posted on the site: Yes

Are part time jobs posted on the site: Yes

Are contract jobs posted on the site: Yes

Are consulting jobs posted on the site: Yes

Resume Services

Are resumes or profiles stored on the site: Yes (resumes only)

Recruiters

Is there an automated resume agent: Yes

Is banner advertising available: Yes

Other Employment Services

Is a discussion forum or blog offered on the site: Yes

Are assessment instruments offered on the site: Yes

Job Seekers

Is there an automated job agent: Yes

Is career info provided: Yes

ClearedJobs.Net

SITE'S SELF-DESCRIPTION

ClearedJobs.Net is a veteran-owned career site and job fair company committed to providing outstanding customer service to security cleared job seekers and cleared facilities employers. Based in Falls Church, Virginia, ClearedJobs.Net offers thousands of cleared positions across the country and around the world.

GENERAL INFORMATION

URL: www.clearedjobs.net

Date the site was activated online: 2004

Parent organization of the site: ClearedJobs.Net, Inc.

What field, industry or location does the site cover: Wide variety with U.S. Government security clearance

Is the site an IAEWS Member: Yes

Employment Opportunities

Are full time jobs posted on the site: Yes

Are part time jobs posted on the site: Yes

Are contract jobs posted on the site: Yes

Are consulting jobs posted on the site: Yes

Resume Services

Are resumes or profiles stored on the site: Yes

Other Employment Services

Is a discussion forum or blog offered on the site: Yes

Are assessment instruments offered on the site: No

Recruiters

Is there an automated resume agent: Yes

Is banner advertising available: Yes

Job Seekers

Is there an automated job agent: Yes

Is career info provided: Yes

CollegeRecruiter.com

SITE'S SELF-DESCRIPTION

CollegeRecruiter.com is the leading job board for college students searching for internships and recent graduates hunting for entry-level and other career opportunities. Features tens of thousands of pages of employment-related articles, blogs, videos, podcasts and other such content.

GENERAL INFORMATION

URL: www.collegerecruiter.com

Date the site was activated online: 1996

Parent organization of the site: CollegeRecruiter.com

What field, industry or location does the site cover: EN, SM, Internships

Is the site an IAEWS Member: Yes

Employment Opportunities

Are full time jobs posted on the site: Yes

Are part time jobs posted on the site: Yes

Are contract jobs posted on the site: Yes

Are consulting jobs posted on the site: Yes

Resume Services

Are resumes or profiles stored on the site: No

Recruiters

Is there an automated resume agent: No

Is banner advertising available: Yes

Other Employment Services

Is a discussion forum or blog offered on the site: Yes

Are assessment instruments offered on the site: Yes

Job Seekers

Is there an automated job agent: Yes

Is career info provided: Yes

ConstructionJobs.com

SITE'S SELF-DESCRIPTION

ConstructionJobs.com is the nation's premier employment resource for the construction, design and building industries. Endorsed by nine industry associations as their preferred partner for online recruiting, our award-winning job board and resume database provide a cost-effective solution that makes advertising open positions and locating qualified candidates faster and easier.

GENERAL INFORMATION

URL: www.constructionjobs.com

Date the site was activated online: 2000

Parent organization of the site: Construction Jobs, Inc.

What field, industry or location does the site cover: Construction

Is the site an IAEWS Member: Yes

Employment Opportunities

Are full time jobs posted on the site: Yes

Are part time jobs posted on the site: Yes

Are contract jobs posted on the site: Yes

Are consulting jobs posted on the site: Yes

Resume Services

Are resumes or profiles stored on the site: Yes

Recruiters

Is there an automated resume agent: Yes

Is banner advertising available: Yes

Other Employment Services

Is a discussion forum or blog offered on the site: No

Are assessment instruments offered on the site: Yes

Job Seekers

Is there an automated job agent: Yes

Is career info provided: Yes

Cool Works

SITE'S SELF-DESCRIPTION

Cool Works® is about finding a seasonal job or career in some of the greatest places on Earth. We offer thousands of jobs in national and state parks, summer and ski resorts, camps, ranches, adventure travel companies and more. Our 5,700-member social network provides a place to compare and share work and life experiences in these unique places.

GENERAL INFORMATION

URL: www.coolworks.com

Date the site was activated online: 1995

Parent organization of the site: CW, Inc.

What field, industry or location does the site cover: MG, Food & Beverage, Housekeeping

Is the site an IAEWS Member: Yes

Employment Opportunities

Are full time jobs posted on the site: Yes

Are part time jobs posted on the site: Yes

Are contract jobs posted on the site: Yes

Are consulting jobs posted on the site: No

Resume Services

Are resumes or profiles stored on the site: No

Recruiters

Is there an automated resume agent: No

Is banner advertising available: Yes

Other Employment Services

Is a discussion forum or blog offered on the site: Yes

Are assessment instruments offered on the site: No

Job Seekers

Is there an automated job agent: No

Is career info provided: Yes

Dice.com

SITE'S SELF-DESCRIPTION

Dice, a Dice Holdings, Inc. service, is the leading career site for technology and engineering professionals. With a 20-year track record of meeting the needs of technology professionals, companies and recruiters, our specialty focus and exposure to highly skilled professional communities enable employers to reach hard-to-find, experienced and qualified candidates.

GENERAL INFORMATION

URL: www.dice.com

Date the site was activated online: 1990

Parent organization of the site: Dice Holdings, Inc.

What field, industry or location does the site cover: EN, IS, Technology

Is the site an IAEWS Member: Yes

Employment Opportunities

Are full time jobs posted on the site: Yes

Are part time jobs posted on the site: Yes

Are contract jobs posted on the site: Yes

Are consulting jobs posted on the site: Yes

Resume Services

Are resumes or profiles stored on the site: Yes

Recruiters

Is there an automated resume agent: Yes

Is banner advertising available: Yes

Other Employment Services

Is a discussion forum or blog offered on the site: Yes

Are assessment instruments offered on the site: No

Job Seekers

Is there an automated job agent: Yes

Is career info provided: Yes

disABLEDperson.com

SITE'S SELF-DESCRIPTION

We are a public charity organization whose primary focus is disability employment. We want to help you, a person with a disability find employment. Our portal connects individuals with disabilities with proactive employers. So come, post your resume and look for a job. It's free! Our goal is to get as many jobs for people with disabilities as possible.

GENERAL INFORMATION

URL: www.disabledperson.com

Date the site was activated online: 2002

Parent organization of the site: disABLEDperson, Inc.

What field, industry or location does the site cover: Wide variety

Is the site an IAEWS Member: Yes

Employment Opportunities

Are full time jobs posted on the site: Yes

Are part time jobs posted on the site: No

Are contract jobs posted on the site: No

Are consulting jobs posted on the site: No

Resume Services

Are resumes or profiles stored on the site: Yes

Other Employment Services

Is a discussion forum or blog offered on the site: No

Are assessment instruments offered on the site: No

Recruiters

Is there an automated resume agent: No

Is banner advertising available: Yes

Job Seekers

Is there an automated job agent: No

Is career info provided: Yes

DiversityJobs.com

SITE'S SELF-DESCRIPTION

Developed by LatPro, Inc., DiversityJobs.com holds the #1 ranking on Google, Yahoo! and Bing for the search term "diversity jobs." Our mission is to equip African-Americans, women, Hispanics, veterans, persons with disabilities, Asian-Americans, Native Americans, members of the LGBT community and others with current jobs from employers dedicated to a diverse workforce.

GENERAL INFORMATION

URL: www.diversityjobs.com

Date the site was activated online: 2006

Parent organization of the site: LatPro, Inc.

What field, industry or location does the site cover: AD, HR, SM, Healthcare

Is the site an IAEWS Member: Yes

Employment Opportunities

Are full time jobs posted on the site: Yes

Are part time jobs posted on the site: Yes

Are contract jobs posted on the site: Yes

Are consulting jobs posted on the site: Yes

Resume Services

Are resumes or profiles stored on the site: No

Other Employment Services

Is a discussion forum or blog offered on the site: Yes

Are assessment instruments offered on the site: Yes

Recruiters

Is there an automated resume agent: Yes

Is banner advertising available: Yes

Job Seekers

Is there an automated job agent: Yes

Is career info provided: Yes

eFinancialCareers.com

SITE'S SELF-DESCRIPTION

eFinancialCareers, a Dice Holdings, Inc. company, serves the global financial community as the leading network of career sites for professionals working in banking and the financial markets and those firms seeing to employ them. For financial service professionals, our mission is to provide the best job opportunities, job market news and analysis, salary surveys and career advice. For our customers, our mission is to help companies engage with and hire the most qualified finance professionals around the world.

GENERAL INFORMATION

URL: www.efinancialcareers.com

Date the site was activated online: 2000

Parent organization of the site: Dice Holdings, Inc.

What field, industry or location does the site cover: Financial markets

Is the site an IAEWS Member: Yes

Employment Opportunities

Are full time jobs posted on the site: Yes

Are part time jobs posted on the site: Yes

Are contract jobs posted on the site: Yes

Are consulting jobs posted on the site: Yes

Resume Services

Are resumes or profiles stored on the site: Yes

Recruiters

Is there an automated resume agent: Yes

Is banner advertising available: Yes

Other Employment Services

Is a discussion forum or blog offered on the site: No

Are assessment instruments offered on the site: No

Job Seekers

Is there an automated job agent: Yes

Is career info provided: Yes

EHSCareers.com

SITE'S SELF-DESCRIPTION

EHSCareers.com has been the leading job board for the environmental, occupational health and safety profession since 2003. The site is free to job seekers. Recruiters and employers pay a fee for job postings and access to job seeker profiles. EHSCareers.com is also the official job board for the National Safety Council and the National Association of EHS Managers.

GENERAL INFORMATION

URL: www.ehscareers.com

Date the site was activated online: 2003

Parent organization of the site: EHSCareers.com, Inc.

What field, industry or location does the site cover: Environment, Safety, Occupational Health

Is the site an IAEWS Member: Yes

Employment Opportunities

Are full time jobs posted on the site: Yes

Are part time jobs posted on the site: Yes

Are contract jobs posted on the site: Yes

Are consulting jobs posted on the site: Yes

Resume Services

Are resumes or profiles stored on the site: Yes

Other Employment Services

Is a discussion forum or blog offered on the site: No

Are assessment instruments offered on the site: No

Recruiters

Is there an automated resume agent: Yes

Is banner advertising available: Yes

Job Seekers

Is there an automated job agent: Yes

Is career info provided: Yes

EmployeeBenefitsJobs.com

SITE'S SELF-DESCRIPTION

Online since 1996, EmployeeBenefitsJobs.com has high Google visibility and a loyal audience. A link to each job is published in email newsletters sent to 25,000 subscribers daily by affiliate BenefitsLink.com, the leading and first Web-site for the employee benefits community, where an advertisement for the job board appears on every page.

GENERAL INFORMATION

URL: www.employeebenefitsjobs.com

Date the site was activated online: 1996

Parent organization of the site: BenefitsLink.com, Inc.

What field, industry or location does the site cover: Employee Benefits & Administration

Is the site an IAEWS Member: Yes

Employment Opportunities

Are full time jobs posted on the site: Yes

Are part time jobs posted on the site: Yes

Are contract jobs posted on the site: Yes

Are consulting jobs posted on the site: Yes

Resume Services

Are resumes or profiles stored on the site: Yes

Other Employment Services

Is a discussion forum or blog offered on the site: Yes

Are assessment instruments offered on the site: No

Recruiters

Is there an automated resume agent: No

Is banner advertising available: Yes

Job Seekers

Is there an automated job agent: Yes

Is career info provided: Yes

EmploymentGuide.com

SITE'S SELF-DESCRIPTION

Partnered with The Employment Guide weekly publication, EmploymentGuide.com is the comprehensive online recruiting solution for employers looking to fill hourly and entry-level to mid-management positions. Widely recognized for its ease of use, EmploymentGuide.com offers an optimum combination of hiring solutions and job search options across all industries nationwide.

GENERAL INFORMATION

URL: www.employmentguide.com

Date the site was activated online: 1995

Parent organization of the site: Dominion Enterprises

What field, industry or location does the site cover: Wide variety, hourly to middle management

Is the site an IAEWS Member: No

Employment Opportunities

Are full time jobs posted on the site: Yes

Are part time jobs posted on the site: Yes

Are contract jobs posted on the site: Yes

Are consulting jobs posted on the site: Yes

Resume Services

Are resumes or profiles stored on the site: Yes (profiles only)

Other Employment Services

Is a discussion forum or blog offered on the site: Yes

Are assessment instruments offered on the site: Yes

Recruiters

Is there an automated resume agent: Yes

Is banner advertising available: Yes

Job Seekers

Is there an automated job agent: Yes

Is career info provided: Yes

ExecuNet

SITE'S SELF-DESCRIPTION

ExecuNet is a private membership network for business leaders who believe that the right connections can produce extraordinary results in their careers and organizations. Since 1988, it has provided members access to confidential six-figure job opportunities, proprietary research and pragmatic advice.

GENERAL INFORMATION

URL: www.execunet.com

Date the site was activated online: 1995

Parent organization of the site: ExecuNet

What field, industry or location does the site cover: HR, IS, MG, SM

Is the site an IAEWS Member: No

Employment Opportunities

Are full time jobs posted on the site: Yes

Are part time jobs posted on the site: No

Are contract jobs posted on the site: Yes

Are consulting jobs posted on the site: No

Resume Services

Are resumes or profiles stored on the site: Yes

Other Employment Services

Is a discussion forum or blog offered on the site: Yes

Are assessment instruments offered on the site: Yes

Recruiters

Is there an automated resume agent: Yes

Is banner advertising available: No

Job Seekers

Is there an automated job agent: Yes

Is career info provided: Yes

FlexJobs

SITE'S SELF-DESCRIPTION

FlexJobs is an innovative job site dedicated to bringing legitimate, flexible telecommuting jobs – and the work-life, economic, and environmental benefits they offer – to the people who want them. FlexJobs provides job-seekers a way to find qualified, hand-screened jobs quickly, easily, and safely and is a free resource for employers to recruit top-notch candidates.

GENERAL INFORMATION

URL: www.flexjobs.com

Date the site was activated online: 2007

Parent organization of the site: FlexJobs Corporation

What field, industry or location does the site cover: Telecommuting and flexible jobs

Is the site an IAEWS Member: Yes

Employment Opportunities

Are full time jobs posted on the site: Yes

Are part time jobs posted on the site: Yes

Are contract jobs posted on the site: Yes

Are consulting jobs posted on the site: Yes

Resume Services

Are resumes or profiles stored on the site: Yes

Recruiters

Is there an automated resume agent: Yes

Is banner advertising available: No

Other Employment Services

Is a discussion forum or blog offered on the site: No

Are assessment instruments offered on the site: No

Job Seekers

Is there an automated job agent: Yes

Is career info provided: No

Great Insurance Jobs

SITE'S SELF-DESCRIPTION

Great Insurance Jobs operates the insurance industry's leading career site. Functional products and services create the ultimate solution for a variety of hiring needs. Employers can reach the most qualified candidates by posting jobs or by searching our database of insurance-only professionals.

GENERAL INFORMATION

URL: www.greatinsurancejobs.com

Date the site was activated online: 2001

Parent organization of the site: Great Insurance Jobs, Inc.

What field, industry or location does the site cover: Insurance-related

Is the site an IAEWS Member: Yes

Employment Opportunities

Are full time jobs posted on the site: Yes

Are part time jobs posted on the site: Yes

Are contract jobs posted on the site: Yes

Are consulting jobs posted on the site: Yes

Resume Services

Are resumes or profiles stored on the site: Yes

Recruiters

Is there an automated resume agent: Yes

Is banner advertising available: Yes

Other Employment Services

Is a discussion forum or blog offered on the site: No

Are assessment instruments offered on the site: No

Job Seekers

Is there an automated job agent: Yes

Is career info provided: Yes

Hcareers

SITE'S SELF-DESCRIPTION

Are you looking for a hotel, restaurant, food service, or any other hospitality job? Find your next hospitality career on Hcareers, the leading online job board for the hospitality industry. Hcareers attracts over 800,000 unique job seeker visitors each month – more than any other niche job board. Employers can also review over 160,000 resumes posted by job seekers.

GENERAL INFORMATION

URL: www.hcareers.com

Date the site was activated online: 1998

Parent organization of the site: onTargetjobs, Inc.

What field, industry or location does the site cover: MG, OP, Hotel, Restaurant

Is the site an IAEWS Member: Yes

Employment Opportunities??

Are full time jobs posted on the site: Yes

Are part time jobs posted on the site: Yes

Are contract jobs posted on the site: Yes

Are consulting jobs posted on the site: Yes

Resume Services

Are resumes or profiles stored on the site: Yes

Recruiters

Is there an automated resume agent: Yes

Is banner advertising available: Yes

Other Employment Services

Is a discussion forum or blog offered on the site: No

Are assessment instruments offered on the site: Yes

Job Seekers

Is there an automated job agent: Yes

Is career info provided: No

Health Callings

SITE'S SELF-DESCRIPTION

Health Callings, a Dice Holdings, Inc. service, is a leading online career site dedicated to matching healthcare professionals with the best career opportunities in their profession. Recruiters and employers can post jobs targeting specific fields within the healthcare industry including allied health, nursing, laboratory, pharmacy and medicine.

GENERAL INFORMATION

URL: www.healthcallings.com

Date the site was activated online: 2005

Parent organization of the site: Dice Holdings, Inc.

What field, industry or location does the site cover: MG, Nursing, Allied Health

Is the site an IAEWS Member: Yes

Employment Opportunities

Are full time jobs posted on the site: Yes

Are part time jobs posted on the site: Yes

Are contract jobs posted on the site: No

Are consulting jobs posted on the site: No

Resume Services

Are resumes or profiles stored on the site: Yes

Other Employment Services

Is a discussion forum or blog offered on the site: No

Are assessment instruments offered on the site: No

Recruiters

Is there an automated resume agent: Yes

Is banner advertising available: Yes

Job Seekers

Is there an automated job agent: Yes

Is career info provided: Yes

HEALTHeCAREERS Network

SITE'S SELF-DESCRIPTION

HEALTHeCAREERS Network is a unique recruitment tool made possible through partnerships with more than 70 healthcare associations. The Network gives employers a single point of access to recruit from participating associations and hundreds of partner Web-sites. Services also include online print campaign management and access to association career fairs.

GENERAL INFORMATION

URL: www.healthecareers.com

Date the site was activated online: 1999

Parent organization of the site: onTargetjobs, Inc.

What field, industry or location does the site cover: AD, Healthcare, Physician, Nurse

Is the site an IAEWS Member: Yes

Employment Opportunities

Are full time jobs posted on the site: Yes

Are part time jobs posted on the site: Yes

Are contract jobs posted on the site: Yes

Are consulting jobs posted on the site: Yes

Resume Services

Are resumes or profiles stored on the site: Yes

Other Employment Services

Is a discussion forum or blog offered on the site: Yes

Are assessment instruments offered on the site: Yes

Recruiters

Is there an automated resume agent: Yes

Is banner advertising available: Yes

Job Seekers

Is there an automated job agent: Yes

Is career info provided: Yes

HealthJobsNationwide.com

SITE'S SELF-DESCRIPTION

Health Jobs Nationwide is the largest healthcare job board/talent acquisition resource in the nation. We are dedicated to a quality user experience with a focus on reach, relevancy and results for the healthcare professional and employment provider.

GENERAL INFORMATION

URL: www.healthjobsnationwide.com

Date the site was activated online: 2003

Parent organization of the site: Healthcare Staffing Innovations, LLC

What field, industry or location does the site cover: Healthcare

Is the site an IAEWS Member: Yes

Employment Opportunities

Are full time jobs posted on the site: Yes

Are part time jobs posted on the site: Yes

Are contract jobs posted on the site: Yes

Are consulting jobs posted on the site: Yes

Resume Services

Are resumes or profiles stored on the site: Yes

Other Employment Services

Is a discussion forum or blog offered on the site: Yes

Are assessment instruments offered on the site: Yes

Recruiters

Is there an automated resume agent: Yes

Is banner advertising available: Yes

Job Seekers

Is there an automated job agent: Yes

Is career info provided: Yes

HigherEdJobs

SITE'S SELF-DESCRIPTION

HigherEdJobs is the leading source for jobs and career information in academia. During 2010, more than 4,200 colleges and universities posted over 79,000 job postings to the company's Web-site. Serving higher education since 1996, HigherEdJobs now receives two million visits a month from 780,000 unique visitors representing both higher education professionals and couples.

GENERAL INFORMATION

URL: www.higheredjobs.com

Date the site was activated online: 1996

Parent organization of the site: Internet Employment Linkage, Inc.

What field, industry or location does the site cover: Higher Education (All Departments)

Is the site an IAEWS Member: Yes

Employment Opportunities

Are full time jobs posted on the site: Yes

Are part time jobs posted on the site: Yes

Are contract jobs posted on the site: No

Are consulting jobs posted on the site: No

Resume Services

Are resumes or profiles stored on the site: Yes

Other Employment Services

Is a discussion forum or blog offered on the site: No

Are assessment instruments offered on the site: No

Recruiters

Is there an automated resume agent: No

Is banner advertising available: Yes

Job Seekers

Is there an automated job agent: Yes

Is career info provided: Yes

HIMSS JobMine

SITE'S SELF-DESCRIPTION

HIMSS JobMine is offered to the members of the Healthcare Information and Management Systems Society (HIMSS). HIMSS represents more than 50,000 individual members and over 570 corporate members that represent organizations employing millions of people. Members are senior executives and IT management at hospitals and other providers, payers, consulting firms, IT vendors and more. 57% hold CIO, CTO or other IT titles, while 21% hold CEO, COO, CFO or other administration titles.

GENERAL INFORMATION

URL: http://jobmine.himss.org

Date the site was activated online: 2008

Parent organization of the site: HIMSS

What field, industry or location does the site cover: AD, IT, Healthcare

Is the site an IAEWS Member: No

Employment Opportunities

Are full time jobs posted on the site: Yes

Are part time jobs posted on the site: Yes

Are contract jobs posted on the site: Yes

Are consulting jobs posted on the site: Yes

Resume Services

Are resumes or profiles stored on the site: Yes

Other Employment Services

Is a discussion forum or blog offered on the site: Yes

Are assessment instruments offered on the site: Yes

Recruiters

Is there an automated resume agent: No

Is banner advertising available: Yes

Job Seekers

Is there an automated job agent: Yes

Is career info provided: Yes

Hospital Dream Jobs

SITE'S SELF-DESCRIPTION

Hospital Dream Jobs is unique in offering tens of thousands of healthcare jobs, cutting-edge technology, and original in-depth healthcare resources all in one place for healthcare professionals! Our updated services in social media marketing get results through branding, blogs, Twitter and Facebook. Our team has more than 20 years of experience in healthcare recruiting and Web-site technology.

GENERAL INFORMATION

URL: www.hospitaldreamjobs.com

Date the site was activated online: 2009

Parent organization of the site: Healthcare Communications, LLC

What field, industry or location does the site cover: Healthcare

Is the site an IAEWS Member: Yes

Employment Opportunities

Are full time jobs posted on the site: Yes

Are part time jobs posted on the site: Yes

Are contract jobs posted on the site: Yes

Are consulting jobs posted on the site: Yes

Resume Services

Are resumes or profiles stored on the site: Yes

Other Employment Services

Is a discussion forum or blog offered on the site: Yes

Are assessment instruments offered on the site: Yes

Recruiters

Is there an automated resume agent: Yes

Is banner advertising available: Yes

Job Seekers

Is there an automated job agent: Yes

Is career info provided: Yes

Hospital Jobs Online

SITE'S SELF-DESCRIPTION

Hospitaljobsonline.com is the #1 hospital job board and the leader in healthcare career resources for doctors, nurses, allied health, and administration job seekers. Employers receive pre-qualified leads and resumes sent daily, access to the resume database and unlimited job postings via bulk upload.

GENERAL INFORMATION

URL: www.hospitaljobsonline.com

Date the site was activated online: 2001

Parent organization of the site: Internet Brands, Inc.

What field, industry or location does the site cover: Nurses, Physicians, Allied Health

Is the site an IAEWS Member: Yes

Employment Opportunities

Are full time jobs posted on the site: Yes

Are part time jobs posted on the site: Yes

Are contract jobs posted on the site: Yes

Are consulting jobs posted on the site: Yes

Resume Services

Are resumes or profiles stored on the site: Yes

Other Employment Services

Is a discussion forum or blog offered on the site: No

Are assessment instruments offered on the site: No

Recruiters

Is there an automated resume agent: Yes

Is banner advertising available: Yes

Job Seekers

Is there an automated job agent: Yes

Is career info provided: Yes

icrunchdata

SITE'S SELF-DESCRIPTION

Icrunchdata is a community of top professionals in data, analytics, and technology! Whether you are looking to hire talent or promote your brand, we can help you reach your advertising goals.

GENERAL INFORMATION

URL: www.icrunchdata.com

Date the site was activated online: 2003

Parent organization of the site: icrunchdata

What field, industry or location does the site cover: Data, Analytics, Statistics

Is the site an IAEWS Member: Yes

Employment Opportunities

Are full time jobs posted on the site: Yes

Are part time jobs posted on the site: No

Are contract jobs posted on the site: Yes

Are consulting jobs posted on the site: Yes

Resume Services

Are resumes or profiles stored on the site: Yes

Recruiters

Is there an automated resume agent: Yes

Is banner advertising available: Yes

Other Employment Services

Is a discussion forum or blog offered on the site: No

Are assessment instruments offered on the site: No

Job Seekers

Is there an automated job agent: Yes

Is career info provided: Yes

IEEE Job Site

SITE'S SELF-DESCRIPTION

Use the IEEE Job Site to post jobs, search resumes and pre-screen candidates, all of whom are pre-qualified, highly skilled members of the Institute of Electrical & Electronics Engineers (IEEE). Place banner ads on the site or classified and display advertising in IEEE print publications. Our unique "smart job" technology will find you the best candidates available.

GENERAL INFORMATION

URL: www.ieee.org/jobs

Date the site was activated online: 2001

Parent organization of the site: Institute of Electrical & Electronics Engineers (IEEE)

What field, industry or location does the site cover: EN, IS, MG, Scientist

Is the site an IAEWS Member: Yes

Employment Opportunities

Are full time jobs posted on the site: Yes

Are part time jobs posted on the site: Yes

Are contract jobs posted on the site: No

Are consulting jobs posted on the site: No

Resume Services

Are resumes or profiles stored on the site: Yes

Recruiters

Is there an automated resume agent: Yes

Is banner advertising available: Yes

Other Employment Services

Is a discussion forum or blog offered on the site: No

Are assessment instruments offered on the site: No

Job Seekers

Is there an automated job agent: Yes

Is career info provided: Yes

iHire.com

SITE'S SELF-DESCRIPTION

iHire job seekers enjoy access to over 850,000 jobs from over 4,300 sources, as well as personalized, daily job feeds, resume and cover letter assistance, and interview and salary negotiation coaching. iHire's industry-specific focus, money-back guarantee, and resume matching technologies provide employers with a risk-free, effective alternative to conventional job boards.

GENERAL INFORMATION

URL: www.ihire.com

Date the site was activated online: 1999

Parent organization of the site: iHire, LLC

What field, industry or location does the site cover: Wide variety

Is the site an IAEWS Member: Yes

Employment Opportunities

Are full time jobs posted on the site: Yes

Are part time jobs posted on the site: Yes

Are contract jobs posted on the site: Yes

Are consulting jobs posted on the site: Yes

Resume Services

Are resumes or profiles stored on the site: Yes

Other Employment Services

Is a discussion forum or blog offered on the site: No

Are assessment instruments offered on the site: Yes

Recruiters

Is there an automated resume agent: Yes

Is banner advertising available: No

Job Seekers

Is there an automated job agent: Yes

Is career info provided: Yes

Indeed

SITE'S SELF-DESCRIPTION

Indeed is the #1 job site worldwide, with over 40 million unique visitors per month from more than 50 countries in 24 languages. Job seekers perform more than 1 billion job searches on Indeed each month. Since 2004, Indeed has given job seekers free access to millions of jobs from thousands of company Web-sites and job boards.

GENERAL INFORMATION

URL: www.indeed.com

Date the site was activated online: 2004

Parent organization of the site: Recruit Co.

What field, industry or location does the site cover: Wide variety

Is the site an IAEWS Member: Yes

Employment Opportunities

Are full time jobs posted on the site: Yes

Are part time jobs posted on the site: Yes

Are contract jobs posted on the site: Yes

Are consulting jobs posted on the site: Yes

Resume Services

Are resumes or profiles stored on the site: No

Recruiters

Is there an automated resume agent: No

Is banner advertising available: No

Other Employment Services

Is a discussion forum or blog offered on the site: Yes

Are assessment instruments offered on the site: Yes

Job Seekers

Is there an automated job agent: Yes

Is career info provided: Yes

Inside Higher Ed

SITE'S SELF-DESCRIPTION

Inside Higher Ed is the daily news Web-site for higher education professionals. Featuring breaking news, commentary, career advice, blogs, and thousands of faculty, administrative and executive job postings, more than 750,000 unique readers visit the site each month. Job content is integrated throughout the site, reaching passive candidates with related jobs.

GENERAL INFORMATION

URL: www.insidehighered.com

Date the site was activated online: 2005

Parent organization of the site: Inside Higher Ed

What field, industry or location does the site cover: Higher Education Faculty, Staff & Other

Is the site an IAEWS Member: Yes

Employment Opportunities

Are full time jobs posted on the site: Yes

Are part time jobs posted on the site: Yes

Are contract jobs posted on the site: Yes

Are consulting jobs posted on the site: No

Resume Services

Are resumes or profiles stored on the site: Yes

Other Employment Services

Is a discussion forum or blog offered on the site: No

Are assessment instruments offered on the site: No

Recruiters

Is there an automated resume agent: Yes

Is banner advertising available: Yes

Job Seekers

Is there an automated job agent: Yes

Is career info provided: Yes

JAMA Career Center®

SITE'S SELF-DESCRIPTION

JAMA Career Center® is a resource for active and passive physician job seekers. The site presents physician career opportunities, news, and resources relevant to the full spectrum of medical practice. Recruiters will find a range of posting options including multi-job packs, site wrapping, employer profiles, banner ads, and print plus online combos.

GENERAL INFORMATION

URL: www.jamacareercenter.com

Date the site was activated online: 2005

Parent organization of the site: American Medical Association

What field, industry or location does the site cover: Physician

Is the site an IAEWS Member: Yes

Employment Opportunities

Are full time jobs posted on the site: Yes

Are part time jobs posted on the site: Yes

Are contract jobs posted on the site: Yes

Are consulting jobs posted on the site: Yes

Resume Services

Are resumes or profiles stored on the site: Yes

Other Employment Services

Is a discussion forum or blog offered on the site: No

Are assessment instruments offered on the site: Yes

Recruiters

Is there an automated resume agent: Yes

Is banner advertising available: Yes

Job Seekers

Is there an automated job agent: Yes

Is career info provided: Yes

Job.com

SITE'S SELF-DESCRIPTION

Based out of Fredericksburg, VA and one of the fastest growing career portals on the Internet, Job.com connects great people across the U.S. with great companies. Job.com is consistently recognized as a top 4 career site on the Internet by Internet audience measurement leader comScore Media Metrix.

GENERAL INFORMATION

URL: www.job.com

Date the site was activated online: 2001

Parent organization of the site: Job.com, Inc.

What field, industry or location does the site cover: AD, FA, IS, SM

Is the site an IAEWS Member: Yes

Employment Opportunities

Are full time jobs posted on the site: Yes

Are part time jobs posted on the site: Yes

Are contract jobs posted on the site: Yes

Are consulting jobs posted on the site: Yes

Resume Services

Are resumes or profiles stored on the site: Yes

Recruiters

Is there an automated resume agent: Yes

Is banner advertising available: Yes

Other Employment Services

Is a discussion forum or blog offered on the site: No

Are assessment instruments offered on the site: Yes

Job Seekers

Is there an automated job agent: Yes

Is career info provided: Yes

Jobing

SITE'S SELF-DESCRIPTION

A three-time Inc. 500 fastest-growing company, Jobing.com is the nation's largest locally-focused job board community whose mission is to connect local employers and job seekers through a variety of resources such as job postings, resume search, employment branding banners and advertising, event listings and advanced company profiles.

GENERAL INFORMATION

URL: www.jobing.com

Date the site was activated online: 2000

Parent organization of the site: Jobing

What field, industry or location does the site cover: Wide variety

Is the site an IAEWS Member: Yes

Employment Opportunities

Are full time jobs posted on the site: Yes

Are part time jobs posted on the site: Yes

Are contract jobs posted on the site: Yes

Are consulting jobs posted on the site: Yes

Resume Services

Are resumes or profiles stored on the site: Yes

Recruiters

Is there an automated resume agent: Yes

Is banner advertising available: Yes

Other Employment Services

Is a discussion forum or blog offered on the site: Yes

Are assessment instruments offered on the site: Yes

Job Seekers

Is there an automated job agent: Yes

Is career info provided: Yes

JobMonkey

SITE'S SELF-DESCRIPTION

Since 1999, JobMonkey.com has been a leader in matching employers with jobseekers looking for great summer, seasonal and year-round jobs in the U.S. and abroad. JobMonkey has 6,000+ pages of industry guides directing jobseekers to the "coolest jobs" available. Primary Users: age 18-40 Site Traffic: Over 1 million page views per month. Jobs also promoted via Facebook, Twitter and newsletters.

GENERAL INFORMATION

URL: www.jobmonkey.com

Date the site was activated online: 1999

Parent organization of the site: JobMonkey, Inc.

What field, industry or location does the site cover: SM, Hospitality, Hourly, Entry Level, Retail

Is the site an IAEWS Member: Yes

Employment Opportunities

Are full time jobs posted on the site: Yes

Are part time jobs posted on the site: Yes

Are contract jobs posted on the site: Yes

Are consulting jobs posted on the site: Yes

Resume Services

Are resumes or profiles stored on the site: Yes

Other Employment Services

Is a discussion forum or blog offered on the site: Yes

Are assessment instruments offered on the site: No

Recruiters

Is there an automated resume agent: Yes

Is banner advertising available: Yes

Job Seekers

Is there an automated job agent: Yes

Is career info provided: Yes

Jobs2Careers.com

SITE'S SELF-DESCRIPTION

Jobs2Careers is a comprehensive job search engine attracting millions of job seekers nationwide. Our Web-site gives job seekers free access to easily search through millions of open positions from thousands of company Web-sites and job boards all at once in a fast, intuitive display. We update our job content daily to deliver the freshest jobs to job seekers. Use our site to search for jobs and launch your career!

GENERAL INFORMATION

URL: www.jobs2careers.com

Date the site was activated online: 2010

Parent organization of the site: InsidersReferral.com, Inc.

What field, industry or location does the site cover: Wide variety

Is the site an IAEWS Member: Yes

Employment Opportunities

Are full time jobs posted on the site: Yes

Are part time jobs posted on the site: Yes

Are contract jobs posted on the site: Yes

Are consulting jobs posted on the site: Yes

Resume Services

Are resumes or profiles stored on the site: No

Other Employment Services

Is a discussion forum or blog offered on the site: No

Are assessment instruments offered on the site: No

Recruiters

Is there an automated resume agent: No

Is banner advertising available: No

Job Seekers

Is there an automated job agent: Yes

Is career info provided: No

JobServe

SITE'S SELF-DESCRIPTION

The JobServe group of companies is an international network of employment Web-sites servicing clients across the globe, and incorporating renowned international brands CareerBoard.com, ComputerWork.com, ComputerJobs.com, JobShark.com and JobNetcom. au. JobServe has sites covering Europe, Australia, Asia, the US and Canada.

GENERAL INFORMATION

URL: www.jobserve.com

Date the site was activated online: 1993

Parent organization of the site: JobServe Limited

What field, industry or location does the site cover: Wide variety

Is the site an IAEWS Member: Yes

Employment Opportunities

Are full time jobs posted on the site: Yes

Are part time jobs posted on the site: Yes

Are contract jobs posted on the site: Yes

Are consulting jobs posted on the site: Yes

Resume Services

Are resumes or profiles stored on the site: Yes

Other Employment Services

Is a discussion forum or blog offered on the site: Yes

Are assessment instruments offered on the site: Yes

Recruiters

Is there an automated resume agent: Yes

Is banner advertising available: Yes

Job Seekers

Is there an automated job agent: Yes

Is career info provided: Yes

JobsInBenefits.com

SITE'S SELF-DESCRIPTION

JobsInBenefits.com brings together qualified benefits/HR professionals with the companies that seek them. Because this job site is hosted by a respected association, recruiters can expect to find resumes from highly qualified benefits/HR professionals. Recruiters looking to fill multiple positions can save with the purchase of a Job Pack.

GENERAL INFORMATION

URL: www.jobsinbenefits.com

Date the site was activated online: 1998

Parent organization of the site: International Foundation of Employee Benefit Plans (IFEBP)

What field, industry or location does the site cover: HR, MG, Benefits, Compensation

Is the site an IAEWS Member: Yes

Employment Opportunities

Are full time jobs posted on the site: Yes

Are part time jobs posted on the site: Yes

Are contract jobs posted on the site: Yes

Are consulting jobs posted on the site: Yes

Resume Services

Are resumes or profiles stored on the site: Yes

Other Employment Services

Is a discussion forum or blog offered on the site: Yes

Are assessment instruments offered on the site: No

Recruiters

Is there an automated resume agent: No

Is banner advertising available: No

Job Seekers

Is there an automated job agent: No

Is career info provided: Yes

JobsInLogistics.com

SITE'S SELF-DESCRIPTION

JobsInLogistics.com is North America's largest and most cost effective career and recruiting job board for the logistics, supply chain, manufacturing, transportation, distribution, purchasing, materials management and warehousing professions. JobsInLogistics.com conducts extensive target marketing to attract the top quality candidates in this niche area.

GENERAL INFORMATION

URL: www.jobsinlogistics.com

Date the site was activated online: 2000

Parent organization of the site: JobsInLogistics.com, Inc.

What field, industry or location does the site cover: Logistics, Transportation, Warehousing

Is the site an IAEWS Member: Yes

Employment Opportunities

Are full time jobs posted on the site: Yes

Are part time jobs posted on the site: Yes

Are contract jobs posted on the site: Yes

Are consulting jobs posted on the site: Yes

Resume Services

Are resumes or profiles stored on the site: Yes

Other Employment Services

Is a discussion forum or blog offered on the site: No

Are assessment instruments offered on the site: No

Recruiters

Is there an automated resume agent: Yes

Is banner advertising available: Yes

Job Seekers

Is there an automated job agent: Yes

Is career info provided: Yes

Jobsintheus.com

SITE'S SELF-DESCRIPTION

JobsInTheUS (JIUS) is a network of state-specific, locally branded, general employment Web-sites dedicated to connecting local, high-quality and eminently real employers with equally high-quality and real job-seeking candidates.

GENERAL INFORMATION

URL: www.jobsintheus.com

Date the site was activated online: 1999

Parent organization of the site: JiUS, Inc.

What field, industry or location does the site cover: Northeast USA (Maine, New Hampshire, Rhode Island, Vermont and Massachusetts)

Is the site an IAEWS Member: Yes

Employment Opportunities

Are full time jobs posted on the site: Yes

Are part time jobs posted on the site: Yes

Are contract jobs posted on the site: Yes

Are consulting jobs posted on the site: Yes

Resume Services

Are resumes or profiles stored on the site: Yes

Other Employment Services

Is a discussion forum or blog offered on the site: No

Are assessment instruments offered on the site: No

Recruiters

Is there an automated resume agent: No

Is banner advertising available: Yes

Job Seekers

Is there an automated job agent: Yes

Is career info provided: Yes

JobsinTrucks

SITE'S SELF-DESCRIPTION

JobsInTrucks.com is the #1 driver job board used by employers to hire experienced drivers and owner-operators across the USA and Canada. More than 200,000 drivers visit the site each month to find jobs for Class A and Class B company driver and owner-operator positions for long distance, regional and local delivery.

GENERAL INFORMATION

URL: www.jobsintrucks.com

Date the site was activated online: 2004

Parent organization of the site: JobsinLogistics.com

What field, industry or location does the site cover: Truck Driver

Is the site an IAEWS Member: Yes

Employment Opportunities

Are full time jobs posted on the site: Yes

Are part time jobs posted on the site: Yes

Are contract jobs posted on the site: Yes

Are consulting jobs posted on the site: Yes

Resume Services

Are resumes or profiles stored on the site: Yes

Other Employment Services

Is a discussion forum or blog offered on the site: No

Are assessment instruments offered on the site: No

Recruiters

Is there an automated resume agent: No

Is banner advertising available: Yes

Job Seekers

Is there an automated job agent: Yes

Is career info provided: Yes

JobsRadar

SITE'S SELF-DESCRIPTION

JobsRadar is a one-stop Web-site for job seekers and a user-friendly recruitment resource for HR groups. We not only host resumes but build and host Web-sites for registered users from which they can manage their professional online identity. In addition to job search, a career directory and sales discovery, career advancement, education and scholarship tools are available.

GENERAL INFORMATION

URL: www.jobsradar.com

Date the site was activated online: 2009

Parent organization of the site: Percipio Media, LLC

What field, industry or location does the site cover: Wide variety

Is the site an IAEWS Member: Yes

Employment Opportunities

Are full time jobs posted on the site: Yes

Are part time jobs posted on the site: Yes

Are contract jobs posted on the site: Yes

Are consulting jobs posted on the site: Yes

Resume Services

Are resumes or profiles stored on the site: Yes

Other Employment Services

Is a discussion forum or blog offered on the site: No

Are assessment instruments offered on the site: Yes

Recruiters

Is there an automated resume agent: Yes

Is banner advertising available: Yes

Job Seekers

Is there an automated job agent: Yes

Is career info provided: Yes

JobWings.com

SITE'S SELF-DESCRIPTION

jobWings.com is the Internet reference for employment in the fields of finance, accounting and management for intermediate to senior level positions in Canada. Founded in February, 2001, jobWings.com quickly established itself as the leader in that field and remains so today with more than 53,000 visitors per month.

GENERAL INFORMATION

URL: www.jobwings.com

Date the site was activated online: 2001

Parent organization of the site: jobWings.com

What field, industry or location does the site cover: FA, MG

Is the site an IAEWS Member: Yes

Employment Opportunities

Are full time jobs posted on the site: Yes

Are part time jobs posted on the site: No

Are contract jobs posted on the site: No

Are consulting jobs posted on the site: No

Resume Services

Are resumes or profiles stored on the site: No

Other Employment Services

Is a discussion forum or blog offered on the site: No

Are assessment instruments offered on the site: No

Recruiters

Is there an automated resume agent: No

Is banner advertising available: Yes

Job Seekers

Is there an automated job agent: Yes

Is career info provided: Yes

Juju

SITE'S SELF-DESCRIPTION

Juju's goal is to make job search easier. We search jobs found on thousands of employer sites and job boards around the Web and offer features that help you find the one you're looking for more efficiently. We also offer recruitment advertising that allows employers to reach millions of targeted job seekers, enhance their employment brand, and lower their cost-per-hire.

GENERAL INFORMATION

URL: www.juju.com

Date the site was activated online: 2006

Parent organization of the site: Juju, Inc.

What field, industry or location does the site cover: Wide variety

Is the site an IAEWS Member: Yes

Employment Opportunities

Are full time jobs posted on the site: Yes

Are part time jobs posted on the site: Yes

Are contract jobs posted on the site: Yes

Are consulting jobs posted on the site: Yes

Resume Services

Are resumes or profiles stored on the site: No

Other Employment Services

Is a discussion forum or blog offered on the site: No

Are assessment instruments offered on the site: No

Recruiters

Is there an automated resume agent: No

Is banner advertising available: No

Job Seekers

Is there an automated job agent: Yes

Is career info provided: No

LatPro

SITE'S SELF-DESCRIPTION

Established in 1997, LatPro is the worldwide leader in providing online employment resources for Hispanic and bilingual professionals. With over 330,000 registered candidates and 90 of the Fortune 100 companies using its award-winning service, LatPro.com (available in English, Spanish and Portuguese) is the premier career destination for Latino and bilingual professionals.

GENERAL INFORMATION

URL: www.latpro.com

Date the site was activated online: 1997

Parent organization of the site: LatPro, Inc.

What field, industry or location does the site cover: CS, EN, FA, SM, Diversity

Is the site an IAEWS Member: Yes

Employment Opportunities

Are full time jobs posted on the site: Yes

Are part time jobs posted on the site: Yes

Are contract jobs posted on the site: Yes

Are consulting jobs posted on the site: Yes

Resume Services

Are resumes or profiles stored on the site: Yes

Other Employment Services

Is a discussion forum or blog offered on the site: Yes

Are assessment instruments offered on the site: Yes

Recruiters

Is there an automated resume agent: Yes

Is banner advertising available: Yes

Job Seekers

Is there an automated job agent: Yes

Is career info provided: Yes

LinkedIn

SITE'S SELF-DESCRIPTION

LinkedIn is the world's largest professional network with 200 million members in 200 countries and territories around the globe. Our mission is simple: connect the world's professionals to make them more productive and successful. When you join LinkedIn, you get access to people, jobs, news, updates, and insights that help you be great at what you do.

GENERAL INFORMATION

URL: www.linkedin.com

Date the site was activated online: 2003

Parent organization of the site: LinkedIn Corporation

What field, industry or location does the site cover: Wide variety

Is the site an IAEWS Member: No

Employment Opportunities

Are full time jobs posted on the site: Yes

Are part time jobs posted on the site: Yes

Are contract jobs posted on the site: Yes

Are consulting jobs posted on the site: Yes

Resume Services

Are resumes or profiles stored on the site: Yes

Other Employment Services

Is a discussion forum or blog offered on the site: Yes

Are assessment instruments offered on the site: No

Recruiters

Is there an automated resume agent: No

Is banner advertising available: Yes

Job Seekers

Is there an automated job agent: No

Is career info provided: Yes

LiveCareer

SITE'S SELF-DESCRIPTION

LiveCareer's career experts have focused goals: to give job seekers all the tools needed to win the job and to connect them with the perfect employer. That's why we created our award winning Resume Builder, the easiest way to build a professional resume. Plus, our cover letter builder, career tests, job postings and interview guides provide all the tools needed for a successful job search.

GENERAL INFORMATION

URL: www.livecareer.com

Date the site was activated online: 2004

Parent organization of the site: LiveCareer, Ltd.

What field, industry or location does the site cover: Call Center, CS, SM

Is the site an IAEWS Member: Yes

Employment Opportunities

Are full time jobs posted on the site: Yes

Are part time jobs posted on the site: Yes

Are contract jobs posted on the site: Yes

Are consulting jobs posted on the site: Yes

Resume Services

Are resumes or profiles stored on the site: Yes

Other Employment Services

Is a discussion forum or blog offered on the site: Yes

Are assessment instruments offered on the site: Yes

Recruiters

Is there an automated resume agent: Yes

Is banner advertising available: No

Job Seekers

Is there an automated job agent: Yes

Is career info provided: Yes

LocumTenens.com

SITE'S SELF-DESCRIPTION

LocumTenens.com is a leading provider of locum tenens physicians and CRNAs nationwide. It is the only full-service locum tenens recruiting agency offering a free Internet job board (for both permanent and interim positions) and an array of "unbundled" services including a CV builder, a credentialing warehouse and online resource centers for both physicians and facilities.

GENERAL INFORMATION

URL: www.locumtenens.com

Date the site was activated online: 1999

Parent organization of the site: LocumTenens.com, Inc.

What field, industry or location does the site cover: Physician, Certified Registered Nurse Anesthetist (CRNA)

Is the site an IAEWS Member: Yes

Employment Opportunities

Are full time jobs posted on the site: Yes

Are part time jobs posted on the site: Yes

Are contract jobs posted on the site: Yes

Are consulting jobs posted on the site: Yes

Resume Services

Are resumes or profiles stored on the site: Yes (resumes only)

Recruiters

Is there an automated resume agent: Yes

Is banner advertising available: No

Other Employment Services

Is a discussion forum or blog offered on the site: No

Are assessment instruments offered on the site: Yes

Job Seekers

Is there an automated job agent: Yes

Is career info provided: Yes

Matchpoint Careers

SITE'S SELF-DESCRIPTION

Matchpoint Careers presents an innovative, break-through solution for recruitment and career guidance. We match people and jobs based on the factors that predict performance in each job, with industry-leading, validated, assessments. We end "hire on skill, fire on fit." Employers get performance-predicting job and candidate profiles, ranked for top performance. Candidates receive self-knowledge and guidance to best-fit careers.

GENERAL INFORMATION

URL: www.matchpointcareers.com

Date the site was activated online: 2011

Parent organization of the site: Matchpoint Careers, Inc.

What field, industry or location does the site cover: Wide variety

Is the site an IAEWS Member: Yes

Employment Opportunities

Are full time jobs posted on the site: Yes

Are part time jobs posted on the site: Yes

Are contract jobs posted on the site: Yes

Are consulting jobs posted on the site: Yes

Resume Services

Are resumes or profiles stored on the site: Yes

Other Employment Services

Is a discussion forum or blog offered on the site: Yes

Are assessment instruments offered on the site: Yes

Recruiters

Is there an automated resume agent: No

Is banner advertising available: No

Job Seekers

Is there an automated job agent: Yes

Is career info provided: Yes

Mediabistro

SITE'S SELF-DESCRIPTION

Mediabistro is the number one destination to reach job seekers in the media industry. Our members/users hear about us through word-of-mouth and our invitation-only cocktail parties (we don't advertise) so our candidates are savvy, and our traffic is targeted. Post your job online and reach out to over 400,000 registered creative and business-side professionals.

GENERAL INFORMATION

URL: www.mediabistro.com

Date the site was activated online: 1997

Parent organization of the site: WebMediaBrands

What field, industry or location does the site cover: Journalism, Media

Is the site an IAEWS Member: No

Employment Opportunities

Are full time jobs posted on the site: Yes

Are part time jobs posted on the site: Yes

Are contract jobs posted on the site: No

Are consulting jobs posted on the site: No

Resume Services

Are resumes or profiles stored on the site: Yes (profiles only)

Recruiters

Is there an automated resume agent: No

Is banner advertising available: Yes

Other Employment Services

Is a discussion forum or blog offered on the site: Yes

Are assessment instruments offered on the site: No

Job Seekers

Is there an automated job agent: Yes

Is career info provided: Yes

Medreps

SITE'S SELF-DESCRIPTION

MedReps.com has been connecting industry employers and recruiters with medical and pharmaceutical sales, marketing, and management professionals since the year 2000. Experienced job seekers know they can find the most sought-after medical jobs on MedReps.com, and big name industry employers and recruiters continue to trust MedReps.com to deliver top-performing sales people.

GENERAL INFORMATION

URL: www.medreps.com

Date the site was activated online: 2000

Parent organization of the site: Healthcare Staffing Technologies, LLC

What field, industry or location does the site cover: SM, Medical device and pharmaceutical

Is the site an IAEWS Member: Yes

Employment Opportunities

Are full time jobs posted on the site: Yes

Are part time jobs posted on the site: Yes

Are contract jobs posted on the site: Yes

Are consulting jobs posted on the site: Yes

Resume Services

Are resumes or profiles stored on the site: Yes

Other Employment Services

Is a discussion forum or blog offered on the site: No

Are assessment instruments offered on the site: No

Recruiters

Is there an automated resume agent: Yes

Is banner advertising available: Yes

Job Seekers

Is there an automated job agent: Yes

Is career info provided: Yes

MEP Jobs

SITE'S SELF-DESCRIPTION

MEP Jobs is the leading career site for the mechanical, electrical and plumbing industries. Each day, thousands of HVAC, facilities, electrical and plumbing professionals and employers find each other on MEP Jobs.

GENERAL INFORMATION

URL: www.mepjobs.com

Date the site was activated online: 1996

Parent organization of the site: Industry People Group

What field, industry or location does the site cover: EN, HVAC, Construction

Is the site an IAEWS Member: Yes

Employment Opportunities

Are full time jobs posted on the site: Yes

Are part time jobs posted on the site: Yes

Are contract jobs posted on the site: Yes

Are consulting jobs posted on the site: Yes

Resume Services

Are resumes or profiles stored on the site: Yes

Other Employment Services

Is a discussion forum or blog offered on the site: No

Are assessment instruments offered on the site: No

Recruiters

Is there an automated resume agent: Yes

Is banner advertising available: Yes

Job Seekers

Is there an automated job agent: Yes

Is career info provided: Yes

MilitaryConnection.com

SITE'S SELF-DESCRIPTION

We are called the "Go To" site for jobs, resources, articles and more for military veterans and their families. We offer clients the opportunity to repeat their message in additional and creative ways. We are excellent at reaching passive job seekers too. Users average 25 minutes on-site according to Alexa, drawn by the most up-to-date resources and databases for transition.

GENERAL INFORMATION

URL: www.militaryconnection.com

Date the site was activated online: 2006

Parent organization of the site: MilitaryConnection.com

What field, industry or location does the site cover: Wide variety

Is the site an IAEWS Member: Yes

Employment Opportunities

Are full time jobs posted on the site: Yes

Are part time jobs posted on the site: Yes

Are contract jobs posted on the site: Yes

Are consulting jobs posted on the site: Yes

Resume Services

Are resumes or profiles stored on the site: Yes

Recruiters

Is there an automated resume agent: No

Is banner advertising available: Yes

Other Employment Services

Is a discussion forum or blog offered on the site: Yes

Are assessment instruments offered on the site: Yes

Job Seekers

Is there an automated job agent: No

Is career info provided: Yes

MilitaryHire.com

SITE'S SELF-DESCRIPTION

MilitaryHire.com is the leading Internet job board for military personnel. As of 2011, we represent nearly 500,000 military candidates. MilitaryHire.com was developed by veterans, for veterans! We specialize in the military experienced candidate. The departing military candidate has the skills that are crucial in today's competitive business environment.

GENERAL INFORMATION

URL: www.militaryhire.com

Date the site was activated online: 1999

Parent organization of the site: The Mentor Group, Inc.

What field, industry or location does the site cover: IS, Defense, Security Clearance

Is the site an IAEWS Member: Yes

Employment Opportunities

Are full time jobs posted on the site: Yes

Are part time jobs posted on the site: Yes

Are contract jobs posted on the site: Yes

Are consulting jobs posted on the site: Yes

Resume Services

Are resumes or profiles stored on the site: Yes

Other Employment Services

Is a discussion forum or blog offered on the site: Yes

Are assessment instruments offered on the site: Yes

Recruiters

Is there an automated resume agent: Yes

Is banner advertising available: Yes

Job Seekers

Is there an automated job agent: Yes

Is career info provided: Yes

Monster.com

SITE'S SELF-DESCRIPTION

Monster.com® , the leading job matching engine, is dedicated to matching talent to opportunity with unrivaled precision. Monster offers employers a full array of online products and services for building and growing a talented workforce and matches seekers to meaningful careers, inspiring them to improve their lives through the world of work.

GENERAL INFORMATION

URL: www.monster.com

Date the site was activated online: 1994

Parent organization of the site: Monster Worldwide, Inc.

What field, industry or location does the site cover: Wide variety

Is the site an IAEWS Member: Yes

Employment Opportunities

Are full time jobs posted on the site: Yes

Are part time jobs posted on the site: Yes

Are contract jobs posted on the site: Yes

Are consulting jobs posted on the site: Yes

Resume Services

Are resumes or profiles stored on the site: Yes

Other Employment Services

Is a discussion forum or blog offered on the site: Yes

Are assessment instruments offered on the site: Yes

Recruiters

Is there an automated resume agent: Yes

Is banner advertising available: Yes

Job Seekers

Is there an automated job agent: Yes

Is career info provided: Yes

National Healthcare Career Network

SITE'S SELF-DESCRIPTION

The National Healthcare Career Network is the fastest growing healthcare association job board network available. The Network links job boards of more than 200 leading healthcare associations, which are the preferred resource for healthcare talent. We serve employers in filling positions ranging from volunteers and hourly staff to physicians and executive management.

GENERAL INFORMATION

URL: www.nhcnnetwork.org

Date the site was activated online: 2007

Parent organization of the site: Boxwood Technology

What field, industry or location does the site cover: Nurse, Physician, Allied Health

Is the site an IAEWS Member: Yes

Employment Opportunities

Are full time jobs posted on the site: Yes

Are part time jobs posted on the site: Yes

Are contract jobs posted on the site: Yes

Are consulting jobs posted on the site: Yes

Resume Services

Are resumes or profiles stored on the site: Yes

Other Employment Services

Is a discussion forum or blog offered on the site: Yes

Are assessment instruments offered on the site: Yes

Recruiters

Is there an automated resume agent: Yes

Is banner advertising available: Yes

Job Seekers

Is there an automated job agent: Yes

Is career info provided: Yes

NationJob.com

SITE'S SELF-DESCRIPTION

NationJob.com is the leading provider of community-based recruitment. Our core business is our Community Job Network, a partnership between NationJob.com and membership-based organizations offering members significant discounts and creating a custom job site for member employers.

GENERAL INFORMATION

URL: www.nationjob.com

Date the site was activated online: 1995

Parent organization of the site: NationJob Network, Inc.

What field, industry or location does the site cover: Wide variety

Is the site an IAEWS Member: Yes

Employment Opportunities

Are full time jobs posted on the site: Yes

Are part time jobs posted on the site: Yes

Are contract jobs posted on the site: Yes

Are consulting jobs posted on the site: Yes

Resume Services

Are resumes or profiles stored on the site: Yes

Other Employment Services

Is a discussion forum or blog offered on the site: No

Are assessment instruments offered on the site: Yes

Recruiters

Is there an automated resume agent: No

Is banner advertising available: Yes

Job Seekers

Is there an automated job agent: Yes

Is career info provided: Yes

NCAA Market

SITE'S SELF-DESCRIPTION

The National Collegiate Athletic Association (NCAA) is the national governing body for almost 1,300 member institutions, athletics conferences and affiliated organizations.Use the NCAA Market to find the career in intercollegiate athletics that you've been seeking. Review job postings from colleges and universities across the country. You can establish an account, post a resume and create search tools that will let you know when a career match is posted.

GENERAL INFORMATION

URL: http://ncaamarket.ncaa.org

Date the site was activated online: 2007

Parent organization of the site: National Collegiate Athletic Association

What field, industry or location does the site cover: College Athletics

Is the site an IAEWS Member: No

Employment Opportunities

Are full time jobs posted on the site: Yes

Are part time jobs posted on the site: Yes

Are contract jobs posted on the site: Yes

Are consulting jobs posted on the site: No

Resume Services

Are resumes or profiles stored on the site: Yes

Other Employment Services

Is a discussion forum or blog offered on the site: No

Are assessment instruments offered on the site: No

Recruiters

Is there an automated resume agent: Yes

Is banner advertising available: Yes

Job Seekers

Is there an automated job agent: Yes

Is career info provided: No

Net-Temps

GENERAL INFORMATION

URL: www.net-temps.com

Date the site was activated online: 1996

Parent organization of the site: Net-Temps, Inc.

What field, industry or location does the site cover: AD, FA, IS, MG, Retail

Is the site an IAEWS Member: Yes

Employment Opportunities

Are full time jobs posted on the site: Yes

Are part time jobs posted on the site: Yes

Are contract jobs posted on the site: Yes

Are consulting jobs posted on the site: Yes

Resume Services

Are resumes or profiles stored on the site: Yes

Other Employment Services

Is a discussion forum or blog offered on the site: Yes

Are assessment instruments offered on the site: Yes

Recruiters

Is there an automated resume agent: Yes

Is banner advertising available: Yes

Job Seekers

Is there an automated job agent: Yes

Is career info provided: Yes

Openreq

SITE'S SELF-DESCRIPTION

Openreq is a specialized career portal for the staffing, recruiting & HR industry with news, content, featured articles and a career center. The site includes a branded LinkedIn group with 35,000+ members and a Facebook page and Twitter page for full professional and social networking. Organizations looking to hire staffing, recruiting & HR professionals can showcase their employment opportunities, culture and brand.

GENERAL INFORMATION

URL: www.openreq.com

Date the site was activated online: 1999

Parent organization of the site: eCareer Holdings, Inc.

What field, industry or location does the site cover: Staffing, Recruiting & HR

Is the site an IAEWS Member: Yes

Employment Opportunities

Are full time jobs posted on the site: Yes

Are part time jobs posted on the site: Yes

Are contract jobs posted on the site: Yes

Are consulting jobs posted on the site: Yes

Resume Services

Are resumes or profiles stored on the site: Yes

Other Employment Services

Is a discussion forum or blog offered on the site: Yes

Are assessment instruments offered on the site: Yes

Recruiters

Is there an automated resume agent: Yes

Is banner advertising available: Yes

Job Seekers

Is there an automated job agent: Yes

Is career info provided: Yes

PharmaDiversity Job Board

SITE'S SELF-DESCRIPTION

PharmaDiversity Job Board is the only job board that specifically connects minority, diverse and multilingual job seekers with ALL types of jobs in pharma, biotech and healthcare business. In business for seven years, we boast a 95% renewal rate among advertisers. PharmaDiversity Job Board has a proven track record for focused talent acquisition while expanding our featured employer's diversity branding. PharmaDiversity, an all-inclusive, global job board, is free for job seekers.

GENERAL INFORMATION

URL: www.pharmadiversityjobboard.com

Date the site was activated online: 2007

Parent organization of the site: PharmaDiversity

What field, industry or location does the site cover: Diversity, Pharmacuetical, Biotech, Healthcare

Is the site an IAEWS Member: Yes

Employment Opportunities

Are full time jobs posted on the site: Yes

Are part time jobs posted on the site: Yes

Are contract jobs posted on the site: Yes

Are consulting jobs posted on the site: Yes

Resume Services

Are resumes or profiles stored on the site: Yes

Other Employment Services

Is a discussion forum or blog offered on the site: No

Are assessment instruments offered on the site: No

Recruiters

Is there an automated resume agent: Yes

Is banner advertising available: Yes

Job Seekers

Is there an automated job agent: Yes

Is career info provided: Yes

Physics Today Jobs

SITE'S SELF-DESCRIPTION

Physics Today Jobs is part of the AIP Career Network. Network partners include the American Association of Physicists in Medicine, American Association of Physics Teachers, American Physical Society, AVS Science and Technology, IEEE Computer Society, and the Society of Physics Students and Sigma Pi Sigma.

GENERAL INFORMATION

URL: www.physicstoday.org/jobs

Date the site was activated online: 1993

Parent organization of the site: American Institute of Physics (AIP)

What field, industry or location does the site cover: EN, Science, Computing

Is the site an IAEWS Member: Yes

Employment Opportunities

Are full time jobs posted on the site: Yes

Are part time jobs posted on the site: Yes

Are contract jobs posted on the site: Yes

Are consulting jobs posted on the site: Yes

Resume Services

Are resumes or profiles stored on the site: Yes

Recruiters

Is there an automated resume agent: Yes

Is banner advertising available: Yes

Other Employment Services

Is a discussion forum or blog offered on the site: No

Are assessment instruments offered on the site: No

Job Seekers

Is there an automated job agent: Yes

Is career info provided: Yes

PracticeLink.com

SITE'S SELF-DESCRIPTION

PracticeLink.com, the online physician job bank and magazine, is the most widely used physician recruitment Web-site among physicians and staff physician recruiters. Each year, more than 20,000 physicians and advanced practitioners register with PracticeLink.com in their search for a new practice. Thousands more use the site each month to confidentially search for opportunities at the 5,000+ facilities that rely on PracticeLink to find the providers they need.

GENERAL INFORMATION

URL: www.practicelink.com

Date the site was activated online: 1995

Parent organization of the site: PracticeLink, Ltd.

What field, industry or location does the site cover: Physicians, Advanced Practitioners and other health care professionals

Is the site an IAEWS Member: Yes

Employment Opportunities

Are full time jobs posted on the site: Yes

Are part time jobs posted on the site: Yes

Are contract jobs posted on the site: Yes

Are consulting jobs posted on the site: Yes

Resume Services

Are resumes or profiles stored on the site: Yes

Other Employment Services

Is a discussion forum or blog offered on the site: No

Are assessment instruments offered on the site: No

Recruiters

Is there an automated resume agent: Yes

Is banner advertising available: Yes

Job Seekers

Is there an automated job agent: Yes

Is career info provided: Yes

PRSA Jobcenter

SITE'S SELF-DESCRIPTION

The PRSA Public Relations and Communications Jobcenter is the most targeted community of public relations and communications jobs. Post a job of any length for a discounted flat fee. Whether you are posting PR jobs, community relations, corporate communications, or similar positions, PRSA Jobcenter connects you with more than 77,000 potential employees.

GENERAL INFORMATION

URL: www.prsa.org/jobcenter

Date the site was activated online: 2008

Parent organization of the site: The Public Relations Society of America (PRSA)

What field, industry or location does the site cover: Public Relations, Corporate Communications

Is the site an IAEWS Member: Yes

Employment Opportunities

Are full time jobs posted on the site: Yes

Are part time jobs posted on the site: Yes

Are contract jobs posted on the site: Yes

Are consulting jobs posted on the site: Yes

Resume Services

Are resumes or profiles stored on the site: Yes

Recruiters

Is there an automated resume agent: Yes

Is banner advertising available: Yes

Other Employment Services

Is a discussion forum or blog offered on the site: Yes

Are assessment instruments offered on the site: Yes

Job Seekers

Is there an automated job agent: Yes

Is career info provided: Yes

PsycCareers

SITE'S SELF-DESCRIPTION

Since re-launching the site six years ago, PsycCareers has established itself as THE place to find top quality candidates. It is the one stop shop for career information, jobs, and recruitment for the American Psychological Association.

GENERAL INFORMATION

URL: www.psyccareers.com

Date the site was activated online: 2006

Parent organization of the site: American Psychological Association

What field, industry or location does the site cover: Psychology

Is the site an IAEWS Member: Yes

Employment Opportunities

Are full time jobs posted on the site: Yes

Are part time jobs posted on the site: Yes

Are contract jobs posted on the site: Yes

Are consulting jobs posted on the site: Yes

Resume Services

Are resumes or profiles stored on the site: Yes

Recruiters

Is there an automated resume agent: Yes

Is banner advertising available: Yes

Other Employment Services

Is a discussion forum or blog offered on the site: No

Are assessment instruments offered on the site: No

Job Seekers

Is there an automated job agent: Yes

Is career info provided: Yes

RegionalHelpWanted.com

SITE'S SELF-DESCRIPTION

RegionalHelpWanted.com partners with local broadcast radio stations to design, build and maintain recruitment Web-sites throughout the United States and Canada. RegionalHelpWanted.com operates over 400 regional sites.

GENERAL INFORMATION

URL: www.regionalhelpwanted.com

Date the site was activated online: 1999

Parent organization of the site: onTargetjobs, Inc.

What field, industry or location does the site cover: Wide variety

Is the site an IAEWS Member: Yes

Employment Opportunities

Are full time jobs posted on the site: Yes

Are part time jobs posted on the site: Yes

Are contract jobs posted on the site: Yes

Are consulting jobs posted on the site: Yes

Resume Services

Are resumes or profiles stored on the site: Yes (resumes only)

Recruiters

Is there an automated resume agent: Yes

Is banner advertising available: Yes

Other Employment Services

Is a discussion forum or blog offered on the site: No

Are assessment instruments offered on the site: No

Job Seekers

Is there an automated job agent: Yes

Is career info provided: Yes

RetirementJobs.com

SITE'S SELF-DESCRIPTION

RetirementJobs.com is a career portal for Baby Boomers. Its mission is to deliver opportunity, inspiration, community and counsel to people over age 50 seeking work that matches their lifestyle needs. The site is free for job seekers. It makes money by charging placement fees to employers and advertisers.

GENERAL INFORMATION

URL: www.retirementjobs.com

Date the site was activated online: 2006

Parent organization of the site: RetirementJobs.com, Inc.

What field, industry or location does the site cover: CS, SM

Is the site an IAEWS Member: Yes

Employment Opportunities

Are full time jobs posted on the site: Yes

Are part time jobs posted on the site: Yes

Are contract jobs posted on the site: No

Are consulting jobs posted on the site: No

Resume Services

Are resumes or profiles stored on the site: Yes

Recruiters

Is there an automated resume agent: Yes

Is banner advertising available: Yes

Other Employment Services

Is a discussion forum or blog offered on the site: No

Are assessment instruments offered on the site: No

Job Seekers

Is there an automated job agent: Yes

Is career info provided: Yes

Security Jobs Network™

SITE'S SELF-DESCRIPTION

Security Jobs Network™ is a subscription-based service providing up-to-date information based on comprehensive research and the collection of current executive, professional-level security and asset protection opportunities, including corporate security and loss prevention; public, private, civil or criminal investigation; executive protection and other similar positions.

GENERAL INFORMATION

URL: www.securityjobs.net

Date the site was activated online: 1998

Parent organization of the site: Security Jobs Network, Inc.

What field, industry or location does the site cover: Individual and corporate security

Is the site an IAEWS Member: Yes

Employment Opportunities

Are full time jobs posted on the site: Yes

Are part time jobs posted on the site: No

Are contract jobs posted on the site: No

Are consulting jobs posted on the site: No

Resume Services

Are resumes or profiles stored on the site: No

Other Employment Services

Is a discussion forum or blog offered on the site: No

Are assessment instruments offered on the site: No

Recruiters

Is there an automated resume agent: No

Is banner advertising available: No

Job Seekers

Is there an automated job agent: No

Is career info provided: No

SeniorHousingJobs.com

SITE'S SELF-DESCRIPTION

SeniorHousingJobs.com is the premier niche career site for senior housing, long-term care and assisted living. Founded in 2003, SeniorHousingJobs.com connects senior care job seekers and employers. Employers advertise jobs and search resumes at a fraction of the cost of large job sites. Job seekers post resumes, create job alerts and search/ apply for jobs.

GENERAL INFORMATION

URL: www.seniorhousingjobs.com

Date the site was activated online: 2003

Parent organization of the site: www.seniorhousingjobs.com

What field, industry or location does the site cover: Senior Living and Long-Term Care industries to include Assisted Living, Independent Living, CCRC, Retirement Housing, Home Health, Hospice

Is the site an IAEWS Member: Yes

Employment Opportunities

Are full time jobs posted on the site: Yes

Are part time jobs posted on the site: Yes

Are contract jobs posted on the site: Yes

Are consulting jobs posted on the site: Yes

Resume Services

Are resumes or profiles stored on the site: Yes

Other Employment Services

Is a discussion forum or blog offered on the site: No

Are assessment instruments offered on the site: Yes

Recruiters

Is there an automated resume agent: Yes

Is banner advertising available: Yes

Job Seekers

Is there an automated job agent: Yes

Is career info provided: Yes

SHRM HR Jobs

SITE'S SELF-DESCRIPTION

The Society for Human Resource Management (SHRM) is the world's largest professional association devoted to human resource management. Our mission is to serve the needs of HR professionals by providing the most current and comprehensive resources, and to advance the profession by promoting HR's essential strategic role.

GENERAL INFORMATION

URL: www.shrm.org/jobs

Date the site was activated online: 1999

Parent organization of the site: Society for Human Resource Management (SHRM)

What field, industry or location does the site cover: HR

Is the site an IAEWS Member: Yes

Employment Opportunities

Are full time jobs posted on the site: Yes

Are part time jobs posted on the site: Yes

Are contract jobs posted on the site: Yes

Are consulting jobs posted on the site: Yes

Resume Services

Are resumes or profiles stored on the site: Yes

Other Employment Services

Is a discussion forum or blog offered on the site: No

Are assessment instruments offered on the site: No

Recruiters

Is there an automated resume agent: No

Is banner advertising available: No

Job Seekers

Is there an automated job agent: Yes

Is career info provided: Yes

Simply Hired

SITE'S SELF-DESCRIPTION

With more than seven million job listings worldwide, Simply Hired is the world's largest job search engine and recruitment advertising network. The company powers jobs on over 10,000 network partner sites, and operates global sites in 22 countries and 11 languages on six continents.

GENERAL INFORMATION

URL: www.simplyhired.com

Date the site was activated online: 2005

Parent organization of the site: Simply Hired, Inc.

What field, industry or location does the site cover: Healthcare, Technology

Is the site an IAEWS Member: Yes

Employment Opportunities

Are full time jobs posted on the site: Yes

Are part time jobs posted on the site: Yes

Are contract jobs posted on the site: Yes

Are consulting jobs posted on the site: Yes

Resume Services

Are resumes or profiles stored on the site: No

Other Employment Services

Is a discussion forum or blog offered on the site: Yes

Are assessment instruments offered on the site: Yes

Recruiters

Is there an automated resume agent: No

Is banner advertising available: Yes

Job Seekers

Is there an automated job agent: Yes

Is career info provided: Yes

SnagAJob.com

SITE'S SELF-DESCRIPTION

SnagAJob.com, the nation's largest job search site and online community, has helped connect hourly workers with quality full-time and part-time jobs in a wide range of industries since 2000. Headquartered in Richmond, VA, SnagAJob.com also provides both job seekers and employers with valued insights and a cutting-edge interface that are unique to hourly employment.

GENERAL INFORMATION

URL: www.snagajob.com

Date the site was activated online: 2000

Parent organization of the site: SnagAJob.com, Inc.

What field, industry or location does the site cover: Wide variety

Is the site an IAEWS Member: No

Employment Opportunities

Are full time jobs posted on the site: Yes

Are part time jobs posted on the site: Yes

Are contract jobs posted on the site: No

Are consulting jobs posted on the site: No

Resume Services

Are resumes or profiles stored on the site: Yes

Other Employment Services

Is a discussion forum or blog offered on the site: Yes

Are assessment instruments offered on the site: Yes

Recruiters

Is there an automated resume agent: Yes

Is banner advertising available: Yes

Job Seekers

Is there an automated job agent: Yes

Is career info provided: Yes

SPIE Career Center

SITE'S SELF-DESCRIPTION

Your source for optics and photonics jobs and talent. Recruit your next hire or find your next job on the SPIE Career Center. Job seekers can search job listings, set up email alerts, and view the 'Advice+Tools' section. Employers may post jobs and gain access to a resume database, create a Resume Alert, and participate in job fairs held at SPIE conferences.

GENERAL INFORMATION

URL: www.spie.org/careercenter

Date the site was activated online: 2001

Parent organization of the site: SPIE - The International Society for Optics and Photonics

What field, industry or location does the site cover: EN

Is the site an IAEWS Member: Yes

Employment Opportunities

Are full time jobs posted on the site: Yes

Are part time jobs posted on the site: Yes

Are contract jobs posted on the site: Yes

Are consulting jobs posted on the site: Yes

Resume Services

Are resumes or profiles stored on the site: Yes

Other Employment Services

Is a discussion forum or blog offered on the site: No

Are assessment instruments offered on the site: No

Recruiters

Is there an automated resume agent: Yes

Is banner advertising available: Yes

Job Seekers

Is there an automated job agent: Yes

Is career info provided: Yes

TopUSAJobs.com

SITE'S SELF-DESCRIPTION

TopUSAJobs.com, the first pay-per-click job search engine, is a leading provider of targeted candidate traffic to hundreds of job boards, companies and staffing agencies. Since 2003, TopUSAJobs has given job seekers free access to millions of jobs nationwide with our easy-to-use search functionalities.

GENERAL INFORMATION

URL: www.topusajobs.com

Date the site was activated online: 2003

Parent organization of the site: TopUSAJobs.com, Inc.

What field, industry or location does the site cover: Wide variety

Is the site an IAEWS Member: Yes

Employment Opportunities

Are full time jobs posted on the site: Yes

Are part time jobs posted on the site: Yes

Are contract jobs posted on the site: Yes

Are consulting jobs posted on the site: Yes

Resume Services

Are resumes or profiles stored on the site: No

Recruiters

Is there an automated resume agent: No

Is banner advertising available: Yes

Other Employment Services

Is a discussion forum or blog offered on the site: No

Are assessment instruments offered on the site: No

Job Seekers

Is there an automated job agent: No

Is career info provided: Yes

VetJobs

SITE'S SELF-DESCRIPTION

Veterans of Foreign Wars sponsored VetJobs is the leading military-related job board on the Internet. The jobs database is available to anyone who visits the site, but to post a resume a candidate must have been associated with the military family. Thousands of veterans worldwide have found jobs with the hundreds of employers who use VetJobs to reach the veteran market.

GENERAL INFORMATION

URL: www.vetjobs.com

Date the site was activated online: 1999

Parent organization of the site: VetJobs.com, Inc.

What field, industry or location does the site cover: AD, EN, IS, MG, OP, Defense

Is the site an IAEWS Member: Yes

Employment Opportunities

Are full time jobs posted on the site: Yes

Are part time jobs posted on the site: Yes

Are contract jobs posted on the site: Yes

Are consulting jobs posted on the site: Yes

Resume Services

Are resumes or profiles stored on the site: Yes

Other Employment Services

Is a discussion forum or blog offered on the site: No

Are assessment instruments offered on the site: Yes

Recruiters

Is there an automated resume agent: No

Is banner advertising available: Yes

Job Seekers

Is there an automated job agent: No

Is career info provided: Yes

WallStJobs.com

SITE'S SELF-DESCRIPTION

WallStJobs.com is nationally recognized as the leading provider of Web-based career information and resources for the financial services industry. Unlike the big-box job boards, WallStJobs.com serves only industry-specific professionals with the experience and skills our clients need.

GENERAL INFORMATION

URL: www.wallstjobs.com

Date the site was activated online: 1999

Parent organization of the site: WallStJobs.com, Inc.

What field, industry or location does the site cover: Financial Services

Is the site an IAEWS Member: Yes

Employment Opportunities

Are full time jobs posted on the site: Yes

Are part time jobs posted on the site: Yes

Are contract jobs posted on the site: Yes

Are consulting jobs posted on the site: Yes

Resume Services

Are resumes or profiles stored on the site: Yes (resumes only)

Recruiters

Is there an automated resume agent: Yes

Is banner advertising available: Yes

Other Employment Services

Is a discussion forum or blog offered on the site: No

Are assessment instruments offered on the site: Yes

Job Seekers

Is there an automated job agent: Yes

Is career info provided: Yes

Work In Sports

SITE'S SELF-DESCRIPTION

Work In Sports is the complete sports employment resource, working with pro teams, leagues, facilities, NCAA athletic departments and other organizations in the sports industry. Employers can post unlimited jobs and internships and search the resume database of qualified applicants at no charge.

GENERAL INFORMATION

URL: www.workinsports.com

Date the site was activated online: 2000

Parent organization of the site: Work In Sports, LLC

What field, industry or location does the site cover: CS, MG, SM, Sports-related

Is the site an IAEWS Member: Yes

Employment Opportunities

Are full time jobs posted on the site: Yes

Are part time jobs posted on the site: Yes

Are contract jobs posted on the site: No

Are consulting jobs posted on the site: No

Resume Services

Are resumes or profiles stored on the site: Yes

Recruiters

Is there an automated resume agent: No

Is banner advertising available: No

Other Employment Services

Is a discussion forum or blog offered on the site: No

Are assessment instruments offered on the site: No

Job Seekers

Is there an automated job agent: Yes

Is career info provided: Yes

Workopolis

SITE'S SELF-DESCRIPTION

Workopolis.com is the Canadian leader in the Internet recruitment and career transition solutions field. We're committed to transforming the recruitment industry by launching innovative new ways for employers and candidates to find and get to know each other better online.

GENERAL INFORMATION

URL: www.workopolis.com

Date the site was activated online: 2000

Parent organization of the site: Toronto Star Newspapers & Gesca, Lt.

What field, industry or location does the site cover: Wide variety, Canada

Is the site an IAEWS Member: Yes

Employment Opportunities

Are full time jobs posted on the site: Yes

Are part time jobs posted on the site: Yes

Are contract jobs posted on the site: Yes

Are consulting jobs posted on the site: Yes

Resume Services

Are resumes or profiles stored on the site: Yes (resumes only)

Recruiters

Is there an automated resume agent: Yes

Is banner advertising available: Yes

Other Employment Services

Is a discussion forum or blog offered on the site: No

Are assessment instruments offered on the site: Yes

Job Seekers

Is there an automated job agent: Yes

Is career info provided: Yes

WorkplaceDiversity.com

SITE'S SELF-DESCRIPTION

WorkplaceDiversity.com, the source for diversity talent®, is the preeminent job search Web-site for corporate recruiters who are seeking experienced diverse talent. Our goal is to create a connection between companies that support diversity and experienced, distinct candidates by providing one location for recruiters to post open positions.

GENERAL INFORMATION

URL: www.workplacediversity.com

Date the site was activated online: 1999

Parent organization of the site: WorkplaceDiversity.com, LLC

What field, industry or location does the site cover: Wide variety, Diversity

Is the site an IAEWS Member: Yes

Employment Opportunities

Are full time jobs posted on the site: Yes

Are part time jobs posted on the site: Yes

Are contract jobs posted on the site: Yes

Are consulting jobs posted on the site: Yes

Resume Services

Are resumes or profiles stored on the site: Yes

Other Employment Services

Is a discussion forum or blog offered on the site: No

Are assessment instruments offered on the site: Yes

Recruiters

Is there an automated resume agent: Yes

Is banner advertising available: Yes

Job Seekers

Is there an automated job agent: Yes

Is career info provided: Yes

ZipRecruiter

SITE'S SELF-DESCRIPTION

ZipRecruiter streamlines the hiring process by enabling companies to post a job on 40+ leading job boards with one click and manage all applicants in one place. By providing a central location for finding, screening and tracking applicants, employers can quickly make the best hiring decisions, at a fraction of the cost of traditional job boards.

GENERAL INFORMATION

URL: www.ziprecruiter.com

Date the site was activated online: 2010

Parent organization of the site: ZipRecruiter, Inc.

What field, industry or location does the site cover: Wide variety

Is the site an IAEWS Member: Yes

Employment Opportunities

Are full time jobs posted on the site: Yes

Are part time jobs posted on the site: Yes

Are contract jobs posted on the site: Yes

Are consulting jobs posted on the site: Yes

Resume Services

Are resumes or profiles stored on the site: Yes

Other Employment Services

Is a discussion forum or blog offered on the site: Yes

Are assessment instruments offered on the site: No

Recruiters

Is there an automated resume agent: Yes

Is banner advertising available: No

Job Seekers

Is there an automated job agent: Yes

Is career info provided: Yes

WEDDLE's

Guide
to
Employment Sites
on the Internet

> ## The
> # Best &
> # the Rest

A Directory of 10,000+ Employment Sites

The enclosed database includes job boards, aggregators, career portals, social media sites, blogs, employment-related search engines, and other online job search and recruitment resources, totalling over 9,000 entries organized by occupational field, industry and geographic focus. The URLs listed for the entries were tested and found operational as of January 2013.

Site Categories

-A-

Administrative/Clerical/Secretarial (see also Classifieds)
Advertising/Public Relations
Agriculture
Archeology/Anthropology
Architecture
Arts
Association-Professional & Trade/Affinity Group
Astronomy
Automotive
Aviation

-B-

Banking
Bilingual/Multilingual Professionals/Translation Professionals
Biology/Biomedical/Biotechnology
Blogs-Job Search/Careers
Blogs-Recruiting
Building Industry-Construction/Management (see also Construction)
Business

-C-

Call Center
Career Counseling/Job Search Services
Chemistry
Child & Elder Care
Classifieds-Newspaper & Magazine
College/Internships/Entry-Level/Graduate School Graduates
Computer (see also High Tech/Technical/Technology and Information Technology/Information Systems)
Computer-Aided Design, Manufacturing & Engineering
Construction (see also Engineering)
Consultants
Contract Employment/Part Time Employment (see also Search Firms)

Cosmetology
Culinary/Food Preparation (see also Hospitality)

-D-

Data Processing
Defense (see also Military Personnel Transitioning into the Private Sector)
Dental
Diversity

-E-

Economists
Education/Academia
Employee Referral
Energy & Utilities
Engineering
Entertainment/Acting
Environmental
Equipment Leasing
Exchanges-Recruiter/Employer/Job Seeker
Executive/Management

-F-

Fashion
Feminism
Fiber Optics
Finance & Accounting (see also Banking, Insurance)
Free Lance/Free Agents
Funeral Industry/Services

-G-

Gaming
General-All Career Fields, Industries & Locations
Graphic Arts/Electronic & Traditional (see also Journalism & Media)

-H-

Healthcare/Medical
High Tech/Technical/Technology
Hospitality (see also Culinary/Food Preparation)
Hourly (see also Classifieds-Newspaper)
Human Resources (see also Recruiters' Resources)

-I-

Industrial/Manufacturing
Information Technology/Information Systems
Insurance
International
Investment/Brokerage (see also Finance & Accounting)

-J-

Job Fairs Online
Journalism & Media (see also Graphic Arts)

-L-

Law/Legal
Law Enforcement & Fire Departments
Library & Information Science
Linguistics
Logistics & Maintenance

-M-

Military Personnel Transitioning into the Private Sector (see also Defense)
Mining
Modeling
Music

-N-

Networking (see also Social Media)
Non-Profit

-O-

Outdoors/Recreation/Sports

-P-

Packaging-Food & Drug
Pharmaceutical
Physics
Printing & Bookbinding
Public Sector/Government
Publishing
Purchasing

-Q-

Quality/Quality Control

-R-

Real Estate
Recruiters' Resources
Recruitment Advertising-Non-Newspaper Print & Online
Regional-USA
Religion
Retail

-S-

Sales & Marketing
Science/Scientists
Search Engines-Employment
Search Firms/Staffing Agencies/Recruiters
Security-Building & Business
Senior Workers/Mature Workers/"Retired" Workers
Social Media Sites (see also Associations)
Social Service/Human Service
Statistical & Math

-T-

Telecommunications
Telecommuting
Trade Organizations
Training
Transportation-Land & Maritime
Travel & Tourism

-V-

Video-Resume & Interview
Volunteer Positions

-Y-

Young Adult/Teen Positions

-A-

Administrative/Clerical/Secretarial (See also Classifieds)

Adminstractive Carreers	http://www.administrativecareers.com
Admin Careers	http://www.admincareers.com
AdminJob.ca [Canada]	http://www.adminjob.ca
AdminJobs.ie [Ireland]	http://www.adminjobs.ie
The Association of Executive & Administrative Professionals	http://www.theaeap.com
4Secretarial Jobs	http://www.4secretarialjobs.com
Front Recruitment [United Kingdom]	http://www.frontrecruitment.co.uk
Get File Clerk Jobs	http://www.getfileclerkjobs.com
GxPJobs.com [United Kingdom]	http://www.gxpjobs.com
iHireMedicalSecretaries.com	http://www.ihiremedicalsecretaries.com
iHireSecretarial.com	http://www.ihiresecretarial.com
International Association of	http://www.jobs.iaap-hq.org
Jobs4Clerical	http://www.jobs4clerical.com
LondonOfficeJobs.co.uk [United Kingdom]	http://www.londonofficejobs.co.uk
LondonSecretarialJobs.co.uk [United Kingdom]	http://www.londonsecretarialjobs.co.uk
NextJobAtHome	http://www.nextjobathome.com
Office Recruit [United Kingdom]	http://www.officerecruit.com
ReceptionistJobStore.com	http://www.receptionistjobstore.com
Secrecruit.co.uk [United Kingdom]	http://www.secrecruit.co.uk
SecretarialCareers.co.uk [United Kingdom]	http://www.secretarialcareers.co.uk
SecretarialJobsBoard.co.uk [United Kingdom]	http://www.secretarialjobsboard.co.uk
Secretary Help Wanted	http://www.secretaryhelpwanted.com
SecretaryJobStore	http://www.secretaryjobstore.com
Secsinthecity [United Kingdom]	http://www.secsinthecity.com
VirtualAssistants.com	http://www.virtualassistants.com

Advertising/Public Relations

Ad Age	http://www.adage.com
Ad Agency Jobs	http://www.adagencyjobs.net
Adholes.com	http://www.adholes.com
Ad Week	http://www.adweek.com
The American Advertising Federation	http://www.aaf.org/jobs
Association of National Advertisers Job Opportunities	http://www.ana.net/careers/content/careers
Capital Communicator	http://www.capitalcommunicator.com
Communicators & Marketers Jobline	http://www.cmjobline.org
Council of Public Relations Firms	http://www.prfirms.org
CreativeJobsCentral.com	http://www.creativejobscentral.com
Direct Marketing Association	http://www.the-dma.org/careercenter
eMarketing & Commerce's Job Connection	http://www.jobs.emarketingandcommerce.com
Get Advertising Jobs	http://www.getadvertisingjobs.com
iHire Advertising	http://www.ihireadvertising.com
International Association of Business Communicators Job Centre	http://jobs.iabc.com/
International Classified Management Association	http://www.icmaonline.org
The Internet Advertising Bureau Job Board	http://www.iab.net/jobs
MarketingHire.com	http://www.marketinghire.com
MassMediaJobs.com	http://www.massmediajobs.com
mediabistro	http://www.mediabistro.com
Media Job Market	http://www.mediajobmarket.com
Media Jobs	http://www.mediajobs.com
MediaRecruiter.com	http://www.mediarecruiter.com
NationJob Network-Advertising & Media Jobs Page	http://www.nationjob.com/media
Opportunities in Public Affairs	http://www.opajobs.com
PaidContent.org	http://www.jobs.paidcontent.org
PRCrossing	http://www.prcrossing.com
ProductionHUB	http://www.productionhub.com
PR News Online Job Center	http://www.prnewsonline.com

Promotion Marketing Association Job Bank	http://www.pmalink.org
PRWeek Jobs [United Kingdom]	http://www.prweekjobs.co.uk
Public Relations Society of America Job Center	http://www.prsa.org
SimplyPRJobs.co.uk [United Kingdom]	http://www.simplyprjobs.co.uk
TalentZoo.com	http://www.talentzoo.com
Television Bureau of Advertising	http://www.tvb.org/nav/build_frameset.aspx
Tiger Jobs	http://www.tigerjobs.com
Women Executives in Public Relations	http://www.wepr.org
Work in PR	http://www.workinpr.com

Agriculture

AgCareers.com	http://www.agcareers.com
Agriculture Industry Now	http://www.agricultureindustrynow.com
AgricultureJobs.com	http://www.agriculturejobs.com
Agri-Management	http://agri-man.com
AgriSeek.com	http://www.agriseek.com
AgriSupport Online	http://www.agrisupportonline.com
American Society of Agricultural and Biological Engineers	http://www.asabe.org
American Society of Agronomy	http://www.agronomy.org
American Society of Animal Science	http://www.asas.org
American Society of Horticultural Science HortOpportunities	http://www.ashs.org
California Agricultural Technical Institute ATI-Net	http://www.atinet.org/jobs.asp
Dairy Network Career Center	http://www.dairynetwork.com
FarmRanchJobs.com	http://www.farmranchjobs.com
FarmSittersUSA	http://www.farmsittersusa.com
Farms.com	http://www.farms.com/
Jobs in Horticulture	http://www.hortjobs.com
PMA Foundation Job Bank	http://www.pmafit.com
Texas A&M Poultry Science Department	http://www.gallus.tamu.edu/careerops.htm

The Outdoor Job   http://www.theoutdoorjob.com

Weed Science Society of America WeedJobs: http://www.wssa.net/WSSA/Students/index.htm

Archeology/Anthropology

Archeology Jobs   http://www.archaeologycareers.jobamatic.com/a/
                                                jobs/find-jobs

Anthropology Jobs   http://anthropologyjobs.org/

American Anthropology Association   http://www.aaanet.org/profdev/careercenter.cfm

Society for American Archeology Careers,   http://www.saa.org/careers/index.html
Opportunities & Jobs

Architecture

AEC Job Bank   http://www.aecjobbank.com

AEJob.com   http://www.aejob.com

American Institute of Architects Online   http://www.aia.org

Archinect   http://www.archinect.com

Architect Job Source   http://www.architectjobsource.com

ArchitectJobs.com   http://www.architectjobs.com

ArchitectJobsOnline   http://www.architectjobsonline.com

ArchitectureJobs.co.uk   http://www.architecturejobs.co.uk

ArchitectJobsOnline   http://www.architectjobsonline.com

Arkitectum.com   http://www.arkitectum.com

CreativeJobsCentral.com   http://www.creativejobscentral.com

Environmental Construction Engineering   http://www.eceajobs.com
Architectural Jobs Online

IT Architect Jobs   http://www.itarchitectjobs.com

ReferWork-Jobs.com   http://www.referwork-jobs.com

Residential Architect Magazine   http://www.residentialarchitect.com

Society of Naval Architects and Marine Engineers http://www.sname.org

World Architecture News   http://www.worldarchitecturenews.com

Arts

American Art Therapy Association	http://careercenter.americanarttherapy association.org
ArtInfo	http://www.artinfo.com
ArtJob	http://www.artjob.org
Art Libraries Society of North America JobNet	http://www.arlisna.org/jobnet.html
ArtNetwork	http://www.artmarketing.com
The Art Newspaper	http://www.theartnewspaper.com
ArtSearch	http://www.artsearch.us
The Arts Deadline List	http://www.artdeadlineslist.com
Artshub.com.au [Australia]	http://www.artshub.com.au
ArtsJobsOnline.com [United Kingdom]	http://www.artsjobsonline.com
Arts Opportunities	http://www.artsopportunities.org
Creative Shake	http://www.creativeshake.com
Dance USA	http://www.danceusa.org
HireCulture	http://www.hireculture.org
iHireCommercialArt	http://www.ihirecommercialart.com
New York Foundation for the Arts	http://www.nyfa.org

Association-Professional & Trade/Affinity Group

AcademyHealth	http://www.academyhealth.org
Academy of Correctional Health Professionals	http://careers.correctionalhealth.org
Academy of Family Physicians CareerLink	http://www.aafpcareerlink.org
Academy of Managed Care Pharmacy	http://www.amcp.org
Academy of Management Placement Services	http://aom.org/placement/
Academy of Medical-Surgical Nurses	http://www.medsurgnurse.org
The Advanced Computing Systems Association	http://www.usenix.org
Adventure Travel Trade Association	http://www.adventuretravel.biz
Alexander Graham Bell Association for the Deaf and Hard of Hearing	http://careers.agbell.org
Allegheny County Medical Society	http://www.acms.org

Alliance of Merger and Acquisition Advisors	http://www.amaaonline.com
American College of Cardiology	http://www.acc.org
American Academy of Cardiology - Colorado Chapter	http://careers.coloradoacc.org
American Academy of Dermatology	http://www.aad.org
American Academy of Family Physicians	http://www.aafp.org
American Academy of Health Care Providers in the Addictive Disorders	http://careers.americanacademy.org
American Academy of Otolaryngology- Head & Neck Surgery	http://www.entnet.org/Community/ public/careers.cfm
American Academy of Ambulatory Care Nursing	http://www.aaacn.org
American Academy of Cardiovascular and Pulmonary Rehabilitation	http://www.aacvpr.org
American Academy of Hospice and Palliative Medicine	http://jobmart.aahpm.org
American Academy of Medical Administrators	http://joblink.aameda.org
American Academy of Neurology	http://careers.aan.com
American Academy of Nurse Practitioners	http://www.aanp.org
American Academy of Ophthalmology	http://ophthjobs.aao.org
American Academy of Pain Medicine	http://careercenter.painmed.org
American Academy of Pediatrics PedJobs	http://jobs.pedjobs.org
American Academy of Pediatrics - Illinois Chapter	http://careers.illinoisaap.org
American Academy of Pediatrics - Kansas Chapter	http://jobboard.kansasaap.org
American Academy of Pediatrics - Kentucky Chapter	http://careercenter.kyaap.org
American Academy of Pediatics - Maine Chapter	http://careers.maineaap.org
American Academy of Pediatrics - Missouri Chapter	http://careers.moapp.org
American Academy of Pediatrics - Ohio Chapter	http://careers.ohioaap.org
American Academy of Pediatrics - Washington Chapter	http://careers.wcaap.org
American Academy of Pediatrics - Wisconsin Chapter	http://careers.wisapp.org
American Academy of Pharmaceutical Physicians & Investigators	http://www.appinet.org
American Academy of Physical Medicine & Rehabilitation Job Board	http://jobboard.aapmr.org
American Academy of Physician Assistants	http://www.aapa.org

American Academy of Professional Coders   http://www.aapc.com

American Accounting Association Career Center   http://commons.aaahq.org

The American Advertising Federation   http://www.aaf.org/jobs/index.html

American Agricultural Economic Association   https://www.aaea.execinc.com/classifieds
Employment Service

American Alliance of Museums jobHQ   http://www.aam-us.org/resources/careers

American Anthropology Association   http://www.aaanet.org/profdev/careercenter.cfm

American Art Therapy Association   http://careercenter.americanarttherapyassociation.
                                                    org

American Assisted Living Nurses Association   http://careers.alnursing.org

American Association of Brewing Chemists   http://www.asbcnet.org

American Association for Budget and Program Analysis http://www.aabpa.org/main/careerdev.htm#jobs

American Association of Cardiovascular   http://www.aacvpr.org
and Pulmonary Rehabilitation

American Association of Cereal Chemists   http://www.aaccnet.org/membership/
                                                    careerplacement.asp

American Association of Clinical Chemistry Career Center http://careercenter.aacc.org

American Association of Colleges of   http://jobs.aacom.org
Osteopathic Medicine

American Association of Critical Care Nurses   http://www.aacn.org

American Association of Diabetes   http://careernetwork.diabeteseducator.org
Educators CareerNetwork

American Association of Finance & Accounting   http://www.aafa.com/careers.htm

American Association of Gynecologic Laparoscopists http://www.aagl.org

American Association of Heart Failure Nurses   http://careers.aahfn.org

American Association of Hip and Knee Surgeosn   http://careers.aahks.org

American Association of Integrated   http://careers.aaihds.org
Heatlhcare Delivery Systems

American Association of Law Libraries   http://www.aallnet.org/hotline/hotline.asp
Job Placement Hotline

American Association of Managed Care Nurses   http://careers.aamcn.org

American Association for Marriage and Family Therapy http://jobconnection.aamft.org

American Association of Medical Assistants   http://www.aama-ntl.org

American Association of Neurological Surgeons	http://www.aans.org
American Association of Neuromuscular & Electrodiagnostic Medicine	http://www.aanem.org
American Association of Neuroscience Nurses	http://careercenter.aann.org
American Association of Occupational Health Nurses	http://www.aaohn.org
American Association of Oral & Maxillofacial Surgeons	http://www.aaoms.org
American Association of Orthopaedic Executives	http://careers.aaoe.net
American Association of Pharmaceutical Sales Professionals	http://www.pharmaceuticalsales.org
American Association of Pharmaceutical Scientists	http://www.aaps.org
American Association of Physics Teachers	http://www.aapt.org
American Association of Respiratory Care	http://www.aarc.org
American Association for the Study of Liver Diseases	http://careercenter.aasld.org
American Astronomical Society Job Register	http://www.aas.org/career
American Bankers Association	http://www.aba.careerbank.com
American Bankruptcy Institute Career Center	http://www.abiworld.org
American Board of Quality Assurance and Utilization Review Physicians	http://careers.abqaurp.org
American Chemical Society	http://www.portal.acs.org
American Chiropractic Association	http://careers.acatoday.org
American Cleft Palate-Craniofacial Association	http://careers.acpa-cpf.org
American College of Allergy, Asthma & Immunology	http://www.acaai.org
American College of Audiology HearCareers	http://hearcareers.audiology.org
American College of Cardiology	http://www.acc.org
American College of Cardiology - Alabama Chapter	http://careers.alacc.org
American College of Cardiology - Arizona Chapter	http://careers.acc-az.org
American College of Cardiology - California Chapter	http://careers.caacc.org
American College of Cardiology - Colorado Chapter	http://careers.coloradoacc.org
American College of Cardiology - Florida Chapter	http://careers.accfl.org
American College of Cardiology - Indiana Chapter	http://careers.inacc.org
American College of Cardiology - Iowa Chapter	http://careers.iaacc.org
American College of Cardiology - Maryland Chapter	http://cardio-careers.marylandacc.org

American College of Cardiology - Michigan Chapter	http://careers.accmi.org
American College of Cardiology - Missouri Chapter	http://careers.moacc.org
American College of Cardiology - North Carolina Chapter	http://careercenter.ncacc.org
American College of Cardiology - Ohio Chapter	http://careers.ohioacc.org
American College of Cardiology - Pennsylvania Chapter	http://careers.pcacc.org
American College of Cardiology - Virginia Chapter	http://cardio-careers.vcacc.org
American College of Cardiology - Washington State Chapter	http://careers.accwa.org
American College of Cardiology - West Virginia Chapter	http://careers.accwv.org
American College of Chest Physicians	http://www.chestnet.org
American College of Clinical Pharmacology	http://www.accp1.org
American College of Clinical Pharmacy	http://www.accp.com
American College of Emergency Physicians	http://www.acep.org
American College of Foot and Ankle Surgeons	http://www.acfas.org
American College of Healthcare Executives Employment Service	http://www.ache.org
American College of Medical Quality	http://careers.acmq.org
American College of Nurse Midwives	http://www.acnw.org
American College of Obstetricians and Gynecologists	http://www.acog.org
American College of Occupational and Environmental Medicine	http://www.acoem.org
American College of Osteopathic Family Physicians Career Center	http://www.acofp.org/Membership/Career_Center
American College of Osteopathic Emergency Physicians	http://careers.acoep.org
American College of Physicians	http://www.acponline.org/career_connection
American College of Physician Executives	http://www.acpe.org
American College of Preventive Medicine	http://www.acpm.org
American College of Rheumatology	http://www.rheumatology.org
American College of Surgeons	http://www.facs.org
American Congress of Rehabilitation Medicine	http://careers.acrm.org
American Correctional Health Services Association	http://careers.achsa.org

American Counseling Association · http://www.counseling.org

American Dental Hygienists' Association · http://www.adha.org/careerinfo/index.html

American Design Drafting Association · http://www.adda.org

American Dietetic Association · http://www.eatright.org

American Economic Association · http://www.aeaweb.org/joe

American Educational Research Association Job Openings · http://www.jobtarget.com/home/index.cfm?site_id=557

American Evaluation Association · http://www.eval.org/Programs/careercenter.asp

American Forest & Paper Association · http://www.afandpa.org

American Foundation for the Blind · http://www.afb.org

American Gastroenterological Association · http://www.healthecareers.com/site_templates/AGA/index.asp?aff=AGA&SPLD=AGA

American Geriatrics Society · http://www.americangeriatrics.org

American Group Psychotherapy Association · http://careers.agpa.org

American Health Care Association · http://careers.ahcancal.org

The American Health Quality Association · http://careers.ahqa.org

American Health Information Management Association CareerAssist · http://careerassist.ahima.org

American Healthcare Radiology Administrators · http://www.ahraonline.org

American Hotel and Lodging Association · http://www.ahla.com

American Industrial Hygiene Association · http://www.aiha.org

American Institute of Architects Online · http://www.aia.org

American Institute of Biological Sciences · http://www.aibs.org

American Institute of Certified Public Accountants Career Center · http://www.cpa2biz.com/AST/AICPA_CPA2BIZ_Browse/Additional_Resources/CareerCenter.jsp

American Institute of Chemical Engineers CareerEngineer · http://careerengineer.aiche.org

The American Institute of Chemists · http://www.theaic.org

American Institute of Graphic Arts · http://www.aiga.org

American Institute of Ultrasound in Medicine · http://careers.aium.org

American Library Association Library Education and Employment Menu Page · http://www.ala.org/ala/education/educationcareers.cfm

American Marketing Association Career Center	http://www.marketingpower.com/Careers/Pages/JobBoard.aspx
American Medical Association JAMA Career Center	http://www.ama-assn.org
American Medical Athletic Association	http://careers.amaasportsmed.org
American Medical Society for Sports Medicine	http://careers.amssm.org
American Medical Technologists	http://www.amtl.com
American Mental Health Counselors Career Center	http://careers.amhca.org
American Meteorological Society Employment Announcements	http://www.ametsoc.org
American Nurses Association	http://www.nursingworld.org
American Occupational Therapy Association	http://www.aota.org
American Optometric Association	http://www.excelod.com/career-center
American Pain Society	http://www.americanpainsociety.org/resources/content/aps-career-center.html
American Pharmaceutical Association	http://www.aphanet.org
American Psychiatric Association JobCentral	http://jobs.psychiatry.org
American Psychiatric Nurses Association	http://www.apna.org
American Physical Society	http://www.aps.org/careers/index.cfm
American Physical Therapy Association	http://www.apta.org
American Psychological Association PsycCareers	http://www.apa.org/careers/index.aspx
American Psychological Society Observer Job Listings	http://www.psychologicalscience.org/jobs
American Public Health Association CareerMart	http://careers.apha.org/
American Registry of Diagnostic Medical Sonographers	http://www.ardms.org
American Registry of Radiologic Technologists	http://www.arrt.org
American Roentgen Ray Society	http://careercenter.arrs.org
American Society of Addiction Medicine	http://careers.asam.org
American Society of Agricultural and Biological Engineers	http://www.asabe.org
American Society of Agronomy	http://www.agronomy.org
American Society of Anesthesiologists	http://careers.asahq.org
American Society of Animal Science	http://www.fass.org/job.asp
American Society of Association Executives CareerHQ	http://www.careerhq.org

American Society of Business Press Editors	http://www.asbpr.org
American Society for Cell Biology	http://www.ascb.org
American Society for Clinical Laboratory Science	http://www.ascls.org
American Society for Clinical Pathology	http://www.ascp.org
American Society of Clinical Pharmacology and Therapeutics	http://www.ascpt.org
American Society of Consultant Pharmacists	http://bt.myrxcareer.com
American Society of Cytopathology	http://cytojobs.cytopathology.org
American Society for Cytotechnology	http://careercenter.asct.com
American Society for Gastrointestinal Endoscopy	http://careers.asge.org
American Society of Gene Therapy	http://www.asgt.org
American Society of General Surgeons	http://www.theasgs.org
American Society for Healthcare Human Resource Management	http;//careers.ashhra.org
American Society for Healthcare Risk Management	http://careers.ashrm.org
American Society of Horticultural Science HortOpportunities	http://www.ashs.org/careers.html
American Society for Information Science & Technology	http://www.asis.org
American Society of Interior Designers Job Bank	http://www.asid.org/career_center/ job_opp/job.asp
American Society of Journalists & Authors	http://www.freelancewritersearch.com
American Society for Law Enforcement Training	http://www.aslet.org
American Society of Mechanical Engineers Career Center	http://www.asme.org/jobs
American Society for Microbiology	http://www.asm.org
American Society for Nutrition	http://jobs.nutrition.org
American Society of Pediatric Hematology/Oncology	http://careercenter.aspho.org
American Society of PeriAnesthesia Nurses	http://www.aspan.org
American Society of Pharmacognosy	http://www.phcog.org
American Society for Pharmacology & Experimental Therapeutics	http://careers.aspet.org
American Society of Plant Biologists	http://www.aspb.org
American Society of Professional Estimators	http://www.aspenational.com

American Society for Radiation Oncology	http://careers.astro.org
American Society of Radiologic Technologists	http://www.asrt.org
American Society for Training & Development Job Bank	http://www.jobs.astd.org
American Society of Transplant Surgeons	http://careercenter.asts.org
American Society of Travel Agents	http://www.asta.org
American Society of Women Accountants Employment Opportunities	http://www.aswact.org
American Speech-Language-Hearing Career Center	http://www.asha.org/careers
American Statistical Association Statistics Career Center	http://www.amstat.org/careers
American Thoracic Society	http://careers.thoracic.org
American Urogynecologic Society	http://careercenter.augs.org
American Urological Association JobFinder	http://careercenter.auanet.org
American Veterinary Medical Association Career Center	http://www.jobs.avma.org
American Water Works Association Career Center (Water Jobs)	http://www.awwa.org
Apartment Association of Greater Dallas	http://www.aagdallas.org
Apartment Association of Tarrant County	http://www.aatcnet.org/subsite/CareerCenter/careercenterindex.htm
Arizona Orthopaedic Society	http://careers.azortho.org
Arizona Public Health Association	http://healthcarecareers.azpha.org
Art Libraries Society of North America JobNet	http://www.arlisna.org/jobs.html
Association of Air Medical Services	http://careercenter.aams.org/
Association of American Medical Colleges CareerConnect	https://www.aamc.org/services/careerconnect/
Association for Applied Human Pharmacology [Germany]	http://www.agah-web.de
Association of Black Cardiologists	http://careers.abcardio.org
Association of Career Professionals International	http://www.acpinternational.org
Association of Certified Fraud Examiners Career Center	http://www.acfe.com/career/career.asp
Association of Clinical Research Professionals Career Center	http://www.acrpnet.org
Association of Clinicians for the Underserved	http://careers.clinicians.org
Association for Community Health Improvement	http://careers.communityhlth.org

Association for Computing Machinery Career Resource Center	http://www.acm.org
Association for Educational Communications and Technology Job Center	http://www.aect.org
Association for Environmental and Outdoor Education	http://www.aeoe.org
The Association of Executive & Administrative Professionals	http://www.theaeap.com
Association of Executive Search Consultants	http://www.bluesteps.com
Association of ex-Lotus Employees	http://www.axle.org
Association for Experential Education	http://aee.org
Association of Finance Professionals Career Services	http://www.afponline.org/pub/cs/career_services.html
Association of Graduate Careers Advisory Service [United Kingdom]	http://www.agcas.org.uk
Association for Healthcare Documentation Integrity	http://careerconnection.ahdionline.org
Association for Healthcare Environment	http://careerlink.ahe.org
Association for Healthcare Volunteer Resource Professionals	http://careers.ahvrp.org
The Association for Institutional Research	http://www.airweb.org
Association of Internet Professionals National Job Board	http://www.internetprofessionals.org
AssociationJobBoards.com	http://www.associationjobboards.com
Association of Latino Professionals in Finance & Accounting Job Postings	http://www.alpfa.org
Association of Management Consulting Firms	http://www.amcf.org
Association of MBAs	http://www.mbaworld.com
Association of National Advertisers Job Opportunities	http://www.ana.net/careers/content/careers
Association of Perioperative Registered Nurses Online Career Center	http://www.aorn.org/CareerCenter
Association for Play Therapy	http://careercenter.a4pt.org
Association for Professionals in Infection Control & Epidemiology	http://careers.apic.org
Association of Rehabilitation Nurses	http://careercenter.rehabnurse.org
Association of Research Libraries	http://www.arl.org
Association of Staff Physician Recruiters	http://www.aspr.org

Association for Strategic Planning	http://www.strategyplus.org
Association of Surgical Technicians	http://careercenter.ast.org
Association of Teachers of Technical Writing	http://www.cms.english.ttu.edu/ATTW
Association of University Teachers [United Kingdom]	http://www.AUT4Jobs.com
Association for Women in Computing	http://www.awc-hq.org
Association of Women's Health, Obstetric & Neonatal Nurses	http://www.awhonn.org
Bank Administration Institute	http://www.bai.org
Bank Marketing Association	http://www.bmanet.org
Bay Bio	http://www.baybio.org
Biomedical Engineering Society	http://www.bmes.org
Biotechnology Association of Alabama	http://www.bioalabama.com
Biotechnology Association of Maine	http://www.mainebiotech.org
Biotechnology Council of New Jersey	http://www.newjerseybiotech.org
Black Data Processing Association Online	http://www.bdpa.org
Board of Pharmaceutical Specialties	http://www.bpsweb.org
Board of Registered Polysomnographic Technologists	http://careers.brpt.org
Business Marketing Association	http://www.marketing.org
California Academy of Family Physicians	http://www.fpjobsonline.org
California Agricultural Technical Institute ATI-Net AgJobs	http://www.atinet.org/jobs.asp
California Dental Hygienists' Association Employment Opportunities	http://www.cdha.org/employment/index.html
California Mortgage Brokers Association Career Center	http://www.cambweb.org
California Psychological Association	http://careers.cpapsych.org
California Radiological Society	http://careers.calrad.org
California Separation Science Society	http://www.casss.org
Canadian Society of Biochemistry/Molecular/ Cellular Biologists Job Listing	http://www.medicine.mcgill.ca/expmed/emjl/ expmed_whoislinking.htm
Capital Markets Credit Analysts Society Resume Service	http://www.cmcas.org
Cardiothoracic Surgery Network	http://www.ctsnet.org
Case Management Society	http://www.cmsa.org
Casualty Actuarial Society Career Center	http://careers.casact.org

Chicago Medical Society	http://www.cmsdocs.org
College of American Pathologists	http://www.cap.org
College and University Personnel Association JobLine	http://www.cupahr.org/jobline
Colorado Academy of Family Physicians	http://www.fpjobsonline.org
Colorado Health and Hospital Association	http://www.cha.com
Computing Research Association Job Announcements	http://www.cra.org/ads
Connecticut Orthopaedic Society	http://careers.ctortho.org
Connecticut State Medical Society	http://careers.csms.org
Controlled Release Society	http://www.controlledrelease.org
Council for Advancement & Support of Education Career Central	http://www.case.org/career_central.html
Council of Public Relations Firms	http://www.prfirms.org
Delaware Nurses Association	http://nursejobs.denurses.org
Dermatology Nurses' Association	http://www.dnanurse.org
Design Management Institute Job Bank	http://www.dmi.org/dmi/html/jobbank/jobbank_d.jsp
Digital Printing and Imaging Association Employment Exchange (with the Screenprinting & Graphic Imaging Association International)	http://www.sgia.org/employment
DirectEmployers Association	http://www.directemployers.org
Direct Marketing Association	http://www.the-dma.org/careercenter
District of Columbia Health Care Association	http://careers.dchca.org
Drilling Research Institute Classifieds	http://www.drillers.com/Visitor/Drilling_JobSearch.aspx
Drug Information Association Employment Opportunities	http://www.diahome.org/DIAHome/Resources/FindJob.aspx
Editorial Freelancers Association	http://www.the-efa.org
Emergency Medical Services Association of Colorado	http://jobs.emsac.org
Emergency Medicine Residents Association	http://www.emra.org
Emergency Nurses Association	http://enacareercenter.ena.org
Employers Resource Association	http://www.hrxperts.org
Financial Executives Institute Career Center	http://www.financialexecutives.org

Financial Management Association International Placement Services	http://www.fma.org/Placement
Financial Managers Society Career Center	http://www.fmsinc.org/cms/?pid=1025
Financial Women International Careers	http://www.fwi.org
FindMortgageJobs.com	http://www.findmortgagejobs.com
Florida Academy of Family Physicians	http://www.fpjobsonline.org
Florida Naturopathic Physicians Association	http://careers.fnpa.org
Florida Psychological Association	http://careercenter.flapsych.com
Global Association of Risk Professionals Career Center	http://www.garp.com/careercenter/index.asp
Georgia Academy of Family Physicians	http://www.fpjobsonline.org
Georgia Association of Personnel Services	http://70.85.148.53:5574/JobBoard/tabid/53/Default.aspx
Georgia Orthopaedic Society	http://careers.georgiaorthosociety.org
Georgia Pharmacy Association	http://www.gpha.org
Graphic Artists Guild JobLine	http://www.graphicartistsguild.org
Harris County Medical Society	http://www.hcms.org
Healthcare Businesswomen's Association	http://www.hbanet.org
Healthcare Information and Management Systems Society JobMine	http://jobmine.himss.org
Healthcare Financial Management Association	http://www.hfma.org
Healthcaare Human Resources Management Association of California	http://careers.hhrmac.org
Health Industry Group Purchasing Association	http://careers.supplychainassociation.org
Health Occupations Students of America	http://careers.hosa.org
Heart Rhythm Society	http://careers.hrsonline.org
Hispanic American Police Command Officers Association	http://www.hapcoa.org
History of Science Society	http://www.hssonline.org
HIV Medicine Association	http://www.hivma.org
HTML Writers Guild HWG-Jobs	http://www.hwg.org/lists/hwg-jobs
Human Resource Association of the National Capital Area Job Bank Listing	http://www.hra-nca.org/job_list.asp

Human Resource Independent Consultants (HRIC) On-Line Job Leads	http://www.hric.org
Human Resource Management Association of Mid Michigan Job Postings	http://www.hrmamm.com/jobpostings/index.php
Illinois Academy of Family Physicians	http://www.fpjobsonline.org
Illinois Nurses Association	http://careers.illinoisnurses.com
Illinois Psychological Assocation	http://careers.illinoispsychology.org
Illinois Recruiters Association	http://www.illinoisrecruiter.ning.com
Independent Human Resource Consultants Association	http://www.ihrca.com
Infectious Diseases Society of America	http://www.idsa.org
Infusion Nurses Society	http://careercenter.ins1.org
Institute of Electrical & Electronics Engineers Job Site	http://www.ieee.org/web/careers/home/index.html
Institute of Food Science & Technology	http://www.ifst.org
Institute of Internal Auditors Audit Career Center	https://na.theiia.org/about-us/Pages/Audit-Career-Center.aspx
Institute of Management Accountants Career Center	http://www.imanet.org/development_career.asp
Institute of Management and Administration's Supersite	http://www.ioma.com
Institute of Real Estate Management Jobs Bulletin	http://www.irem.org
Institute for Supply Management Career Center	http://www.ism.ws/CareerCenter/index.cfm
The Instrumentation, Systems and Automation Society Online ISA Jobs	http://www.isa.org/isa_es
International Association of Administrative Professionals Job Board	http://www.jobs.iaap-hq.org
International Association of Business Communicators Job Centre	http://jobs.iabc.com
International Association of Conference Centers Online (North America)	http://www.iacconline.org
International Association for Commercial and Contract Management	http://www.iaccm.com
International Association of Forensic Nurses	http://careercenter.iafn.org
International Association for HR Information Management Job Central	http://www.hrim.hrdpt.com
International Classified Management Association	http://www.icmaonline.org
International Code Council	http://www.iccsafe.org

International Customer Service Association Job Board	http://www.icsatoday.org
International Foundation of Employee Benefit Plans Job Postings	http://www.ifebp.org
International Health Economics Association	http://www.healtheconomics.org
International Pediatric Transplant Association	http://careers.iptaonline.org
International Society for Molecular Plant-Microbe Interactions	http://www.ismpminet.org/career
International Society for Performance Improvement Job Bank	http://www.ispi.org
International Society for Pharmaceutical Engineering	http://www.ispe.org
International Society for Pharmacoepidemiology	http://careers.pharmacoepi.org
Iowa Biotechnology Association	http://www.iowabiotech.org
Kansas Hospital Association	http://kshealthjobs.net
Kansas Psychological Association	http://careers.kspsych.org
Latinos in Information Sciences and Technology Association	http://www.a-lista.org
LeadingAge	http://careers.leadingage.org
Louisiana Assisted Living Association	http://careers.laassisted.org
Louisiana Occupational Therapy Association	http://www.lota.org
Louisiana State Medical Society	http://careers.lsms.org
Marine Executive Association	http://www.marineea.org
Maryland Association of CPAs Job Connect	http://www.macpa.org/content/classifieds/public/search.aspx
Maryland State Dental Association	http://careers.dentalcompany.com
Maryland Orthopaedic Association	http://jobboard.mdortho.org
The Maryland State Medical Society	http://careers.medchi.org
Massachusetts Biotechnology Council	http://www.massbio.org
Massachusetts Environmental Education Society	http://www.massmees.org
Massachusetts Healthcare Human Resources Association	http://www.mhhra.org
Mathematical Association of America	http://www.mathclassifieds.com
MdBio, Inc. (Maryland Bioscience)	http://www.techcouncilmd.com/mdbio

Media Communications Association International Job Hotline	http://www.mca-i.org
Media Human Resources Association	http://www.jobs/shrm.org
Medical-Dental-Hospital Business Association	http://www.mdhba.org
Medical Device Manufacturers Association Career Center	http://careers.medicaldevices.org
Medical Fitness Association	http://www.medicalfitness.org/networking
Medical Group Management Association	http://www.mgma.com
Medical Marketing Association	http://www.mmanet.org
Medical Society of New York - Sixth District Branch	http://www.jobbank.medsocieties.org
Medical Society of Virginia	http://jobboard.msv.org
Mental Health America	http://careers.mentalhealthamerica.net
Metroplex Association of Personnel Consultants	http://www.recruitingfirms.com
MichBIO	http://www.michbio.org
Military Officers Association of America	http://www.moaa.org
The Minerals, Metals, Materials Society JOM	http://www.tms.org
Minnesota Medical Association	http://careercenter.mnmed.org
Mississippi Ambulatory Surgery Center Association	http://jobboard.masca-ms.org
Mississippi Nurses Association	http://careers.msnurses.org
Missouri Academy of Family Physicians	http://www.fpjobsonline.org
Missouri Pharmacy Association	http://www.morx.com
Music Library Association Job Placement	http://www.musiclibraryassoc.org/ employmentanded/joblist/index.shtml
National Alliance of State Broadcasters Associations CareerPage	http://www.careerpage.org
National Alliance of Wound Care	http://woundcare.careers.nawccb.org
National Apartment Association	http://www.naahq.org
National Association of Black Accountants, Inc. Career Center	http://www.nabacareercenter.nabainc.org
National Association of Boards of Pharmacy	http://www.nabp.net
National Association of Chronic Disease Directors	http://nacddhealthjobs.chronicdisease.org
National Association for College Admission Counseling Career Opportunities	http://www.nacac.com/classifieds.cfm

National Association of Colleges & Employers (NACE)	http://www.nacelink.com
National Association of County and City Health Officials	http://careers.naccho.org
National Association for Female Executives	http://www.nafe.com
National Association for Healthcare Quality	http://careercenter.nahq.org
National Association of Healthcare Transport Management	http://careers.nahtm.org
National Association of Health Services Executives	http://careers.nahse.org
National Association of Hispanic Nurses Houston Chapter	http://www.nahnhouston.org
National Association of Hispanic Publications Online Career Center	http://www.nahp.org
National Associatiion of Managed Care Physicians	http://careers.namcp.org
National Association of Medical Staff Services	http://careers.namss.org
National Association of Neonatal Nurses	http://careercentral.nann.org
National Association of Orthopaedic Nurses	http://www.orthonurse.org
National Association of Pharmaceutical Sales Representatives	http://www.napsronline.org
National Association for Printing Leadership	http://www.napl.org
National Association of Printing Ink Manufacturers	http://www.napim.org
National Association of Sales Professionals Career Center	http://www.nasp.com
National Association of School Psychologists	http://www.nasponline.org
National Association of Securities Professionals Current Openings	http://www.nasphq.org/career.html
National Association of Securities Professionals (Atlanta) Current Openings	http://www.naspatlanta.org/career.html
National Association of Securities Professionals Underground Railroad	http://www.nasp-ny.org
National Association of Social Workers Joblink	http://www.socialworkers.org/joblinks/default.asp
National Athletic Trainers Association	http://jobs.nata.org
National Black Police Association	http://www.blackpolice.org
National Community Pharmacists Association Pharmacy Matching Service	http://www.ncpanet.org
National Confectioners' Association	http://www.candyusa.com

National Contract Management Association   http://www.ncmahq.org

National Defense Industrial Association   http://www.ndia.monster.com

National Environmental Health Association   http://www.neha.org

National Federation of Paralegal Associations Career Center   http://www.paralegals.org

National Field Selling Association   http://www.nfsa.com

National Fire Prevention Association Online Career Center   http://www.nfpa.org

National Funeral Directors Association   http://www.nfda.org

National Gerontological Nursing Association   http://careercenter.ngna.org

National Hispanic Medical Association   http://jobs.nhmamd.org

National Hospice and Palliative Care Organization   http://careers.nhpco.org

National Insurance Recruiters Association Online Job Database   http://www.nirassn.com

National Kidney Association Career Center   http://www.careers.kidney.org

National Latino Peace Officers Association   http://www.nlpoa.org

National League for Nursing   http://www.nln.org

National Medical Association   http://career.nmanet.org/

National Organization of Black Law Enforcement Executives   http://www.noblenational.org

National Organization of Black Chemists and Chemical Engineers   http://www.engin.umich.edu/societies/nobcche

National Parking Association   http://www.careers.npapark.org

National Rural Health Association   http://careers.ruralhealthweb.org

National Rural Recruitment & Retention Network   http://www.3rnet.org

National Society of Black Engineers   http://www.national.nsbe.org

National Society of Black Physicists   http://www.nsbp.org

National Society of Collegiate Scholars Career Connection   http://www.nscs.org

National Society of Genetic Counselors   http://jobconnection.nsgc.org

National Society of Hispanic MBAs Career Center   http://www.nshmba.org

National Society of Professional Engineers Employment   http://www.nspe.org/Employment/index.html

National Sporting Goods Association   http://www.nsga.org

National Venture Capital Association	http://www.nvca.org
National Weather Association Job Corner	http://www.nwas.org
National Women's Studies Association	http://www.nwsa.org
National Writers Union Job Hotline	http://www.nwu.org
Nationwide Process Servers Association	http://www.processserversassociation.com
Network of Commercial Real Estate Women Job Bank	http://www.crewnetwork.org
New Jersey Metro Employment Management Association	http://www.njmetroema.org
New Jersey Human Resource Planning Group	http://www.njhrpg.org
New Jersey Psychological Association	http://careers.psychologynj.org
New Mexico Center for Nursing Excellence	http://healthcarecareers.nmnursingexcellence.org
New Mexico Medical Society	http://healthcarecareers.nmms.org
New Mexico Osteopathic Medical Association	http://healthcarecareers.nmoma.org
The New York Biotechnology Association	http://www.nyba.org
New York Society of Association Executives Career Center	http://www.nysaenet.org
New York Society of Security Analysts Career Resources	http://www.nyssa.org/AM/Template. cfm?Section=career_development
New York State Academy of Family Physicians	http://www.fpjobsonline.org
New York State Society of Orthopaedic Surgeons	http://careers.nyssos.org
Newspaper Association of America Newspaper CareerBank	http://www.naa.org/classified/index.html
North American Association for Environmental Education	http://www.naaee.org
North American Spine Society	http://www.spine.org
North Carolina Medical Society	http://careers.ncmedsoc.org
North Carolina Orthopaedic Association	http://careers.ncorthopaedics.org
North Carolina Pediatric Society	http://www.ncpeds.org/job-listings
Northeast Human Resource Association	http://www.nehra.org
Ohio Nurses Association	http://jobs.ohiorncareers.com
Ohio Orthopaedic Society	http://careers.ohioorthosociety.org
Ohio Psychological Association	http://careers.ohpsych.org
Oklahoma State Medical Association	http://www.osmaonline.org

Orleans Parish Medical Society	http://www.opms.org
Oncology Nursing Society	http://careers.ons.org
Oregon Bioscience Association	http://www.oregon-bioscience.com
Outpatient Ophthalmic Surgery Society	http://careerhq.ooss.org
Pediatric Academic Societies	http://careers.pas-meeting.org
Pennsylvania Academy of Family Physicians	http://www.fpjobsonline.org
Pennsylvania Ambulatory Surgery Association	http://http://careers.pasa-asf.org
Pennsylvania Medical Society	http://jobbank.pamedsoc.org
Pennsylvania Orthopaedic Society	http://careers.paorthosociety.org
Pennsylvania Psychological Association	http://careers.papsy.org
Petroleum Services Association of Canada Employment	http://www.psac.ca
Pharmacy Benefit Management Institute	http://careers.pbmi.com
PhysicsToday.org	http://www.physicstoday.org
Practice Greenhealth	http://careers.practicegreenhealth.org
Professional Association of Health Care Office Management	http://careercenter.pahcom.com
Project Management Institute Career Headquarters	http://www.pmi.org
Promotion Marketing Association Job Bank	http://www.pmalink.org/jobbank/default.asp
Public Responsibility in Medicine and Research	http://careers.primr.org
Radiological Society of North America	http://www.rsna.org
Radiology Business Management Association	http://www.rbma.org
Real Estate Lenders Association	http://www.rela.org
Regulatory Affairs Professionals Society Regulatory Career Connections	http://regulatorycareers.raps.org
Renal Physicians Association	http://careers.renalmd.org
Risk & Insurance Management Society Careers	http://www.rims.org/resources/careercenter
Sales & Marketing Executives International Career Center	http://www.smei.org
San Bernardino County Medical Society / Riverside County Medical Society	http://healthcarecareers.sbcms.org
Screenprinting & Graphic Imaging Association International	http://www.sgia.org/employment

Securities Industry Association Career Resource Center	http://www.sifma.com/services/career_center/career_center.html
Sheet Metal and Air Conditioning Contractor's Association	http://www.smacna.org
Society for American Archeology Careers, Opportunities & Jobs	http://www.saa.org/careers/index.html
Society of Automotive Engineers Job Board	http://www.sae.org/careers/recrutad.htm
Society for Clinical Research Sites	http://careers.myscrs.org
Society of Competitive Intelligence Professionals Job Marketplace	http://www.scip.org/CareerCenter
Society of Correctional Physicians	http://jobnet.corrdocs.org
Society of Critical Care Medicine	http://careercentral.sccm.org
Society of Diagnostic Medical Sonographers	http://www.sdms.org
Society of Gastroenterology Nurses & Associates	http://www.sgna.org
Society of General Internal Medicine	http://careers.sgim.org
Society for Healthcare Consumer Advocacy	http://careercenter.shca-aha.org
Society of Hispanic Professional Engineers Career Services	http://www.shpe.org
Society of Hospital Medicine Career Center	http://www.hospitalmedicine.org
Society for Human Resource Management HRJobs	http://www.jobs/shrm.org
Society for Imaging Informatics in Medicine	http://careers.siimweb.org
Society for Industrial & Organizational Psychology JobNet	http://www.siop.org/JobNet
Society for Laboratory Automation and Screening	http://careers.slas.org
Society of Manufacturing Engineers Jobs Connection	http://jobsconnection.sme.org
Society of Mexican American Engineers and Scientists	http://www.maes-natl.org
Society of Naval Architects and Marine Engineers	http://www.sname.org
Society for Neuroscience	http://neurojobs.sfn.org
Society of Nuclear Medicine	http://www.snm.org
Society of Petrologists & Well Log Analysts Job Opportunities	http://www.spwla.org
Society for Radiation Oncology Administrators	http://careers.sroa.org
Society for Research in Child Development	http://careers.srcd.org

Society of Risk Analysis Opportunities	http://www.sra.org/opportunities.php
Society of Satellite Professionals International Career Center	http://www.sspi.broadbandcareers.com/Default.asp
Society of Women Engineers Career Services	http://www.careers.swe.org
South Carolina Medical Association	http://careers.scmedical.org
South Carolina Orthopaedic Association	http://www.scoanet.org
SPIE Web-International Society for Optical Engineering	http://www.spieworks.com
Strategic Account Management Association Career Resources	http://www.strategicaccounts.org
Student Conservation Association	http://www.thesca.org
Teachers of English to Speakers of Other Languages Job Finder	http://www.tesol.org
Technical Association of the Pulp & Paper Industry Career Center	http://www.tappi.org/careercenter/careercenter.asp
Telecommunication Industry Association Online	http://www.tiaonline.org
Texas Academy of Family Physicians	http://www.fpjobsonline.org
Texas Apartment Association	http://www.taa.org/member/industry/careerCenter
Texas Association for Home Care & Hospice	http://careers.tahch.org
Texas Healthcare & Bioscience Institute	http://www.thbi.org
Texas Medical Association	http://www.texmed.org
United States & Canadian Academy of Pathology	http://careers.uscap.org
Urgent Care Association of America	http://jobs.ucaoa.org
U.S. Psychiatric Rehabilitation Association	http://careers.uspra.org
Utah Life Sciences Association	http://www.utahlifescience.com
Utah Medical Association	http://docjobs.utahmed.org
Virginia Biotechnology Association	http://www.vabio.org
Washington Biotechnology & Biomedical Association	http://www.wabio.com
Washington Multi-Family Housing Association	http://www.careers.wmfha.org
Washington State Radiological Society	http://careers.wsrs.org
Weed Science Society of America WeedJobs: Positions in Weed Science	http://www.wssa.net/WSSA/Students/index.htm
West Virginia Orthopaedic Society	http://careers.wvos.org

Wisconsin Academy of Family Physicians	http://www.fpjobsonline.org
Wisconsin Biotechnology Association	http://www.wisconsinbiotech.org
Wisconsin Dental Association	http://careers.wda.org
Wisconsin Medical Society	http://www.wisconsinmedicalsociety.org
Women in Technology	http://www.womenintechnology.org
Women in Technology International (WITI) 4Hire	http://www.witi4hire.com
Women Executives in Public Relations	http://www.wepr.org
The Working Group for Electronic Data Interchange	http://careers.wedi.org
Space-Careers.com	http://www.space-careers.com
SpaceJobs.com	http://www.spacejobs.com

Astronomy

American Astronomical Society Job Register	http://www.aas.org/career
Board of Physics & Astronomy	http://www7.nationalacademies.org
HigherCareers.com	http://www.highercareers.com
The Chronicle of Higher Education	http://www.chronicle.com/jobs
Physicstoday	http://careers.physicstoday.org/jobs
Physics & Astronomy Online	http://www.physlink.com
Space-Careers.com	http://www.space-careers.com
SpaceJobs.com	http://www.spacejobs.com

Automotive

Autocareers	http://www.autocareers.com
Auto Head Hunter	http://www.autoheadhunter.net
Auto Industry Central	http://www.autoindustrycentral.com
AutoJobs.com	http://www.autodealerjobs.com
Auto Jobs	http://www.autodealerjobs.com
Auto Staffing	http://www.actautostaffing.com
Automotive Aftermarket Jobs	http://www.customtrucks.net

Automotive Careers Today	http://www.autocareerstoday.net
Automotive JobBank	http://www.automotivejobbank.com
AutomotiveJobs.com	http://www.automotivejobs.com
AutomotiveJobsOnline.com	http://www.automotivejobsonline.com
Automotive News	http://www.autonews.com
Best Auto Jobs	http://www.bestautojobs.com
CarDealerJobs.com	http://www.cardealerjobs.com
CareerRPM.com	http://www.careerrpm.com
Dealer Classified	http://www.dealerclassified.com
DieselMechanicJobs.com	http://www.dieselmechanicjobs.com
Great Auto Jobs	http://www.greatautojobs.com
InAutomotive.com [United Kingdom]	http://www.inautomotive.com
Motor Careers	http://www.motorcareers.com
Motor Sports Employment	http://www.motorsportsemployment.com
NeedTechs.com	http://www.needtechs.com
Racing Jobs	http://www.racingjobs.com
ShowroomToday.com	http://www.showroomtoday.com

Aviation

Aeroindustryjobs	http://www.aeroindustryjobs.com
AeroSpaceNews.com	http://www.aerospacenews.com
AerotAge Jobs	http://www.aerotagejobs.com
AircraftEngineers.com [United Kingdom]	http://www.aircraftengineers.com
AirJobsDaily.com	http://www.airjobsdigest.com
AirlineJobFinder.com	http://www.airlinejobfinder.com
AirlinePilotJobs.com	http://www.airlinepilotjobs.com
All Port Jobs	http://pwww.allportjobs.com
Association of Air Medical Services	http://careercenter.aams.org
AVCrew.com	http://www.avcrew.com
AVjobs.com	http://www.avjobs.com

AviaNation.com	http://www.avianation.com
AviationCareers	http://www.aviationcareers.net
Aviation Employment.com	http://www.aviationemployment.com
Aviation Employment Board	http://www.aviationemploymentboard.net
Aviation Employment NOW	http://www.aenworld.com
Aviation Employment Placement Service	http://www.aeps.com
AviationJobSearch.com	http://www.aviationjobsearch.com
Aviation Jobs Central	http://www.aviationjobscentral.com
Aviation Jobs Online	http://www.aviationjobsonline.com
Aviation Tire	http://www.aviationtire.com
Aviation Today	http://www.aviationtoday.com
Aviation Week	http://www.aviationweek.com
Aviation World Services	http://www.aviationworldservices.com
Best Aviation	http://www.bestaviation.net
Blue Collar Jobs	http://www.bluecollarjobs.com
Careers in Aviation	http://www.aec.net
Climbto350.com	http://www.climbto350.com
CopterJobs	http;//www.copterjobs.com
Federal Aviation Administration Resumes	http://www.faa.gov
Find A Pilot	http://www.findapilot.com
Flightdeck Recruitment	http://www.flightdeckrecruitment.com
Flight Global	http://www.flightglobal.com
FliteJobs.com	http://www.flitejobs.com
Fly Contract	http://www.flycontract.com
Get Pilot Jobs	http://www.getpilotjobs.com
JS Firm	http://www.jsfirm.com
Just Helicopters	http://www.justhelicopters.com
Landings	http://www.landings.com
NationJob Network-Aviation	http://www.nationjob.com/aviation
Pilot Career Center	http://www.pilotcareercenter.com

Pilot Jobs	http://www.pilotjobs.com
Space Careers	http://www.space-careers.com
Worldwide 747 Pilots & Operators Job Portal	http://www.747pilotjobs.org

-B-

Banking

Alliance of Merger and Acquisition Advisors	http://www.amaaonline.com
American Banker Online Career Zone	http://www.americanbanker.com/Careerzone.html
American Bankers Association	http://www.aba.careerbank.com
American Bankruptcy Institute Career Center	http://www.abiworld.org
Bank Administration Institute	http://www.bai.org
Bank Gigs	http://www.bankgigs.com
Bank Jobs	http://www.bankjobs.com
Bank Marketing Association	http://www.bmanet.org
BankingBoard.com	http://www.bankingboard.com
Banking Careers	http://www.bankingcareers.com
Banking & Financial Services Career Network	http://www.searchbankingjobs.com
Banking Job Site	http://www.bankingjobsite.com
Banking Job Store	http://www.bankingjobstore.com
CareerBank.com	http://www.careerbank.com
CreditCardJobs.net	http://www.creditcardjobs.net
Credit Union Board	http://www.creditunionboard.net
eFinancialCareers.com	http://www.efinancialcareers.com
FinancialJobBank	http://www.financialjobbank.com
Financial Job Network	http://www.fjn.com
FINANCIALjobs.com	http://www.financialjobs.com
Financial Women International Careers	http://www.fwi.org
The Finance Beat	http://www.business.searchbeat.com/finance.htm

FindMortgageJobs.com	http://www.findmortgagejobs.com
Florida Banking Jobs Online	http://www.bankjobsflorida.com
GetBankTellerJobs	http://www.getbanktellerjobs.net
GTNews [United Kingdom]	http://www.gtnews.com
iHireBanking.com	http://www.ihirebanking.com
InvestmentBankingJobs.com	http://www.investmentbankingjobs.com
Jobs4Banking.com	http://www.jobs4banking.com
JobsinCredit [United Kingdom]	http://www.jobsincredit.com
Loan Closer Jobs	http://www.loancloserjobs.com
LoanOfficerJobs.com	http://www.loanofficerjobs.com
Loan Originator Jobs	http://www.loanoriginatorjobs.com
LoanProcessorJobs.com	http://www.loanprocessorjobs.com
LoanServicingJobs.com	http://www.loanservicingjobs.com
MortgageBoard	http://www.mortgageboard.com
Mortgage Job Store	http://www.mortgagejobstore.com
National Banking Network	http://nbn-jobs.com
Real Estate Finance Jobs	http://www.realestatefinancejobs.com
Real Estate Lenders Association	http://www.rela.org
Search Banking Jobs	http://www.searchbankingjobs.com
Society of Risk Analysis Opportunities	http://www.sra.org/opportunities.php
TitleBoard.net	http://www.titleboard.net
TopBankingJobs	http://www.topbankingjobs.com
True Careers	http://www.truecareers.com
UnderwritingJobs.com	http://www.underwritingjobs.com

Bilingual/Multilingual/Translation Professionals

Asianet	http://www.asianetglobal.com
Asian-Jobs.com	http://www.asian-jobs.com
BilingualCareer.com	http://www.bilingualcareer.com
BilingualJobBoard	http://www.bilingualjobboard.com

Bilingual-Jobs	http://www.bilingual-jobs.com
CHALLENGEUSA	http://www.challengeusa.com
Eflweb	http://www.eflweb.com
Euroleaders	http://www.euroleaders.com
ExposureJobs [Europe]	http://www.exposurejobs.com
FreeLancerSupport	http://www.freelancersupport.com
GetBilingualJobs	http://www.getbilingualjobs.net
Hispanic Chamber of Commerce	http://www.ushcc.com
Hispanic-Jobs.com	http://www.hispanic-jobs.com
iHispano	http://www.ihispano.com
Language123	http://www.language123.com
LatPro	http://www.latpro.com
National Society of Hispanic MBAs Career Center	http://www.nshmba.org
SaludosWeb	http://www.saludos.com
Society of Hispanic Professional Engineers Career Services	http://www.shpe.org
Tomedes	http;//www.tomedes.com
Top Language Jobs [Europe]	http://www.toplanguagejobs.co.uk
TRADUguide	http;//www.traduguide.com
Translators Café	http://www.translatorscafe.com
Translators Town	http://www.translatorstown.com
Two Lingos	http://www.twolingos.com
Zhaopin.com	http://www.zhaopin.com

Biology/Biomedical/Biotechnology

American Chemical Society	http://www.portal.acs.org
American Institute of Biological Sciences	http://www.aibs.org
American Society of Agricultural and Biological Engineers	http://www.asabe.org
American Society for Cell Biology	http://www.ascb.org
American Society of Gene Therapy	http://www.asgt.org

American Society for Gravitational and Space Biology	http://www.asgsb.org/index.php
American Society of Limnology and Oceanography	http://www.aslo.org
American Society for Microbiology	http://www.asm.org
American Society of Plant Biologists	http://www.aspb.org
Bay Bio	http://www.baybio.org
Bermuda Biological Station for Research, Inc.	http://www.bios.edu
Biocareer.com	http://www.biocareer.com
BioCareers.co.za [South Africa]	http://www.biocareers.co.za
BioExchange.com	http://www.bioexchange.com
Biofind	http://www.biofind.com
BioFlorida	http://www.bioflorida.com
BioJobNet.com	http://www.biojobnet.com
BiologyJobs.com	http://www.biologyjobs.com
Biomedical Engineering Society	http://www.bmes.org
BioOptics World	http://www.bioopticsowrld.com
Bio Research Online	http://www.bioresearchonline.com
BioSource Technical Service	http://www.biosource-tech.com
BioSpace Career Center	http://www.biospace.com
BioTech Job Site	http://www.biotechjobsite.com
BiotechSales/Chemistry Career Search	http://www.biotechsaleschemistry.com
Biotechnology Association of Alabama	http://www.bioalabama.com
Biotechnology Association of Maine	http://www.mainebiotech.org
Biotechnology Calendar, Inc.	http://www.biotech-calendar.com
Biotechnology Council of New Jersey	http://www.newjerseybiotech.org
Biotechnology Industry Organization	http://www.bio.org
BioView	http://www.bioview.co.il/HTMLs/Home.aspx
Canadian Society of Biochemistry/Molecular/ Cellular Biologists Job Listing	http://www.medicine.mcgill.ca/expmed/emjl/ expmed_whoislinking.htm
CanMed [Canada]	http://www.canmed.com
Cell Press Online	http://www.cell.com/cellpress
ChemJobs.net	http://www.chemjobs.net

ChemPharma	http://www.chempharma.net
Connecticut's BioScience Cluster	http://www.curenet.org
Drug Information Association Employment Opportunities	http://www.diahome.org/DIAHome/Resources/FindJob.aspx
GxPJobs.com [United Kingdom]	http://www.gxpjobs.com
HireBio.com	http://www.hirebio.com
HireLifeScience	http://www.hirelifescience.com
Iowa Biotechnology Association	http://www.iowabiotech.org
Jobscience Network	http://www.jobs.jobscience.com
The London Biology Network [United Kingdom]	http://www.biolondon.org.uk
Massachusetts Biotechnology Council	http://www.massbio.org
MdBio, Inc. (Maryland Bioscience)	http://www.techcouncilmd.com/mdbio
Medzilla	http://www.medzilla.com
MichBIO	http://www.michbio.org
Nature	http://www.nature.com
The New York Biotechnology Association	http://www.nyba.org
North Carolina Biotechnology Center	http://www.ncbiotech.org
North Carolina Genomics & Bioinformatics	http://www.ncgbc.org
Oregon Bioscience Association	http://www.oregon-bioscience.com
Organic-Chemistry	http://www.organic-chemistry.org
PharmacyWeek	http://www.pharmacyweek.com
PharmaOpportunities	http://www.pharmaopportunites.com
Public Responsibility in Medicine and Research	http://careers.primr.org
RPhrecruiter.com	http://www.rphrecruiter.com
Rx Career Center	http://www.rxcareercenter.com
Science Careers	http://www.sciencecareers.sciencemag.org
Sciencejobs.com	http://www.newscientistjobs.com
The Science Jobs	http://www.thesciencejobs.com
SCIENCE Online	http://www.scienceonline.org
Scijobs.com	http://www.sciencecareers.sciencemag.org
SciWeb Biotechnology Career Center	http://www.biocareers.com

Texas Healthcare & Bioscience Institute	http://www.thbi.org
Utah Life Sciences Association	http://www.utahlifescience.com
Virginia Biotechnology Association	http://www.vabio.org
Washington Biotechnology & Biomedical Association	http://www.wabio.com
Wisconsin Biotechnology Association	http://www.wisconsinbiotech.org

Blogs-Job Search/Careers

Baily WorkPlay	http://www.baileyworkplay.com
BlogEmploi [France]	http://www.cadresonline.com/coaching/blog/index_blog_emploi.php
BoldCareer.com	http://www.boldcareer.com
Boston.com	http://www.boston.com/jobs
Career Advice & Resources Blog	http://www.resumelines.com/blog
Career Assessment Goddess	http://www.blog.careergoddess.com
Career Chaos	http://www.coachmeg.typepad.com/career_chaos
CareerHub	http://www.careerhub.typepad.com/main
Career and Job Hunting Blog	http://www.quintcareers.com/career_blog
CollegeRecruiter.com Insights By Candidates Blog	http://www.collegerecruiter.com/insightblog
Dave Opton's Blog at ExecuNet	http://www.execunet.com
DearAnyone.com	http://www.dearanyone.com/work
Dr. Bamster's Blog	http://www.drbamstersblog.squarespace.com
Dream Big	http://www.letsdreambig.blogspot.com
Employment Digest	http://www.employmentdigest.net
Find A New Job	http://www.findnewjob.blogspot.com
From the Inside Out	http://www.iyjnjen.blogspot.com
Get That Job	http://www.getthatjob.blogspot.com
GetTheJob's Job Seeker Blog	http://www.getthejob.com
Guerrilla Job Hunting	http://www.guerrillajobhunting.typepad.com/guerrilla_job_hunting
Heather's Blog at Microsoft	http://www.blogs.msdn.com/b/heatherleigh

HireBlog	http://www.hireblog.blogspot.com
IWorkWithFools.com	http://www.iworkwithfools.com
Job Search Opportunity Tips & Advice	http://www.job-search-opportunity.blogspot.com
Jobs Blog/Technical Careers at Microsoft	http://www.blogs.msdn.com/b/jobsblog
Jobs, Job Seekers, Employers & Recruiters	http://www.employment.typepad.com
Knock 'em Dead Blog	http://www.bknock-em-dead.blogspot.com
Life@Work	http://www.dbcs.typepad.com
The Monster Blog	http://www.monster.typepad.com/monsterblog
My Blog By Jan Melnik	http://www.myblog.janmelnik.com
The Occupational Adventure	http://www.curtrosengren.typepad.com/occupationaladventure
Peter Weddle's WorkStrong Blog	http://www.weddles.com/workstrong
Retail Anonymous	http://www.retailanonymous.blogspot.com
Secrets of the Job Hunt	http://www.secretsofthejobhunt.blogspot.com
SecurityClearanceJobsBlog.com	http://www.securityclearancejobsblog.com
TechLawAdvisor.com Job Postings	http://www.techlawadvisor.com/jobs
The Virtual Handshake	http://www.thevirtualhandshake.com/blog
WildJobSafari	http://www.wildjobsafari.blogspot.com
WorkBloom	http://www.workbloom.com/default.aspx
Workers Work	http://www.workerswork.com
Wurk	http://www.wurk.net
Yaps4u.net	http://www.yaps4u.net

Blogs-Recruiting

Advanced Online Recruiting Techniques	http://www.recruiting-online.spaces.live.com
Amitai Givertz's Recruitomatic Blog	http://www.recruitomatic.wordpress.com
The Asia Pacific Headhunter	http://www.searchniche.blogs.com
Bells and Whistles	http://www.rcirs.com/blog
Blog Indeed	http://www.blog.indeed.com
Digability by Jim Stroud	http://www.digability.blogspot.com

Hiring Technical People	http://www.jrothman.com/blog/htp
JobBoarders.com	http://www.jobboarders.com
Jobster	http://www.jobster.com
MarketingHeadhunter.com	http://www.marketingheadhunter.com
Mini Microsoft	http://www.minimsft.blogspot.com
MN Headhunter	http://www.mnheadhunter.com
PassingNotes.com	http://www.passing-notes.com
Peter Weddle's WorkStrong Blog	http://www.weddles.com/workstrong
Recruiting.com	http://www.recruiting.com
RecruitingAnimal.com	http://www.recruitinganimal.com
RecruitingBlogs.com	http://www.recruitingblogs.com
Seth Godin's Blog	http://www.sethgodin.typepad.com
SimplyHired Blog	http://www.blog.simplyhired.com
Talentism	http://www.jjhunter.typepad.com
TechCrunch	http://www.techcrunch.com

Building Construction/Management (See also Construction)

Air Conditioning Heating Refrigeration News	http://www.achrnews.com
Air Conditioning Jobs	http://www.airconditioningjobs.com
AffordableHousingJobs.com	http://www.affordablehousingjobs.com
AllHousingJobs.co.uk [United Kingdom]	http://www.allhousingjobs.co.uk
Apartment Association of Greater Dallas	http://www.aagdallas.org
Apartment Association of Tarrant County	http://www.aatcnet.org/subsite/CareerCenter/careercenterindex.htm
ApartmentCareerHQ.org	http://www.apartmentcareerHQ.org
ApartmentCareers.com	http://www.apartmentcareers.com
ApartmentJobs.com	http://www.apartmentjobs.com
Apartment Jobz	http://www.apartmentjobz.com
BuilderJobs	http://www.builderjobs.com
Builder Magazine	http://www.builderonline.com

Building Industry Exchange	http://www.building.org
Construction4Professionals.co.uk [United Kingdom]	http://www.construction4professionals.co.uk
Contract Design Magazine	Http://contractdesign.com
Custom Home Magazine	http://www.customhomeonline.com
EstimatorJobs.com	http://www.estimatorjobs.com
HelmetstoHardhats.com	http://www.helmetstohardhats.com
HVACagent.com	http://www.hvacagent.com
HVAC Industry	http://www.hvac-industry.com
The HVAC Source	http://www.thehvacsource.com
iHireBuildingTrades.com	http://www.ihirebuildingtrades.com
International Code Council	http://www.iccsafe.org/Pages/default.aspx
JobsinConstruction [United Kingdom]	http://www.jobsinconstruction.co.uk
JobsinSurveying [United Kingdom]	http://www.jobsinsurveying.co.uk
JustEngineers.net [Australia]	http://www.justengineers.net
Kitchen & Bath Business	http://www.kbbonline.com
MaintenanceEmployment.com	http://www.maintenanceemployment.com
National Apartment Association	http://www.naahq.org/Pages/welcome.aspx
NewHomeSalesJobs.com	http://www.newhomesalesjobs.com
ProjectManagerJobs.com	http://www.projectmanagerjobs.com
Senior Housing Jobs	http://www.seniorhousingjobs.com
SuperintendentJobs.com	http://www.superintendentjobs.com
Texas Apartment Association	http://www.taa.org/sitemap
QCEmployMe.com	http://www.regionalhelpwanted.com/quad-cities-il-ia-jobs
Sheet Metal and Air Conditioning Contractor's Association	http://www.smacna.org
Tools of the Trade Magazine	http://www.toolsofthetrade.net
TopBuildingJobs.com	http://www.topbuildingjobs.com
UtilityJobSearch.com [United Kingdom]	http://www.utilityjobsearch.com
Washington Multi-Family Housing Association	http://www.careers.wmfha.org

Business

Alliance of Merger and Acquisition Advisors	http://www.amaaonline.com
American Bankruptcy Institute Career Center	http://www.abiworld.org//AM/Template.cfm?Section=Home
American Society for Quality	http://www.asq.org/career
APICS	http://www.apics.org/default.htm
Association of Executive and Administration Professionals	http://www.theaeap.com
Association of MBAs	http://www.mbaworld.com
Association for Strategic Planning	http://www.strategyplus.org
Barron's Online	http://www.online.barrons.com/home-page
Big Charts	http://www.bigcharts.marketwatch.com
Billboard	http://www.billboard.com
Biz Journals	http://www.bizjournals.com/jobs
Bloomberg.com	http://www.bloomberg.com
BPOJobSite.com [India]	http://www.bpojobsite.com
Business Finance	http://www.businessfinancemag.com
Business Marketing Association	http://www.marketing.org/i4a/pages/index.cfm?pageid=1
Capital Hill Blue	http://www.chblue.com
CareerMarketplace.com	http://www.careermarketplace.com
Career Network	http://www.careernetwork.com/section/Home/5
Careers In Business	http://www.careers-in-business.jobsinthemoney.com
CNBC/Career Center	http://www.cnbc.com
CNNMoney.com	http://www.money.cnn.com/
CommNexus	http://www.commnexus.com
CondeNet	http://www.condenastdigital.com/index.html
Corporate Finance Net	http://www.corpfinet.com
Corporate Watch	http://www.corpwatch.org
CreditCardJobs.net	http://www.creditcardjobs.net
Crain's Chicago	http://www.chicagobusiness.com

Customer Service Management	http://www.csm-us.co/mhc3.asp
Customer Service University	http://www.customerserviceuniversity.com
Degree Hunter	http://www.degreehunter.net
Dow Jones	http://www.dowjones.com
e-Marketer	http://www.e-marketer.com
Entrepreneur	http://www.entrepreneur.com/magazine/entrepreneur/index.html
ForeignMBA.com	http://www.foreignmba.com
Fortune	http://www.money.cnn.com/magazines/fortune
Global Careers	http://www.globalcareers.com
Harvard Business Review	http://www.hbsp.Harvard.edu
Hollywood Reporter	http://www.hollywoodreporter.com/hr/index.jsp
HomeOfficeJob.com	http://www.homeoffice.com
Hoover's Online	http://www.hoovers.com
iHireSecurity.com	http://www.ihiresecurity.com
Inc.	http://www.inc.com
Industry Week	http://www.industryweek.com
International Association of Business Communicators	http://www.iabc.com
International Association for Commercial and Contract Management	http://www.iaccm.com
International Customer Service Association Job Board	http://www.icsatoday.org
Internet News	http://www.internetnews.com
Jane's Information Group	http://www.janes.com
JobsinRisk.com [United Kingdom]	http://www.jobsinrisk.com
Journal of Commerce	http://www.joc.com
Kiplinger	http://www.kiplinger.com
latinMBA.com	http://www.latinmba.com
MBA Careers	http://www.mbacareers.com
MBA-Exchange.com	http://www.mba-exchange.com/candidates/mba_jobs.php
MBA Free Agents	http://www.mbafreeagents.com
MBAGlobalNet	http://www.mbaglobalnet.com

MBAJobs.net	http://www.mbajobs.net
MBAmatch.com [United Kingdom]	http://www.mbamatch.com
MBA Style Magazine	http://www.mbastyle.com
MBATalentWire.com	http://www.mbatalentwire.com
MeetingJobs.com	http://www.meetingjobs.com
MinorityMBAs	http://www.minoritymbas.com
Multiunitjobs.com	http://www.multiunitjobs.com
National Society of Hispanic MBAs Career Center	http://www.nshmba.org
New York Black MBA	http://www.nyblackmba.org
P-Jobs	http://www.pjobs.org
Pro2Net	http://www.accounting.smartpros.com
Product Development & Management Association	http://www.pdma.org
ReceptionistJobStore.com	http://www.receptionistjobstore.com
Red Herring	http://www.redherring.com
Securities Industry Association Career Resource Center	http://www.sifma.com/services/career_center/career_center.html
Smart Money	http://www.smartmoney.com
Society of Competitive Intelligence Professionals Job Marketplace	http://www.scip.org/CareerCenter
Strategy+Business	http://www.strategy-business.com
The Street	http://www.thestreet.com
TANG	https://www.nyustern.campusgroups.com/home
Top Startups	http://www.topstartups.com
VAR Business	http://www.crn.com/cwb/careers
Vault	http://www.vault.com/wps/portal/usa
WetFeet.com	http://www.wetfeet.com

-C-

Call Center

AnswerStat	http://www.answerstat.com
Cactussearch.co.uk [United Kingdom]	http://www.cactussearch.co.uk
CallCenterCareers.com	http://www.callcentercareers.com/index.jsp
CallCenterClassifieds	http://www.callcenterclassifieds.com
CallCenterJob.ca [Canada]	http://www.callcenterjob.ca
CallCenterJobs.com	http://www.callcenterjobs.com
CallCenterOps.com	http://www.callcenterops.com
CallCenterProfi.de [Germany]	http://www.callcenterprofi.de/index.php;sid=5df09 c06c9fdf1810ce006b8f9beab9f
Get Call Center Jobs	http://www.getcallcenterjobs.com
JobsinContactCentres [United Kingdom]	http://www.jobsincontactcentres.com
Teleplaza	http://www.teleplaza.com/jp.html

Career Counseling/Job Search Services

America's Career InfoNet	http://www.acinet.org
American Evaluation Association	http://www.eval.org/programs/careercenter.asp
AskNaukri.com [India]	http://www.asknaukri.com
Association of Career Professionals International	http://www.iacpm.org
Association of Graduate Careers Advisory Service [United Kingdom]	http://www.agcas.org.uk
Association of Executive Search Consultants	http://www.bluesteps.com
BrainBench	http://www.brainbench.com
BrazenCareerist	http://www.brazencareerist.com
Bright.com	http://www.bright.com
Canadian Association of Career Educators & Employers	http://www.cacee.com
CanadianCareers.com	http://www.canadiancareers.com

CareerDNA	http://www.careerdna.netstatic/home
CareerHarmony.com	http://www.careerharmony.com
Career Management International	http://www.cmi-lmi.com
CareerVoyages.gov	http://www.careervoyages.gov
CareersUSA.com	http://www.careersusa.com
Computing Technology Industry Association Career Compass	http://www.tcc.comptia.org
CVTips.com	http://www.cvtips.com
DDI	http://www.ddiworld.com
Eggsprout	http://www.eggsprout.com
eLance	http://www.elance.com
The Engineering Specific Career Advisory Problem-Solving Environment	https://www.engineering.purdue.edu/Engr
ePredix	http://www.previsor.com
Executive Agent	http://www.myresumeagent.com
ExecutiveResumes.com	http://www.executiveresumes.com
Exxceed	http://www.exxceed.com
FaceCV [Italy]	http://www.facecv.it
FreeLancingProjects.com	http://www.freelancingprojects.com
Get Me A Job	http://www.getmeajob.com
GetMoreJobOffers.com [United Kingdom]	http://www.getmorejoboffers.com
GlassDoor.com	http://www.glassdoor.com/index.htm
GotResumes.com	http://www.gotresumes.com
Gray Hair Management LLC	http://www.grayhairmanagement.com
Guru.com	http://www.guru.com
Hoovers Online	http://www.hoovers.com
JibberJobber.com	http://www.jibberjobber.com/login.php
JobBait.com	http://www.jobbait.com
JobConnect.org	http://www.jobconnections.org
Jobfiler.com	http://www.jobfiler.com
Job Hunter's Bible	http://www.jobhuntersbible.com

JobSearchNews.com	http://www.jobsearchnews.com
JobseekersAdvice.com [United Kingdom]	http://www.jobseekersadvice.com
JobStar	http://www.jobstar.org/index.php
JobVoting.com [Germany]	http://www.jobvoting.com
JobsRadar	http://www.jobsradar.com
Kaplan Career Services	http://www.kaplan.com/pages/default.aspx
Kelzen.com [Austria]	http://www.kelzen.com/en
Kununu.com [Austria]	http://www.kununu.com
The Limited	http://www.thelimited.com
LiveCareer	http://www.livecareer.com
MyWebCareer	http://www.mywebcareer.com
National Association of Colleges & Employers	http://www.jobweb.com
National Association for College Admission Counseling Career Opportunities	http://www.nacac.com/classifieds.cfm
National Association of Colleges & Employers (NACE)	http://www.nacelink.com
National Board for Certified Counselors	http://www.nbcc.org
National Career Development Association	http://www.ncda.org
ThePhoenixLink.com	http://www.thephoenixlink.com
PitchYourTalent [Southeast Asia]	http://www.pitchyourtalent.com
Pursut.com	http://www.pursut.com
Ready Minds	http://www.readyminds.com
Real-Home-Employment	http://www.real-home-employment.com
RentaCoder.com	http://www.vworker.com/RentACoder/DotNet/default.aspx
ResumeBlaster	http://www.resumeblaster.com
ResumeBomber	http://www.resumebomber.com
ResumeBucket	http://www.resumebucket.com
ResumeXPRESS	http://www.resumexpress.com
Resume Network	http://www.resume-network.com
The Resume Place, Inc.	http://www.resume-place.com
ResumeRabbit.com	http://www.resumerabbit.com

Resume2Hire.com	http://www.resume2hire.com
Resumes on the Web	http://www.resweb.com
Resume Workz	http://www.resumeworkz.com
The Riley Guide	http://www.rileyguide.com
Rypple.com	http://www.rypple.com
Salary.com	http://www.salary.com
Seidbet Associates	http://www.seidbet.com
SingleMindedWomen.com	http://www.singlemindedwomen.com
Skill Scape	http://www.skillscape.com
SoloGig	http://www.sologig.com
Tweetajob	http://www.tweetajob.com
TweetMyJobs.com	http://www.tweetmyjob.com
Vault	http://www.vault.com/wps/portal/usa
Vizibility	http://www.vizibility.com
WEDDLE's Newsletters, Guides & Directories	http://www.weddles.com
Wetfeet.com	http://www.wetfeet.com
WorkBloom.com	http://www.workbloom.com
WorkMinistry.com	http://www.workministry.com
Yourcha.de [Germany]	http://www.yourcha.com/de/employee/home/s
ZoomInfo.com	http://www.zoominfo.com

Chemistry

American Chemical Society	http://portal.acs.org/portal/acs/corg/content
American Chemical Society Rubber Division	http://www.rubber.org
American Association of Brewing Chemists	http://www.asbcnet.org/placement/jobs.htm
American Association of Cereal Chemists careerplacement.asp	http://www.aaccnet.org/membership/
American Association of Clinical Chemistry Career Center	http://careercenter.aacc.org/
American Institute of Chemical Engineers CareerEngineer	http://careerengineer.aiche.org/

The American Institute of Chemists	http://www.theaic.org/DesktopDefault.aspx
BiotechSales/Chemistry Career Search	http://www.biotechsaleschemistry.com
Chememploy	http://www.chemweek.com/chemploy
Chemical Industry Central	http://www.chemicalindustrycentral.com
Chemical Week	http://www.chemweek.com
Chemist Jobs	http://www.chemistjobs.com
Chemistry & Industry	http://www.soci.org/Chemistry-and-Industry/Cnl-Data/2010/11
ChemJobs.net	http://www.chemjobs.net/chemjobs.html
ChemPeople.com [United Kingdom]	http://www.chempeople.com
ChemPharma	http://www.chempharma.net
ChemSeer	http://www.chemseer.com
Chem Web	http://www.chemweb.com
HireLifeScience	http://www.hirelifescience.com
iHireChemists.com	http://www.ihirechemists.com
Intratech	http://www.intratech1.com
Jobscience Network	http://jobs.jobscience.com
Jobs in Chemistry	http://www.jobsinchemistry.com
Nature	http://www.nature.com
New Scientist Jobs	http://www.newscientistjobs.com
Organic Chemistry	http://www.organic-chemistry.org
Organic Chemistry Jobs Worldwide [Belgium]	http://www.organicworldwide.net/jobs
PlasticsJobsForum.com	http://www.plasticsjobsforum.com
Poly Sort	http://www.polysort.com
Science Careers	http://sciencecareers.sciencemag.org
Scijobs.org	http://sciencecareers.sciencemag.org
ScienceJobs.org	http://www.sciencejobs.org

Child & Elder Care

AuPair In Europe	http://www.planetaupair.com/aupaireng.htm
CareGuide	http://www.careguide.net
4Nannies.com	http://www.4nannies.com
Nannyjob.co.uk [United Kingdom]	http://www.nannyjob.co.uk
NurseryWorldJobs.co.uk [United Kingdom]	http://www.nurseryworldjobs.co.uk
SitterByZip	http://www.sitterbyzip.com

Classifieds-Newspaper & Magazine

International

BioPharm International	http://www.biopharminternational.com
Jobb24.se [Sweden]	http://www.jobb24.se
Laser Focus World	http://www.laserfocusworld.com
TheLondonPaper.com [United Kingdom]	http://www.thelondonpaper.com
MediaWeek [United Kingdom]	http://www.mediaweek.co.uk
Mobiljob [France]	http://www.topannonces.fr/petites-annonces--offres-d-emploi-interim.html
Offshore Magazine	http://offshore-mag.com
Oil & Gas Journal	http://www.ogj.com
TimesJobs.com [India]	http://www.timesjobs.com
Vlan [Belgium]	http://www.vlan.be
TheWest.com.au [Australia]	http://au.news.yahoo.com/thewest

National

AdWeek	http://www.adweek.com
American Lawyer Magazine	http://www.americanlawyer.com
Automotive News	http://www.autonews.com
BackStage	http://www.backstage.com
Billboard.com	http://www.billboard.com
BioOptics World	http://www.bioopticsowrld.com

Builder Magazine	http://www.builderonline.com
CareerCast.com	http://www.careercast.com
Chain Store Age	http://www.chainstoreage.com
Consulting Magazine	http://www.consultingmag.com
Contract Magazine	http://www.contractdesign.com
Corporate Counsel	http://www.law.com/corporatecounsel
Custom Home Magazine	http://www.customhomeonline.com
Deadline Hollywood	http://www.deadline.com/hollywood
Diversity Classifieds	http://www.diversityclassifieds.com
Drug Store News	http://www.drugstorenews.com
EDN Network	http://www.edn.com
EE Times	http://www.eetimes.com
Event Design Magazine	http://www.eventdesignmag.com
Folio Magazine	http://www.foliomag.com
Hollywood Reporter	http://www.hollywoodreporter.com
Home Channel News	http://www.homechannelnews.com
Impre Media	http://www.impremedia.com
Industrial Laser Solutions	http://industrial-lasers.com
Law Technology News	http://www.law.com/lawtechnologynews
Multifamily Executive Magazine	http://www.multifamilyexecutive.com
National Law Journal	http://www.law.com/jsp/nlj/index.jsp
PharmacyTimes	http://www.pharmacytimes.com
PharmacyWeek	http://www.pharmacyweek.com
Public Works Magazine	http://www.pwmag.com
Residential Architect Magazine	http://www.residentialarchitect.com
Retailing Today	http://www.retailingtoday.com
Test & Measurement World	http://www.tmworld.com
Tools of the Trade Magazine	http://www.toolsofthetrade.net
Vision Systems Design	http://www.vision-systems.com
The Wall Street Journal	http://online.wsj.com/home-page

USA Today	http://www.usatoday.com
Vista Magazine	http://www.vistamagazine.com
Women's Wear Daily Careers	http://www.wwd.com/wwdcareers

Alabama

AL.com	http://www.al.com
Birmingham News	http://www.bhamnews.com
Huntsville Times	http://www.htimes.com
Mobile Register Online	http://www.mobileregister.com
Montgomery Advertiser	http://www.montgomeryadvertiser.com
The Tuscaloosa News	http://www.tuscaloosanews.com

Alaska

Anchorage Daily News	http://www.adn.com
Fairbanks Daily News	http://fairbanks.abracat.com
Frontiersman	http://www.frontiersman.com
Juneau Empire	http://www.juneauempire.com
Nome Nugget	http://www.nomenugget.com

Arizona

Arizona Daily Sun (Flagstaff)	http://www.azdailysun.com
The Daily Courier (Prescott)	http://www.dcourier.com
East Valley Tribune (Mesa)	http://www.eastvalleytribune.com
Geebo	http://www.geebo.com
Phoenix News Times	http://www.phoenixnewtimes.com
Today's News-Herald (Lake Havasu City)	http://www.havasunews.com

Arkansas

ArkansasOnline	http://www.arkansasonline.com
Benton Courier	http://www.bentoncourier.com
Jonesboro Sun	http://www.jonesborosun.com

NWAonline   http://www.nwaonline.com

The Sentinel-Record (Hot Springs)   http://www.hotsr.com

California

BayAreaClassifieds.com   http://www.bayareaclassifieds.com

El Mensajero (San Francisco)   http://www.elmensajero.com

Geebo   http://www.geebo.com

Inland Valley Daily Bulletin   http://www.dailybulletin.com

La Opinion (Los Angeles)   http://www.laopinion.com

Los Angeles Daily News   http://www.dailynews.com

Los Angeles Times   http://www.latimes.com

Mercury News (San Jose)   http://www.bayarea.com

Orange County Register   http://www.ocregister.com

Pasadena Star-News   http://www.pasadenastarnews.com

The Press Enterprise   http://www.pe.com

Press Telegram of Long Beach   http://www.presstelegram.com

The Recorder   http://www.law.com/jsp/ca/index.jsp

Recordnet.com   http://www.recordnet.com

Redlands Daily Facts   http://www.redlandsdailyfacts.com

Sacramento Bee   http://www.sacbee.com

San Diego Reader   http://www.sandiegoreader.com

San Bernadino Sun   http://www.sbsun.com

San Francisco Chronicle   http://www.sfgate.com

San Gabriel Valley Tribune   http://www.sgvtribune.com

Whittier Daily News   http://www.whittierdailynews.com

Colorado

Aspen Daily News   http://www.aspendailynews.com

Colorado Springs Independent   http://www.csindy.com

The Daily Sentinel (Grand Junction)   http://www.gjsentinel.com

Denver Post   http://www.denverpost.com

Durango Herald   http://www.durangoherald.com

Rocky Mountain News   http://www.rockymountainnews.com/jobs

Connecticut

The Advocate (Stamford)   http://www.stamfordadvocate.com

Connecticut Law Tribune   http://www.ctlawtribune.com

Danbury News-Times   http://www.newstimes.com

TheDay.com (New London)   http://www.theday.com

Hartford Courant   http://www.courant.com

New Haven Register   http://www.newhavenregister.com

Waterbury Republican American   http://www.rep-am.com

Delaware

Delaware Law Weekly   http://www.delawarelawweekly.com

Dover Post   http://www.doverpost.com

The News Journal (Wilmington)   http://www.delawareonline.com

District of Columbia

Afro-American   http://.afro.com

Geebo   http://www.geebo.com

JobFetch.com   http://www.jobfetch.com

RC Jobs, The Newspaper of Capital Hill   http://www.rcjobs.com

The Washington Post   http://www.washingtonpost.com

Washington Times   http://www.washingtontimes.com

Florida

Daily Business Review (Miami)   http://www.dailybusinessreview.com

Daytona Beach News-Journal   http://www.news-journalonline.com

Florida Times Union (Jacksonville)   http://jacksonville.com

Geebo   http://www.geebo.com

La Prensa (Orlando)   http://www.laprensafl.com

Miami Herald — http://www.miami.com

Orlando Sentinel — http://www.orlandosentinel.com

Pensacola News Journal — http://www.pnj.com

St. Petersburg Times — http://www.sptimes.com

Georgia

The Albany Herald — http://www.albanyherald.net/classbrowse.htm

Atlanta Journal and Constitution — http://www.ajc.com

Augusta Chronicle — http://chronicle.augusta.com

Clayton News Daily — http://www.news-daily.com

Daily Report (Atlanta) — http://www.dailyreportonline.com

Gwinnett Daily Post — http://www.gwinnettdailypost.com

Henry Daily Herald — http://www.henryherald.com

Macon Telegraph — http://www.macon.com

Newton Citizen — http://www.newtoncitizen.com

Rockdale Citizen — http://www.rockdalecitizen.com

Savannah Morning News — http://www.savannahnow.com

Hawaii

Hawaii Tribune-Herald (Hilo) — http://www.hawaiitribune-herald.com/index.html

Honolulu Advertiser — http://www.honoluluadvertiser.com

Honolulu Star-Bulletin — http://www.starbulletin.com

Maui News — http://www.mauinews.com

West Hawaii Today (Kailua) — http://www.westhawaiitoday.com

Idaho

Cedar Rapids Gazette — http://www.gazetteonline.com

The Daily Nonpareil (Council Bluffs) — http://southwestiowanews.com/council_bluffs/front

Des Moines Register — http://www.desmoinesregister.com

Quad City Times (Davenport) — http://qctimes.com

Sioux City Journal   http://www.siouxcityjournal.com

Illinois

Chicago Tribune   http://www.chicagotribune.com

The Daily Register (Canton)   http://www.cantondailyledger.com

Geebo   http://www.geebo.com

Herald & Review (Decatur)   http://www.herald-review.com

La Raza (Chicago)   http://www.laraza.com

The News-Gazette (Champaign)   http://www.news-gazette.com

Register-News (Mount Vernon)   http://register-news.com

The State Journal Register (Springfield)   http://www.sj-r.com

Indiana

The Elkhart Truth   http://www.etruth.com

The Herald-Times (Bloomington)   http://www.heraldtimesonline.com

Indianapolis Star News   http://www.indystar.com

The News-Sentinel (Fort Wayne)   http://www.fortwayne.com

Post-Tribune (Gary)   http://www.post-trib.com/index.html

South Bend Tribune   http://www.sbinfo.com

Kansas

Daily Union (Junction City)   http://www.thedailyunion.net

Kansas City Kansan   http://www.kansascitykansan.com

Salina Journal   http://www.saljournal.com

The Topeka Capital Journal   http://www.cjonline.com

Wichita Eagle   http://www.kansas.com

Kentucky

The Courier-Journal (Louisville)   http://www.courier-journal.com

The Daily News (Bowling Green)   http://www.bgdailynews.com

Grayson County News-Gazette (Leitchfield)   http://www.gcnewsgazette.com

Lexington Herald Leader http://www.kentucky.com

Sentinel News (Shelbyville) http://www.sentinelnews.com

Louisiana

The Advocate (Baton Rouge) http://www.theadvocate.com

The Times (Shreveport) http://www.shreveporttimes.com

The Times-Picayune (New Orleans) http://www.nola.com

Maine

Bangor Daily News http://www.bangordailynews.com

Kennebec Journal (Augusta) http://www.kjonline.com

Lewiston Sun Journal http://www.sunjournal.com

Portland Press Herald http://www.portland.com

Sanford News http://www.fosters.com/apps/pbcs.dll/
section?category=SANNEWS

The Times Record (Brunswick) http://www.timesrecord.com

York County Coast News http://www.seacoastonline.com

Maryland

Afro-American (Baltimore) http://www.afro.com

Baltimore Sun http://www.baltimoresun.com

The Capital (Annapolis) http://www.hometownannapolis.com

Gazette.net http://www.gazette.net

The Herald-Mail (Hagerstown) http://www.herald-mail.com

JobFetch.com http://www.jobfetch.com

The Star Democrat (Easton) http://www.stardem.com

Massachusetts

Barnstable Patriot http://barnstablepatriot.com

The Boston Globe http://www.boston.com/bostonglobe

CapeCodSummerJobs.com http://www.capecodsummerjobs.com

Cape Cod Times | http://www.capecodonline.com

The Eagle-Tribune (Lawrence) | http://www.eagletribune.com

Fall River Spirit | http://www.southcoasttoday.com

Geebo | http://www.geebo.com

The Sun (Lowell) | http://www.lowellsun.com

The Salem News | http://www.salemnews.com

Union-News & Sunday Republican (Springfield) | http://www.masslive.com

Michigan

Ann Arbor News | http://www.mlive.com/annarbornews

Bay City News | http://www.mlive.com/bctimes

Detroit Free Press | http://www.freep.com

Flint Journal | http://www.mlive.com/flintjournal

Grand Rapids Press | http://www.mlive.com/grpress

Jackson Citizen Patriot | http://www.mlive.com/citpat

Kalamazoo Gazette | http://www.mlive.com/kzgazette

Lansing State Journal | http://www.lansingstatejournal.com

Muskegon Chronicle | http://www.mlive.com/chronicle

Saginaw News | http://www.mlive.com/saginawnews

Minnesota

Duluth News-Tribune | http://www.duluthnewstribune.com

Elk River Star News | http://www.erstarnews.com

The Journal (New Ulm) | http://www.oweb.com

Minneapolis Star Tribune | http://www.startribune.com

Saint Paul Pioneer Press | http://www.twincities.com

Mississippi

The Clarion Ledger (Jackson) | http://www.clarionledger.com

Gulflive.com | http://www.gulflive.com

Meridian Star | http://www.meridianstar.com

The Natchez Democrat http://www.natchezdemocrat.com

The Sun Herald (Biloxi) http://www.sunherald.com

The Vicksburg Post http://www.vicksburgpost.com

Missouri

The Examiner (Independence) http://www.examiner.net

Hannibal Courier-Post http://www.hannibal.net

Jefferson City News Tribune http://www.newstribune.com

JobsinStJoe.com http://www.jobsinstjoe.com

Joplin Globe http://www.joplinglobe.com

Springfield News-Leader http://www.news-leader.com

Montana

Billings Gazette http://billingsgazette.com

Bozeman Daily Chronicle http://www.bozemandailychronicle.com

Helena Independent Record http://www.helenair.com

Missoulian http://www.missoulian.com

The Montana Standard (Butte) http://www.mtstandard.com

Nebraska

Columbus Telegram http://www.columbustelegram.com

Lincoln Journal Star http://www.journalstar.com

North Platte Telegraph http://www.nptelegraph.com

Omaha World-Herald http://www.omaha.com

Scotts Bluff Star-Herald http://www.starherald.com

Nevada

Elko Daily Free Press http://www.elkodaily.com

Las Vegas Business Press http://www.lvbusinesspress.com

Las Vegas Review-Journal http://www.lvrj.com

Las Vegas Sun http://www.lasvegassun.com

Nevada Appeal (Carson City)   http://www.nevadaappeal.com

Reno Gazette Journal   http://www.rgj.com

New Hampshire

Concord Monitor   http://www.concordmonitor.com

Foster's Daily Democrat   http://www.fosters.com

Keene Sentinel   http://www.keenesentinel.com

Portsmouth Herald   http://www.seacoastonline.com

The Telegraph (Nashua)   http://www.nashuatelegraph.com

The Union Leader (Manchester)   http://www.theunionleader.com

New Jersey

Asbury Park Press   http://www.app.com

CentralJersey.com   http://www.centraljersey.com

Courier-Post (Cherry Hill)   http://www.courierpostonline.com

The Montclair Times   http://www.northjersey.com/towns/Montclair.html

The Star Ledger (Newark)   http://www.nj.com

The Trentonian   http://www.trentonian.com

New Mexico

Albuquerque Journal   http://www.abqjournal.com

The Gallup Independent   http://www.gallupindependent.com

Los Alamos Monitor   http://www.lamonitor.com

Santa Fe New Mexican   http://www.santafenewmexican.com

The Silver City Daily Press   http://www.scdailypress.com/ee/
silvercitydailypress/index.php

New York

Albany Democrat Herald   http://www.democratherald.com

El Diario New York   http://www,eldiariony.com

Geebo   http://www.geebo.com

Ithaca Times   http://www.zwire.com/site/news.
cfm?brd=1395&nr=1&nostat=1

Middletown Times Herald-Record	http://www.recordonline.com
New York Law Journal	http://www.newyorklawjournal.com
New York Post	http://www.nypost.com
The New York Times	http://www.nytimes.com
The Post-Standard (Syracuse)	http://www.syracuse.com/poststandard
Staten Island Advance	http://www.silive.com/advance
Syracuse New Times	http://www.newtimes.com

North Carolina

Charlotte Observer	http://www.charlotteobserver.com/943
Greensboro News-Record	http://www.news-record.com
News & Observer (Raleigh)	http://www.newsobserver.com
StarNewsOnline.com	http://www.starnewsonline.com
Winston-Salem Journal	http://www2.journalnow.com/home

North Dakota

Bismarck Tribune	http://www.bismarcktribune.com
Grand Forks Herald	http://www.grandforks.com
The Jamestown Sun	http://www.jamestownsun.com
Minot Daily News	http://www.minotdailynews.com

Ohio

Cincinnati Enquirer	http://www.enquirer.com
The Cleveland Nation	http://www.clnation.com
Cleveland Plain Dealer	http://www.cleveland.com/plaindealer
Columbus Dispatch	http://www.dispatch.com/live/content/index.html
Dayton Daily News	http://www.daytondailynews.com
Springfield News Sun	http://www.springfieldnewssun.com
Sun Newspapers (Cleveland)	http://www.sunnews.com
Youngstown Vindicator	http://www.vindy.com

Oklahoma

Altus Times	http://www.altustimes.com
Lawton Constitution	http://www.lawton-constitution.com
The Oklahoman (Oklahoma City)	http://www.newsok.com
OKC.gov	http://www.okc.gov
Ponca City News	http://www.poncacitynews.com
Tulsa World	http://www.tulsaworld.com

Oregon

Ashland Daily Tidings	http://www.dailytidings.com
East Oregonian (Pendleton)	http://eastoregonian.com/index.asp
eSouthernOregon.com	http://www.esouthernoregon.com
Eugene Register-Guard	http://www.registerguard.com
Medford Mail Tribune	http://www.mailtribune.com
The Oregonian (Portland)	http://www.oregonlive.com/oregonian
The Register-Guard (Eugene)	http://www.registerguard.com/web/news/index.csp
Springfield News	http://www.hometownnews.com
Statesman Journal (Salem)	http://www.statesmanjournal.com

Pennsylvania

Canonsburg Almanac	http://www.thealmanac.net/ALM
CityPaperJobs.net	http://www.citypaper.net/jobs/index.php
Erie Daily Times-News	http://www.goerie.com
The Express Times (Lehigh Valley)	http://www.lehighvalleylive.com
Geebo	http://www.geebo.com
Lancaster New Era	http://lancasteronline.com
The Patriot-News	http://www.pennlive.com
The Philadelphia Inquirer	http://www.philly.com
Pittsburg Post-Gazette	http://www.post-gazette.com
Pocono Record	http://www.poconorecord.com

Scranton Times Tribune

http://thetimes-tribune.com

The Times Leader (Wilkes-Barre)

http://www.timesleader.com

Washington Observer-Reporter

http://www.observer-reporter.com

Rhode Island

The Narragansett Times (Wakefield)

http://www.narragansetttimes.com

The Pawtucket Times

http://www.pawtuckettimes.com

Providence Journal

http://www.projo.com/projojobs

Sakonnet Times (Portsmouth)

http://www.eastbayri.com

South Carolina

Camden Chronicle Independent

http://www.chronicle-independent.com/site/news.cfm?brd=1382

Free Times (Columbia)

http://www.free-times.com

The Greenville News

http://www.greenvilleonline.com

The Post and Courier (Charleston)

http://www.postandcourier.com

The Sun Times (Myrtle Beach)

http://www.thesunnews.com/myrtlebeachonline

South Dakota

Argus Leader (Sioux Falls)

http://www.argusleader.com

Brookings Daily Register

http://www.brookingsregister.com/v2_main_page.php

The Capital Journal (Pierre)

http://www.capjournal.com

The Freeman Courier

http://www.freemansd.com

Huron Plainsman

http://www.plainsman.com/v2_main_page.php

Tennessee

Chattanooga Times Free Press

http://www.timesfreepress.com/home

Daily Post-Athenian

http://www.dpa.xtn.net

Knoxville News Sentinel

http://www.knoxnews.com

Memphis Flyer

http://www.memphisflyer.com

The Tennessean (Nashville)

http://www.tennessean.com

Texas

Austin American-Statesman	http://www.austin360.com
Dallas Morning News	http://www.dallasnews.com
El Paso Times	http://www.elpasotimes.com
Geebo	http://www.geebo.com
Houston Chronicle	http://www.chron.com
Matagorda Advocate	http://www.matagordaadvocate.com
Rumbo (Houston)	http://www.rumbotx.com
San Antonio Express News	http://www.mysanantonio.com
Victoria Advocate	http://www.victoriaadvocate.com

Utah

The Daily Herald (Provo)	http://www.heraldextra.com
Herald Journal (Logan)	http://www.hjnews.com
Salt Lake Tribune	http://www.sltrib.com
Standard-Examiner (Ogden)	http://www.standard.net

Vermont

Addison County Independent (Middlebury)	http://www.addisonindependent.com
Burlington Free Press	http://www.burlingtonfreepress.com
Deerfield Valley News (West Dover)	http://www.dvalnews.com
Stowe Reporter	http://www.stowetoday.com
Valley News (White River Junction)	http://www.vnews.com

Virginia

The Daily Progress (Charlottesville)	http://www2.dailyprogress.com
Danville Register Bee	http://www2.godanriver.com
Fairfax Times	http://www.fairfaxtimes.com
HamptonRoads.com	http://www.hamptonroads.com
JobFetch.com	http://www.jobfetch.com
The News-Advance (Lynchburg)	http://www2.newsadvance.com

Richmond Times-Dispatch	http://www2.timesdispatch.com
Roanoke Times	http://www.roanoke.com
Virginian-Pilot (Norfolk)	http://pilotonline.com

Washington

The Columbian (Vancouver)	http://www.columbian.com
Everett Daily Herald	http://seattletimes.com
Geebo	http://www.geebo.com
The News Tribune (Tacoma)	http://www.thenewstribune.com
The Olympian (Olympia)	http://www.theolympian.com
Seattle Post-Intelligencer	http://www.seattlepi.com
Seattle Times	http://seattletimes.com
The Spokesman-Review (Spokane)	http://www.spokane.net
Yakima Herald-Republican	http://www.yakima-herald.com

West Virginia

Charlestown Daily Mail	http://www.dailymail.com
Clarksburg Exponent Telegram	http://www.cpubco.com
The Dominion Post (Morgantown)	http://www.dominionpost.com
Times West Virginian (Fairmont)	http://timeswv.com
Wheeling News-Register	http://www.news-register.com

Wisconsin

GMToday.com (Greater Milwaukee)	http://www.gmtoday.com
Green Bay Press Gazette	http://www.greenbaypressgazette.com
The Journal Times (Racine)	http://www.journaltimes.com
Kenosha News	http://www.kenoshanews.com/home
La Crosse Tribune	http://www.lacrossetribune.com
Milwaukee Journal Sentinel	http://www.jsonline.com
Ozaukee Press	http://www.ozaukeepress.com
Wisconsin State Journal (Madison)	http://host.madison.com

Wyoming

Douglas Budget — http://www.douglas-budget.com

Wyoming Tribune-Eagle — http://www.wyomingnews.com

College/Internships/Entry Level/ Graduate School Graduates

Entry-Level

Aboutjobs.com — http://www.aboutjobs.com

Activate.co.uk [United Kingdom] — http://www.activate.co.uk

AfterCollege.com — http://www.aftercollege.com

AtCollegeJobs — http://www.atcollegejobs.com

Barefootstudent.com — http://www.barefootstudent.com/directory/search/students

THE BLACK COLLEGIAN Online — http://www.blackcollegian.com

Campus Career Center — http://www.campuscareercenter.com

Campus Grotto — http://www.campusgrotto.com

CampusRN.com — http://www.campusrn.com

Canadian Association of Career Educators & Employers — http://www.cacee.com

Career Conferences — http://www.careerconferences.com

CareerEdge [Canada] — http://www.careeredge.ca

Career Explorer — https://access.bridges.com/auth/login.do?targetUri=%2Fportal%2FlandingPage.do

Careerfair.com — http://www.careerfair.com

College Central Network — http://www.collegecentral.com

CollegeGrad.com — http://www.collegegrad.com

CollegeHelpers.com — http://www.collegehelpers.com

College Job Bank — http://www.collegejobbank.com

College Job Board — http://www.collegejobboard.com/cjb/index.cfm

College News Online — http://www.collegenews.com/college_careers

College PowerPrep — http://www.powerprep.com

CollegeRecruiter.com — http://www.collegerecruiter.com

Colleges	http://www.colleges.com
Current Jobs for Graduates	http://www.graduatejobs.com
EntryLevelJobs.net	http://www.entryleveljobs.net
Experience	http://www.experience.com
FuseJobs.co.uk [United Kingdom]	http://www.fusejobs.co.uk
Get.hobsons.co.uk [United Kingdom]	http://www.get.hobsons.co.uk
Thegraduate.co.uk [United Kingdom]	http://www.thegraduate.co.uk
Graduate Jobs	http://www.graduatejobs.com
Graduating Engineer & Computer Careers Online	http://www.graduatingengineer.com
GrooveJob.com	http://www.groovejobs.com
Historic Black Colleges & Universities Connect	http://www.hbcuconnect.com
TheJobBox.com	http://www.thejobbox.com/tjb/index.cfm?page=main
job-hunt.org	http://www.job-hunt.org
JobPostings.net	http://www.jobpostings.net
JobScribble.com	http://www.jobscribble.com
JustClick.co.uk [United Kingdom]	http://www.justclick.co.uk
Mapping Your Future	http://mappingyourfuture.org
MBAGlobalNet	http://www.mbaglobalnet.com
MBAmatch.com [United Kingdom]	http://www.mbamatch.com
MBA Style Magazine	http://www.mbastyle.com
Milkround.com [United Kingdom]	http://www.milkround.com
Monster Campus	http://college.monster.com
National Association of Colleges & Employers	http://www.nacelink.com
National Society of Collegiate Scholars Career Connection	http://www.nscs.org
National Society of Hispanic MBAs Career Center	http://www.nshmba.org
New England Higher Education Recruitment Consortium	http://www.newenglandherc.org/home/index.cfm?site_id=660
New York Black MBA	http://www.nyblackmba.org
OverseasJobs.com	http://www.overseasjobs.com
Peterson's	http://www.petersons.com

Princeton Review Online	http://www.princetonreview.com
Prospects.ac.uk [United Kingdom]	http://www.prospects.ac.uk
SallieMae/TrueCareers	http://www.truecareers.com
SnagAJob	http://www.snagajob.com
Student Affairs	http://www.studentaffairs.com
Student Central	http://www.studentcentral.com
UniJobs.at [Austria]	http://www.unijobs.at
Vault.com [Europe]	http://www.vault.com/wps/portal/usa

Internships

CollegeHelpers.com	http://www.collegehelpers.com
InternJobs.com	http://www.internjobs.com
Internship Programs	http://www.internshipprograms.com
Internships	http://www.internships.com
Internships4You	http://www.internships4you.com
Internweb	http://www.internweb.com
Paid Internships	http://www.paidinternships.com
Urban Interns	http://www.urbaninterns.com

Summer Jobs

Barefootstudent.com	http://www.barefootstudent.com/directory/search/students
CollegeJobs.co.uk [United Kingdom]	http://www.collegejobs.co.uk
CoolWorks	http://www.coolworks.com
ResortJobs.com	http://www.resortjobs.com
Student Awards	http://www.studentawards.com
StudentJobs.gov	http://www.usajobs.gov/studentjobs
Study Abroad	http://www.studyabroad.com
SummerJobs.com	http://www.summerjobs.com
Super College	http://www.supercollege.com
Teens 4 Hire	http://www.teens4hire.org

TenStepsforStudents.org — http://www.tenstepsforstudents.org

University Directories — http://www.universitydirectories.com/career-partners.asp

University Links — http://www.ulinks.com

Youth@Work — http://www.youthatwork.org

College/University Affiliated

California State University - Chico — http://www.csuchico.edu/careers

Career Development Center at Rensselaer Polytechnic Institute — http://www.rpi.edu/dept/cdc

Case Western Reserve University — http://www.cwru.edu

The Catholic University of America Career Services Office — http://careers.cua.edu

Clemson University — http://www.clemson.edu

Columbia University [Master of Science in Construction Administration] — http://www.theconstructionjob.com

Drake University — http://www.drake.edu

Drexel University — http://www.drexel.edu

Duke University Job Resources — http://career.studentaffairs.duke.edu

Emory University Rollins School of Public Health — http://www.sph.emory.edu/cms/current_students/career_services/index.html

Foothill-De Anza Community College — http://www.fhda.edu/jobs

Georgia State University Career Services — http://www.gsu.edu/career

Georgia Tech Career Services Office — http://www.career.gatech.edu

Loyola College — http://www.loyola.edu/thecareercenter/index.html

Nova Southeastern University — http://www.nova.edu

Oakland University — http://www.oakland.edu/careerservices

Profiles Database — http://www.profilesdatabase.com

Purdue University Management Placement Office — http://www.krannert.purdue.edu/departments/gcs

San Francisco State University Instructional Technologies — http://www.itec.sfsu.edu

University of Arkansas — http://www.uark.edu/home

U.C. Berkeley Work-Study Programs — http://workstudy.berkeley.edu

University of Virginia Career Planning & Placement	http://www.hrs.virginia.edu
University of Wisconsin-Madison School of Business Career Center	http://www.bus.wisc.edu/career
Washington and Lee University	http://www.wlu.edu/x6.xml
Worcester Polytechnic Institute	http://www.wpi.edu

Computer (See High Tech/Technical/Technology and Information Technology/Information Systems)

Computer-Aided Design, Manufacturing & Engineering

American Design Drafting Association	http://www.adda.org
Auto CAD Job Network	http://www.acjn.com
Computer-Aided Three-Dimensional Interactive Application Job Network	http://www.catjn.com
e-Architect	http://www.e-architect.com
GetCADJobs.com	http://www.getcadjobs.com
Just CAD Jobs	http://www.justCADjobs.com
ManufacturingJobs.com	http://www.manufacturingjobs.com
Manufacturing.Net	http://www.manufacturing.net
PLMjobs	http://www.plmjobs.com
UG Job Network (Unigraphics)	http://www.ugjn.com

Construction (See also Engineering)

A/E/C JobBank	http://www.aecjobbank.com
AGC Iowa Careers	http://www.agciajobs.com
Air Conditioning-Heating-Refrigeration News	http://www.achrnews.com
AirConditioningJobs.com	http://www.airconditioningjobs.com
Akhtaboot [Jordan]	http://www.akhtaboot.com
Aljazeerajobs.com [Middle East]	http://www.aljazeerajobs.com
All Port Jobs	http://www.allportjobs.com

American Society of Heating, Refrigerating and Air-conditioning Engineers	http://www.ashraejobs.com
American Society of Professional Estimators	http://www.aspenational.org
Arch + Design	http://www.archdesignjobs.com
ASHRAEjobs.com (Heating, Refrigeration, Air Conditioning)	http://www.ashraejobs.com
Bayt.com [United Arab Emirates]	http://www.bayt.com
Bconstructive [United Kingdom]	http://www.bconstructive.co.uk
Blue Collar Jobs	http://www.bluecollarjobs.com
Build Find	http://www.buildfind.com
BuilderJobs	http://www.builderjobs.com
Builder Magazine	http://www.builderonline.com
Builder Online	http://www.builder.hw.net
Building.com	http://www.building.com
Building Services [United Kingdom]	http://www.buildingservicesjobs.co.uk
Building Trades Jobs	http://www.tradesjobs.com
Careerjunctionme.com [Middle East]	http://www.careerjunctionme.com
Careers In Construction	http://www.careersinconstruction.com
CarpenterJobs.com	http://www.carpenterjobs.com
CarpenterJobsite.com	http://www.carpenterjobsite.com
Construction/Careers	http://www.construction.com
ConstructionEducation.com	http://www.constructioneducation.com
Construction Executive Online	http://www.constructionexecutive.com
Construction4Professionals.co.uk [United Kingdom]	http://www.construction4professionals.co.uk
Construction Gigs	http://www.constructiongigs.com
Construction Industry Central	http://www.constructionindustrycentral.com
TheConstructionJob [Columbia University]	http://www.theconstructionjob.com
ConstructionJobForce	http://www.constructionjobforce.com
Construction Job Search [United Kingdom]	http://www.constructionjobsearch.co.uk
ConstructionJobs.com	http://www.constructionjobs.com/index_eng.cfm
ConstructionJobsNow [United Kingdom]	http://www.constructionjobsnow.co.uk

Construction Work	http://www.constructionwork.com
ConstructionWorkforce.net	http://www.constructionwork.com
Constructor [United Kingdom]	http://www.constructor.co.uk
Contract Design Magazine	Http://contractdesign.com
Custom Home Magazine	http://www.customhomeonline.com
ElectricalAgent	http://www.electricalagent.com
Electrical Jobs	http://www.electricityforum.com/careers.htm
Electrical Employment	http://www.cossin.com/page3.html
Engineering News Record	http://enrconstruction.com
Environmental Construction Engineering Architectural Jobs Online	http://www.eceajobs.com
Estimator Jobs	http://www.estimatorjobs.com
GeneralConstructionJobs.com	http://www.generalconstructionjobs.com
GetElectricianJobs.com	http://www.getelectricianjobs.com
go4constructionJobs	http://www.go4constructionjobs.com
Grist.org	http://jobs.grist.org
HelmetstoHardhats.com	http://www.helmetstohardhats.com
HomeBuilderJobs.com	http://www.bigbuildercareers.com
HVACagent.com	http://www.hvacagent.com
HVAC Industry	http://www.hvac-industry.com
HVAC Mall	http://www.hvacmall.com
The HVAC Source	http://www.thehvacsource.com
iHireBuildingTrades.com	http://www.ihirebuildingtrades.com
iHireConstruction.com	http://www.ihireconstruction.com
Just Construction [United Kingdom]	http://www.justconstruction.net
JustEngineers.net [Australia]	http://www.justengineers.net
JobsinConstruction [United Kingdom]	http://www.jobsinconstruction.co.uk
JobsinSurveying [United Kingdom]	http://www.jobsinsurveying.co.uk
Jobsite.co.uk [United Kingdom]	http://www.jobsite.co.uk
Kitchen & Bath Business	http://www.kbbonline.com
Maintenance Engineer	http://www.maintenanceemployment.com

Materials Jobs	http://www.welding-engineer.com
Maxim Recruitment [United Kingdom]	http://www.maximrecruitment.co.uk
MEPjobs.com [mechanical, electrical, plumbing]	http://www.mepjobs.com/%28S%28wkttyv31uqwii2nncqhtqbml%29%29/default.aspx
Metal Working Portal	http://metal-working.tradeworlds.com
Misco Jobs	http://www.miscojobs.com
MonsterGulf.com [Middle East]	http://www.monstergulf.com
MyConstructionJobs.net	http://www.myconstructionjobs.net
National Association of Women in Construction	http://www.nawic.org/nawic/Default.asp
NaukriGulf.com [Middle East]	http://www.naukrigulf.com
Offsite Jobs [United Kingdom]	http://www.offsitejobs.co.uk
PlumbingAgent	http://www.plumbingagent.com
Plumbing Careers	http://www.plumbingcareers.com
PlumbingGigs.com	http://www.plumbinggigs.com
PlumbingHelper.com	http://www.plumbinghelper.com
PLUMBjob.com	http://www.plumbjobs.com
ProjectManagerJobs.com	http://www.projectmanagerjobs.com
QCEmployMe.com	http://regionalhelpwanted.com/quad-cities-il-ia-jobs
RecruitConstruction [United Kingdom]	http://www.recruitconstruction.com
ReferWork-Jobs.com	http://www.referwork-jobs.com
RefrigeJobs.com	http://www.refrigejobs.com
Right of Way	http://www.rightofway.com
SkilledWorkers.com [Canada]	http://www.skilledworkers.com
SuperintendentJobs.com	http://www.superintendentjobs.com
Tools of the Trade Magazine	http://www.toolsofthetrade.net
TopBuildingJobs.com	http://www.topbuildingjobs.com
TradesJobs.com	http://www.tradesjobs.com
Trade Jobs Online	http://www.tradejobsonline.com
UtilityJobSearch.com [United Kingdom]	http://www.utilityjobsearch.com
Utility Jobs Online	http://www.utilityjobsonline.com

Welding Jobs	http://www.weldingjobs.com

Consultants

American Society of Consultant Pharmacists	http://bt.myrxcareer.com
AndersenAlumni.net	http://www.andersenalumni.net
Architect, Engineering & Environmental Consultants Jobs	http://www.aejob.com
Association of Management Consulting Firms	http://www.amcf.org
Career Lab	http://www.careerlab.com
CEWeekly.com	http://www.ceweekly.com
Computerwork.com	http://www.computerwork.com
ConsultLink.com	http://www.consultlink.com
ConsultantsBoard.com [United Kingdom]	http://www.consultantsboard.com
Consulting Career Quest	http://www.consultingcareerquest.com
Consulting Magazine	http://www.consultingmag.com
GenerationMom.com	http://www.generationmom.com
GlenRecruitment.co.uk [United Kingdom]	http://www.glenrecruitment.co.uk
HotGigs.com	http://www.hotgigs.com
The Independent Consultants Network	http://www.inconet.com
JobNews.at [Austria]	http://www.jobnews.at
Medical Consultants Network	http://www.mcn.com
SoloGig.com	http://www.sologig.com
Top-Consultant.com	http://www.top-consultant.com/UK/career/appointments.asp
TrainingConsortium.com	http://www.trainingconsortium.com

Contract Employment/Part Time Employment (See also Search Firms)

AllFreeLanceWork.com	http://www.allfreelancework.com
Ants	http://www.ants.com
AutomationTechies.com	http://www.automationtechies.com

Camp Jobs	http://www.campjobs.com
Camp Staff	http://www.campstaff.com
CanadaParttime.com [Canada]	http://www.canadaparttime.com/content/flash
CollegeHelpers.com	http://www.collegehelpers.com
ContractCareers.com	http://www.contractcareers.com
Contract Employment Weekly Jobs Online	http://www.ceweekly.com
ContractJob.net	http://www.contractjob.net
Contract Job Hunter	http://www.cjhunter.com
contractjobs.com	http://www.contractjobs.com
ContractJobsite.com	http://www.contractjobsite.com
ContractedWork	http://www.contractedwork.com
ContractingCareers	http://www.contractingcareers.com
Contracts247 [United Kingdom]	http://www.contracts247.co.uk
Creative Freelancers	http://www.freelancers.com
DangerZoneJobs	http://www.dangerzonejobs.com
DoaAProject.com	http://www.doaproject.com
eLance	http://www.elance.com
eMoonlighter	http://www.moonlighter.com
ExperienceNet.com	http://www.experiencenet.com
Flexjobs.com	http://www.flexjobs.com
Fly Contract	http://www.flycontract.com
Freelancer	http://www.freelancer.com
Game Contractor	http://www.gamecontractor.com
Go Freelance	http://www.gofreelance.com
GrooveJob.com	http://www.groovejobs.com
Guru.com	http://www.guru.com
HireMeNow.com	http://www.hiremenow.com
Homeworkers	http://www.homeworkers.org
HotGigs.com	http://www.hotgigs.com
iFreelance	http://www.ifreelance.com

Jobble	http://www.jobble.net
JobsinLogistics.com	http://www.jobsinlogistics.com
Labor Ready	http://www.laborready.com
LifeguardingJobs.com	http://www.lifeguardingjobs.com
mediabistro	http://www.mediabistro.com
Net-Temps	http://www.net-temps.com
ProductionBase.co.uk [United Kingdom]	http://www.productionbase.co.uk
Project4Hire.com	http://www.project4hire.com
Ready People	http://www.readypeople.eu
RoadTechs.com	http://www.roadtechs.com
Software Contractors Guild	http://www.scguild.com
Sheet Metal and Air Conditioning Contractor's Association	http://www.smacna.org
SnagAJob	http://www.snagajob.com
Sologig	http://www.sologig.com
Subcontract.com	http://www.subcontract.com
Summer Jobs	http://www.summerjobs.com
Talent Connections	http://www.talentconnections.net
TelecommutingJobs	http://www.tjobs.com
Temps Online.co.uk [United Kingdom]	http://www.tempsonline.co.uk
Training Consortium	http://www.trainingconsortium.net
Travel Per Diem Contract	http://www.travelperdiemcontract.com
U Bid Contract Contracting Portal	http://www.ubidcontract.com

Cosmetology

BeautyJobs	http://www.beautyjobs.com
BehindtheChair.com	http://www.behindthechair.com
SalonEmployment.com	http://www.salonemployment.com
Salon Gigs	http://www.salongigs.com
SalonJobStore	http://www.salonjobstore.com

Salon Jobs	http://www.salonjobs.com
SalonPost.com	http://www.salonpost.com
Salon Search	http://www.salonsearch.com
Spa and Salon Jobs	http://www.spaandsalonjobs.com

Culinary/Food Preparation (See also Hospitality)

American Association of Brewing Chemists	http://www.scisoc.org
American Association of Cereal Chemists	http://www.scisoc.org
American Culinary Federation	http://www.acfchefs.org
Bakery-Net	http://www.bakerynet.com
BookaChef.co.uk [United Kingdom]	http://www.bookachef.co.uk
Careers in Food	http://www.careersinfood.com
Caterer.com [United Kingdom]	http://www.caterer.com
Chef Jobs [United Kingdom]	http://www.chefjobs.co.uk
Chef Jobs Network	http://chefjobsnetwork.com
Chef2Chef.com	http://www.chef2chef.com
Chefs Employment	http://www.chefsemployment.com
Escoffier Online	http://escoffier.com
FineDiningJobs.com	http://www.finediningjobs.com
Focus-management [United Kingdom]	http://www.focusmanagement.co.uk
Food And Drink Jobs.com	http://www.foodanddrinkjobs.com
Food Industry Jobs	http://www.foodindustryjobs.com
Hcareers	http://www.hcareers.com
iHireChefs.com	http://www.ihirechefs.com
JobsinCatering [United Kingdom]	http://www.jobsincatering.com
JobsinHotels [United Kingdom]	http://www.jobsinhotels.com
Jobstore [United Kingdom]	http://www.jobstore.co.uk
National Confectioners' Association	http://www.candyusa.com
National Restaurant Association	http://www.restaurant.org/careers
Restaurant Jobs [United Kingdom]	http://www.restaurantjobs.co.uk

RollingPinJobs.com	http://www.rollingpinjobs.com
SommelierJobs.com	http://www.sommelierjobs.com
Star Chefs	http://www.starchefs.com
WineJobsOnline [New Zealand]	http://www.winejobsonline.con
Wine & Hospitality Jobs	http://www.wineandhospitalityjobs.com
YachtChefs.com	http://www.yachtchefs.com

-D-

Data Processing

Black Data Processing Association Online	http://www.bdpa.org
DataNewsJobs.com [Belgium]	http://datanews.rnews.be/datanews/nl/jobs
Dice	http://www.dice.com
Jobvertise	http://www.jobvertise.com

Defense (See also Military Personnel Transitioning into the Private Sector)

AeroIndustryJobs.com	http://www.aeroindustryjobs.com
Aerospace & Defense Jobs	http://www.aerospacedefensejobs.com
AerotAge	http://www.aerotagejobs.com
Aviation Week	http://www.aviationweek.com
ClearanceJobs.com	http://www.clearancejobs.com
ClearedJobs.net	http://www.clearedjobs.net
ClearedConnections.com	http://www.clearedconnections.com
DangerZoneJobs	http://www.dangerzonejobs.com
Defense Industry Central	http://www.defenseindustrycentral.com
The Defense Talent Network	http://www.defensetalent.com
Dice	http://www.dice.com

GovJobs.com   http://www.govjobs.com

IntelJobs.com   http://www.inteljobs.com

Intelligence.gov   http://www.intelligence.gov

IntelligenceCareers.com   http://www.intelligencecareers.com

Military.com   http://www.military.com

Military Connection   http://www.militaryconnection.com

Military Connections   http://www.militaryconnections.com

MilitaryHire.com   http://www.militaryhire.com

SecurityClearanceJobsBlog   http://www.securityclearancejobsblog.com

SecurityClearedJobs.com [United Kingdom]   http://www.securityclearedjobs.com

Security Job Zone   http://www.securityjobzone.com

SpaceJobs.com   http://www.spacejobs.com

Transition Careers   http://www.transitioncareers.com

USA Jobs   http://www.usajobs.com

VetJobs   http://www.vetjobs.com

Dental

American Dental Hygienists' Association   http://www.adha.org/careerinfo

California Dental Hygienists' Association   http://cdha.org/employment

Dental Economics   http://www.dentaleconomics.com/index.html

DentalJobs.com   http://www.dentaljobs.com

DentalPost.com   http://www.dentalpost.com

Foothill College Biological & Health Sciences   http://www.foothill.fhda.edu/bio/jobs.php

iHireDental.com   http://www.ihiredental.com

Jobscience Network   http://jobs.jobscience.com

Maryland State Dental Association   http://careers.dentalcompany.com/

MedHunters Dental Hygiene   http://www.medhunters.com

Medical-Dental-Hospital Business Association   http://www.mdhba.org

OverseasDentist.com   http://www.overseasdentist.com

SmileJobs.com   http://www.smilejobs.com

Wisconsin Dental Association	http://careers.wda.org

Diversity

Diversity-General

Affirmative Action Register	http://www.insightintodiversity.com
Anchorage Diversity	http://www.anchoragediversity.com
Career Moves	http://www.jvs-boston.org
CommunityConnectJobs.com	http://www.communityconnectjobs.com
Corporate Diversity Search	http://www.corpdiversitysearch.com
Diversity.com	http://www.diversity.com
DiversityAlliedHealth.com	http://www.diversityalliedhealth.com
Diversity Careers	http://www.diversitycareers.com
Diversity Careers [Canada]	http://www.diversitycareers.ca
Diversity Central	http://www.diversityhotwire.com
Diversity Classifieds	http://www.diversityclassifieds.com
DiversityConnect	http://www.diversityconnect.com
Diversity Employment	http://www.diversityemployment.com
Diversity Events	http://www.diversityevents.com
DiversityInc.com	http://www.diversityinc.com
DiversityJobFairs.com	http://www.diversityjobfairs.com
Diversity Job Network	http://www.diversityjobnetwork.com
DiversityJobs.com	http://diversityjobs.com
DiversityLink	http://www.diversitylink.com
DiversityNursing.com	http://www.diversitynursing.com
Diversity Search	http://www.diversitysearch.com
DiversityWorking	http://www.diversityworking.com
DiversityZone.com	http://www.diversityzone.com
EmployDiversity	http://www.employdiversity.com
Equal Opportunity Publications, Inc.	http://www.eop.com
HireDiversity.com	http://www.hirediversity.com

IMDiversity.com	http://www.imdiversity.com
Insight Into Diversity	http://www.insightintodiversity.com
Jobs4Diversity.com	http://www.jobs4diversity.com
LeadingDiversity.com	http://leadingdiversity.ning.com
MinnesotaDiversity.com	http://www.minnesotadiversity.com
The Multicultural Advantage	http://www.multicuturaladvantage.com
National Diversity Newspaper Job Bank	http://www.newsjobs.net
Society for Human Resource Management Diversity Page	http://www.shrm.org/hrdisciplines/Diversity/Pages/default.aspx/
WorkplaceDiversity.com	http://www.workplacediversity.com

Age

Age Positive Jobs [United Kingdom]	http://www.agepositivejobs.com
Canada's Fifty-Plus	http://www.fifty-plus.net
Encore	http://www.encore.org
Forty Plus	http://www.fortyplus.org
GeezerJobs.com	http://www.geezerjobs.com
National Commission on Aging	http://www.ncoa.org
PrimeCB.com	http://www.primecb.com
RetiredBrains	http://www.retiredbrains.com/default.aspx
RetirementJobs.com	http://www.retirementjobs.com
Workforce50	http://www.workforce50.com

Bilingual Persons

Asianet	http://www.asianetglobal.com
Asian-Jobs.com	http://www.asian-jobs.com
BilingualCareer.com	http://www.bilingualcareer.com
Bilingual-Jobs	http://www.bilingual-jobs.com
CHALLENGEUSA	http://www.challengeusa.com
Eflweb	http://www.eflweb.com
Euroleaders	http://www.euroleaders.com

Hispanic Chamber of Commerce	http://www.ushcc.com
iHispano	http://www.ihispano.com
Hispanic-Jobs.com	http://www.hispanic-jobs.com
LatPro	http://www.latpro.com
National Society of Hispanic MBAs Career Center	http://www.nshmba.org
SaludosWeb	http://www.saludos.com
Society of Hispanic Professional Engineers Career Services	http://www.shpe.org
Top Language Jobs [Europe]	http://www.toplanguagejobs.co.uk

Ethnicity

Afro-American (Washington, D.C.)	http://www.afro.com
Alianza (Latino)	http://www.alianza.org
A Mighty River	http://www.amightyriver.com
Asianet	http://www.asianetglobal.com
AsianAve.com	http://www.asianave.com
Association of Black Cardiologists	http://careers.abcardio.org
Association of Latino Professionals in Finance & Accounting Job Postings	http://www.alpfa.org
Black Career Women Online	http://www.bcw.org
THE BLACK COLLEGIAN Online	http://www.blackcollegian.com
Black Data Processing Association Online	http://www.bpda.org
Black Enterprise Magazine Career Center	http://www.blackenterprise.com
Blackgeeks	http://www.blackgeeks.com
BlackPlanet.com	http://www.blackplanet.com
Black Voices	http://www.blackvoices.com
Black World	http://www.blackworld.com
Chicago Chinese Computing Professional Assn	http://www.cccpa.org
El Diario New York	http://www,eldiariony.com
El Mensajero - San Francisco, CA	http://www.elmensajero.com
El Nuevo Herald	http://www.elnuevoherald.com

Ethnicity	http://www.ethnicity.com
Ethnicjobsite.co.uk [United Kingdom]	http://www.ethnicjobsite.co.uk
GoldSea	http://www.goldsea.com/Text
HierosGamos	http://www.hg.org
Hispanic American Police Command Officers Association	http://www.hapcoa.org
Historic Black Colleges & Universities Connect	http://www.hbcuconnect.com
Hispanic Business.com	http://www.hispanicbusiness.com/Redirect/Welcome.asp
Hispanic Chamber of Commerce	http://www.ushcc.com
Hispanic-Jobs.com	http://www.hispanic-jobs.com
Hispanic Online	http://www.hispaniconline.com
iHispano.com	http://www.ihispano.com
Impre Media	http://www.impremedia.com
JournalismNext.com	http://www.journalismnext.com
latinMBA.com	http://www.latinmba.com
LatinoHire.com	http://www.latinohire.com
Latinos in Information Sciences and Technology Association	http://www.a-lista.org
La Opinion - Los Angeles, CA	http://www.laopinion.com
La Prensa - Orlando, FL	http://www.laprensafl.com
Latin MBA	http://www.latinmba.com
LatPro	http://www.latpro.com
La Raza - Chicago, IL	http://www.laraza.com
MiGente.com	http://www.migente.com
Minorities Job Bank	http://www.imdiversity.com
MinorityAffairs.com	http://www.minorityaffairs.com
MinorityITJobs.com	http://www.minorityitjobs.com
Minority Jobs	http://www.minorityjobs.net
MinorityJobsite.com	http://www.minorityjobsite.com
Minority Career Network	http://www.minoritycareernet.com
Minority MBAs	http://www.minoritymbas.com

MinorityNurse.com	http://www.minoritynurse.com
Minority Professional Network	http://www.minorityprofessionalnetwork.com
NAACP Job Fair	http://www.naacpjobfair.com
National Association of Hispanic Nurses Houston Chapter	http://www.nahnhouston.org
National Association of African Americans in Human Resources	http://www.naaahr.us/default.aspx
National Association of Black Accountants, Inc. Career Center	http://nabacareercenter.nabainc.org
National Association of Hispanic Publications Online Career Center	http://www.nahp.org
National Black MBA Association, Inc.	http://www.nbmbaa.org
National Black MBA Association New York Chapter	http://www.nyblackmba.org
National Hispanic Medical Association	http://http://jobs.nhmamd.org
National Latino Peace Officers Association	http://www.nlpoa.org
National Organization of Black Law Enforcement Executives	http://www.noblenational.org
National Organization of Black Chemists and Chemical Engineers	http://www.engin.umich.edu/societies/nobcche
National Society of Black Engineers	http://national.nsbe.org
National Society of Black Physicists	http://www.nsbp.org
National Society of Hispanic MBAs Career Center	http://www.nshmba.org
National Urban League	http://www.nul.org
NativeAmericanJobs.com	http://www.nativeamericanjobs.com
NetNoir	http://www.netnoir.com
PharmaDiversity	http://www.pharmadiversity.com
Rumbo (Houston)	http://www.rumbotx.com
Saludos Web Site	http://www.saludos.com
Society of Hispanic Professional Engineers Career Services	http://www.shpe.org
Society of Mexican American Engineers and Scientists	http://www.maes-natl.org
Vista Magazine	http://www.vistamagazine.com
Worksfm.com [United Kingdom]	http://www.worksfm.com

Gender

The Ada Project	http://women.cs.cmu.edu/ada
AdvancingWomen	http://www.advancingwomen.com
American Society of Women Accountants Employment Opportunities	http://www.aswact.org
Association for Women in Communications	http://www.womcom.org
Association for Women in Computing	http://www.awc-hq.org
Career Women	http://www.careerwomen.com
DCWebWomen	http://www.dcwebwomen.org
Electra	http://electra.com
Feminist Majority Foundation Career Center	http://www.feminist.org/911/jobs/joblisting.aspp
Financial Women International Careers	http://www.fwi.org
Healthcare Businesswomen's Association	http://www.hbanet.org/home.aspx
JobsandMoms.com	http://www.jobsandmoms.com
National Association of Women in Construction	http://www.nawic.org/nawic/Default.asp
National Female Executives	http://www.nafe.com
Sistahspace	http://groups.yahoo.com/group/SistahSpace
Society of Women Engineers Career Services	http://careers.swe.org
Webgrrls International	http://www.webgrrls.com
Women Connect.com	http://www.womenconnect.com
Women In Communications Washington, D.C. Chapter	http://www.awic-dc.org
Women in Federal Law Enforcement	http://www.wifle.org
WomenforHire.com	http://www.womenforhire.com
Women in Technology	http://www.womenintechnology.org
Women in Technology International (WITI) 4Hire	http://www.witi4hire.com
Women Work! The National Network for Women's Employment	http://www.womenwork.org
Women's Executive Network	http://www.thewen.com
Women's Finance Exchange	http://www.wfedallas.org
WomensJobList.com	http://www.womensjoblist.com
WomenSportsJobs.com	http://www.womensportjobs.com

Women's Sport Services	http://www.wiscnetwork.com
Women's Wear Daily	http://www.wwd.com
Womens-work	http://www.womans-work.com
Women Executives in Public Relations	http://www.wepr.org
Worksfm.com [United Kingdom]	http://www.worksfm.com

National Origin

Iconjob [India]	http://www.iconjob.com
Job-Quest.net [United Kingdom]	http://www.job-quest.net
VISA Jobs	http://www.h1visajobs.com

Physical Disability

AbilityEdge [Canada]	http://overview.careeredge.ca/index.asp?FirstTime=True&context=0&FromContext=2&language=1
AbilityJobs.com	http://www.abilityjobs.com
Disability Job Board	http://www.disabilityjobboard.com
Disability Job Site	http://www.disabilityjobsite.com
disABLEDperson.com	http://www.disabledperson.com
Disabled-World	http://www.disabled-world.com
GettingHired.com	http://www.gettinghired.com
Job Ability	http://www.jobability.com
JobAccess.org	http://www.jobaccess.org
Job Accommodation Network	http://askjan.org/
Job Opportunities for Disabled American Veterans	http://www.jofdav.com
NBDC	http://www.business-disability.com/index.aspx
New Mobility	http://www.newmobility.com
RecruitDisability.org	http://www.recruitdisability.org
Return 2 Work	http://www.return2work.org

Religion

Christian Jobs Online   http://www.christianjobs.com

Jewish Vocational Service Jobs Page   http://www.jvs-boston.org/index.
                                                   php?option=com_content&task=view&id=104

Sexual Orientation

Career Proud   http://www.careerproud.com

LGBTjobs   http://www.lgbtjobs.com

Out & Equal   http://www.outandequal.org

Pride Source   http://www.pridesource.com

Veterans

Army Career & Alumni Program   http://www.acap.army.mil

Blue-to-Gray   http://www.corporategray.com

Center for Employment Management   http://www.cfainstitute.org/pages/index.aspx

ClearanceJobs.com   http://www.clearancejobs.com

ClearedJobs.net   http://www.clearedjobs.net

Corporate Gray Online   http://www.corporategrayonline.com

The Defense Talent Network   http://www.defensetalent.com

Green-to-Gray   http://www.corporategray.com

HelmetstoHardhats.com   http://www.helmetstohardhats.com

Hire Quality   http://www.hire-quality.com

HireVetsFirst.gov   http://www.dol.gov/vets

Job Opportunities for Disabled American Veterans   http://www.jofdav.com

Jobs4Vets.com   http://www.jobs4vets.com

Landmark Destiny Group   http://www2.recruitmilitary.com

Military.com   http://www.military.com

Military Careers   http://www.todaysmilitary.com/careers

Military Connection   http://www.militaryconnection.com

Military Connections   http://www.militaryconnections.com

MilitaryHire.com   http://www.militaryhire.com

MilitaryExits	http://www.militaryexits.com
Military JobZone	http://www.militaryjobzone.com
Military Spouse Corporate Career Network	http://www.msccn.org
Military Spouse Job Search	http://jobsearch.spouse.military.com
MilitaryStars.com	http://www.militarystars.com
My Future	http://www.myfuture.com
Operation Transition	https://www.dmdc.osd.mil/appj/dwp/index.jsp
RecruitAirForce.com	https://www2.recruitmilitary.com
RecruitMarines.com	https://www2.recruitmilitary.com
RecruitMilitary.com	https://www2.recruitmilitary.com
RecruitNavy.com	https://www2.recruitmilitary.com
Reserve Officers Association	http://www.roa.org/site/PageServer
Stripes.com	http://www.stripes.com
Transition Assistance Online	http://www.taonline.com
Veterans Today	http://www.veteranstoday.com
VetJobs	http://www.vetjobs.com

-E-

Economists

American Agricultural Economics Association	http://www.aaes.org
American Economic Association	http://www.aeaweb.org/joe
EconCareers	http://www.econcareers.com
Econ-Jobs.com	http://www.econ-jobs.com
Economist.com	http://www.economist.com
Health Economics	http://www.healtheconomics.org
Inomics	http://www.inomics.com
International Health Economics Association	http://www.healtheconomics.org

Education/Academia

About.com	http://www.about.com/careers
Academic Careers Online	http://www.academiccareers.com
Academic Employment Network	http://www.academploy.com
Academic Jobs Today	http://academicjobs.net
AcademicKeys	http://www.academickeys.com
Academic Physician & Scientist	http://www.acphysci.com
Academic Position Network	http://www.apnjobs.com
Academic360	http://www.academic360.com
Affirmative Action Register	http://www.insightintodiversity.com
American Association of Colleges of Osteopathic Medicine	http://jobs.aacom.org
American Association of Diabetes Educators CareerNetwork	http://careernetwork.diabeteseducator.org
American Association of Physics Teachers	http://www.aapt.org
American Bankruptcy Institute Career Center	http://www.abiworld.org//AM/Template. cfm?Section=Home
American Educational Research Association Job Openings	http://www.jobtarget.com/home/ index.cfm?site_id=557
American Psychological Society Observer Job Listings	http://www.psychologicalscience.org/jobs
ArtJob Online	http://www.artjob.org/cgi-local/displayPage. pl?page=index.html
Association of American Medical Colleges CareerConnect	https://www.aamc.org/services/careerconnect/
Association for Environmental and Outdoor Education	http://www.aeoe.org
Association for Experential Education	http://aee.org
Association of Graduate Careers Advisory Service [United Kingdom]	http://www.agcas.org.uk
The Association for Institutional Research	http://www.airweb.org
Association of Teachers of Technical Writing	http://english.ttu.edu/ATTW
Association of University Teachers [United Kingdom]	http://www.AUT4Jobs.com
ATeacherJobSearch.com	http://www.ateacherjobsearch.com
BizSchoolJobs	http://www.bizschooljobs.com

Campus Review	http://www.campusreview.com.au
Canadian Society of Biochemistry and Molecular and Cellular Biologists	http://www.medicine.mcgill.ca/expmed/emjl/expmed_whoislinking.htm
ChristianUniversityJobs.com	http://www.christianuniversityjobs.com
ccJobsOnline.com	http://www.ccjobsonline.com
The Chronicle of Higher Education	http://www.chronicle.com/jobs
College and University Personnel Association JobLine	http://www.cupahr.org/jobline
CommunityCollegeJobs.com	http://www.communitycollegejobs.com
Community College Week	http://www.ccweek.com
Community Learning Network	http://www.cln.org
Computing Research Association Job Announcements	http://www.cra.org/ads
Council for Advancement & Support of Education Career Central	http://www.case.org/career_central.html
Dave's ESL Café	http://www.eslcafe.com
The Directory Recruitment Service [Australia]	http://www.thedirectory.aone.net.au/page8.htm
EdJoin	http://www.edjoin.org
Education America Network	http://www.educationamerica.net
Education Bug	http://www.educationbug.org
EducationJobs.com	http://www.educationjobs.com
Education Week on the Web	http://www.edweek.org/ew/index.html
Education World Jobs	http://www.educationworld.com/jobs
EFLWEB: English as a Second or Foreign Language	http://www.eflweb.com
e-Math	http://www.ams.org/home/page
The ESL Café's Job Center	http://www.eslcafe.com/jobs
ESL Worldwide	http://www.eslworldwide.com
Eteach.com [United Kingdom]	http://www.eteach.com
FacultyJob.com	http://www.facultyjob.com
FEcareers.co.uk [United Kingdom]	http://www.fecareers.co.uk
FEjobs.com [United Kingdom]	http://www.fejobs.com
Foothill-De Anza Community College District	http://www.fhda.edu/jobs
GeoWebServices-RocketHire	http://www.geowebservices.com

GreatInfo.com	http://greatinfo.com
Grist.org	http://jobs.grist.org
Higher Careers.com	http://www.highercareers.com
HigherEdJobs.com	http://www.higheredjobs.com
The Higher Education Recruitment Consortium	http://www.hercjobs.org
HireEd.com	http://www.hireed.com
History of Science Society	http://www.hssonline.org
HotEducationJobs	http://www.hoteducationjobs.com
Hudson Institute	http://www.hudson.org
Humanities and Social Sciences Online	http://www.h-net.org
Independent School Management	http://isminc.com
I Need a Library Job	http://www.inalj.com
Inside Higher Ed	http://www.insidehighered.com
Jaeger's Ince-Math	http://www.ams.org/home/page/employment
JOE: Job Opportunities for Economists	http://www.aeaweb.org/joe
JobsinEducation [United Kingdom]	http://www.jobsineducation.com
Jobs in Linguistics	http://linguistlist.org/jobs
Jobs.ac.uk [United Kingdom]	http://www.jobs.ac.uk
K-12 Jobs	http://www.k12jobs.com
Library Job Postings	http://www.libraryjobpostings.org
Massachusetts Environmental Education Society	http://www.massmees.org
Mathematical Association of America	http://www.mathclassifieds.org
Math-Jobs	http://www.math-jobs.com
The Minerals, Metals, Materials Society JOM	http://www.tms.org/TMSHome.aspx
MinorityNurse.com	http://www.minoritynurse.com
Music Library Association Job Placement	http://www.musiclibraryassoc.org/employmentanded/joblist/index.shtml
NationJob Network-Education Job Openings	http://www.nationjob.com/education
National Association for College Admission Counseling Career Opportunities	http://www.nacac.com/classifieds.cfm
National Council of Teachers of Math Jobs	http://www.nctm.org

National Information Services and Systems [United Kingdom]	http://www.hero.ac.uk/uk/home/index.cfm
National Teacher Recruitment	http://www.recruitingteachers.com
National Women's Studies Association	http://www.nwsa.org
New England Higher Education Recruitment Consortium	http://www.newenglandherc.org/home/index.cfm?site_id=660
The New Jersey Higher Education Recruitment Consortium	http://www.njepadeherc.org/home/index.cfm?site_id=685
North American Association for Environmental Education	http://www.naaee.org
Now Hiring Teachers	http://www.nowhiringteachers.com
Pediatric Academic Societies	http://careers.pas-meeting.org
PhDjobs.com	http://www.phdjobs.com
Phds.org	http://www.phds.org
PhysicsToday.org	http://www.physicstoday.org
PLATO	http://www.skillsnet.com
RISE: Resources for Indispensable Schools and Educators	http://www.risenetwork.org
Scholarly Jobs	http://www.scholarlyjobs.com
School-Jobs	http://www.school-jobs.net
SchoolSpring.com	http://www.schoolspring.com
School Staff	http://www.schoolstaff.com
Scoted Jobs [Scotland]	http://www.scotedjobs.com
Superintendent Jobs	http://www.superintendentjobs.com
Teach for America	http://www.teachforamerica.org
Teach Network [United Kingdom]	http://www.teachnetwork.co.uk
Teacher Jobs	http://www.teacherjobs.com
Teachers of English to Speakers of Other Languages Job Finder	http://www.tesol.org/s_tesol/index.asp
Teachers Support Network	http://www.teacherssupportnetwork.com
Teachers-Teachers	http://www.teachers-teachers.com
TeachingJobs.com	http://www.teachingjobs.com
TedJob: Top Higher-Education Jobs	http://www.tedjob.com

Top School Jobs	http://www.topschooljobs.org
Tefl-jobs.co.uk [United Kingdom]	http://www.tefl-jobs.co.uk
University of Illinois at Urbana-Champaign Grad School of Library & Information Science Placement Online-Library Job Service	http://www.lis.illinois.edu/careers
University of Wisconsin School of Education	http://careers.education.wisc.edu
University Job Bank	http://www.universityjobs.com
UniversityJobs.com	http://www.universityjobs.com

Employee Referral

G2Bux	http://g2bux.ourtoolbar.com
H3.com	http://www.h3.com
Interview Exchange ReferredHire	http://www.interviewexchange.com
Jobster	http://www.jobster.com
JobThread.com	http://www.jobthread.com
JobTonic.com [United Kingdom]	http://www.jobtonic.com
Jobvite	http://recruiting.jobvite.com
KarmaOne	http://www.karmaone.com

Energy & Utilities

Akhtaboot [Jordan]	http://www.akhtaboot.com
Aljazeerajobs.com [Middle East]	http://www.aljazeerajobs.com
Bayt.com [United Arab Emirates]	http://www.bayt.com
Careerjunctionme.com [Middle East]	http://www.careerjunctionme.com
Careers in Wind	http://www.careersinwind.com
Dakota Oil Jobs	http://www.dakotaoiljobs.com
Drilling Research Institute Classifieds	http://www.drillers.com/pages/view/jobs
Earthworks-Jobs.com [United Kingdom]	http://www.earthworks-jobs.com
Energy Careers	http://www.energycareers.com
Energy Central Jobs	http://www.energycentraljobs.com

Energy Industry Central	http;//www.energyindustrycentral.com
EnergyJobsNetwork	http://www.energyjobsnetwork.com
Energy Jobs Portal	http://www.energyjobsportal.com
Electric Net	http://www.electricnet.com
Get Utility Jobs	http://www.getutilityjobs.com
Green Energy Jobs	http://www.greenenergyjobs.com
GreenEnergyJobsOnline.com	http://www.greenenergyjobsonline.com
iHireUtilities	http://www.ihireutilities.com
Jobs in Biofuels	http://www.jobsinbiofuels.com
Jobs in Solar Power	http://www.jobsinsolarpower.com
Jobs in Wind Power	http://www.jobsinwindpower.com
NaukriGulf.com [Middle East]	http://www.naukrigulf.com
NukeWorker.com	http://www.nukeworker.com
Offshore Magazine	http://www.offshore-mag.com
Oil Career	http://www.oilcareer.com
OilCareers.com	http://www.oilcareers.com
Oil Exec	http://www.oilexec.com
Oil & Gas Jobs	http://www.earthworks-jobs.com
OilandGasJobSearch	http://www.oilandgasjobsearch.com
Oil & Gas Journal	http://www.ogj.com
Oil Industry Jobs	http://www.oilsurvey.com
Oil Job	http://www.oiljob.com
Oil Job Finder	http://www.oiljobfinder.com
Oil-Offshore Marine	http://www.oil-offshore-marine.com
PennEnergyJobs.com	http://www.pennenergyjobs.com
Petroleum & Mining Job Portal	http://www.pmjobs.net
Power Careers	http://www.power-careers.com
Power Magazine	http://www.powermag.com
Power Online	http://www.poweronline.com
Power Plant Pro	http://www.powerplantpro.com

Professional Energy Jobs	http://www.professionalenergyjobs.com
RenewableEnergyJobs.com [United Kingdom]	http://www.renewableenergyjobs.com
RenewableEnergyWorld.com	http://www.renewableenergyworld.com
RigZone	http://www.rigzone.com
SecurityClearedJobs.com [United Kingdom]	http://www.securityclearedjobs.com
SkilledWorkers.com [Canada]	http://www.skilledworkers.com
SustainableBusiness.com	http://www.sustainablebusiness.com
Think Network	http://www.globalenergyjobs.com
UtilityHire	http://www.utilityhire.com
Utility Jobs Online	http://www.utilityjobsonline.com
Utility Worker	http://www.utility-worker.com
World Oils	http://www.worldoils.com
WorldwideWorker	http://www.worldwideworker.com

Engineering

Engineering-General

AEJob.com	http://www.aejob.com
A1A Jobs	http://www.a1ajobs.com
All4Engineers.de [Germany]	http://www.all4engineers.com
AmericanJobs.com	http://www.americanjobs.com
Balfour Betty Rail UK [United Kingdom]	http://www.bbrailjobs.com
Bayt.com [United Arab Emirates]	http://www.bayt.com
Beechwood Recruit [United Kingdom]	http://www.beechwoodrecruit.com
Career Marketplace Network	http://www.careermarketplace.com
Degree Hunter	http://degreehunter.net
Dice	http://www.dice.com
Discover Jobs	http://www.discover-jobs.com
The Engineer [United Kingdom]	http://www.theengineer.co.uk
Engineer.net	http://www.engineer.net
EngineerBoard [United Kingdom]	http://www.engineerboard.co.uk

EngineerJobs.com	http://www.engineerjobs.com
Engineering Central	http://www.engcen.com/jobbank.htm
Engineering Classifieds	http://www.engineeringclassifieds.com/Main/Default.asp
Engineering Giant	http://www.engineergiant.com
Engineering Institute of Canada	http://www.eic-ici.ca
EngineeringJobs.com	http://www.engineeringjobs.com
EngineeringJobs.co.uk [United Kingdom]	http://www.engineeringjobs.co.uk
EngineeringJobsNow [United Kingdom]	http://www.engineeringjobsnow.co.uk
Engineering Jobs Site	http://www.engineering-job-site.com
Engineering News Record	http://enrconstruction.com
Engineer Web	http://www.engineerweb.com
The Engineering Specific Career Advisory Problem-Solving Environment	https://engineering.purdue.edu/Engr
The Engineering Technology Site [United Kingdom]	http://www.engineers4engineers.co.uk
4EngineeringJobs	http://www.4engineeringjobs.com
iHireEngineering.com	http://www.ihireengineering.com
In Automotive [United Kingdom]	http://www.inautomotive.com
interEC.net	http://www.interec.net
Jim Finder [United Kingdom]	http://www.jimfinder.com
Job Net	http://www.jobnet.org
Job Search for Engineers	http://www.interec.net
Jobs 4 Engineers	http://www.ajob4engineers.com
JobsinConstruction [United Kingdom]	http://www.jobsinconstruction.co.uk
JobsinSurveying [United Kingdom]	http://www.jobsinsurveying.co.uk
JustEngineers.net [Australia]	http://www.justengineers.net
National Society of Professional Engineers Employment	http://www.nspe.org/Employment/index.html
PennEnergyJobs.com	http://www.pennenergyjobs.com
PlanetRecruit [United Kingdom]	http://www.planetrecruit.com
QualityEngineerJobs.com	http://www.qualityengineerjobs.com
Rail Job Search [United Kingdom]	http://www.railjobsearch.com/index.html

ReferWork-Jobs.com   http://www.referwork-jobs.com

SecurityClearedJobs.com [United Kingdom]   http://www.securityclearedjobs.com

Tech Employment   http://www.techemployment.com

ThaiEngineeringJobs.com [Thailand]   http://www.thaiengineerjobs.com/en/index.asp

Think Network   http://www.thinkjobs.com

Utility Job Search [United Kingdom]   http://www.utilityjobsearch.com

Worldwide Worker   http://www.worldwideworker.com

Aeronautical/Aviation

Aeroindustryjobs   http://www.aeroindustryjobs.com

Aeronautical Engineering Jobs [United Kingdom]   http://www.aeronauticalengineeringjobs.co.uk

Aerospace Jobs   http://hometown.aol.com/aerojobs

AeroSpaceNews.com   http://www.aerospacenews.com

AircraftEngineers.com [United Kingdom]   http://www.aircraftengineers.com

Agricultural

American Society of Agricultural and Biological   http://www.asabe.org
Engineers

Chemical

American Chemical Society   http://portal.acs.org/portal/acs/corg/content

American Institute of Chemical Engineers   http://careerengineer.aiche.org/
CareerEngineer

Chemical Engineer   http://www.chemicalengineer.com

ChemJobs.net   http://www.chemjobs.net/chemjobs.html

Jobs in Chemistry   http://www.jobsinchemistry.com

National Organization for Black Chemists and   http://www.engin.umich.edu/societies/nobcche
Chemical Engineers

Civil

American Society of Civil Engineers   http://www.asce.org

Civil Engineering Central   http://www.civilengineeringcentral.com

Civil Engineering Jobs	http://www.civilengineeringjobs.com
CIVILjobs.com	http://www.civiljobs.com
iCivil Engineer	http://www.icivilengineer.com/jobs

Construction

A/E/C Job Bank	http://www.aecjobbank.com
Arch + Design	http://www.archdesignjobs.com
CED Magazine	http://www.cedmagazine.com
Contract Design Magazine	Http://contractdesign.com
Custom Home Magazine	http://www.customhomeonline.com
Kitchen & Bath Business	http://www.kbbonline.com
PlumbingCareers.com	http://www.plumbingcareers.com
PLUMBjob.com	http://www.plumbjobs.com
Structural Engineer Job Source	http://www.structuralengineerjobsource.com
Tools of the Trade Magazine	http://www.toolsofthetrade.net
Utility Jobs Online	http://www.utilityjobsonline.com

Diversity

National Society of Black Engineers	http://national.nsbe.org
Society of Hispanic Professional Engineers Career Services	http://www.shpe.org
Society of Mexican American Engineers and Scientists	http://www.maes-natl.org
Society of Women Engineers Career Services	http://careers.swe.org

Electrical/Electronics

EDN Network	http://www.edn.com
eeProductCenter	http://cmpmedia.globalspec.com
EE Times	http://www.eetimes.com
Electric Net	http://www.electricnet.com
Electrical Engineer	http://www.electricalengineer.com

ElectroMagneticCareers.com	http://www.electromagneticcareers.com
Electronic News Online	http://www.edn.com
Electronics Weekly	http://www.electronicsweekly.com
Institute of Electrical & Electronics Engineers Job Site	http://www.ieee.org/education_careers/index.html
National Electrical Contractors Association	http://www.necanet.org
Radio-Electronics.com	http://www.radio-electronics.com
RF Globalnet	http://www.rfglobalnet.com
Test & Measurement World	http://www.tmworld.com
UG Job Network (Unigraphics CAD/CAM/CAE)	http://www.ugjn.com
Yaps4u.net	http://www.yaps4u.net

Environmental

Earthworks-Jobs.com [United Kingdom]	http://www.earthworks-jobs.com
Environmental Construction Engineering Architectural Jobs Online	http://www.eceajobs.com
GeoWebServices-RocketHire	http://www.geowebservices.com
Grist.org	http://jobs.grist.org

Industrial/Manufacturing

AutomationTechies.com	http://www.automationtechies.com
iHireManufacturingEngineers.com	http://www.ihiremanufacturingengineers.com
Industrial Engineer	http://www.industrialengineer.com
Materials Engineer	http://www.materialsengineerjobs.com
NukeWorker.com	http://www.nukeworker.com
Plastics Jobs Forum.com	http://www.plasticsjobsforum.com
Power Magazine	http://www.powermag.com
Society of Manufacturing Engineers Jobs Connection	http://jobsconnection.sme.org

Mechanical

American Society of Mechanical Engineers Career Center   http://www.asme.org/jobs

Jobs for Mechanical Engineers   http://www.mechanicalengineer.com

Mechanical Engineers Magazine Online   http://www.memagazine.org

Mining/Petroleum

Drilling Research Institute Classifieds   http://www.drillers.com/pages/view/jobs

Ethanol-Jobs.com   http://www.ethanol-jobs.com

Job Oil   http://www.joboil.com

The Minerals, Metals, Materials Society JOM   http://www.tms.org/TMSHome.aspx

Oil & Gas Jobs   http://www.earthworks-jobs.com/comm.htm

Oil Career   http://www.oilcareer.com

Oil Industry Jobs   http://www.oilsurvey.com

Oil Job   http://www.oiljob.com

RigZone.com   http://www.rigzone.com

Software

Career Center @ Semiconductor Online   http://www.semiconductoronline.com

Computer-Aided Three-Dimensional Interactive Application Job Network   http://www.catjn.com

Semi Web   http://www.semiweb.com

Systems

The Instrumentation, Systems and Automation Society Online ISA Jobs   http://www.isa.org/isa_es

Society for Information Display   http://www.sid.org/jobmart/jobmart.html

Transportation

Right Of Way   http://www.rightofway.com

RoadTechs.com   http://www.roadtechs.com

Society of Automotive Engineers Job Board   http://www.sae.org/careers/recruitad.htm

Society of Naval Architects and Marine Engineers   http://www.sname.org/SNAME/SNAME/Home

Other Specialty

Biodiesel-Jobs	http://www.biodiesel-jobs.com
Biomedical Engineering Society	http://www.bmes.org/aws/BMES/pt/sp/home_page
CFD Online (Computational Fluid Dynamics)	http://www.cfd-online.com
Contract Employment Weekly	http://www.ceweekly.com
Design Engineering Jobs	http://www.designengineeringjobs.com
Design News	http://www.designnews.com
Electromagnetic Careers	http://www.electromagneticcareers.com
Graduating Engineer & Computer Careers Online	http://www.graduatingengineer.com
Human Factors Careers	http://www.hfcareers.com
International Society for Pharmaceutical Engineering	http://www.ispe.org
JustCADJobs.com	http://www.justcadjobs.com
MaterialsEngineerJobs.com	http://www.materialsengineeerjobs.com
National Association of Grad & Prof Students	http://www.nagps.org
National Association of Radio and Telecommunications Engineers	http://www.narte.org
QA Engineer Jobs	http://www.qaengineerjobs.com
QualityEngineerJobs.com	http://www.qualityengineerjobs.com
ScientistWorld.com [United Kingdom]	http://www.scientistworld.com
Space Jobs	http://www.spacejobs.com
SPIE Web-International Society for Optical Engineering	http://spie.org/app/buyersguide/index.aspx
Wireless Design Online	http://www.wirelessdesignonline.com

Entertainment/Acting

Airwaves Media Web	http://www.airwaves.com
Airwaves Media Web	http://www.airwaves.com
Answers4Dancers.com	http://www.answers4dancers.com
ArtJob Online	http://www.artjob.org
Backstage.com	http://www.backstage.combso/index.jsp
BestRad!oJobs	http://www.bestradiojobs.com

Billboard.com	http://www.billboard.com
Casting-America	http://www.castingsociety.com
Casting Daily	http://www.castingnet.com
CreativeJobsCentral.com	http://www.creativejobscentral.com
CrewNet	http://www.crewnet.com
CruiseShipJobs.com	http://www.cruiseshipjobs.com
Dance USA	http://www.danceusa.org
Deadline Hollywood	http://www.deadline.com/hollywood
Designer Max	http://www.designermax.com
Entertainment Careers	http://www.entertainmentcareers.net
EntertainmentJobs.com	http://www.entertainmentjobs.com
Employment Network	http://www.employnow.com
Filmbiz.com	http://www.filmbiz.com
4 Entertainment Jobs	http://www.4entertainmentjobs.com
Grapevine Jobs [United Kingdom]	http://www.grapevinejobs.com/home.asp
The Hollywood Reporter	http://www.hollywoodreporter.com
Hollywood Web	http://www.hollywoodweb.com
JobMonkey.com	http://www.jobmonkey.com
Mass Media Jobs	http://www.massmediajobs.com
Media Communications Association International Job Hotline	http://www.mca-i.org
Media Week [United Kingdom]	http://www.mediaweek.co.uk
National Association of Broadcasters	http://www.nab.org
New England Film	http://www.newenglandfilm.com/jobs.htm
Opportunities Online [United Kingdom]	http://www.opps.co.uk
PlanetSharkProductions.com	http://www.planetsharkproductions.com
Playbill On-Line	http://www.playbill.com
ProductionBase.co.uk [United Kingdom]	http://www.productionbase.co.uk
ProductionHUB	http://www.productionhub.com
Radio Online	http://menu.radio-online.com/cgi-bin/rolmenu.exe/menu

Showbizjobs.com	http://www.showbizjobs.com
Show Biz Data	http://www.showbizdata.com
Showreel	http://www.showreel.tv
Society of Broadcast Engineers	http://www.sbe.org
Theatre Jobs	http://www.theatrejobs.com
TVjobs.com	http://www.tvjobs.com
TV and Radio Jobs	http://www.tvandradiojobs.com
VarietyCareers.com	http://thebiz.variety.com/home/index.cfm?site_id=7307
Voice of Dance	http://www.voiceofdance.com/v1/index.cfm

Environmental

AEJob.com	http://www.aejob.com
American College of Occupational and Environmental Medicine	http://www.acoem.org
American Water Works Association Career Center (Water Jobs)	http://www.awwa.org
APSnet-Plant Pathology Online	http://www.apsnet.org
Association for Environmental and Outdoor Education	http://www.aeoe.org
Association for Healthcare Environment	http://careerlink.ahe.org
AutomationTechies.com	http://www.automationtechies.com
Biodiesel-Jobs	http://www.biodiesel-jobs.com
Bright Green Talent	http://www.brightgreentalent.com
Conservation Job Board	http://www.conservationjobboard.com
Earthworks-Jobs.com [United Kingdom]	http://www.earthworks-jobs.com
Eco.org	http://www.eco.org
EE-Link: The Environmental Education Web Server	http://eelink.net/pages/EE+Jobs+Database
EHScareers.com	http://www.ehscareers.com
EnviroNetwork	http://www.environetwork.org/default.aspx
EnvironmentalCareer Center	http://www.environmentalcareer.com
Environmental Career Opportunities	http://www.ecojobs.com

Environmental Careers Bulletin Online	http://www.ecbonline.com
Environmental Careers Organization	http://www.eco.org
Environmental Careers World	http://www.environmentaljobs.com
Environmental Construction Engineering Architectural Jobs Online	http://www.eceajobs.com
Environmental Data Interactive Exchange Job Centre [United Kingdom]	http://www.edie.net
Environmental Employment Pages	http://www.datacorinc.com/employment.php
Environmental Engineer	http://www.environmentalengineer.com
Environmental-Expert.com	http://www.environmental-expert.com
Environmental Jobs	http://www.environmentaljobs.com
Environmental Jobs & Careers	http://www.ejobs.org
Environmental Nes	http://www.enn.com
EnviroWorld	http://www.enviroworld.com
Ethanol-Jobs.com	http://www.ethanol-jobs.com
GeoWebServices-RocketHire	http://www.geowebservices.com
GIS Jobs Clearinghouse	http://www.gjc.org
Great Green Careers	http://www.greatgreencareers.com
GreenBiz.com	http://jobs.greenbiz.com
Green Dream Jobs	http://www.sustainablebusiness.com
Green Energy Jobs	http://www.greenenergyjobs.com
GreenEnergyJobsOnline.com	http://www.greenenergyjobsonline.com
GreenJobs.com	http://www.greenjobs.com
Green Jobs Online [United Kingdom]	http://www.greenjobsonline.co.uk
Green Jobs Ready	http://www.greenjobsready.com
Job.com	http://www.job.com
Jobs In Waste [United Kingdom]	http://www.jobsinwaste.co.uk
Massachusetts Environmental Education Society	http://www.massmees.org
Misco Jobs	http://www.miscojobs.com
National Environmental Health Association	http://www.neha.org
Nevada Mining	http://www.nevadamining.org

New Scientist Jobs	http://www.newscientistjobs.com
North American Association for Environmental Education	http://www.naaee.org
Organic-Chemistry	http://www.organic-chemistry.org
Pollution Online	http://www.pollutiononline.com
Power Online	http://www.poweronline.com
Practice Greenhealth	http://careers.practicegreenhealth.org
Public Works	http://www.publicworks.com
Pulp & Paper Online	http://www.pulpandpaperonline.com
PureGreenJobs.com	http://www.puregreenjobs.com
RenewableEnergyJobs	http://www.renewableenergyjobs.net
RenewableEnergyWorld.com	http://www.renewableenergyworld.com
The Science Jobs	http://www.thesciencejobs.com
SkilledWorkers.com [Canada]	http://www.skilledworkers.com
Solar Jobs [United Kingdom]	http://www.solarjobs.com
Solid Waste	http://www.solidwaste.com
Student Conservation Association	http://www.thesca.org
SustainableBusiness.com	http://www.sustainablebusiness.com
Universities Water Information Network	http://www.ucowr.siu.edu
Water Online	http://www.wateronline.com

Equipment Leasing

Equipment Leasing and Finance Association	http://www.elfaonline.org
Jobvertise	http://www.jobvertise.com
Leasing News	http://www.leasingnews.org/Classified/Jwanted/Jwanted.htm

Exchanges-Recruiter/Employer/Job Seeker

America's Job Exchange	http://www.americasjobexchange.com
@Recruiter.com	http://www.atrecruiter.com
Avoxa.com	http://www.avoxa.fr/v2/htm

Dealsplit.com	http://www.dealsplit.com
eLance	http://www.elance.com
FreelancingProjects.com	http://www.freelancingprojects.com
Guru.com	http://www.guru.com
HotGigs	http://www.hotgigs.com
JobCentral.com	http://www.jobcentral.com
RentaCoder.com	http://www.vworker.com/RentACoder/DotNet/default.aspx
Sologig.com	http://www.sologig.com
US.jobs	http://www.us.jobs

Executive/Management

Executive-General

AllExecutiveJobs.com [United Kingdom]	http://www.allexecutivejobs.com
TheBigChair.com.au [Australia]	http://thebigchair.com.au
B7 Appointments [United Kingdom]	http://www.business7.co.uk/b7-appointments
Association of Executive Search Consultants	http://www.bluesteps.com
CFO.com	http://www.cfo.com
CFO Jobsite	http://www.cfojobsite.com
CIO	http://itjobs.cio.com/a/all-jobs/list?source=top_nav/
Consultants Board [United Kingdom]	http://www.consultantsboard.com
Consultants United [United Kingdom]	http://www.consultantsunited.com
CVTrumpet.co.uk [United Kingdom]	http://www.cvtrumpet.co.uk
eChannelLinecareers.com [Canada]	http://www.echannellinecareers.com
Exec2Exec.com [United Kingdom]	http://www.exec2exec.com
ExecuNet	http://www.execunet.com
execSearches.com	http://www.execsearches.com
TheExecutiveClub.com [United Kingdom]	http://www.theexecutiveclub.com
Executive-i.com [United Kingdom]	http://www.executive-i.com
ExecutiveOpenings.com [United Kingdom]	http://www.executiveopenings.com

Executive Placement Services	http://www.execplacement.com
Executive Registry	http://www.executiveregistry.com
Executive Taskforce [New Zealand]	http://executivetaskforce.org
Executives Online [United Kingdom]	http://www.executivesonline.co.uk
ExecutivesontheWeb.com [United Kingdom]	http://www.executivesontheweb.com
ExecutivesOnly.com	http://www.executivesonly.com
Experteer.co.uk [United Kingdom]	http://www.experteer.co.uk
FazJob.net [Germany]	http://fazjob.net
50kandup.com	http://jobs.50kandup.com/home/index.cfm?site_id=2167
GoldJobs [United Kingdom]	http://www.goldjobs.com/overview/default.asp
Grist.org	http://jobs.grist.org
High Tech Partners [United Kingdom]	http://www.hightechpartners.com
Ivy Exec	http://www.ivyexec.com
NetShare	http://www.netshare.com
New Life Network [United Kingdom]	http://www.newlifenetwork.co.uk
PlatinumJobs.com [United Kingdom]	http://www.platinumjobs.com/overview/default.asp
RiteSite.com	http://www.ritesite.com/Login/index.cfm
Score	http://www.scn.org/civic/score-online
Seek Executive [Australia]	http://executive.seek.com.au
Top-Consultant.com [United Kingdom]	http://www.top-consultant.com/UK/career/appointments.asp

Management-General

Academy of Management Placement Services	http://aom.org/placement
The American Management Association Management Jobs	http://management-jobs.amanet.org
Association of MBAs	http://www.mbaworld.com
CardBrowser.com	http://www.cardbrowser.com
CareerFile	http://www.careerfile.com
Corporate Alumni	http://www.selectminds.com

Eclectic [Netherlands]	http://www.eclectic.eu
Futurestep	http://www.futurestep.com
Institute of Management & Administration's Supersite	http://www.ioma.com
International Economic Development Council	http://www.iedconline.org
Jobs.ac.uk [United Kingdom]	http://www.jobs.ac.uk
Jobs4Managers.com	http://www.jobs4managers.com
TheLadders.com	http://www.theladders.com
Latin MBA	http://www.latinmba.com
MBA Careers	http://www.mbacareers.com
MBA Exchange [Switzerland]	http://www.mba-exchange.com
MBA Global Net	http://www.mbaglobalnet.com
Monster Management	http://www.monster.com
Multiunitjobs.com	http://www.multiunitjobs.com
National Black MBA Association	http://www.nbmbaa.org
Net Expat	http://www.netexpat.com
PMjob.ca [Canada]	http://www.pmjob.ca
6FigureJobs	http://www.6figurejobs.com
Stern Alumni Outreach Career	http://www.stern.nyu.edu
TopJobs.ch [Switzerland]	http://www.topjobs.ch
Zhaopin.com [China]	http://www.zhaopin.com

Career Field-Specific

CM Today	http://www.cmcrossroads.com
Compliance Jobs	http://www.compliancejobs.com
Construction Executive Online	http://www.constructionexecutive.com
Financial Executives Institute Career Center	http://www.financialexecutives.org
Ft.com-Financial Times [United Kingdom]	http://www.ft.com
Hispanic American Police Command Officers Association	http://www.hapcoa.org
National Organization of Black Law Enforcement Executives	http://www.noblenational.org
NursingExecutives.com	http://www.nursingexecutives.com

Industry-Specific

Agri-Management	http://agri-man.com
American Bankers Association	http://aba.careerbank.com
American College of Healthcare Executives	http://ache.org
American College of Physician Executives	http://www.acpe.org
American Society of Association Executives CareerHQ	http://www.careerhq.org
boardnetUSA	http://www.boardnetusa.org/public/home.asp
The Brass Key	http://www.thepoliceexecutive.com
Case Management Society	http://www.cmsa.org/
CFO Publishing	http://cfonet.com
Chain Store Age	http://www.chainstoreage.com
HospitalityExecutive.com	http://www.hospitalityexecutive.com
Medical Group Management Association	http://www.mgma.com
Multifamily Executive Magazine	http://www.multifamilyexecutive.com
National Association of Health Services Executives	http://careers.nahse.org
New York Society of Association Executives Career Center	http://www.nysaenet.org/NYSAENET/NYSAENET/Home
Pharmaceutical Executive	http://www.pharmexec.com
Women Executives in Public Relations	http://www.wepr.org
GxPJobs.com [United Kingdom]	http://www.gxpjobs.com

-F-

Fashion

Be The 1	http://www.bethe1.com/en
DrapersOnline [United Kingdom]	http://www.drapersonline.com
Fashion Career Center	http://www.fashioncareercenter.com
Fashion Group International	http://www.fgi.org
Fashion Net	http://www.fashion.net/jobs

CreativeJobsCentral.com	http://www.creativejobscentral.com
Footware News	http://www.wwd.com/footware-news
RagTradeJobs.com [Australia]	http://www.ragtradejobs.com
Women's Wear Daily Careers	http://www.wwd.com/wwdcareers

Feminism

FeministCampus.org	http://www.feministcampus.org
Feminist Majority Foundation Online	http://www.feminist.org

Fiber Optics

The Fiber Optic Association	http://www.thefoa.org/foanewsletter.html#anchor651744
Fiber Optic Marketplace	http://www.fiberoptic.com
Fiber Optics Online	http://www.fiberopticsonline.com

Finance & Accounting (See also Banking, Insurance)

Accounting-General

AccountancyAgeJobs.com [United Kingdom]	http://www.accountancyagejobs.com
AccountancyJobsBoard [United Kingdom]	http://www.accountancyjobsboard.co.uk
Accountant Careers	http://www.accountantcareers.com
Accountant Gigs	http://www.accountantgigs.com
AccountantJobs.com	http://www.accountantjobs.com
Accountant Jobs Chicago	http://www.accountantjobschicago.com
AccountManager.com	http://www.accountmanager.com
Accounting.com	http://www.accounting.com
Accounting & Finance Jobs	http://www.accountingjobs.com
AccountingBoard.com	http://www.accountingboard.com
Accounting Career Network	http://www.searchaccountingjobs.com
Accounting Classifieds	http://www.accountingclassifieds.com/Main/Default.asp

AccountingGigs.com	http://www.accountinggigs.com
Accounting Jobs in New York	http://www.accounting-jobs-in-new-york.com
Accounting Jobs Online	http://www.accountingjobsonline.com
Accounting Jobs Today	http://www.accountingjobstoday.com
AccountingNet	http://www.accountingnet.com
Accounting Now	http://www.accountingnow.com
Accounting Professional	http://www.accountingprofessional.com
Ambition [Australia]	http://www.ambition.com.au
American Accounting Association Career Center	http://commons.aaahq.org/
American Society of Women Accountants	http://www.aswact.org
AndersenAlumni.net	http://www.andersenalumni.net
Antsjobs.ie [Ireland]	http://www.antsjobs.ie
Awesome Accountants	http://www.awesomeaccountants.comh/aa.asp
Bean Brains	http://www.beanbrains.com
CA Magazine	http://www.camagazine.com
Careers in Accounting	http://www.careers-in-accounting.com
CASource [Canada]	http://www.casource.com
Certified Management Accountants of Canada	http://www.cma-canada.org
iHire Accounting	http://www.ihireaccounting.com
JobsFinancial [United Kingdom]	http://www.jobsfinancial.com
Jobs4Accounting	http://www.jobs4accounting.com
MyAccountancyJobs [United Kingdom]	http://www.myaccountancyjobs.com
MyAccountingJobs.net	http://www.myaccountingjobs.net
National Association of Black Accountants, Inc. Career Center	http://nabacareercenter.nabainc.org/index.cfm?
National Society of Accountants	http://www.nsacct.org/index.asp
Search Accounting Jobs	http://www.searchaccountingjobs.com
ThaiFinanceJobs.com [Thailand]	http://www.thaifinancejobs.com/en/index.asp
TotallyFinancial.com.au [Australia]	http://www.totallyfinancial.com/australia

Accountants-Certified Public Accountants

American Association of Hispanic Certified Public Accountants	http://www.aahcpa.org
American Institute of Certified Public Accountants Career Center	http://www.cpa2biz.com
CPA Jobs	http://www.cpajobs.com
CPANet	http://www.cpanet.com
Illinois CPA Society Career Center	http://www.icpas.org/hc-career-center.aspx?id=2178
Institute of Management Accountants Career Center	http://www.imanet.org/development_career.asp
Inside Careers Guide to Chartered Accountancy [United Kingdom]	http://www.insidecareers.co.uk
Institute of Chartered Accountants of Alberta [Canada]	http://www.albertacas.ca/Home.aspx
Maryland Association of CPAs Job Connect	http://www.macpa.org/content/classifieds/public/search.aspx
New Jersey Society of CPAs	http://www.njscpa.org
New York State Society of CPAs	http://www.nysscpa.org/classified/main.cfm
Tennessee Society of CPA's	http://www.tscpa.com

Audit

AccountantAuditor.net	http://www.accountantauditor.net
Audit Jobs Chicago	http://www.auditjobschicago.com
Audit Net	http://www.auditnet.org
AuditProfessional.com	http://www.auditprofessional.com
AuditorJobs.com	http://www.auditorjobs.com
Institute of Internal Auditors Audit Career Center	https://na.theiia.org/about-us/Pages/Audit-Career-Center.aspx
InternalAuditJobs.net [United Kingdom]	http://www.internalauditjobs.net

Brokerage/Investment

Advocis	http://www.advocis.ca
Annuitiesnet.com	http://www.annuitiesnet.com/v2
Association for Investment Management and Research	http://www.cfainstitute.org

Bond Buyer	http://www.bondbuyer.com
BrokerHunter.com	http://www.brokerhunter.com
International Association for Registered Financial Planners	http://careers.iarfc.org
Investment Management and Trust Exchange	http://www.antaeans.com
National Venture Capital Association	http://www.nvca.org
New York Society of Security Analysts Career Resources	http://www.nyssa.org/AM/Template.cfm?Section=career_development
Securities Industry Association Career Resource Center	http://www.sifma.com/services/career_center/career_center.html
Society of Actuaries	http://www.soa.org
Society of Risk Analysis Opportunities	http://www.sra.org/opportunities.php
WallStJobs.com	http://www.wallstjobs.com

Finance-General

American Association of Finance & Accounting	http://www.aafa.com/careers.html
American Bankruptcy Institute Career Center	http://www.abiworld.org
Association of Finance Professionals Career Services	http://www.afponline.org/pub/cs/career_services.html
Association of Latino Professionals in Finance & Accounting Job Postings	http://www.alpfa.org
Banking and Financial Services Career Center	http://www.searchbankingjobs.com
Bloomberg.com	http://www.bloomberg.com
Business Finance Magazine	http://businessfinancemag.com
Business-Money Magazine	http://www.business-money.com
CareerBank.com	http://www.careerbank.com
CareerJournal.com	http://online.wsj.com/public/page/news-career-jobs.html
CareerJournal.com Europe	http://online.wsj.com/public/page/news-career-jobs.html
Careers in Finance	http://www.careers-in-finance.com
CFO.com	http://www.cfo.com
CFOEurope.com	http://www.cfoeurope.com

CFO and CPA Jobs	http://www.cfoandcpajobs.com
CFO Publishing	http://cfonet.com
eFinancial Careers	http://www.efinancialcareers.com
eFinancialCareers.fr [France]	http://www.efinancialcareers.fr
The Finance Beat	http://www.search-beat.com/finance.htm
Finance and Commerce	http://www.finance-commerce.com
Finance Job Network	http://www.financialjobnet.com
Finance Job Store	http://www.financejobstore.com
FinanceJobs.net	http://www.financejobs.net
Financial Executives Institute Career Center	http://www.financialexecutives.org
Financial Executive Networking Group	http://www.thefeng.org
Financial Job Bank	http://www.financialjobbank.com
Financial Job Network	http://www.fjn.com
FinancialJobs.com	http://www.financialjobs.com
Financial Management Association International Placement Services	http://www.fma.org/Placement
Financial Managers Society Career Center	http://www.fmsinc.org/default.aspx
Financial Positions	http://www.financialpositions.com/Main/Default.asp
Financial Women International Careers	http://www.fwi.org
Fortune	http://money.cnn.com/magazines/fortune
Ft.com -Financial Times [United Kingdom]	http://www.ft.com
GAAP Web [United Kingdom]	http://www.gaapweb.com
Healthcare Financial Management Association	http://www.hfma.org
iHire Finance	http://www.ihirefinance.com
JobWings.com	http://www.jobwings.com
JobsFinancial.com [United Kingdom]	http://www.jobsfinancial.com
jobsinthemoney.com	http://www.jobsinthemoney.com
TheLadders.com	http://www.theladders.com
NationJob Network: Financial Jobs Page	http://www.nationjob.com/financial
PfJobs [United Kingdom]	http://www.pfjobs.co.uk

QUANTster.com [United Kingdom]	http://www.quantster.com
Smart Pros FinanceJobs.com	http://accounting.smartpros.com/x10522.xml

Financial Analysis

Actuary.com	http://www.actuary.com
Alliance of Merger and Acquisition Advisors	http://www.amaaonline.com
American Association for Budget and Program Analysis	http://www.aabpa.org/main/careerdev.htm#jobs
Capital Markets Credit Analysts Society Resume Service	http://www.cmcas.org
CFA Institute	http://www.cfainstitute.org
Global Association of Risk Professionals Career Center	http://www.garp.com/careercenter/index.asp
Hedge Fund Intelligence LLC [United Kingdom]	http://www.hedgefundintelligence.com
JobsinRisk.com [United Kingdom]	http://www.jobsinrisk.com
QuantFinanceJobs.com	http://www.quantfinancejobs.com
QUANTster.com	http://www.quantster.com
Risk & Insurance Management Society Careers	http://www.rims.org/resources/careercenter/Pages/default.aspx
Risk Management Web	http://www.riskmanagementweb.com
Toronto Society of Financial Analysts [Canada]	http://www.tsfa.ca
UnderwritingJobs.com	http://www.uwjobs.com

Finance-Banking

American Bankers Association	http://aba.careerbank.com
BankingBoard.com	http://www.bankingboard.com
BankJobs	http://www.bankjobs.com
Canadian Association of Accredited Mortgage Professionals	http://www.caamp.org
CreditJobs.com	http://creditjobs.com/index.asp
CreditUnionBoard.com	http://www.creditunionboard.net
Escrowboard.com	http://www.escrowboard.net
FindMortgageJobs.com	http://www.findmortgagejobs.com

JobsinCredit [United Kingdom]	http://www.jobsincredit.com
MortgageBoard.com	http://www.mortgageboard.com
MortgageCareers.org	http://www.mortgagecareers.org
Mortgage Job Store	http://www.mortgagejobstore.com
National Banking Network	http://www.banking-financejobs.com
Titleboard.net	http://www.titleboard.net

Finance-Controller

Cash Management Career Center	http://www.amgi.com
Controller Jobs	http://www.controllerjobs.com

Finance-Other

BookkeeperJobs.com	http://www.bookkeeperjobs.com
Fund Raising Jobs	http://www.fundraisingjobs.com
Healthcare Financial Management Association	http://www.hfma.org
IFSjobs.com	http://www.ifsjobs.com
JobsinCredit [United Kingdom]	http://www.jobsincredit.com
JobsinRisk.com [United Kingdom]	http://www.jobsinrisk.com
MBA Careers	http://www.mbacareers.com
MBA-Exchange.com	http://www.mba-exchange.com
MBA Free Agents	http://www.mbafreeagents.com
MBAGlobalNet	http://www.mbaglobalnet.com
MBAJobs.net	http://www.mbajobs.net/
MBAmatch.com [England]	http://www.mbamatch.com
MBA Style Magazine	http://www.mbastyle.com
MBATalentWire.com	http://www.mbatalentwire.com
National Black MBA Association, Inc.	http://www.nbmbaa.org
National Society of Hispanic MBAs Career Center	http://www.nshmba.org

Real Estate Finance Jobs   http://www.realestatefinancejobs.com

Smart Money   http://www.smartmoney.com

Tax

CareersinAudit [Europe]   http://www.careersinaudit.com/home/home.aspx

Planet Audit [United Kingdom]   http://www.planetaudit.net

eTaxjobs.com   http://www.etaxjobs.com

Tax Jobs   http://www.taxjobs.com

Tax Jobs Chicago   http://www.taxjobschicago.com

Tax-Talent.com   http://www.tax-talent.com

Free Lance/Free Agents

AF Work   http://www.allfreelancework.com

AllFreeLance.com   http://www.allfreelance.com

American Society of Journalists & Authors   http://www.freelancewritersearch.com

Editorial Freelancers Association   http://www.the-efa.org

eLance   http://www.elance.com

FreeLanceMom.com   http://www.freelancemom.com

FreeLanceWriting.com   http://www.freelancewriting.com

FreeLancers Network [United Kingdom]   http://www.freelancers.net

Freelancer   http://www.freelancer.com

FreeLancingProjects.com   http://www.freelancingprojects.com

Go Freelance   http://www.gofreelance.com

Guru.com   http://www.guru.com

HotGigs.com   http://www.hotgigs.com

iFreelance.com   http://www.ifreelance.com

Real-Home-Employment   http://www.real-home-employment.com

RentaCoder.com   http://www.vworker.com

SoloGig   http://www.sologig.com

Training Consortium   http://www.trainingconsortium.net

Telecommuting Jobs   http://www.tjobs.com

Funeral Industry/Services

Abbott and Hast Classifieds   http://www.abbottandhast.com/classads.html

FuneralNet   http://www.funeralnet.com

FuneralWire.com   http://www.funeralwire.com

National Funeral Directors Association   http://www.nfda.org

-G-

Gaming

BlueFoxJobs.com   http://www.bluefoxjobs.com

Casino Careers Online   http://www.casinocareers.com

CroupierLink.com   http://www.croupierlink.com

Game Jobs   http://www.gamejobs.com

General-All Career Fields, Industries & Locations

50kandup.com   http://jobs.50kandup.com

555-1212   http://www.555-1212.com

About Jobs   http://www.aboutjobs.com

Abracat   http://www.abracat.com

ActiJob   http://www.act1staff.com

Adicio   http://www.adicio.com

Adquest 3D   http://www.adquest3d.com

AECPII   http://www.aecpii.com

Alianza (Latino)   http://www.alianza.org

AllStarJobs   http://www.allstarjobs.com

AmericanJobs.com	http://www.americanjobs.com
American Preferred Jobs	http://www.preferredjobs.com
AmpleJobs	http://www.amplejobs.com
Ants.com	http://www.ants.com
Any Who	http://www.anywho.com
Asianet	http://www.asianetglobal.com
Association Job Source	http://www.jobsourcenetwork.com
AssociationJobBoards.com	http://www.associationjobboards.com
Authoria	http://www.authoria.com
Available Jobs	http://www.availablejobs.com
BaseJobs.com [Canada]	http://www.basejobs.com
Bayt.com [United Arab Emirates]	http://www.bayt.com
BDOJobs.com	http://www.bdojobs.com
Best Jobs USA	http://www.bestjobsusa.com
Best Local Jobs	http://www.bestlocaljobs.com
Big Dog Hub	http://www.bigdoghub.com
Biz Journals	http://www.bizjournals.com/jobs
Black Career Women Online	http://www.bcw.org
THE BLACK COLLEGIAN Online	http://www.blackcollegian.com
BlowSearch	http://www.blowsearch.com
Blue Collar Jobs	http://www.bluecollarjobs.com
Boldface Jobs	http://www.boldfacejobs.com
Boston Globe	http://www.boston.com/bostonglobe
Branch Staff Online	http://www.branchstaffonline.com
Business Week Online	http://www.businessweek.com/managing/career
Career.com	http://www.career.com
CareerBoard	http://www.careerboard.com
CareerBuilder.com	http://www.careerbuilder.com
CareerLink.com	http://america.careerlink.com
Career Center	http://www.careercenters.com

The Career Connection	http://www.career-connection.com
CareerExposure	http://www.careerexposure.com
Careerfile.com	http://www.careerfile.com
Career Giant	http://www.careergiant.com
CareerLife Connection	http://www.careerlifeconnection.com
Career Magazine	http://www.careermag.com
Careermetasearch.com	http://www.careermetasearch.com
Career Network	http://www.career-network.com
Career Quest	http://careerquestusa.com
Career Resource Center	http://www.careers.org
CareerShop	http://www.autohiresoftware.com
Careers.org	http://www.careers.org
Career Span	http://careerspan.com/hc3.asp
Career Talk	http://www.careertalkguys.com
Career Xchange	http://www.careerxchange.com
CareerMVP.com	http://www.careermvp.com
CBCJobs.com	http://www.cbcjobs.com
Chain Store Guide	http://www.chainstoreguide.com
Chattanooga Publishing	http://www.chatpub.com
Chowk	http://www.chowk.com
City Search.com	http://www.citysearch.com
Classifieds 2000	http://www.classifieds2000.com
Classified Solutions Group	http://www.classifiedsolutionsgroup.com
Community Associations Institute	http://www.caionline.org/Pages/Default.aspx
Contract Employment Connection	http://www.ntes.com
Contract-Jobs.com	http://www.contract-jobs.com
craigslist	http://www.craigslist.org
Creative Hotlist	http://www.creativehotlist.com
Customer Service Management	http://www.csm-us.co
Cuzie Corporation	http://www.cuzie.com

Daily Digest	http://www.le-digest.com
Database America	http://www.infousa.com
Delphi Forums	http://delphi.com
DirectEmployers Association	http://www.directemployers.org
Direct Marketing Association	http://www.the-dma.org/careercenter
Diversity Careers	http://www.diversitycareers.com
Diversity Employment	http://www.diversityemployment.com
DiversityLink	http://www.diversitylink.com
Diversity Search	http://www.diversitysearch.com
eBullpen.com	http://www.ebullpen.com
e-learning Jobs	http://www.e-learningjobs.com
ePage Internet Classifieds	http://epage.com
eCom Recruitment	http://www.ecomrecruitment.com
eJobResource.com	http://www.ejobresource.com
Employers Online	http://www.employersonline.com
Employmax	http://www.employmax.com
Employment	http://www.employment.com
Employment-inc.com	http://www.employment-inc.com
Employment 911	http://www.employment911.com
EmploymentGuide.com	http://www.employmentguide.com
EmploymentSource	http://www.employmentsource.net
Employment Spot	http://www.employmentspot.com
Employment Weekly	http://www.employment-weekly.com
eNeighborhoods	http://www.eneighborhoods.com
The EPages Classifieds	http://www.ep.com
Ephron Taylor	http://ephren.typepad.com
First Market Research	http://firstmarket.com
FlipDog.com	http://www.flipdog.com
4Jobs	http://www.4jobs.com
Fresh Jobs	http://www.freshjobs.comemp/Home

Friday-Ad [United Kingdom]	http://www.friday-ad.co.uk
Fun Jobs	http://www.funjobs.com
Future Access Employment Guide	http://www.futureaccess.com
Garage.com	http://www.garage.com
Get A Job	http://www.getajob.com
GettheJob	http://www.getthejob.com
Go Jobs	http://www.gojobs.com
Google.com	http://www.google.com
Got A Job	http://www.gotajob.com
HelpWanted	http://www.helpwanted.com
Help-Wanted.net	http://www.help-wanted.net
Hire Web	http://www.hireweb.comHW2CP.aspx
Hiring Network	http://www.hiringnetwork.com/common/tips.asp
How2FindAJob.com	http://www.how2findajob.com
Hot Resumes	http://www.hotresumes.com
Hennepin County Job Openings	http://www.co.hennepin.mn.us
HispanicBusiness.com	http://www.hispanicbusiness.com
100 Hot	http://www.100hot.com
Human-Intelligence.com	http://www.human-intelligence.com
iHireJobNetwork	http://www.iHireJobNetwork.com
Ideal Jobs.com	http://www.idealjobs.com
InfoSpace.com	http://www.infospace.com/ispace/ws/index
Insta Match	http://www.instamatch.com
International Career Employment Center	http://www.internationaljobs.org
International Customer Service Association Job Board	http://www.icsatoday.org
Internet Career Connection	http://www.iccweb.com
Internet Traffic Report	http://www.internettrafficreport.com
Iowa Smart Idea	http://www.smartcareermove.com
Job.com	http://www.job.com
Job Ads1	http://www.jobads1.com

JobaLot	http://www.jobalot.com
Job Animal	http://www.jobanimal.com
JobBank	http://www.jobbank.com
JobBank USA	http://www.jobbankusa.com
Job Catalog	http://www.jobcatalog.com
JobCenterUSA.com	http://www.jobcenterusa.com
JobCentral	http://www.jobcentral.com
JobCrank.com	http://www.jobcrank.com
JobDango	http://www.jobdango.com
JobDig	http://www.jobdig.com
JobDiscover.com	http://www.jobdiscover.com
Job Exchange	http://www.jobexchange.com
JobFind.com	http://www.bostonherald.com/jobfind
Job Fly	http://www.jobfly.com
Job Front	http://www.jobfront.com
Job-Hunt	http://www.job-hunt.org
Job Hunt	http://www.jobhunt.com
Jobing.com	http://www.jobing.com
JobisJob	http://www.jobisjob.com
Job Launch	http://www.joblaunch.com
Job Lynx	http://www.muchbetterjobs.com
Job Master	http://www.rvp.com/jh
JobNewsRadio.com	http://www.jobnewsradio.com
JobOpenings	http://www.jobopenings.net
Job Point Connection	http://www.jobpoint.com
Job Safari	http://www.jobsafari.com
Job SAT	http://www.jobsat.com
Job-Search-Engine	http://www.job-search-engine.com
JobSeekUSA.com	http://www.jobseekusa.com
Job Sleuth	http://www.jobsleuth.com

Job Sniper	http://www.jobsniper.com
JobSpin.com	http://www.jobspin.com
Job Star	http://jobstar.org/index.php
JobTarget	http://www.jobtarget.com
Jobvertise	http://www.jobvertise.com
Jobs.com	http://www.jobs.com
Jobs Inc.	http://www.jobsinc.com
Jobs+	http://www.jobsplus.org
Jobs America	http://www.us.plusjobs.com
Jobs at Corporations	http://www.searchbeat.com/jobs2.htm
JobsDB [Hong Kong]	http://www.jobsdb.com
JobsDirectUSA	http://www.jobsdirectusa.com
JobsGroup.net	http://www.jobsgroup.net
Jobs Online	http://www.jobsonline.net
Jobs on the Web	http://www.jobsontheweb.com
LatPro	http://www.latpro.com
Liszt	http://www.topica.com
LocalCareers	http://www.localcareers.com
LocalJobNetwork	http://www.localjobnetwork.com
Local Jobs	http://www.localjobs.com
LocalOpenings.com	http://www.localopenings.com
Lycos City Guide	http://lycos.oodle.com/cities
Mail.com	http://corp.mail.com
MegaJobSites	http://www.megajobsites.com
Meta Crawler	http://www.metacrawler.com
Minorities Job Bank	http://www.imdiversity.com
Minority Career Network	http://www.minoritycareernet.com
Monitor	http://www.monitordaily.com
Monster.com	http://www.monster.com
My Job Search	http://www.myjobsearch.com

MySpace	http://www.myspace.com/careers
NationCareer	http://www.nationcareer.com
National Diversity Newspaper Job Bank	http://www.newsjobs.net
NationJob Network	http://www.nationjob.com
NationJobSearch.com	http://www.nationjob.com
Nationwide Consultants	http://www.nationwideconsultants.com
Neighbor Works Net	http://www.nw.org/network/home.asp
NetNoir	http://www.netnoir.com
Net-Temps	http://www.net-temps.com
NewYorkJobs.com	http://www.newyorkjobs.com
NicheClassifieds.com	http://www.nicheclassifieds.com
NicheJobs.com	http://www.nichejobs.com
NotchUp.com	http://www.notchup.com/c/home
NowHiring.com	http://www.nowhiring.com
1to1media.com	http://www.1to1media.com
Online-Jobs	http://www.online-jobs.com
Only-Jobs	http://www.only-jobs.com
PageBites.com	http://www.pagebites.com
People Bank	http://www.peoplebank.com
Personnel Department	http://www.careermachine.com
PlanetRecruit [United Kingdom]	http://www.planetrecruit.com
PlugStar.com	http://www.plugstar.com
PreferredJobs	http://www.preferredjobs.com
Pro Hire.com	http://jobs.prohire.com
QuietHire	http://www.quiethire.com
Quintessential Careers	http://quintcareers.com/index.html
RecruiterConnection	http://www.recruiterconnection.com
Recruiters Online	http://www.recruitersonline.com
Recruiting Shark	http://www.recruitingshark.com
ReferTalent.com	http://www.refertalent.com

RegionalHelpWanted.com	http://www.regionalhelpwanted.com
Rep Resources	http://www.represources.com
Resume Blaster	http://www.resumeblaster.com
ResumeXPRESS	http://www.resumexpress.com
ResumeRabbit.com	http://www.resumerabbit.com
Resumes on the Web	http://www.resweb.com
Resumes2work.com	http://www.resumes2work.com
Resunet	http://www.resunet.com
RetiredBrains	http://www.retiredbrains.com
Revolution.net	http://www.revolution.net
Saludos Web Site	http://www.saludos.com
Searchease	http://www.searchease.com
Second Life Jobfinder	http://www.SLJobFinder.com
See Me Resumes	http://www.seemeresumes.com
Select Minds	http://www.selectminds.com
Skill Hunter	http://www.skillhunter.com
Smuz.com	http://www.smuz.com
Start Up Jobs	http://www.startupjobs.com
Start Up Zone	http://www.startupzone.com
Starting Point	http://www.stpt.com
State Jobs	http://statejobs.com
The Sunday Paper	http://www.sundaypaper.com
SwapJobs.com	http://www.swapjobs.com
Talentology	http://www.peoplefilter.com
Talent Technology	http://www.peoplefilter.com
TargetedJobSites.com	http://www.jobhill.com
Telecommuting Jobs	http://www.tjobs.com
Teleplaza	http://www.teleplaza.com
TeleportJobs.com	http://www.teleportjobs.com
TopJobUSA	http://www.topjobusa.com

Thingama Job	http://www.thingamajob.com
TopUSAJobs	http://www.topusajobs.com
Totaljobs.com	http://www.totaljobs.com
TNTJobz.net	http://www.tntjobz.net
Tripod	http://www.tripod.lycos.com
Union Jobs Clearinghouse	http://www.unionjobs.com
United States Department of Labor	http://www.dol.gov
UpSeek	http://www.upseek.com
US Jobs	http://www.usjobs.com
USJobNet.com	http://www.usjobnet.com
Vault	http://www.vault.com/wps/portal/usa
Vertical Net	http://www.bravosolution.com/cms/us
Virtual Recruiting Network	http://www.dmpmail.com
The Wall Street Journal Careers Page	http://online.wsj.com/public/page/news-career-jobs.html
Web Crawler	http://www.webcrawler.com
Web Reference	http://www.webreference.com
Wetfeet	http://www.wetfeet.com
Wiserworker.com	http://www.wiserworker.com
Womenswire	http://www.womenswire.net
Work at Home Digest	http://www.workathomedigest.com
WorkLife.com	http://www.worklife.com
Work-Web	http://www.work-web.com
Working.ca [Canada]	http://www.working.ca
Workopolis [Canada]	http://www.workopolis.com
The World Wide Web Employment Office	http://www.employmentoffice.net
WorldWorkz.com	http://www.worldworkz.com
Yahoo! HotJobs	http://www.hotjobs.yahoo.com
Yep.com	http://www.yep.com

Graphic Arts/Electronic & Traditional
(See also Journalism & Media)

ACM Siggraph	http://www.siggraph.org
3DSite	http://www.3dsite.com
Adrecruiter	http://www.adrecruiter.com
American Institute of Graphic Arts	http://www.aiga.org
Animation Industry Database	http://www.aidb.com
Animation World Network	http://www.awn.com
Association for Computing Machinery Special Interest Grp Computer Graphics	http://www.siggraph.org
Capital Communicator	http://www.capitalcommunicator.com
CG Society/society of Digital Artists [Australia]	http://www.gcsociety.org
Communication Arts Magazine	http://www.commarts.com
Communications Round Table	http://www.roundtable.org
Computer Graphics + Animation + Visual Effects Job Board	http://www.cggigs.com
Contracted Work	http://www.contractedwork.com
Copy Editor Newsletter	http://jobs.copyeditor.com/home/index.cfm?site_id=502
Coroflot	http://www.coroflot.com
CreativeHeads.net	http://www.creativeheads.net
CreativeShake.com	http://www.creativeshake.com
DesignJobs.co.uk [United Kingdom]	http://www.designjobs.co.uk
Design Sphere Online Job Hunt	http://www.dsphere.net
Desktop Publishing	http://desktoppublishing.com
DigitalMediaJobs.com [United Kingdom]	http://www.digitalmediajobs.com
FolioMag.com	http://www.foliomag.com
Freelance BBS	http://www.freelancebbs.com
GamesIndustry.biz	http://www.gamesindustry.biz
Get a FreeLancer	http://www.freelancer.com
Graphic Artists Guild JobLine	http://www.graphicartistsguild.org
Graphic Design Freelance Jobs	http://www.graphicdesignfreelancejobs.com

iFreelance	http://www.ifreelance.com
Interior Design Jobs	https://interiordesignjobs.sellisp.com/Default.asp
Media Lab	http://www.media.mit.edu
Media Street.com	http://www.mediastreet.com
Mip Map	http://www.mipmap.com
National Association of Printing Ink Manufacturers	http://www.napim.org
Noble Desktop	http://www.nobledesktop.com
PaidContent.org	http://jobs.paidcontent.org
Print Jobs	http://www.printjobs.com
PrintWorkers.com	http://www.printworkers.com
Printing Careers	http://www.printingcareers.com
Screenprinting & Graphic Imaging Association International	http://www.sgia.org/employment
Silicon Alley Insider	http://jobs.businessinsider.com
VFXWorld	http://www.vfxworld.com

-H-

Healthcare/Medical

Healthcare-General

Absolutely Health Care	http://www.healthjobsusa.com
AdvanceWeb	http://www.advanceweb.com
Allegheny County Medical Society	http://www.acms.org
AllHealthcareJobs.com	http://www.allhealthcarejobs.com
America's Health Care Source	http://www.healthcaresource.com
American Health Care Association	http://careers.ahcancal.org
American Medical Association JAMACareerNet	http://jamacareernet.ama-assn.org
American Public Health Association CareerMart	http://careers.apha.org
ANEScareer.com	http://www.anescareer.com

CARDIOcareer.com	http://www.cardiocareer.com
Centers for Disease Control	http://www.cdc.gov
Chicago Medical Society	http://www.cmsdocs.org
Connecticut State Medical Society	http://careers.csms.org
Discover Jobs	http://www.discover-jobs.com
District of Columbia Health Care Association	http://careers.dchca.org
ElsevierHealthCareers.com	http://www.elsevierhealthcareers.com
EMcareer.com	http://www.emcareer.com
ENT-career.com	http://www.ent-career.com
FocusonHealthcare.com	http://www.focusonhealthcare.com
FPCareer.com	http://www.fpcareer.com
GASTROcareer.com	http://www.gastrocareer.com
Georgia Department of Human Resources	http://www.dhrjobs.com
GovMedCareers.com	http://www.govmedcareers.com
GreenLeg.com	http://www.greenleg.com
GxPJobs.com [United Kingdom]	http://www.gxpjobs.com
Harris County Medical Society	http://www.hcms.org/Template.aspx?id=4
HealthAndWellnessJobs.com	http://www.healthandwellnessjobs.com
Healthcare Businesswomen's Association	http://www.hbanet.org/home.aspx
HealthcareCareerWeb.com	http://www.healthcarecareerweb.com
Healthcare Jobs on Display	http://www.healthcarejobsondisplay.com
Health Care Jobs Online	http://www.hcjobsonline.com
Health Care Match	http://www.healthcarematch.com
Health Care Hiring	http://www.healthcarehiring.com
HealthCare Job Store	http://www.healthcarejobstore.com
Healthcare/Monster	http://monster.com
HealthCareRecruitment.com	http://www.healthcarerecruitment.com
Health Care Seeker	http://www.healthcareseeker.com
HealthcareSource	http://www.healthcaresource.com
Healthcare Traveler Jobs	http://www.healthcaretravelerjobs.com

HealthCareerWeb.com	http://www.healthcareerweb.com
HEALTHeCAREERS	http://assoc.healthecareers.com
Health Direction	http://www.healthdirection.com
HealthJobsNationwide.com	http://www.healthjobsnationwide.com
HealthJobsPlus.com	http://www.healthjobsplus.com
HealthJobsUK.com [United Kingdom]	http://www.healthjobsuk.com/select_sector
HealthJobsUSA.com	http://www.healthjobsusa.com
Health Network USA	http://www.unitedsearch.com
Health Seek.com	http://www.healthseek.com
HealthOpps	http://healthcare.careerbuilder.co
HireBio.com	http://www.hirebio.com
HireRX.com	http://www.hirerx.com
HireMedical.com	http://www.hiremedical.com
HireMedics.com	http://www.hiremedics.com
HireNursing.com	http://www.hirenursing.com
HireCentral.com	http://www.hirecentral.com
HOSPITALISTcareer.com	http://www.hospitalistcareer.com
IMcareer.com	http://www.imcareer.com
IMNGMedJobs.com	http://careers.imngmedjobs.com/jobs/browse
Jobscience Network	http://jobs.jobscience.com
Job Span	http://www.jobspan.com
Jobs4Healthcare.com	http://www.jobs4healthcare.com
Jobs4Medical.com	http://www.jobs4medical.com
JobsinHealth [United Kingdom]	http://www.jobsinhealth.co.uk
Jobs in Healthcare	http://www.jobsinhealthcare.com
JobsinNHS [United Kingdom]	http://www.jobsinnhs.co.uk
Louisiana State Medical Society	http://careers.lsms.org
Med Careers	http://www.medcareers.com
Med Connect	http://www.medconnect.com
MedHunters	http://www.medhunters.com

MedHunting.com	http://www.medhunting.com
MedJobFind.com	http://medjobfind.com
MedLaunch	http://www.medlaunch.com
MedMarket	http://www.medical-admart.com
MedReps.com	http://www.medreps.com
MedicSolve.com [United Kingdom]	http://www.medicsolve.com
Medical AdMart	http://www.medical-admart.com
Medical Design Online	http://www.medicaldesignonline.com
MedicalJobList.com	http://www.medicaljoblist.com
Medical Matrix	http://www.medmatrix.org
Medical Society of New York - Sixth District Branch	http://www.jobbank.medsocieties.org
Miedical Society of Virginia	http://jobboard.msv.org
Medical Words	http://www.md123.com
MedicalWorkers.com	http://www.medicalworkers.com
Medicenter.com	http://www.medicenter.com
Medi-Smart	http://www.medi-smart.com/renal4.htm
MEDopportunities.com	http://www.medopportunities.com
MEDSTER.com	http://www.medster.com
MedHunting.com	http://www.medhunting.com
MedWorking.com	http://www.medworking.com
Medzilla	http://www.medzilla.com
Minnesota Medical Association	http://careercenter.mnmed.org
Modern Healthcare	http://www.modernhealthcare.com
Modern Medicine	http://www.modernmedicine.com
MyHealthJobs.com	http://www.myhealthjobs.com
The National Assembly	http://www.nassembly.org
National Association for Health Care Recruitment	http://www.nahcr.com
National Healthcare Career Network	http://www.nhcnnetwork.com
National Medical Association	http://career.nmanet.org
National Rural Health Association	http://careers.ruralhealthweb.org

National Rural Recruitment & Retention Network	http://www.3rnet.org
NEPHcareer.com	http://www.nephcareer.com
NEUROcareer.com	http://www.neurocareer.com
New England Journal of Medicine	http://content.nejm.org
New Mexico Medical Society	http://healthcarecareers.nmms.org
North Carolina Medical Society	http://careers.ncmedsoc.org
TheNursingJobsite.com [United Kingdom]	http://www.thenursingjobsite.com
OBGYNcareer.com	http://www.obgyncareer.com
Oklahoma State Medical Association	http://www.osmaonline.org
ONCOLOGYcareer.com	http://www.oncologycareer.com
OnlyLTCjobs.com	http://www.onlyltcjobs.com
Orleans Parish Medical Society	http://www.opms.org
Pennsylvania Medical Society	http://jobbank.pamedsoc.org
PeopleMenders.com	http://www.peoplemenders.com
Pflegekarriere.de [Germany]	http://www.pflegekarriere.de
PharmaTalentPool.com [United Kingdom]	http://www.pharmatalentpool.com
PhysicianCareerJobs.com	http://www.physiciancareerjobs.com
Public Health Service Jobs	http://www.usphs.gov
RealMedical.com	http://www.realmedical.com
San Bernardino County Medical Society / Riverside County Medical Society	http://healthcarecareers.sbcms.org
South Carolina Medical Association	http://careers.scmedical.org
Texas Medical Association	http://www.texmed.org
Utah Medical Association	http://docjobs.utahmed.org
West Virginia Health Care Association	http://careers.wvhca.org
Wisconsin Medical Society	http://www.wisconsinmedicalsociety.org

Acute Care/Critical Care/Intensive Care

American Association of Critical Care Nurses	http://www.aacn.org
JobICU.com	http://www.jobicu.com
Jobscience Network	http://jobs.jobscience.com

| Society of Critical Care Medicine | http://careercentral.sccm.org |

Addiction/Substance Abuse

Addiction Medicine Jobs	http://www.addictionmedicinejobs.com
American Academy of Health Care Providers in the Addictive Disorders	http://careers.americanacademy.org
Substance Abuse Jobs	http://www.substanceabusejobs.com
American Society of Addiction Medicine	http://careers.asam.org

Administration/Management

American Academy of Medical Administrators	http://joblink.aameda.org
American Association of Orthopaedic Executives	http://careers.aaoe.net
American College of Healthcare Executives	http://ache.org
American College of Physician Executives	http://www.acpe.org
American Society for Healthcare Human Resource Management	http;//careers.ashhra.org
American Society for Healthcare Risk Management	http://careers.ashrm.org
Association of Staff Physician Recruiters	http://www.aspr.org
College of Healthcare Information Management Executives	http://www.cio-chime.org
Commission for Case Manager Certification	http://careercenter.ccmcertification.org
Grist.org	http://jobs.grist.org
Healthcare Businesswomen's Association	http:careers.hbanet.org
Healthcare Financial Management Association	http://www.hfma.org
Healthcaare Human Resources Management Association of California	http://careers.hhrmac.org
Healthcare Information and Management Systems	http://www.himss.org/ASP/index.asp
Healthline Management	http://www.hmistl.com
Managed Healthcare Executive	http://managedhealthcareexecutive.modernmedicine.com
Massachusetts Healthcare Human Resources Association	http://www.mhhra.org
Medical Case Management Jobs	http://www.casemanagementjobs.com

Medical-Dental-Hospital Business Association   http://www.mdhba.org

Medical Economics   http://www.modernmedicine.com/
                                                   practicemanagement

Medical Group Management Association   http://www.mgma.com

Medical Transcription Jobs   http://www.mtjobs.com

National Association of Health Services Executives http://careers.nahse.org

National Association of Healthcare Transport   http://careers.nahtm.org
Management

National Association of Medical Staff Services   http://careers.namss.org

NursingExecutives.com   http://www.nursingexecutives.com

Professional Association of Health Care Office   http://careercenter.pahcom.com
Management

Radiology Business Management Association   http://www.rbma.org

Rehab Management   http://www.rehabpub.com

Senior Housing Jobs   http://www.seniorhousingjobs.com

Society for Radiation Oncology Administrators   http://careers.sroa.org

Allied Health

Allied Health Jobs   http://www.alliedhealthjobs.com

Allied Health Opportunities Directory   http://www.gvpub.com

Allied Travel Careers   http://www.alliedtravelcareers.com

DiversityAlliedHealth.com   http://www.diversityalliedhealth.com

Anesthesiology

American Society of PeriAnesthesia Nurses   http://www.aspan.org

ANEScareer.com   http://www.anescareer.com

CRNAjobs.com   http://www.crnajobs.com

Gas Jobs   http://www.gasjobs.com

IConnect2Anesthesiology.com   http://www.iconnect2anesthesiology.com

Cardiology

American College of Cardiology   http://www.acc.org

American College of Cardiology - Alabama Chapter — http://careers.alacc.org

American College of Cardiology - Arizona Chapter — http://careers.acc-az.org

American College of Cardiology - California Chapter — http://careers.caacc.org

American College of Cardiology - Colorado Chapter — http://careers.coloradoacc.org

American College of Cardiology - Florida Chapter — http://careers.accfl.org

American College of Cardiology - Indiana Chapter — http://careers.inacc.org

American College of Cardiology - Iowa Chapter — http://careers.iaacc.org

American College of Cardiology - Maryland Chapter — http://cardio-careers.marylandacc.org

American College of Cardiology - Michigan Chapter — http://careers.accmi.org

American College of Cardiology - Missouri Chapter — http://careers.moacc.org

American College of Cardiology - North Carolina Chapter — http://careercenter.ncacc.org

American College of Cardiology - Ohio Chapter — http://careers.ohioacc.org

American College of Cardiology - Pennsylvania Chapter — http://careers.pcacc.org

American College of Cardiology - Virginia Chapter — http://cardio-careers.vcacc.org

American College of Cardiology - Washington State Chapter — http://careers.accwa.org

American College of Cardiology - West Virginia Chapter — http://careers.accwv.org

American Association of Cardiovascular and Pulmonary Rehabilitation — http://www.aacvpr.org

Association of Black Cardiologists — http://careers.abcardio.org/

CARDIOcareer.com — http://www.cardiocareer.com

Cardiologist Jobs — http://www.cardiologistjobs.com

Cardioworking.com — http://www.cardioworking.com

Heart Rhythm Society — http://careers.hrsonline.org

Jobscience Network — http://jobs.jobscience.com

Ear, Nose & Throat

American College of Audiology HearCareers — http://hearcareers.audiology.org

American Speech-Language-Hearing Career Center — http://www.asha.org/careers

ENT-career.com — http://www.ent-career.com

Hearing Review — http://www.hearingreview.com

Emergency Medicine

EMcareer.com — http://www.emcareer.com

Emergency Medical Services Association of Colorado — http://jobs.emsac.org

Emergency Medicine Residents Association — http://www.emra.org

Emergency Nurses Association — http://enacareercenter.ena.org

Equipment-Healthcare

American Medical Technologists — http://www.amtl.com

Device Space — http://www.devicespace.com

Emedcareers — http://www.emedcareers.com

iHireMedTechs.com — http://www.ihiremedtechs.com

MDL Career Center — http://careercenter.devicelink.com

Medical Device Manufacturers Association Career Center — http://careers.medicaldevices.org

Medical Device Star — http://www.medicaldevicestar.com

PharmaOpportunities — http://www.pharmaopportunites.com

Hospital

AHACareerCenter.org (American Hospital Association) — http://www.ahacareercenter.org

American Hospital Association — http://careers.aha.org

Arizona Hospital and Healthcare Association AZHealthJobs — http://www.azhha.org

CareerHospital.com — http://www.careerhospital.com

Children's Hospital Association — http://careers.childrenshospitals.net

Colorado Health and Hospital Association — http://www.cha.com

Colorado Hospital Association — http://healthcarecareers.cha.com

Connecticut Hospital Association — http://www.chime.org

Health Facilities Association of Maryland — http://careers.hfam.org

Hospital Association of Sourthern California — http://careers.allhealthinc.com

Hospital Dream Jobs — http://www.hospitaldreamjobs.com

Hospital Jobs Online — http://www.hospitaljobsonline.com

HospitalSoup.com — http://www.hospitalsoup.com

Hospital Web	http://www.hospitallink.com
JobHospital.com	http://www.jobhospital.com
Kansas Hospital Association	http://kshealthjobs.net
Maryland Hospital Association	http://healthcarecareers.mhaonline.org
Medical-Dental-Hospital Business Association	http://www.mdhba.org
Metropolitan Chicago Healthcare Council	http://careerboard.mchc.org
Michigan Health & Hospital Association	http://careers.mha.org
New Jersey Hospital Association	http://healthjobs.njha.com
New Mexico Hospital Association	http://careers.nmhanet.org
Physicians Hospitals of America	http://www.physicianhospitals.org/?CareerOpportunities
Society of Hospital Medicine Career Center	http://www.hospitalmedicine.org
South Florida Hospital and Healthcare Association	http://healthcareers.sfhha.com

Information Management/Systems

American Health Information Management Association CareerAssist	http://careerassist.ahima.org
Association for Healthcare Documentation Integrity	http://careerconnection.ahdionline.org
Healthcare Information and Management Systems Society JobMine	http://jobmine.himss.org

International

CanMed [Canada]	http://www.canmed.com
DERWeb [United Kingdom]	http://www.derweb.co.uk
EMBL Job Vacancies [Germany]	http://www.embl.de
HUM-MOLGEN [Germany]	http://www.hum-molgen.org/positions
International Association of Forensic Nurses	http://careercenter.iafn.org
International Pediatric Transplant Association	http://careers.iptaonline.org
International Society for Pharmaceutical Engineering	http://www.ispe.org
International Society for Pharmacoepidemiology	http://careers.pharmacoepi.org
Medjobsuk.com [United Kingdom]	http://www.medjobsuk.com
Opportunities Online [United Kingdom]	http://www.opps.co.uk

Midwife/Child Birth

American College of Nurse Midwives	http://www.acnw.org
Lamaze International	careers.lamaze.org
MidwifeJobs	http://assoc.healthecareers.com
NMC4Jobs.com [United Kingdom]	http://www.nmc4jobs.com
Professional Information from the American College of Nurse-Midwives	http://www.midwife.org

Nurses/Nursing

Academy of Medical-Surgical Nurses	http://www.medsurgnurse.org
AllNurses.com	http://allnurses.com
American Academy of Ambulatory Care Nursing	http://www.aaacn.org
American Academy of Nurse Practitioners	http://www.aanp.org/AANPCMS2
American Assisted Living Nurses Association	http://careers.alnursing.org
American Association of Critical Care Nurses	http://www.aacn.org
American Association of Heart Failure Nurses	http://careers.aahfn.org
American Association of Managed Care Nurses	http://careers.aamcn.org
American Association of Neuroscience Nurses	http://careercenter.aann.org
American Association of Occupational Health Nurses	http://www.aaohn.org
American College of Nurse Midwives	http://www.acnw.org
American Nurses Association	http://www.nursingworld.org
American Psychiatric Nurses Association	http://www.apna.org
American Society of PeriAnesthesia Nurses	http://www.aspan.org
ANNAlink	http://anna.inurse.com
Association of Pediatric Hematology/Oncology Nurses	http://careercenter.aphon.org
Association of Perioperative Registered Nurses Online Career Center	http://careercenter.aorn.org
Association of Rehabilitation Nurses	http://careercenter.rehabnurse.org
Association of Women's Health, Obstetric & Neonatal Nurses	http://www.awhonn.org
Best Nurse Jobs	http://www.bestnursejobs.com
Camp Nurse Jobs	http://www.campnursejobs.com

CampusRN.com	http://www.campusrn.com
CRNA Jobs	http://www.crnajobs.com
Delaware Nurses Association	http://nursejobs.denurses.org
Dermatology Nurses Association	http://www.dnanurse.org
DiversityNursing.com	http://www.diversitynursing.com
Emergency Nurses Association	http://enacareercenter.ena.org
GraduateNurse.com	http://www.graduatenurse.com
Guaranteed Employment Advertising & Resume Service	http://www.nurse-recruiter.com
HappyCareer.com	http://www.happycareer.com
HealthJobsUSA.com	http://www.healthjobsusa.com
HireNursing.com	http://www.hirenursing.com
Hot Nurse Jobs	http://www.hotnursejobs.com
iHireNursing.com	http://www.ihirenursing.com
Illinois Nurses Association	http://careers.illinoisnurses.com
Infusion Nurses Society	http://careercenter.ins1.org
International Association of Forensic Nurses	http://careercenter.iafn.org
Jobscience Network	http://jobs.jobscience.com
Locum Tenens	http://www.locumtenens.com
MinorityNurse.com	http://www.minoritynurse.com
Mississippi Nurses Association	http://careers.msnurses.org
National Association of Hispanic Nurses Houston Chapter	http://www.nahnhouston.org
National Association of Neonatal Nurses	http://careercentral.nann.org
National Association of Orthopaedic Nurses	http://www.orthonurse.org
National Gerontological Nursing Association	http://careercenter.ngna.org
National League for Nursing	http://www.nln.org
National Rural Recruitment & Retention Network	http://www.3rnet.org
New Mexico Center for Nursing Excellence	http://healthcarecareers.nmnursingexcellence.org
Nurse.com	http://www.nurse.com
Nurse Director Jobs	http://www.directorofnursingjobs.com
NurseJobShop.com	http://www.nursejobshop.com

NurseJobs.com	http://www.nursejobs.com
NurseJobz.com	http://www.nursejobz.com
Nurse Manager Jobs	http://nursemanagerjobs.org
Nurse-Recruiter.com	http://www.nurse-recruiter.com
NurseTown.com	http://www.nursetown.com
NurseUniverse.com	http://www.nurseuniverse.com
NurseZone.com	http://www.nursezone.com
Nurseserve [United Kingdom]	http://www.nurserve.co.uk
Nurses for a Healthier Tomorrow	http://www.nursesource.org
NursingCareersToday.com	http://www.nursingcareerstoday.com
Nursing Center	http://www.nursingcenter.com
NursingExecutives.com	http://www.nursingexecutives.com
NursingJobs.com	http://www.nursingjobs.com
Nursing-Jobs.us	http://www.nursing-jobs.us
NursingMatters.com	http://www.rn.com
NursingNetUK [United Kingdom]	http://www.nursingnetuk.com
Ohio Nurses Association	http://jobs.ohiorncareers.com
Oncology Nursing Society	http://careers.ons.org/
Psychiatric Nurse Jobs	http://psychiatric.nurse.jobs.topusajobs.com
RN.com	http://www.rn.com
RN Journal	http://www.rnjournal.com
RNNetwork	http://www.rnnetwork.com
RNSearch.com	http://www.rnsearch.com
Society of Gastroenterology Nurses & Associates	http://www.sgna.org
TravelNurseSource.com	http://www.travelnursesource.com
TravelNursing.com	http://www.travelnursing.com
TravelNursingUSA.com	http://www.travelnursingusa.com

OBGYN

AdvancedPracticeJobs.com	http://www.healthjobsnationwide.com
American Association of Gynecologic Laparoscopists	http://www.aagl.org

American College of Obstetricians and Gynecologists	http://www.acog.org
Contemporary OBGYN	http://www.modernmedicine.com modernmedicine/Obstetrics/ Gynecology.*Women%27s.Health/home/40157
OBGYNCareer.com	http://www.obgyncareer.com
Obstetric Jobs	http://www.obstetricjobs.com

Oncology

American Society of Pediatric Hematology/Oncology	http://careercenter.aspho.org
American Society for Radiation Oncology	http://careers.astro.org
Association of Pediatric Hematology/Oncology Nurses	http://careercenter.aphon.org
CancerJobs.net [United Kingdom]	http://www.cancerjobs.net
ONCOLOGYcareer.com	http://www.oncologycareer.com
Society for Radiation Oncology Administrators	http://careers.sroa.org

Orthopaedic

American Association of Orthopaedic Executives	http://careers.aaoe.net
Connecticut Orthopaedic Society	http://careers.ctortho.org
Georgia Orthopaedic Society	http://careers.georgiaorthosociety.org
Iowa Orthopaedic Society	http://careers.iowaorthopaedic.org
Maryland Orthopaedic Association	http://jobboard.mdortho.org
North Carolina Orthopaedic Association	http://careers.ncorthopaedics.org
Ohio Orthopaedic Society	http://careers.ohioorthosociety.org
Pennsylvania Orthopaedic Society	http://careers.paorthosociety.org
West Virginia Orthopaedic Society	http://careers.wvos.org

Pediatrics

American Academy of Pediatrics PedJobs	http://jobs.pedjobs.org
American Academy of Pediatrics - Illinois Chapter	http://careers.illinoisaap.org
American Academy of Pediatrics - Kansas Chapter	http://jobboard.kansasaap.org
American Academy of Pediatrics - Kentucky Chapter	http://careercenter.kyaap.org
American Academy of Pediatics - Maine Chapter	http://careers.maineaap.org

American Academy of Pediatrics - Missouri Chapter   http://careers.moapp.org

American Academy of Pediatrics - Ohio Chapter   http://careers.ohioaap.org

American Academy of Pediatrics - Washington Chapter   http://careers.wcaap.org

American Academy of Pediatrics - Wisconsin Chapter   http://careers.wisapp.org

American Society of Pediatric Hematology/Oncology   http://careercenter.aspho.org

Association of Pediatric Hematology/Oncology Nurses   http://careercenter.aphon.org

Children's Hospital Association   http://careers.childrenshospitals.net

Contemporary Pediatrics   http://www.modernmedicine.com/modernmedicine/Pediatrics/home/40165

International Pediatric Transplant Association   http://careers.iptaonline.org

North Carolina Pediatric Society   http://www.ncpeds.org/job-listings

Pediatric Academic Societies   http://careers.pas-meeting.org

Pediatric Jobs   http://www.pediatricjobs.com

Society for Research in Child Development   http://careers.srcd.org

Pharmacist/Pharmacy (See also Pharmaceutical)

American Association of Pharmaceutical Scientists   http://www.aapspharmaceutica.com/index.asp

American Chemical Society   http://portal.acs.org/portal/acs/corg/content

American Pharmaceutical Association   http://www.pharmacist.com

American Society of Consultant Pharmacists   http://bt.myrxcareer.com/

Association for Applied Human Pharmacology [Germany]   http://www.agah.info

BioPharm International   http://www.biopharminternational.com

CenterWatch.com   http://www.centerwatch.com

ChemJobs.net   http://www.chemjobs.net/chemjobs.html

Drug Topics   http://www.drugtopics.modernmedicine.com

Elite Pharmacy Jobs   http://www.elitepharmacyjobs.com

FindPharma.com   http://www.findpharma.com

Formulary Journal   http://www.formularyjournal.modernmedicine.com

HireRX.com   http://www.hirerx.com

iHirePharmacy.com   http://www.ihirepharmacy.com

International Society for Pharmaceutical Engineering   http://www.ispe.org

International Society for Pharmacoepidemiology	http://careers.pharmacoepi.org
Pharmacareers.co.uk [United Kingdom]	http://www.pharmacareers.co.uk
Pharmaceutical Executive	http://www.pharmexec.com
Pharmaceutical Rep Jobs	http://pharmaceuticalrepjobs.org
Pharmacy Benefit Management Institute	http://careers.pbmi.com
PharmacyTimes	http://www.pharmacytimes.com
PharmacyWeek	http://www.pharmacyweek.com
PharmaOpportunities	http://www.pharmaopportunites.com
PharmaTalentPool [United Kingdom]	http://www.pharmatalentpool.com
Pharmiweb.com [United Kingdom]	http://www.pharmiweb.com
PharmTech.com	http://www.pharmtech.com
RPhRecruiter	http://www.rphrecruiter.com
RxCareerCenter	http://www.rxcareercenter.com
Rx Times Pharmacy Magazine	http://careers.rxtimes.com
RxWebportal	http://www.rxwebportal.com

Physical Therapy/Occupational Therapy

American Academy of Cardiovascular and Pulmonary Rehabilitation	http://www.aacvpr.org
American Academy of Physical Medicine & Rehabilitation Job Board	http://jobboard.aapmr.org
American Association of Occupational Health Nurses	http://www.aaohn.org
American College of Occupational and Environmental Medicine	http://www.acoem.org
American Occupational Therapy Association	http://www.aota.org
American Physical Therapy Association	http://www.apta.org
American Society of Clinical Pharmacology and Therapeutics	http://www.ascpt.org
Association of Rehabilitation Nurses	http://careercenter.rehabnurse.org
JobsforPTs.com	http://www.jobsforphysicaltherapists.com
JobsOT.com	http://www.jobsot.com
Louisiana Occupational Therapy Association	http://www.lota.org

PhysicalTherapist.com | http://www.physicaltherapist.com

Physical Therapist Jobs | http://www.physicaltherapistjobs.com

PT Central | http://www.ptcentral.com

PTjobs.com | http://www.ptjobs.com

Rehab License Network | http://www.rehablicense.com

Rehab Options | http://www.rehaboptions.com

RehabWorld | http://www.rehabworld.com

TherapyJobs.com | http://www.therapyjobs.com

UKTherapist.co.uk [United Kingdom] | http://www.uktherapist.co.uk

Physicians/Physician Assistants (See also Surgeons)

Academic Physician & Scientist | http://www.acphysci.com

Academy of Family Physicians CareerLink | http://www.aafpcareerlink.org

American Academy of Physician Assistants | http://www.aapa.org

American Board of Quality Assurance and Utilization Review Physicians | http://careers.abqaurp.org

American College of Chest Physicians | http://www.chestnet.org/accp

American College of Emergency Physicians | http://www.acep.org

American College of Osteopathic Family Physicians Career Center | http://www.acofp.org/Membership/Career_Center

American College of Osteopathic Emergency Physicians | http://careers.acoep.org/

American College of Physicians | http://www.acponline.org/career_connection

American College of Physician Executives | http://www.acpe.org

American Medical Association JAMA CareerCenter | http://jamacareernet.ama-assn.org

California Academy of Family Physicians | http://www.fpjobsonline.org

Colorado Academy of Family Physicians | http://www.fpjobsonline.org

Doc Job | http://www.boston.com/jobs/news/archive/job_doc

Doc on the Web | http://www.webdoc.com

DoctorWork.com | http://www.doctorwork.com

Ed Physician | http://www.edphysician.com

Florida Academy of Family Physicians | http://www.fpjobsonline.org

Florida Naturopathic Physicians Association	http://careers.fnpa.org
Georgia Academy of Family Physicians	http://www.fpjobsonline.org
iHirePhysicians.com	http://www.ihirephysicians.com
JAMA Career Center	http://www.jamacareercenter.com
Illinois Academy of Family Physicians	http://www.fpjobsonline.org
Locum Tenens	http://www.locumtenens.com
MD Job Site	http://www.mdjobsite.com
MD Search	http://www.mdsearch.com
MEDopportunities.com	http://www.medopportunities.com
Missouri Academy of Family Physicians	http://www.fpjobsonline.org
National Associatiion of Managed Care Physicians	http://careers.namcp.org
National Rural Recruitment & Retention Network	http://www.3rnet.org
New England Journal of Medicine Career Center	http://content.nejm.org
New York State Academy of Family Physicians	http://www.fpjobsonline.org
Pennsylvania Academy of Family Physicians	http://www.fpjobsonline.org
Physician Crossroads	http://www.physiciancrossroads.com
Physician Work	http://www.physicianwork.com
Physician's Employment	http://www.physemp.com
Practice Link	http://www.practicelink.com
Profiles Database	http://www.profilesdatabase.com
Renal Physicians Association	http://careers.renalmd.org
Society of Correctional Physicians	http://jobnet.corrdocs.org
Texas Academy of Family Physicians	http://www.fpjobsonline.org
UO Magazine	http://www.uoworks.com
Web MD	http://www.webmd.com
Wisconsin Academy of Family Physicians	http://www.fpjobsonline.org

Psychology/Psychiatry/Mental Health

American Association for Marriage and Family Therapy	http://jobconnection.aamft.org
American Counseling Association	http://www.counseling.org
American Group Psychotherapy Association	http://careers.agpa.org

American Mental Health Counselors Career Center	http://careers.amhca.org
American Psychiatric Association	http://www.psych.org
American Psychiatric Nurses Association	http://www.apna.org
American Psychological Association PsycCareers	http://www.apa.org/careers/psyccareers
American Psychological Society	http://www.psychologicalscience.org/jobs
Association for Play Therapy	http://careercenter.a4pt.org
California Psychological Association	http://careers.cpapsych.org
Florida Psychological Association	http://careercenter.flapsych.com
iHireMentalHealth.com	http://www.ihirementalhealth.com
iHireTherapy.com	http://www.ihiretherapy.com
Illinois Psychological Assocation	http://careers.illinoispsychology.org
Kansas Psychological Association	http://careers.kspsych.org
Mental Health Jobs	http://mentalhealthjobsin.com
Mental Health America	http://careers.mentalhealthamerica.net
Mental Health Net	http://www.mentalhelp.net
National Association of School Psychologists	http://www.nasponline.org
New Jersey Psychological Association	http://careers.psychologynj.org
Ohio Psychological Association	http://careers.ohpsych.org
Pennsylvania Psychological Association	http://careers.papsy.org
Psychiatric Nurse Jobs	http://psychiatric.nurse.jobs.topusajobs.com
Psychiatrist Jobs	http://www.psychiatrists.com
Psychologist Jobs	http://www.psychologistjobs.com
RehabWorld	http://www.rehabworld.com
Social Psychology Network	http://www.socialpsychology.org
SocialService.com	http://www.socialservice.com
U.S. Psychiatric Rehabilitation Association	http://careers.uspra.org

Radiology/Radiologic Technicians

American Healthcare Radiology Administrators	http://www.ahraonline.org
American Registry of Diagnostic Medical Sonographers	http://www.ardms.org
American Registry of Radiologic Technologists	http://www.arrt.org

American Roentgen Ray Society	http://careercenter.arrs.org
American Society for Radiation Oncology	http://careers.astro.org
American Society of Radiologic Technologists	http://www.asrt.org
AuntMinnie.com	http://www.auntminnie.com
California Radiological Society	http://careers.calrad.org
iHireRadiology.com	http://www.ihireradiology.com
Imaging Economics	http://www.imagingeconomics.com
NukeWorker.com	http://www.nukeworker.com
Radiological Society of North America	http://www.rsna.org
Radiology Business Management Association	http://www.rbma.org
RadWorking.com	http://www.radworking.com
RTJobs.com	http://www.allhealthcarejobs.com
Society of Diagnostic Medical Sonographers	http://www.sdms.org
Society of Nuclear Medicine	http://www.snm.org
Society for Radiation Oncology Administrators	http://careers.sroa.org
Washington State Radiological Society	http://careers.wsrs.org

Research

American Society for Clinical Laboratory Science	http://www.ascls.org
American Society for Clinical Pathology	http://www.ascp.org
American Society of Clinical Pharmacology and Therapeutics	http://www.ascpt.org
AppliedClinicalTrialsOnline.com	http://www.appliedclinicaltrialsonline.com
Association for Applied Human Pharmacology [Germany]	http://www.agah.info
Association of Clinical Research Professionals Career Center	http://www.acrpnet.org
Biotechemployment.com	http://www.biotechemployment.com
Biotechnology Industry Organization	http://www.bio.org
Canadian Society of Biochemistry and Molecular and Cellular Biologists Experimental Medicine Job Listing	http://www.medicine.mcgill.ca
History of Science Society	http://www.hssonline.org
American Medical Association JAMA CareerCenter	http://jamacareernet.ama-assn.org

Jobs4dd.com

http://www.jobs4dd.com

Public Responsibility in Medicine and Research

http://careers.primr.org

Society for Clinical Research Sites

http://careers.myscrs.org

Society for Research in Child Development

http://careers.srcd.org

Texas Healthcare & Bioscience Institute

http://www.thbi.org

Retirement Living/Senior Housing/Assisted Living

American Assisted Living Nurses Association

http://careers.alnursing.org

Assisted Living Federation of America

http://www.alfa.org

HealthCallings.com

http://www.healthcallings.com

LeadingAge

http://careers.leadingage.org

LeadingAge Texas

http://careers.leadingagetexas.org

Senior Housing Jobs

http://www.seniorhousingjobs.com

Specialties-Other

Academy of Correctional Health Professionals

http://careers.correctionalhealth.org

Alexander Graham Bell Association for the Deaf and Hard of Hearing

http://careers.agbell.org

Almost Family

http://www.patientcare.com

American Academy of Anesthesiologists

http://careers.asahq.org

American Academy of Dermatology

http://www.aad.org

American Academy of Hospice and Palliative Medicine

http://jobmart.aahpm.org

American Academy of Neurology

http://careers.aan.com

American Academy of Ophthalmology

http://ophthjobs.aao.org

American Academy of Pain Medicine

http://careercenter.painmed.org

American Academy of Professional Coders

http://www.aapc.com

American Art Therapy Association

http://careercenter.americanarttherapyassociation.org

American Association of Cardiovascular and Pulmonary Rehabilitation

http://www.aacvpr.org

American Association of Clinical Chemistry Career Center

http://careercenter.aacc.org

American Association of Colleges of Osteopathic Medicine	http://jobs.aacom.org
American Association of Diabetes Educators Career Network	http://careernetwork.diabeteseducator.org
American Association of Integrated Heatlhcare Delivery Systems	http://careers.aaihds.org
American Association for Marriage and Family Therapy	http://jobconnection.aamft.org
American Association of Medical Assistants	http://www.aama-ntl.org
American Association of Neuromuscular & Electrodiagnostic Medicine	http://www.aanem.org
American Association of Respiratory Care	http://www.aarc.org
American Association for the Study of Liver Diseases	http://careercenter.aasld.org
American Association of Tissue Banks	http:jobcenter.aatb.org
American Chiropractic Association	http://careers.acatoday.org
American Cleft Palate-Craniofacial Association	http://careers.acpa-cpf.org
American College of Audiology HearCareers	http://hearcareers.audiology.org
American College of Occupational and Environmental Medicine	http://www.acoem.org
American Congress of Rehabilitation Medicine	http://careers.acrm.org
American Dietetic Association	http://www.eatright.org
American Industrial Hygiene Association	http://www.aiha.org
American College of Allergy, Asthma & Immunology	http://www.acaai.org
American College of Medical Quality	http://careers.acmq.org
American College of Preventive Medicine	http://www.acpm.org
American College of Rheumatology	http://www.rheumatology.org
American Correctional Health Services Association	http://careers.achsa.org
American Gastroenterological Association	http://assoc.healthecareers.com
American Geriatrics Society	http://www.americangeriatrics.org
The American Health Quality Association	http://careers.ahqa.org
American Institute of Ultrasound in Medicine	http://careers.aium.org
American Medical Athletic Association	http://careers.amaasportsmed.org
American Medical Society for Sports Medicine	http://careers.amssm.org

American Optometric Association	http://www.excelod.com/career-center/
American Osteopathic Association	http://www.osteopathic.org
American Pain Society	http://www.americanpainsociety.org/resources/content/aps-career-center.html
American Society of Anesthesiologists	http://careers.asahq.org
American Society for Clinical Pathology	http://careers.ascp.org
American Society of Cytopathology	http://cytojobs.cytopathology.org
American Society for Cytotechnology	http://careercenter.asct.com
American Society for Gastrointestinal Endoscopy	http://careers.asge.org
American Society of Ichthyologists and Herpetologists	http://www.asih.org
American Society for Microbiology	http://www.asm.org
American Society for Nutrition	http://jobs.nutrition.org
American Society for Pharmacology & Experimental Therapeutics	http://careers.aspet.org
American Speech-Language-Hearing Career Center	http://www.asha.org/careers
American Thoracic Society	http://careers.thoracic.org
American Urogynecologic Society	http://careercenter.augs.org
American Urological Association JobFinder	http://careercenter.auanet.org
AnswerStat	http://www.answerstat.com
Arizona Orthopaedic Society	http://careers.azortho.org
Association of Air Medical Services	http://careercenter.aams.org
Association of Clinicians for the Underserved	http://careers.clinicians.org
Association for Community Health Improvement	http://careers.communityhlth.org
Association for Healthcare Documentation Integrity	http://www.ahdionline.org
Association for Healthcare Environment	http://careerlink.ahe.org
Association for Healthcare Volunteer Resource Professionals	http://careers.ahvrp.org
Association for Professionals in Infection Control & Epidemiology	http://careers.apic.org
Board of Registered Polysomnographic Technologists	http://careers.brpt.org
California Primary Care Association	http://jobs.cliniccareers.org
College of American Pathologists	http://www.cap.org

Dermatology Times	http://www.modernmedicine.com/modernmedicine/Dermatology/home/40160
EHScareers.com	http://www.ehscareers.com
ENT-career.com	http://www.ent-career.com
FieldMedics.com	http://www.fieldmedics.com
FPcareer.com	http://www.fpcareer.com
GASTROcareer.com	http://www.gastrocareer.com
Health Economics	http://www.healtheconomics.org
Health Industry Group Purchasing Association	http://careers.supplychainassociation.org
Hearing Review	http://www.hearingreview.com
HIV Medicine Association	http://www.hivma.org
HOSPITALISTcareer.com	http://www.hospitalistcareer.com
iHireMedicalSecretaries.com	http://www.ihiremedicalsecretaries.com
iHireNutrition.com	http://www.ihirenutrition.com
IMcareer.com	http://www.imcareer.com
Infectious Diseases Society of America	http://www.idsa.org
International Health Economics Association	http://www.healtheconomics.org
Iowa Orthopaedic Society	http://careers.iowaorthopaedic.org
Jobscience Network	http://jobs.jobscience.com
jobsSLP.com	http://www.jobsslp.com
LCGC/Chromotography Online	http://www.chromatographyonline.com
Maryland Orthopaedic Association	http://jobboard.mdortho.org
Medical Consultants Network	http://www.mcn.com
Medical Device Star	http://www.medicaldevicestar.com
Medical Fitness Association	http://www.medicalfitness.org/networking
MedicalSalesJobs.com	http://www.mymedicalsalesjobs.com
MedicalSecretaryJobs.com	http://www.medicalsecretary.com
National Alliance of Wound Care	http://woundcare.careers.nawccb.org
National Association of Chronic Disease Directors	http://nacddhealthjobs.chronicdisease.org
National Association of County and City Health Officials	http://careers.naccho.org
National Association for Healthcare Quality	http://careercenter.nahq.org

National Association of Rehabilitation Providers and Agencies	http://careers.naranet.org
National Environmental Health Association	http://www.neha.org
National Hispanic Medical Association	http://jobs.nhmamd.org
National Hospice and Palliative Care Organization	http://careers.nhpco.org
National Kidney Association Career Center	http://www.careers.kidney.org
National Society of Genetic Counselors	http://jobconnection.nsgc.org
National Sleep Foundation	http://jobs.sleepfoundation.org
NEPHcareer.com	http://www.nephcareer.com
NEUROcareer.com	http://www.neurocareer.com
New Mexico Osteopathic Medical Association	http://healthcarecareers.nmoma.org
North American Spine Society	http://www.spine.org/Pages/Default.aspx
North Carolina Orthopaedic Association	http://careers.ncorthopaedics.org
Ophthalmology Times	http://www.modernmedicine.com/modernmedicine/Ophthalmology/home/40207
Practice Greenhealth	http://careers.practicegreenhealth.org
Public Responsibility in Medicine and Research	http://careers.primr.org
Rehab Management	http://www.rehabpub.com
Renal World	http://www.nephron.org/renalworld
Society of General Internal Medicine	http://careers.sgim.org
Society for Healthcare Consumer Advocacy	http://careercenter.shca-aha.org
Society for Imaging Informatics in Medicine	http://careers.siimweb.org
Society for Laboratory Automation and Screening	http://careers.slas.org
Society for Neuroscience	http://neurojobs.sfn.org
South Carolina Orthopaedic Association	http://www.scoanet.org
Texas Association for Home Care & Hospice	http://careers.tahch.org
Travel Per Diem Contract	http://www.travelperdiemcontract.com
United States & Canadian Academy of Pathology	http://careers.uscap.org
Urgent Care Association of America	http://jobs.ucaoa.org
Urology Times	http://www.modernmedicine.com/modernmedicine/Urology/home/40184
The Working Group for Electronic Data Interchange	http://careers.wedi.org

Students/Recent Graduates

American Medical Association (Resident and Fellow Section)	http://www.ama-assn.org/ama/pub/education-careers.shtml
CampusRN.com	http://www.campusrn.com
Career Espresso	http://www.sph.emory.edu/cms/current_students/career_services/index.html
The College of Education & Human Development at the University of Minnesota	http://www.cehd.umn.edu/career
Degree Hunter	http://degreehunter.net
Health Occupations Students of America	http://careers.hosa.org
Profiles Database	http://www.profilesdatabase.com

Surgery/Surgeons/Surgical Nurses

Ambulatory Surgery Center Association	http://careercenter.ascassociation.org
Academy of Medical-Surgical Nurses	http://www.medsurgnurse.org
American Association of Hip and Knee Surgeosn	http://careers.aahks.org
American Association of Neurological Surgeons	http://www.aans.org
American College of Foot and Ankle Surgeons	http://www.acfas.org
American College of Surgeons	http://www.facs.org
American Society of General Surgeons	http://www.theasgs.org
American Society of Transplant Surgeons	http://careercenter.asts.org
American Association of Oral & Maxillofacial Surgeons	http://www.aoms.org
Association of Surgical Technicians	http://careercenter.ast.org
Cardiothoracic Surgery Network	http://www.ctsnet.org
Contemporary Surgery	http://www.contemporarysurgery.com
Cosmetic Surgery Times	http://www.modernmedicine.com/modernmedicine/Cosmetic+Surgery/home/40174
Florida Society of Ambulatory Surgery Centers	http://careers.fsasc.org
Freestanding Ambulatory Surgery Center Association of Tennessee	http://jobboard.fascatn.org
Georgia Society of Ambulatory Surgery Center	http://jobboard.gsasc.org
Mississippi Ambulatory Surgery Center Association	http://jobboard.masca-ms.org
New York State Society of Orthopaedic Surgeons	http://careers.nyssos.org

Outpatient Ophthalmic Surgery Society   http://careerhq.ooss.org

Pennsylvania Ambulatory Surgery Association   http://careers.pasa-asf.org

South Carolina Ambulatory Surgery Center   http://jobboard.scasc.org

SurgicalAssistants.com   http://www.surgicalassistants.com

High Tech/Technical/Technology

The Ada Project   http://women.cs.cmu.edu/ada

AmericanJobs.com   http://www.americanjobs.com

Association for Educational Communications and   http://www.aect.org
Technology Job Center

ButternutJobs.com [United Kingdom]   http://www.butternutjobs.com

Career Net   http://www.careernet.com

Contract Employment Weekly   http://www.ceweekly.com

CyberMediaDice.com [India]   http://www.cybermediadice.com

High Technology Careers   http://www.hightechcareers.com/hc3.asp

HireAbility.com   http://www.hireability.com

IrishDev.com [Ireland]   http://www.irishdev.com

Job Authority   http://www.jobauthority.com

Job Searching - Technical   http://jobsearchtech.about.com

JobsInSearch.com   http://www.jobsinsearch.com

Just Tech Jobs   http://www.justtechjobs.com

JustTechnicalJobs [United Kingdom]   http://www.jobsgroup.net

TheLadders.com   http://www.theladders.com

Latinos in Information Sciences and Technology   http://www.a-lista.org
Association

LookTech.com   http://www.looktech.com

MEMSNet   http://www.memsnet.org

New Dimensions in Technology, Inc.   http://www.ndt.com

New Mexico High Tech Job Forum   http://www.nmtechjobs.com

RecruTech.ca [Canada]   http://www.recrutech.ca

SalesRecruits.com   http://cardbrowser.com

ScientistWorld.com [United Kingdom]	http://www.scientistworld.com
Society for Technical Communications	http://www.stc.org
Tech Centric	http://www.tech-centric.net
TechJobsScotland	http://www.techjobscotland.com
Technical Recruiters	http://www.technicalrecruiters.com
TechResults	http://www.techresults-nv.com
Tiny Tech Jobs	http://www.tinytechjobs.com
US Tech Jobs	http://www.ustechjobs.com
Virtual Job Fair	http://careerexpo.jobing.com

Hospitality (See also Culinary/Food Preparation)

Hospitality-General

AllHospitality.co.uk [United Kingdom]	http://www.hospitalityonline.co.uk
AnyWorkAnywhere.com [United Kingdom]	http://www.anyworkanywhere.com
Avero	http://www.averoinc.com
Barzone [United Kingdom]	http://www.barzone.co.uk
BlueFoxJobs.com	http://www.bluefoxjobs.com
Carterer Global	http://www.catererglobal.com
Cool Works	http://www.coolworks.com
Hcareers	http://www.hcareers.com
Hospitality Link	http://www.hospitalitylink.com
Hospitality Net Virtual Job Exchange [Netherlands]	http://www.hospitalitynet.org/index.html
Hospitality Online	http://www.hospitalityonline.com
HospitalityRecruitment.co.uk [United Kingdom]	http://www.hospitalityrecruitment.co.uk
Hotel Job Resource	http://www.hoteljobresource.com
Hotel Jobs [United Kingdom]	http://www.hoteljobs.co.uk
Hotel Travel Jobs	http://www.hoteltraveljobs.com
HOTELScareers.com	http://www.catererglobal.com
iHireHospitality.com	http://www.ihirehospitality.com
iHireHospitalityServices.com	http://www.ihirehospitalityservices.com

JobLoft.com [Canada]	http://www.jobloft.com
JobLux [United Kingdom]	http://www.joblux.co.uk
Job Monkey	http://www.jobmonkey.com
JobsinHotels [United Kingdom]	http://www.jobsinhotels.com
MeetingJobs.com	http://www.meetingjobs.com
The Publican [United Kingdom]	http://www.thepublican.com
Resort Work [United Kingdom]	http://www.resortwork.co.uk
SeasonalEmployment.com	http://www.seasonalemployment.com
247recruit.com [United Kingdom]	http://www.247recruit.com

Food Preparation

BookaChef.co.uk [United Kingdom]	http://www.bookachef.co.uk
Careers in Food	http://www.careersinfood.com
CareersinGrocery.com	http://www.careersingrocery.com
Caterer.com [United Kingdom]	http://www.caterer.com
CatererGlobal.com [United Kingdom]	http://www.catererglobal.com
Chef Jobs	http://www.chefjobs.com
Chef2Chef	http;//www.chef2chef.net
Chefs Employment	http://www.chefsemployment.com
FineDiningJobs.com	http://www.finediningjobs.com
Food and Drink Jobs	http://www.foodanddrinkjobs.com
FoodIndustryJobs.com	http://www.foodindustryjobs.com
iHire Chefs	http://www.ihirechefs.com
National Restaurant Association	http://www.restaurant.org/careers
NRNJobPlate.com	http://www.nrnjobplate.com
Restaurant Hospitality	http://www.restuarant-hospitality.com
SommelierJobs.com	http://www.sommelierjobs.com
StarChefs	http://www.starchefs.com
Wine & Hospitality Jobs	http://www.wineandhospitalityjobs.com

Hotel

American Hotel and Lodging Association	http://www.ahla.com
CatererGlobal	http://www.catererglobal.com
Hospitality Design	http://www.hospitalitydesign.com
Hotel Jobs	http://www.hoteljobs.com
Hotel Jobs Network	http://www.hoteljobsnetwork.com
Hotel Restaurant Jobs	http://www.hotelrestaurantjobs.com
LuxuryHotelJobs.com	http://www.luxuryhoteljobs.com

Management

Executive Placement Services	http://www.execplacement.com
Hcareers	http://www.hcareers.com
HospitalityExecutive.com	http://www.hospitalityexecutive.com

Resorts

Cooljobs	http://cooljobs.com
CoolWorks.com	http://www.coolworks.com
HospitalityAdventures.com	http://www.hospitalityadventures.com
Resortjobs.co.uk [United Kingdom]	http://www.resortjobs.co.uk
Resort Work [United Kingdom]	http://www.resortwork.co.uk
SpaOpportunities [United Kingdom]	http://www.spaopportunities.com

Travel

American Society of Travel Agents	http://www.asta.org
TravelJobSearch.com [United Kingdom]	http://www.traveljobsearch.com

Other Specialty

CapeCodSummerJobs.com	http://www.capecodsummerjobs.com
Casino Careers Online	http://www.casinocareers.com
International Association of Conference Centers Online	http://www.iacconline.org
Lifeguardingjobs.com	http://www.lifeguardingjobs.com

MeetingJobs.com   http://www.meetingjobs.com

Museum Jobs   http://www.museumjobs.com

ScottishHospitalityJobs.com [Scotland]   http://www.scottishhospitalityjobs.com

Showbizjobs.com   http://www.showbizjobs.com

SkiingtheNet   http://www.skiingthenet.com

Hourly Workers (See also Classifieds-Newspaper)

CmonJob.fr   http://www.cmonjob.fr

EmploymentGuide.com   http://www.employmentguide.com

GrooveJob.com   http://www.groovejob.com

ParisJob.com   http://www.parisjob.com

SnagaJob   http://www.snagajob.com

YouApplyHere.com   http://www.youapplyhere.com

Human Resources (See also Recruiters' Resources)

Human Resources-General

American Management Association International   http://www.amanet.org

ERE.net   http://www.ere.net

HR Connections   http://www.hrjobs.com

HRjob.ca [Canada]   http://www.humanresourcesjobs.ca

HR Job Net   http://www.hrjobnet.com

HR-Jobs   http://www.hr-jobs.net

HR Staffers   http://www.hrstaffers.com

HR World   http://www.hrworld.com

HRIM Mall   http://www.hrimmall.com

HRM Jobs   http://www.hrmjobs.com

Human Resources.org   http://www.humanresources.org

iHireHR.com   http://www.ihirehr.com

JobBoarders.com   http://www.jobboarders.com

Jobs4HR.com	http://www.jobs4hr.com
TheLadders.com	http://www.theladders.com
NationJob Network: Human Resources Job Page	http://www.nationjob.com/hr
NewHRJobs.com	http://www.newhrjobs.com
PersonnelTodayJobs.com [United Kingdom]	http://www.personneltoday.com
Recruitmentcareeers.co.uk [United Kingdom]	http://www.recruitmentcareers.co.uk
SimplyHRJobs [United Kingdom]	http://www.simplyhrjobs.co.uk
Society for Human Resource Management HRJobs	http://jobs.com
Workforce.com	http://www.workforce.com

Assessment/Evaluation/Selection

American Evaluation Association	http://www.eval.org/programs/careercenter.asp

Compensation & Benefits

BenefitsLink	http://www.benefitslink.com
International Foundation of Employee Benefit Plans Job Postings	http://www.jobsinbenefits.com
Salary.com	http://www.salary.com
WorkersCompensation.com	http://www.workerscompensation.com
World at Work Job Links (American Compensation Association)	http://www.worldatwork.org

Consulting

Human Resource Independent Consultants (HRIC) On-Line Job Leads	http://www.hric.org

Diversity

Career Center for Workforce Diversity	http://www.eop.com
DiversityCareers.com	http://www.diversitycareers.com
Diversity Connect	http://www.diversityconnect.com
DiversityInc.com	http://www.diversityinc.com
DiversityJobs.com	http://www.diversityjobs.com

DiversityWorking.com   http://www.diversityworking.com

IMDiversity.com   http://www.imdiversity.com

WorkplaceDiversity.com   http://www.workplacediversity.com

Industry Specific

Cable and Telecommunications Human Resources   http://www.cthra.com
Association

College and University Personnel Association JobLine   http://www.cupahr.org/jobline

Healthcaare Human Resources Management   http://careers.hhrmac.org
Association of California

HRS Jobs   http://www.hrsjobs.com

Massachusetts Healthcare Human Resources   http://www.mhhra.org
Association

Media Human Resource Association   http://jobs.com

National Association of Colleges & Employers (NACE)   http://www.nacelink.com

Information Systems

HRISjobs.com   http://www.hrisjobs.com

International Association for Human Resource   http://ihrim.hrdpt.com
Information Management

Recruiting

Academy of Healthcare Recruiters   http://www.academyofhealthcarerecruiters.com

Alliance of Medical Recruiters   http://www.physicianrecruiters.com

American Staffing Association   http://www.staffingtoday.net

Arizona Technical Recruiters Association   http://www.atraaz.org/pages/
                                                             recruiterjobopenings.html

Association of Executive Search Consultants   http://www.aesc.org/eweb

Association of Financial Search Consultants   http://www.afsc-jobs.com

Association of Staff Physician Recruiters   http://www.aspr.org

California Staffing Professionals   http://www.catss.org

Canadian Technical Recruiters Network   http://www.ctrn.org

Colorado Technical Recruiters Network   http://www.ctrn.org

Delaware Valley Technical Recruiters Network	http://www.dvtrn.org
ERE.net	http://www.ere.net
Houston High Tech Recruiters Network	http://www.hhtrn.org
Illinois Recruiters Association	http://illinoisrecruiter.ning.com
International Association of Employment Web Sites	http://www.employmentwebistes.org
International Association of Corporate and Professional Recruitment	http://www.iacpr.org
Minnesota Technical Recruiters Network	http://www.mntrn.com
National Association of Executive Recruiters	http://www.naer.org
National Association for Health Care Recruitment	http://www.nahcr.com
National Association of Legal Search Consultants	http://www.nalsc.org
National Association of Personnel Services	http://www.napsweb.org
National Association of Physician Recruiters	http://www.napr.org
National Insurance Recruiters Association Online Job Database	http://www.nirassn.com
New Jersey Metro Employment Management Association	http://www.njmetroema.org
New Jersey Staffing Association	http://www.njsa.com
New Jersey Technical Recruiters Alliance	http://www.njtra.org
Northeast Human Resource Association	http://www.nehra.com
Northwest Recruiters Association	http://www.nwrecruit.org/nwra
OnrecJobs.com [United Kingdom]	http://www.onrecjobs.com
Personnel Management Association of Western New England	http://hrmawne.shrm.org
Recruiters Network	http://www.recruitersnetwork.com
RecruitingJobs.com	http://www.recruitingjobs.com
The Regional Technical Recruiter's Association	http://www.rtra.com
Southeast Employment Network Inc.	http://www.nonprofitdata.com
Technical Recruiters Network	http://www.trnchicago.org
Texas Association of Staffing	http://www.texasstaffing.org
WEDDLE's Research & Publications	http://www.weddles.com

Regional

Central Iowa Chapter, SHRM	http://ci.shrm.org
Chesapeake Human Resources Association	http://www.chra.com
Dallas Human Resource Management Association	http://www.dallashr.org
Houston Human Resource Management Association	http://www.hrhouston.org
Howard County Human Resources Society	http://www.hocohrs.org
HRMA Resource Bank	http://www.hrma.org
Human Resource Association of Broward County	http://www.hrabc.org
Human Resource Association of Central Indiana	http://www.hraci.org
Human Resource Association of Greater Kansas City	http://hrma-kc.org
Human Resource Association of Greater Oak Brook	http://www.hraoakbrook.org
Human Resource Association of the National Capital Area Job Bank Listing	http://hra-nca.org/job_list.asp
Human Resource Association of New York	http://www.nyshrm.org
Human Resource Management Association of Mid Michigan Job Postings	http://hrmamm.com/jobpostings/index.php
Human Resources Online [Russia]	http://www.hro.ru
Illinois Association of Personnel Services	http://www.searchfirm.com
JobsinSearch [United Kingdom]	http://www.jobsinsearch.com
Navigator Online	http://www.lwhra.org
New Jersey Human Resource Planning Group	http://www.njhrpg.org
Northeast Human Resource Association	http://www.nehra.com
Ohio State Council (SHRM)	http://www.ohioshrm.org
Personnel Management Association of Western New England	http://hrmawne.shrm.org
The Portland Human Resource Management Assn	http://www.pbcs.jp
Sacramento Area Human Resources Association	http://www.sahra.org
SHRM Atlanta	http://www.shrmatlanta.org
SHRM Jacksonville	http://www.shrmjax.org
Tri-State Human Resource Management Assn	http://wss3.tristatehr.org/default.aspx
Tulsa Area Human Resources Association	http://www.tahra.org

Training & Development

American Society for Training & Development Job Bank	http://jobs.astd.org
Instructional Systems Technology Jobs	http://education.indiana.edu/ist/students/jobs/joblink.html
International Society for Performance Improvement Job Bank	http://www.ispi.org
Training Consortium	http://www.trainingconsortium.net
Training Forum	http://www.trainingforum.com
Trainingjob.com	http://www.trainingjob.com
TrainingProviderJobs.co.uk [United Kingdom]	http://www.trainingproviderjobs.co.uk

Other Specialty

New Jersey Human Resource Planning Group	http://www.njhrpg.org
OD Network On-line	http://www.odnetwork.org
American Society for Healthcare Human Resource Management	http;//careers.ashhra.org

-|-

Industrial/Manufacturing

American Chemical Society Rubber Division	http://www.rubber.org
American Forest & Paper Association	http://www.afandpa.org
Association of Industrial Metalizers, Coaters & Laminators	http://www.aimcal.org
Auto Glass Magazine	http://www.glass.org
AutomationTechies.com	http://www.automationtechies.com
Blue Collar Jobs	http://www.bluecollarjobs.com
Bluewire Technologies	http://www.bluewire-technologies.com
CastingJobs.com	http://www.castingjobs.com
CoatingsCareers.com	http://www.coatingscareers.com

COBRA	http://www.technologysource.com
Drilling Research Institute	http://www.drillers.com/pages/view/jobs
Bluewire Technologies	http://www.bluewire-technologies.com
Energy Careers	http://www.energycareers.com
Finishing.com	http://www.finishing.com
FM Link-Facilities Management	http://www.fmlink.com
GetMachinistJobs.com	http://www.getmachinistjobs.com
HVACagent.com	http://www.hvacagent.com
iHireManufacturingEngineers.com	http://www.ihiremanufacturingengineers.com
Industrial Laser Solutions	http://industrial-lasers.com
JobsinManufacturing.com	http://www.jobsinmanufacturing.com
Inteletex	http://www.inteletex.com
Iron & Steel Society	http://www.issource.org
Jobwerx	http://www.jobwerx.com
MachinistJobSite.com	http://www.machinistjobsite.com
The Manufacturing Job	http://www.themanufacturingjob.com
ManufacturingJob.com	http://www.manufacturingjob.com
Manufacturing Job Store	http://www.manufacturingjobstore.com
ManufacturingJobs.com	http://www.manufacturingjobs.com
Materials Engineer	http://www.materialsengineerjobs.com
MaterialsJobs.com	http://www.materialsjobs.com
MDL CareerCenter	http://careercenter.devicelink.com
Medical Device Manufacturers Association Career Center	http://careers.medicaldevices.org
MiManufacturingJobs.com	http://www.mimanufacturingjobs.com
MoldingJobs.com	http://www.moldingjobs.com
National Association of Industrial Technology	http://atmae.org
National Defense Industrial Association	http://ndia.monster.com
OilCareer.com	http://www.oilcareer.com
The Oil Directory	http://www.oildirectory.com
Petroleum Services Association of Canada Employment	http://www.psac.ca

Plant Maintenance Resource Center	http://www.plant-maintenance.com
Power Builder Journal	http://pbdj.sys-con.com
Semicon	http://www.semicon.com
Semicon Bay	http://www.semiconbay.com
Sheet Metal and Air Conditioning Contractor's Association	http://www.smacna.org
SkilledWorkers.com [Canada]	http://www.skilledworkers.com
SocialService.com	http://www.socialservice.com
Society of Manufacturing Engineers Jobs Connection	http://jobsconnection.sme.org
Society of Petrologists & Well Log Analysts Job Opportunities	http://www.spwla.org
Subseaexplorer	http://www.subseaexplorer.com
SwissCNCJobs.com	http://www.swisscncjobs.com
Test & Measurement World	http://www.tmworld.com
Top Echelon Network	http://www.topechelon.com
USA Manufactuiring Jobs	http://www.usamanufacturingjobs.com
UtilityJobSearch.com [United Kingdom]	http://www.utilityjobsearch.com
Vision Systems Design	http://www.vision-systems.com

Information Technology/Information Systems

Software, Hardware, Middleware, Client server, Web specialists

Information Technology-General

A1A Computer Jobs Mailing List	http://www.a1acomputerpros.net
A-Z Internet Jobs	http://www.a-zjobs.com
Ace thee Interview	http://www.acetheinterview.com
The Ada Project	http://women.cs.cmu.edu/ada
AD&A Software Jobs Home Page	http://softwarejobs.4jobs.com
The Advanced Computing Systems Association	http://usenix.org
Adviser Zone	http://www.adviserzone.com
AS400 Network	http://systeminetwork.com

Association for Computing Machinery Career Resource Center	http://acpinternational.org
Association for Educational Communications and Technology Job Center	http://www.aect.org
Association of Internet Professionals National Job Board	http://association.org
Asynchrony	http://www.asynchrony.com
Avatar Magazine	http://www.avatarmag.com
Beeline.com	http://www.beeline.com/workforce-solutions
Bluewire Technologies	http://www.bluewire-technologies.com
Brain Buzz	http://www.cramsession.com
Brain Power	http://www.brainpower.com
CanadaIT.com	http://www.canadait.com/cfm/index.cfm
CanadaJobs.com	http://www.canadajobs.com
CardBrowser.com	http://www.cardbrowser.com
CareerFile	http://www.careerfile.com
Career Magic	http://www.careermagic.com
Career Marketplace Network	http://www.careermarketplace.com
Career Shop	http://www.autohiresoftware.com
Cert Review	http://www.itspecialist.com/default.aspx
CIO	http://itjobs.cio.com/a/all-jobs/list?source=top_nav
CM Today (Configuration Management)	http://www.cmcrossroads.com
CNET's Ultimate ISP Guide	http://www.cnet.com
Cobol Jobs	http://www.coboljobs.com
Comforce	http://www.comforce.com
ComputerJobs.com	http://www.computerjobs.com/homepage.aspx
ComputerJobs.ie [Ireland]	http://www.computerjobs.ie
computerjobsbank.com	http://www.computerjobsbank.com
Computerwork.com	http://www.computerwork.com
Computing Research Association Job Announcements	http://www.cra.org/ads
Contract Employment Weekly	http://www.ceweekly.com
Contract Job Hunter	http://www.cjhunter.com

CREN	http://www.computingresources.com
CRN	http://www.crn.com/cwb/careers
Data Masters	http://www.datamasters.com
DevBistro.com	http://www.devbistro.com
Developers.Net	http://www.developers1.net
Devhead	http://www.zdnet.com/?tag=header;header-pri
DICE	http://www.dice.com
Discover Jobs	http://www.discover-jobs.com
Dr. Dobb's	http://www.drdobbs.com
eChannelLinecareers.com [Canada]	http://www.echannellinecareers.com
Eclectic [Netherlands]	http://www.eclectic.eu
eContent	http://www.ecmag.net
Educause	http://www.educause.edu
EE Times	http://www.eetimes.com
E-itsales.com [United Kingdom]	http://www.e-itsales.com
eLance	http://www.elance.com
Embedded.com	http://www.embedded.com
eMoonlighter	http://www.moonlighter.com
The Engineering Technology Site [United Kingdom]	http://www.engineers4engineers.co.uk
eWork Exchange	http://www.ework.com
15 Seconds Job Classifieds	http://www.15seconds.com
FutureGate [Great Britain]	http://www.futuregate.co.uk/internet.html
GetAFreelancer.com	http://www.getafreelancer.com
GisaJob.com [United Kingdom]	http://www.gisajob.com
Gurus.com.au [Australia]	http://gurus.com.au
GxPJobs.com [United Kingdom]	http://www.gxpjobs.com
H1B Sponsors	http://www.h1bsponsors.com
Hi-Tech Careers	http://www.careermarthi-tech.com
Hi-Tech Club	http://www.hitechclub.com
High Technology Careers	http://www.hightechcareers.com/hc3.asp

Hire Ability	http://www.hireability.com
Huntahead	http://www.huntahead.com/index.htm
Iitjobs.com	http://www.iitjobs.com
InfiNet	http://www.infi.net
InformationWeek Career	http://www.informationweek.com/career
In the Middle [United Kingdom]	http://www.inthemiddle.co.uk
Informix Jobs	http://www.premierjobs.com
Intega Online [United Kingdom]	http://www.compucaregroup.com
Inter City Oz	http://interoz.com
Internet.com	http://www.justtechjobs.com
iSmart People	http://www.ismartpeople.com
ITArchtectJobs.com	http://www.itarchitectjobs.com
ITcareers.com	http://itjobs.computerworld.com/a/all-jobs/list
IT Classifieds	http://www.itclassifieds.com/Main/Default.asp
IT Firms	http://www.itfirms.com
IT-JobBank [Denmark]	http://www.it-jobbank.dk
TheITJobBoard.com [United Kingdom]	http://www.theitjobboard.com
ITjobs.com	http://www.itjobs.com
ITjobs.ca [Canada]	http://www.itjob.ca
IT Jobs Online [United Kingdom]	http://www.itjobsonline.com
IT JobsPost [United Kingdom]	http://www.itjobspost.com
IT Jobs Vault	http://www.itjobsvault.co.uk
IT Talent	http://www.ittalent.com
ITVacancies.com [United Kingdom]	http://www.itvacancies.com
IT-webforum.com	http://www.it-webforum.com
JV Search	http://www.jvsearch.com
Job Ads	http://www.jobads.com
Job Authority	http://www.jobauthority.com
JobBoard.IT [United Kingdom]	http://www.jobboardit.com/CareerSite/ jobboardit/index.htm
JobCircle.com	http://www.jobcircle.com

JobEngine	http://www.jobengine.com
The JobFactory	http://www.jobfactory.com
Job Island	http://www.jobisland.com
Jobit [United Kingdom]	http://www.jobit.co.uk
Job Net America	http://www.jobnetamerica.com
Job Serve	http://www.jobserve.us
Job Serve [United Kingdom]	http://www.jobserve.us/homepage.aspx
Job Warriors	http://jobwarriors.com
Job Webs	http://www.jobwebs.com
JobsDB	http://www.jobsdbusa.com
Jobs4IT.com	http://www.jobs4it.com
Jobs-net	http://www.jobs-net.com
JustIT [United Kingdom]	http://www.justit.co.uk
Just Tech Jobs	http://www.justtechjobs.com
KR Solutions [United Kingdom]	http://www.kr-solutions.co.uk
Lan Jobs	http://www.lanjobs.com
Latinos in Information Sciences and Technology Association	http://www.a-lista.org
Lotus Notes Jobs	http://lotusnotesjobs.com
Mojolin	http://www.mojolin.com
Neo Soft Corporation	http://www.neosoftware.com
Net Mechanic	http://www.netmechanic.com
Net-Temps	http://www.net-temps.com
OperationIT	http://www.operationIT.com
Oxygen [United Kingdom]	http://www.oxygenonline.co.uk
PC World	http://www.pcworld.com
PeopleSoft-Resources.com	http://www.peoplesoft-resources.com
The Perl Job Site	http://www.jobs.perl.org
PlanetRecruit [United Kingdom]	http://www.planetrecruit.com
Pracownicy.it [Poland]	http://www.pracownicy.it
PurelyIT.co.uk [United Kingdom]	http://www.purelyit.co.uk

Real-Time Engineering	http://www.realtime-engineering.com
Road Techs	http://www.roadtechs.com
SAS Institute	http://support.sas.com/usergroups
Semiconductor Jobs	http://www.semiconductorjobs.com
Skills Village	https://support.oracle.com/CSP/ui/flash.html
Smarter Work	http://www.smarterwork.com
Society of Computer Professionals Online	http://www.comprof.com
SoftwareJobLink	http://softwarejoblink.com
Southern California Electronic Data Interchange Roundtable	http://www.scedir.org
staffITnow	http://www.staffitnow.com
Swift Jobs	http://www.swiftjobs.com
TechCareers	http://www.techcareers.com
.tech_centric	http://www.tech-centric.net
Tech-Engine	http://techengine.com
Tech Expo USA	http://www.techexpousa.com
TechEmployment.com	http://www.techemployment.com
Techie Gold	http://www.techiegold.com
Tech Job Bank	http://www.techjobbank.com
TechnoJobs [United Kingdom]	http://www.technojobs.co.uk
TechResults	http://www.techresults-nv.com
Tech Target	http://www.techtarget.com
TechWeb	http://www.techweb.com/home
Techs	http://www.techs.com
ThaiITJobs.com [Thailand]	http://www.thaiitjobs.com/en/index.asp
Top IT Consultant [United Kingdom]	http://www.topitconsultant.co.uk
VAR Business	http://www.crn.com/cwb/careers
Virtual Job Fair	http://careerexpo.jobing.com
Wireless Developers	http://www.wirelessdevnet.com
Work Exchange	http://www.workexchange.com
Element K Journals	http://www.elementkjournals.com

AS400

Just AS/400 Jobs   http://www.justas400jobs.com

News400.com   http://systeminetwork.com

Baan

BaanBoard.com   http://www.baanboard.com

Just BAAN Jobs   http://www.justbaanjobs.com

C++

C++ Jobs   http://www.cplusplusjobs.com

C++ Report   http://www.creport.com

C++ Users Group Job Links   http://www.hal9k.com/cug/jobs.htm

C Plus Plus Jobs   http://www.cplusplusjobs.com

Just C Jobs   http://www.justcjobs.com

Cobol

The Cobol Center   http://www.infogoal.com

CobolJobs.com   http://www.coboljobs.com

Just Cobol Jobs   http://www.justcoboljobs.com

Cold Fusion

Atlanta Cold Fusion User Group   http://www.acfug.org

Austin Cold Fusion Users Group   http://austincfug.wordpress.com

CF Programmers   http://www.cfprogrammers.com

Chicago Central ColdFusion User Group   http://www.cccfug.org/cccfug/cccfug.cfm

ColdFusion Support Forums   http://www.adobe.com/cfusion/webforums/forum/index.cfm?forumid=1

House of Fusion   http://www.houseoffusion.com

Just Cold Fusion Jobs   http://www.justcoldfusionjobs.com

Database

Database Jobs	http://www.databasejobs.com
DataNewsJobs.com [Belgium]	http://datanews.rnews.be/datanews/nl/jobs
DBA Support	http://www.dbasupport.com
icrunchdata.com	http://www.icrunchdata.com
International DB2 Users Group	http://www.idug.org
Just DB2 Jobs	http://www.justdb2jobs.com
LazyDBA.com	http://www.lazydba.com
Learn ASP	http://www.learnasp.com/learnasp

Delphi

Delphi Jobs	http://www.delphijobs.com
Just Delphi Jobs	http://www.delphijobs.com

Electric Data Interchange

EDI Jobs Online	http://www.edijobsonline.com
EDI Coordinators & Consultants Clearinghouse	http://www.friend-edi.com
Just Exchange Jobs	http://www.justexchangejobs.com
Southern California Electronic Data Interchange Roundtable	http://www.scedir.org

ERP

ERP Central	http://www.erpcentral.com
ERP Fan Club	http://www.erpfans.com
ERP Jobs [Canada]	http://www.erp-jobs.com
ERP Knowledge Base	http://erp.ittoolbox.com
ERP People	http://www.erp-people.com
ERP Software	http://www.erpsos.com
The ERP Supersite	http://www.techra.com/mambo

Geographic Information Systems

Geo Community	http://www.geocomm.com
GeoJobs.org	http://www.geojobs.org
Get GIS Jobs	http://www.getgisjobs.com
GIScareers.com	http://www.giscareers.com
GIS Connection	http://www.gisconnection.com
GISjobs.com	http://www.gisjobs.com
GISjobs.org	http://www.gisjobs.org
GIS Jobs Clearinghouse	http://www.gjc.org
GISuser.com	http://www.gisuser.com

Java

All-Java-Jobs	http://www.all-java-jobs.com
Digital Cat	http://human.javaresource.com
Java Jobs	http://www.javajobs.com
Java World	http://www.javaworld.com
jGuru	http://www.jguru.com
Just Java Jobs	http://www.justjavajobs.com

Lotus Notes

Association of ex-Lotus Employees	http://www.axle.org
Just Notes Jobs	http://www.justnotesjobs.com
Lavatech	http://www.lotusnotes.com
Lotus Notes Jobs	http://lotusnotesjobs.com

MacIntosh

MacDirectory Job Opportunities	http://www.macdirectory.com
MacTalent.com	http://www.mactalent.com
The Mac Trading Post	http://www.mymac2u.com/themactradingpost

Network/LAN/WAN

iHireNetworkAdministrators.com	http://www.ihirenetworkadministrators.com
Just Netware Jobs	http://www.justnetwarejobs.com
Just Networking Jobs	http://www.justnetworkingjobs.com
LAN Jobs	http://www.lanjobs.com
The Network Engineer.com	http://www.thenetworkengineer.com
Network World Fusion	http://www.networkworld.com/careers

Oracle

Just Oracle Jobs	http://www.justoraclejobs.com
Orca—The Oracle Job Site	http://www.theoraclejobsite.com
Oracle Contractor Database	http://www.cois.com/houg/con.html
Oracle Fan Club	http://www.oraclefans.com
Oracle Fans	http://www.oraclefans.com
OraSearch.com	http://www.orasearch.com

PeopleSoft

Jobs for Programmers	http://www.prgjobs.com/Jobs.cfm/PeopleSoft
Just People Soft Jobs	http://www.justpeoplesoftjobs.com
People Soft Fans	http://www.peoplesoftfans.com
People Soft Links	http://www.itoolbox.com
PSoftPros.com	http://www.psoftpros.com

Power Builder

Just Power Builder Jobs	http://www.justpowerbuilderjobs.com
Power Builder Journal	http://pbdj.sys-con.com/

Programming

Code-Jobs.com	http://www.code-jobs.com
iDevjobs.com	http://www.idevjobs.com
iHireProgrammers.com	http://www.ihireprogrammers.com

Jobs for Programmers	http://www.prgjobs.com
Programmers Heaven	http://www.programmersheaven.com
Programming-Webmaster	http://www.programming.com
RentaCoder.com	http://www.vworker.com/RentACoder/DotNet/default.aspx
Script Lance	http://www.scriptlance.com
SoftwareJoblink.com	http://softwarejoblink.com
Superexpert	http://www.superexpert.com/blog/default.aspx

SAP

A1A Computer Jobs Mailing List	http://www.a1acomputerpros.net
Just SAP Jobs	http://www.justsapjobs.com
SAP Club	http://www.sapclub.com
The SAP Fan Club	http://www.sapfans.com
SAPInfo.net	http://www.sap.com/usa/index.epx
The SAP Job Board [Europe]	http://www.thesapjobboard.com
SAP Professional Organization	http://www.sapprofessionals.org
SAP Solutions	http://www.sap.com/usa/index.epx
The Spot 4 SAP	http://www.thespot4sap.com

Unix

Donohue's RS/6000 & UNIX Employment Site	http://www.s6000.com
Just UNIX Jobs	http://www.justunixjobs.com
Unix Guru Universe	http://www.ugu.com
UNIX admin search	http://www.unixadminsearch.com
Unix Review	http://www.networkcomputing.com
Unix World	http://www.networkcomputing.com

Visual Basic

Just VB Jobs	http://www.justvbjobs.com
V Basic Search	http://www.vbasicsearch.com

VB Code Guru http://codeguru.com/vb

Visual Basic Jobs http://www.visualbasicjobs.com

Web

All Web Jobs http://www.allwebjobs.com

CGI Resource Index http://cgi.resourceindex.com

DevBistro.com http://www.devbistro.com

HTML Writers Guild HWG-Jobs http://www.hwg.org/lists/hwg-jobs

I-Advertising http://internetadvertising.org

Internet Job Store.com http://www.internetjobstore.com

JobsInSearch.com http://www.jobsinsearch.com

Just E-Commerce Jobs http://www.juste-commercejobs.com

Just Web Jobs http://www.justwebjobs.com

Search Hound http://www.searchhound.com

SGML/XML Jobs http://www.eccnet.com/xmlug

Site Experts http://www.siteexperts.com

US Internet Industry http://www.usiia.org

Web Programming Jobs http://www.webprogrammingjobs.com

Web Site Builder http://www.websitebuilder.com

XMLephant http://www.xmlephant.com

Windows

Enterprise IT Planet http://www.enterpriseitplanet.com

Information NT http://www.informationnt.com

Just Tech Jobs http://www.justtechjobs.com

Just Windows Jobs http://www.justwindowsjobs.com

NTPRO http://www.ntpro.org

Other Specialty

American Statistical Association Statistics Career Center http://www.amstat.org/careers

Association for Women in Computing http://www.awc-hq.org

Axaptajobs.com	http://www.axaptajobs.com
Black Data Processing Association Online	http://www.bdpa.org
Blackgeeks	http://www.blackgeeks.com
BroadbandCareers.com	http://www.broadband-careers.com
Carolina Computer Jobs	http://www.carolinacomputerjobs.com
Common Switzerland	http://www.common.ch
Controller Jobs	http://www.controllerjobs.com
CyberMediaDice.com [India]	http://www.cybermediadice.com
Donohue's RS/6000 & UNIX Employment Site	http://www.s6000.com
Ed Barlow's Sysbase Stuff	http://www.edbarlow.com
HeadHuntable	http://www.headhuntable.com
IrishDev.com [Ireland]	http://www.irishdev.com
IT Jobs in New York	http://www.it-jobs-in-new-york.com
Just Access Jobs	http://www.justaccessjobs.com
Just ASP Jobs	http://www.justaspjobs.com
Just Help Desk Jobs	http://www.justhelpdeskjobs.com
Just Informix Jobs	http://www.justinformixjobs.com
Just JD Edwards Jobs	http://www.justjdedwardsjobs.com
Just Mainframe Jobs	http://www.justmainframejobs.com
Just OLAP Jobs	http://www.justolapjobs.com
Just Perl Jobs	http://www.justperljobs.com
Just Progress Jobs	http://www.justprogressjobs.com
Just Project Manager Jobs	http://www.justprojectmanagerjobs.com
Just Q A Jobs	http://www.justqajobs.com
Just Security Jobs	http://www.justsecurityjobs.com
Just Siebel Jobs	http://www.justsiebeljobs.com
Just SQL Server Jobs	http://www.justsqlserverjobs.com
Just Sybase Jobs	http://www.justsybasejobs.com
Just Tech Sales Jobs	http://www.justtechsalesjobs.com
Just Telephony Jobs	http://www.justtelephonyjobs.com

Lapis Software	http://www.lapis.com
MinorityITJobs.com	http://www.minorityitjobs.com
MVShelp.com	http://www.mvshelp.com
NACCB	http://www.techservealliance.org/redirect.cfm
Project Manager	http://www.projectmanager.com
SAS-Jobs.com	http://www.sas-jobs.com
Software Contractor's Guild	http://www.scguild.com
Software Developer	http://www.softwaredeveloper.com
Software Engineer	http://softwareengineer.com
Software & IT Sales Employment Review	http://cardbrowser.com
Software QA and Testing Resource Center	http://www.softwareqatest.com
Sun Microsystems	http://www.oracle.com/index.html
Tech Writers	http://www.techwriters.com
Telecommuting Techies	http://www.telecommuting-techies.com
University of Maryland Computer Science Grads	http://www.cs.umd.edu/users
Texas A&M University Computer Science Grads	http://www.cs.tamu.edu
Women in Technology	http://www.womenintechnology.org
Women in Technology International (WITI) 4Hire	http://www.witi4hire.com

Insurance

Actuary.com	http://www.actuary.com
ActuaryJobs.com	http://www.actuaryjobs.com
Alliance of Merger and Acquisition Advisors	http://www.amaaonline.com
America's Health Insurance Plans	http://careersource.ahiphiwire.org
American Institute for Chartered Property Casualty Underwriters	http://www.aicpcu.org
Casualty Acturial Society Career Center	http://careers.casact.org
Chartered Property Casualty Underwriters	http://www.cpcusociety.org
4 Insurance Jobs	http://www.4insurancejobs.com
Global Association of Risk Professionals Career Center	http://www.garp.com/careercenter/index.asp

Great Insurance Jobs	http://www.greatinsurancejobs.com
Great Insurance Recruiters	http://www.greatinsurancerecruiters.com
IFSjobs.com	http://www.ifsjobs.com
iHireInsurance.com	http://www.ihireinsurance.com
INSData	http://hanbiro.com/index.html
InsuranceClaimsWeb.com	http://www.insuranceclaimsweb.com
Insurance File	http://www.insfile.com
The Insurance Job Bank	http://www.iiin.com/iiinjobs.html
InsuranceJobs.com	http://www.insurancejobs.com
InsurancePathway.com	http://www.insurancepathway.com
InsuranceSalesJobs.com	http://www.insurancesalesjobs.com
InsuranceSalesWeb.com	http://www.insurancesalesweb.com
InsuranceUnderwritingWeb.com	http://www.insuranceunderwritingweb.com
InsuranceWorks.com [Canada]	http://www.insuranceworks.com/bins/index.asp
Jobs4Actuary	http://www.jobs4actuary.com
JobInsurance.ca [Canada]	http://www.jobassurance.ca
LIMRA International	http://www.limra.com
LP Jobs Free	http://www.lpjobsfree.com
National Insurance Recruiters Association Online Job Database	http://www.nirassn.com
NationJob Network: Financial, Accounting and Insurance Jobs Page	http://www.nationjob.com/financial
Online Insurance Jobs [United Kingdom]	http://www.onlineinsurancejobs.co.uk
Property and Casualty	http://www.propertyandcasualty.com
Risk Info	http://www.riskinfo.com
Risk & Insurance Management Society Careers	http://www.rims.org
RiskManagementWeb.com	http://www.riskmanagementweb.com
Ultimate Insurance Jobs	http://www.ultimateinsurancejobs.com
UnderwritingJobs.com	http://www.underwritingjobs.com

International

International-General

AnyWorkAnywhere.com	http://www.anyworkanywhere.com
Campus Review	http://www.campusreview.com.au
CareerBridge	http://http://overview.careeredge.ca
CatererGlobal	http://www.catererglobal.com
Community Learning Network	http://www.cln.org
Danger Zone Jobs	http://www.dangerzonejobs.com
Empowered Network	http://empowerednetworks.com
Escape Artist	http://www.escapeartist.com
Expat Exchange	http://www.expatexchange.com
Expat Focus	http://www.expatfocus.com
ExpatHiring.com	http://www.expathiring.com
Expat Network	http://www.expatnetwork.com
Expatriates.com	http://www.expatriates.com
Escape Artist	http://www.escapeartist.com
Financial Job Network	http://www.financialjobnetwork.com
FT.com -Financial Times	http://www.ft.com
Global Workplace	http://www.qs.com/globalworkplace
International Jobs Center	http://www.internationaljobs.org
International Personnel Management Association	http://www.ipma-hr.org
International Society for Molecular Plant-Microbe Interactions	http://www.ismpminet.org/career
International Union of Food	http://www.iuf.org
JobsAbroad.com	http://www.jobsabroad.com
Jobs 4 All	http://www.jobs4all.com
Net Expat	http://www.netexpat.com
The Network	http://www.the-network.com
Oil Online	http://www.oilonline.com
OneWorld.net	http://us.oneworld.net/jobs
OverseasJobsExpress	http://www.overseasjobs.com

The Internet Pilot to Physics	http://physicsworld.com
Sales & Marketing Executives International Career Center	http://www.smei.org
Space Jobs	http://www.spacejobs.com
Top Jobs	http://www.topjobs.co.uk

Africa-General

AfricaJob.com	http://www.africajob.com
AfricaJobsSite.com	http://www.africajobsite.com
AfricaJobs.net	http://www.africajobs.net
FindaJobinAfrica.com	http://www.findajobinafrica.com
Job Searching for Africa	http://www.africa.upenn.edu
Kazinow.com	http://www.kazinow.com
NetServeAfrica	http://netserveafrica.com/jobs
WazobiaJobs.com	http://www.wazobiajobs.com

Argentina

Bumeran.com	http://www.bumeran.com
Buscares.com	http://www.buscares.com
Empleate.com	http://www2.empleate.com
Empleos.Clarin.com	http://www.empleos.clarin.com/Postulantes
Execuzone.com	http://www.execuzone.com
Jobrapido.ar	http://www.jobrapido.com.ar
Laborum.com	http://www.laborum.com/laborum_com/Default.htm
MineJobs.com	http://www.minejobs.com
TipTopJob.com	http://www.tiptopjob.com
Zeezo.com	http://www.zeezo.com
ZonaJobs.com.ar	http://www.zonajobs.com.ar

Asia-General

Asia Inc.	http://www.asia-inc.com
Asianet	http://www.asianetglobal.com
Asiaco Jobs Center	http://jobs.asiabot.com
Asianpro.com	http://asianpro.com
CareerJournal Asia	http://online.wsj.com/public/page/news-career-jobs.html
Career Next	http://www.careernext.com
JobsDB	http://www.jobsdb.com
Job Street	http://www.jobstreet.com
Panda Career	http://www.pandacareer.com
Recruit.net	http://usa.recruit.net
Wang & Li Asia Resources Online	http://www.wang-li.com

Australia

Ambition	http://www.ambition.com.au
Artshub.com.au	http://www.artshub.com.au/au
The Australian Resume Server	http://www.herenow.com.au
TheBigChair.com.au	http://thebigchair.com.au
Campus Review	http://www.campusreview.com.au
CareerOne	http://www.careerone.com.au
Careers On Line	http://www.careersonline.com.au
Careers.vic.gov.au	http://www.careers.vic.gov.au
CG Society/society of Digital Artists [Australia]	http://www.gcsociety.org
Employment Opportunities In Australia	http://www.employment.com.au
Fairfax Market	http://classifieds.fairfax.com.au
GrapevineJobs.com.au	http://www.grapevinejobs.com/home.asp.au/home.asp
Gurus.com.au	http://gurus.com.au
Jobwire.com.au	http://www.jobwire.com.au/home.aspx
JobsDB	http://www.jobsdb.com

Jobsearch.gov.au	http://www.jobsearch.gov.au
JustEngineers.net	http://www.justengineers.net
LinkedMe	http://www.linkme.com.au
Manpower.com.au	http://www.manpower.com.au
MyCareer.com.au	http://mycareer.com.au
MyMarketingJobs.com.au	http://mymarketingjobs.com.au
Queensland Department of Primary Industries	http://www.dpi.qld.gov.au
RagTradeJobs	http://www.ragtradejobs.com
SEEK	http://www.seek.com.au
TotallyFinancial.com.au	http://www.totallyfinancial.com/australia
TotallyLegal.com.au	http://www.totallylegal.com/australia
TheWest.com.au	http://au.news.yahoo.com/thewest
WorkingIn.com	http://www.workingin.com

Austria

Austria.at	http://www.austria.at
JobNews.at	http://www.jobnews.at
Jobrapido.at	http://www.jobrapido.at
Karriere.de	http://www.karriere.de
Kelzen.com	http://www.kelzen.com/en
Kununu.com	http://www.kununu.com
StepStone	http://www.stepstone.com
UniJobs.at	http://www.unijobs.at

Bahrain

Bayt	http://www.bayt.com
GulfJobsMarket.com	http://www.gulfjobsmarket.com
Gulf Talent	http://www.gulftalent.com

Baltics

CV Market	http://www.cvmarket.net

Bangladesh

JobsDB   http://www.jobsdb.com

Belarus

HeadHunter   http://hh.ru

Belgium

DataNewsJobs.com   http://datanews.rnews.be/datanews/nl/jobs

JobsCareer.be   http://www.jobscareer.be

Organic Chemistry Jobs Worldwide   http://www.organicworldwide.net/jobs

StepStone   http://www.stepstone.com

ToplanguageJobs.be   http://www.toplanguagejobs.be

Vacature.com   http://www.vacature.com

Vlan.be   http://www.vlan.be

Bermuda

Bermuda Biological Station for Research, Inc.   http://www.bios.edu

BermudaJobs.com   http://www.bermudajobs.com

Brazil

Jobrapido.br   http://www.jobrapidobrasil.com

Lartin MBA   http://www.latinmba.com

LatPro   http://www.latpro.com

Zeezo   http://brazil.zeezo.com/jobs.htm

Bulgaria

Jobs.bg   http://www.jobs.bg

Canada

AbilityEdge   http://overview.careeredge.ca

ACREQ   http://www.cre.qc.ca

ActiJob	http://www.act1staff.com
AdminJob.ca	http://www.adminjob.ca
BaseJobs.com	http://www.basejobs.com
Battlefords Job Shop	http://regionalhelpwanted.com/home/279.htm
Calgary Job Shop	http://regionalhelpwanted.com/calgary-jobs
CallCenterJob.ca	http://www.callcenterjob.ca
CanadaIT.com	http://www.canadait.com/cfm/index.cfm
CanadaJobs.com	http://www.canadajobs.com
CanadaParttime.com	http://www.canadaparttime.com/content/flash
Canada's Fifty-Plus	http://www.fifty-plus.net
Canadian Association of Accredited Mortgage Professionals	http://www.caamp.org
Canadian Association of Career Educators & Employers	http://www.cacee.com
Canadian Careers	http://www.canadiancareers.com
Canadian Relocation Systems	http://relocatecanada.com
Canadian Resume' Centre	http://www.canres.com
Canadian Society of Biochemistry and Molecular and Cellular Biologists Experimental Medicine Job Listing	http://www.medicine.mcgill.ca
Canadian Technical Recruiters Network	http://changethatsrightnow.com
Canjobs.com	http://www.canjobs.com
CanMed	http://www.canmed.com
CareerBridge	http://overview.careeredge.ca
CareerBuilder	http://www.careerbuilder.ca/CA/Default.aspx
CareerEdge	http://www.careeredge.ca
Career Internetworking	http://www.careerkey.com
Career Xchange	http://www.careerxchange.com
CASource	http://www.casource.com
Circuit Match	http://www.circuit-search.com/Esearch/applicant_contact.asp
Diversity Careers	http://www.diversitycareers.ca
Eastern Ontario Job Shop	http://regionalhelpwanted.com/eastern-ontario-jobs

eChannelLinecareers.com	http://www.echannellinecareers.com
Edmonton Job Shop	http://regionalhelpwanted.com/edmonton-jobs
Eluta.ca	http://www.eluta.ca
Globe and Mail	http://www.theglobeandmail.com
Grande Prairie Job Shop	http://regionalhelpwanted.com/home/307.htm
Hcareers	http://www.hcareers.ca
HeadHunt.com	http://www.thecounselnetwork.com
HRjob.ca	http://www.humanresourcesjobs.ca/default_en.html
Human Resource Professionals Association of Ontario	http://www.hrpa.ca/Pages/Default.aspx
InfoPresseJobs.com	http://www.infopressejobs.com
Institute of Chartered Accountants of Alberta	http://www.albertacas.ca
InsuranceWorks.com	http://www.insuranceworks.com/bins/index.asp
ITjob.ca	http://www.itjob.ca
Jobboom	http://www.jobboom.com
JobInsurance.ca	http://www.jobassurance.ca
JobLoft.com	http://www.jobloft.com
JobPostings.ca	http://www.jobpostings.ca
JobWings.com	http://www.jobwings.com
Jobs	http://www.jobs.ca
Jobs Abroad	http://www.jobsabroad.com
KW Job Shop	http://regionalhelpwanted.com/kitchener-waterloo-jobs
LegalJob.ca	http://www.legaljob.ca/default_en.html
Lethbridge Job Shop	http://regionalhelpwanted.com/lethbridge-jobs
Medicine Hat Job Shop	http://regionalhelpwanted.com/home/294.htm
Misco Jobs	http;//www.miscojobs.com
Net @ccess	http://www.nac.net
New Brunswick Job Shop	http://regionalhelpwanted.com/new-brunswick-jobs
Newfoundland Labrador Job Shop	http://regionalhelpwanted.com/newfoundland-labrador-jobs

NiceJob.ca	http://www.nicejob.ca
Nova Scotia Job Shop	http://regionalhelpwanted.com/nova-scotia-jobs
Ottawa Area Computer Job Links Page	http://regionalhelpwanted.com/ottawa-jobs/
Ottawa Job Shop	http://regionalhelpwanted.com/ottawa-jobs
Paralegaljob.ca	http://www.paralegaljob.ca
Payroll Jobs	http://www.payrolljobs.com
Petroleum Services Association of Canada	http://www.psac.ca
PMjob.ca	http://www.PMjob.ca
Prince Albert Job Shop	http://regionalhelpwanted.com/home/278.htm
Prince George Job Shop	http://regionalhelpwanted.com/home/309.htm
PubliPac.ca	http://www.publipac.ca
RecruitersCafe.com	http://www.recruiterscafe.com
Recrutech.ca	http://www.recrutech.ca
Red Deer Job Shop	http://regionalhelpwanted.com/home/285.htm
Regina Job Shop	http://regionalhelpwanted.com/regina-jobs
RetailJob.ca	http://www.retailjob.ca
SalesRep.ca	http://www.salesrep.ca
Saskatoon Job Shop	http://regionalhelpwanted.com/saskatoon-jobs
SCWIST Work Pathfinder	http://www.scwist.ca
SkilledWorkers.com	http://www.skilledworkers.com
Sympatico Work Place	http://www.sympatico.ca
Thompson Okanagan Job Shop	http://regionalhelpwanted.com/thompson-okanagan-jobs
Toronto Job Shop	http://regionalhelpwanted.com/toronto-jobs
Toronto Jobs	http://www.toronto.jobs.com
Toronto Society of Financial Analysts	http://www.tsfa.ca
United States & Canadian Academy of Pathology	http://careers.uscap.org
Vancouver Job Shop	http://regionalhelpwanted.com/vancouver-jobs
Vancouver Jobs	http://www.vancouverjobs.com
Victoria Job Shop	http://regionalhelpwanted.com/victoria-jobs
Winnipeg Job Shop	http://regionalhelpwanted.com/winnipeg-jobs

Working.ca   http://www.working.ca

Workopolis   http://www.workopolis.com

Caribbean

CaribCareer.com   http://www.caribcareer.com

Caribbean JobFair   http://www.caribbeanjobfair.com

CaribbeanJobs.com   http://www.caribbeanjobs.com

CaribbeanJobsOnline.com   http://www.caribbeanjobsonline.com

Escape Artist   http://www.escapeartist.com

ResortJobs.com   http://www.resortjobs.com

TropicJobs.com   http://www.tropicjobs.com

Chile

Bumeran.com   http://www.bumeran.com

ChileTech.com   http://www.chiletech.com

Empleate.com   http://www2.empleate.com

Jobrapido.cl   http://www.jobrapido.cl

Laborum.com   http://www.laborum.com/laborum_com/
                               Default.htm

TipTopJob.com   http://www.tiptopjob.com

Zeezo   http://chile.zeezo.com/jobs.htm

China

Asiaco Jobs Center   http://jobs.asiabot.com

CC-Jobs.com   http://www.cc-jobs.com

CJOL   http://www.cjol.com

ChinaHR.com   http://www.chinahr.com/index.htm

DragonSurf.biz   http://dragonsurf.biz

800HR   http://www.800hr.com

51job.com   http://www.51job.com

JobCN   http://www.jobcn.com

Jobkoo	http://www.jobkoo.com
Job168.com	http://www.job168.com
JobSquare	http://www.jobsquare.com
JobsDB	http://www.jobsdb.com
Saongroup.cn	http://www.saongroup.cn
St 701	http://www.st701.com
Zaobao	http://www.zaobao.com
Zhaopin	http://www.zhaopin.com

Colombia

Bumeran.com	http://www.bumeran.com
Empleate.com	http://www2.empleate.com
Laborum.com	http://www.laborum.com/laborum_com/Default.htm
TipTopJob.com	http://www.tiptopjob.com

Croatia

MojPosao	http://www.moj-posao.net

Czech Republic

CV-Online	http://www.cvonline.cz
HotJobs.cz	http://www.hotjobs.cz
Jobs.cz	http://www.jobs.cz
Prace.cz	http://www.prace.cz
Sprace.cz	http://www.sprace.cz/index.fcgi

Denmark

IT-JobBank	http://www.it-jobbank.dk
Job-Index	http://www.jobindex.dk
+Jobs Danmark	http://www.denmark.plusjobs.com
StepStone	http://www.stepstone.com

TopLanguageJobs.dk   http://www.toplanguagejobs.dk

Dubai

GulfJobsMarket.com   http://www.gulfjobsmarket.com

Gulf Talent   http://www.gulftalent.com

UAE Dubai Jobs   http://www.uaedubaijobs.com

Egypt

Bayt   http://www.bayt.com

Estonia

CV Market   http://www.cvmarket.net

CV-Online   http://www.cvonline.cz

Europe-General

AuPair In Europe   http://www.planetaupair.com/aupaireng.htm

CareerJournal Europe   http://online.wsj.com/public/page/
                                        news-career-jobs.html

CareersinAudit   http://www.careersinaudit.com/home/home.aspx

CVO Online   http://www.cvogroup.com

eFinancial Careers   http://www.efinancialcareers.com

Exposure Jobs   http://www.exposurejobs.com

EUjobzone.com   http://www.eujobzone.com

Euroleaders   http://www.euroleaders.com

Jobline International   http://www.jobline.net

The Network   http://www.the-network.com

Russoft.org   http://www.russoft.org

The SAP Job Board   http://www.thesapjobboard.com

StepStone   http://www.stepstone.com

SupplyChainRecruit.com   http://www.supplychainrecruit.com

TipTopJob.com   http://www.tiptopjob.com

Top Language Jobs	http://www.toplanguagejobs.co.uk
Vault	http://www.vault.com/wps/portal/usa
Wideyes	http://www.wideyes.co.uk

Finland

StepStone	http://www.stepstone.com
Uranus	http://www.uranus.fi

France

AdenClassifieds	http://www.adenclassifieds.com
ANPE.fr	http://www.pole-emploi.fr/accueil
BlogEmploi	http://www.cadresonline.com/coaching/blog/index_blog_emploi.php
Cadremploi.fr	http://www.cadremploi.fr
CadresOnline	http://www.cadresonline.com
CEGOS Worldwide	http://www.cegos.fr/Pages/default.aspx
CmonJob.fr	http://www.cmonjob.fr
Cooptin.com	http://www.cooptin.com
DialJob.com	http://www.dialjob.com
eFinancialCareers.fr	http://www.efinancialcareers.fr
eMailJob.com	http://www.emailjob.com
Jobrapido.fr	http://www.jobrapido.fr
KelJob.com	http://www.keljob.com
Les Echos	http://emploi.lesechos.fr
Mobiljob [France]	http://www.topannonces.fr
Monster.fr	http://www.monster.fr
ParisJob.com	http://www.parisjob.com
Purjob.com	http://www.purjob.com
StepStone	http://www.stepstone.fr
TopLanguageJobs.fr	http://www.toplanguagejobs.fr

Germany

All4Engineers.de	http://www.all4engineers.com
Arbeitlife.de	http://www.arbeitlife.de/arbeitlife_v2006
Arbeitsagentur.de	http://www.arbeitsagentur.de
Association for Applied Human Pharmacology	http://www.agah.info
CallCenterProfi.de	http://www.callcenterprofi.de
City Jobs	http://www.cityjobs.com
EMBL Job Vacancies	http://www.embl.de/aboutus/jobs/index.php
FazJob.net	http://fazjob.net
Financial Times Deutschland	http://www.ftd.de
Germany-USA	http://www.germany-usa.com
Getjob.de	http://www.getjob.de
GrapevineJobs.de	http://www.mediajobs.de/home.asp
ICjobs	http://www.icjobs.de
JobBerlin.com	http://www.jobsinberlin.eu
Jobdoo.de	http://www.jobdoo.de
JobDumping.de	http://www.jobdumping.de
Jobline	http://www.jobline.de
JobPilot.de	http://www.jobpilot.de
Jobrapido.de	http://www.jobrapido.de
Jobs.de	http://www.jobs.de
JobScout 24	http://www.jobscout24.de
JobStairs.de	http://www.jobstairs.de
JobVoting.com	http://www.jobvoting.com
Jobware.de	http://www.jobware.de
Kimeta.de	http://www.kimeta.de
Meinestadt.de	http://www.meinestadt.de
Monster.de	http://www.monster.de
Pflegekarriere.de	http://www.pflegekarriere.de
Stellenanzeigen.de	http://www.stellenanzeigen.de
StepStone	http://www.stepstone.com

TopLanguageJobs.de	http://www.toplanguagejobs.de
Undertool.de	http://www.undertool.de
Virtueller Arbeitsmarkt	http://www.arbeitsagentur.de
WorkingOffice.de	http://www.workingoffice.de
Worldwide Jobs	http://www.worldwidejobs.de
Xing	http://www.xing.com
Yourcha.de	http://www.yourcha.com/de/employee/home/s

Greece

Kariera.gr	http://www.kariera.gr/GR/Default.aspx
Skywalker	http://www.skywalker.gr
StepStone	http://www.stepstone.com

Guam

Job Search in Guam	http://www.worldtenant.com

Hong Kong

DragonSurf.biz	http://dragonsurf.biz
Hong Kong Jobs	http://www.hkjobs.com
Hong Kong Standard	http://www.thestandard.com.hk
JobsDB	http://www.jobsdb.com
Monster.com.hk	http://www.monster.com.hk

Hungary

CV-Online	http://www.cvonline.cz
CVO Online	http://www.cvogroup.com
GrapevineJobs.hu	http://www.grapevinejobs.hu/home/home.asp
Profession.hu	http://www.profession.hu
TopJob.hu	http://www.topjob.hu

India

AskNaukri.com	http://asknaukri.com
BPOJobSite.com	http://www.bpojobsite.com
CareerBuilderIndia.com	http://www.careerbuilder.co.in/IN/Default.aspx
Career India	http://jobs.oneindia.in/
Career Mosaic India	http://www.careermosaicindia.com
Cyber India Online	http://www.ciol.com
CyberMediaDice.com	http://www.cybermediadice.com
Icon Job	http://www.iconjob.com
Ikerala	http://www.ikerala.com
JobStreet.com	http://www.jobstreet.com
Jobs Ahead	http://www.jobsahead.com
JobsDB	http://www.jobsdb.com
MonsterIndia	http://www.monsterindia.com
Nasscom.in	http://www.nasscom.in
Naukri.com	http://www.naukri.com
RegisterJobs.com	http://www.registerjobs.com
TimesJobs.com	http://www.timesjobs.com

Indonesia

JobStreet.com	http://www.jobstreet.com.id

Iraq

All Iraq Jobs	http://www.alliraqjobs.com
Bayt	http://www.bayt.com

Ireland

AdminJobs.ie	http://www.adminjobs.ie
Antsjobs.ie	http://www.antsjobs.ie
ComputerJobs.ie	http://www.computerjobs.ie
Corporate Skills	http://www.irishjobs.com

Hcareers	http://www.hcareers.co.uk
IFSCjobs.com	http://www.ifscjobs.com
IrishDev.com	http://www.irishdev.com
Irishjobs	http://www.irishjobs.ie
The Irish Jobs Page	http://www.exp.ie
Jobrapido.ie	http://www.jobrapido.ie
JobSearchNI.com	http://www.jobsearchni.com
JobsinHealth.com	http://www.jobsinhealth.co.uk
JumptoJobs	http://www.jumptojobs.co.uk
Loadzajobs.co.uk	http://www.nijobfinder.co.uk
Northern Ireland Jobs	http://www.nijobs.com
RecruitIreland.com	http://www.recruitireland.com
SalesJobs.ie	http://www.salesjobs.ie/parodia/default.asp
ToplanguageJobs.ie	http://www.toplanguagejobs.ie
TotalJobs.com	http://www.totaljobs.com

Israel

AllJobs	http://www.alljobs.col.il
The Jerusalem Post	http://info.jpost.com/C005/IsraelJobs
JobNet Israel	http://www.jobnet.co.il
Marksman	http://www.marksman.co.il
MyRecruiter.com	http://www.myrecruiter.com

Italy

Annunciveloci.it	http://www.annunciveloci.it
FaceCV	http://www.facecv.it
Infojobs.it	http://www.infojobs.it
Jobcrawler.it	http://www.jobcrawler.it
JobOnline.it	http://www.jobonline.it
Jobrapido	http://www.jobrapido.com
MediaJobs.it	http://www.mediajobs.it/home.asp

Monster.it	http://www.monster.it
StepStone	http://www.stepstone.com
TalentManager	http://www.talentmanager.it
TopLanguageJobs.it	http://www.toplanguagejobs.it
Trovit.it	http://www.trovit.it

Jamaica

CarribeanJobs.com	http://www.carribeanjobs.com
SplashJamaica.com	http://www.splashjamaica.com

Japan

Career Forum	http://www.careerforum.net
Daijob.com	http://www.daijob.com
en-japan inc.	http://employment.en-japan.com
Japanese Jobs	http://www.japanesejobs.com
Job Easy	http://www.jobeasy.com
Mixi, Inc.	http://www.find-job.net
NAUKRI	http://www.naukri.com
O Hayo Sensei	http://www.ohayosensei.com
Tokyo Classified	http://classifieds.metropolis.co.jp

Jordan

Akhtaboot	http://www.akhtaboot.com
Bayt	http://www.bayt.com

Kazakhstan

Headhunter	http://hh.ru

Korea

Asiaco Jobs Center	http://jobs.asiabot.com
Careerxiet	http://www.career.co.kr

Job Korea [not in English]   http://www.jobkorea.co.kr

Peoplenjob   http://www.peoplenjob.com/home

Kuwait

Bayt   http://www.bayt.com

Gulf Talent   http://www.gulftalent.com

Latin America

Asiaco Jobs Center   http://jobs.asiabot.com

Bumeran   http://www.bumeran.com

Latin MBA   http://www.latinmba.com

LatPro   http://www.latpro.com

Latvia

CV Market   http://www.cvmarket.net

CV-Online   http://www.cvonline.cz

Lebanon

Bayt   http://www.bayt.com

Libya

Bayt   http://www.bayt.com

Lithuania

CV Market   http://www.cvmarket.net

CV-Online   http://www.cvonline.cz

Luxembourg

Monster.lu   http://www.monster.lu

StepStone   http://www.stepstone.com

Malaysia

JobStreet.com	http://www.jobstreet.com.my
JobsDB	http://www.jobsdb.com
StarJobs Online	http://www.star-jobs.com

Mexico

ChambaMex.com	http://regionalhelpwanted.com/home/273.htm
Jobrapido.com.mx	http://www.jobrapido.com.mx
Laborum.com	http://www.laborum.com/laborum_com/Default.htm
OCCMundial	http://www.occmundial.com

Middle East

Aljazeerajobs.com	http://www.aljazeerajobs.com
Arabia! Hot Jobs	http://www.arabiahotjobs.com
Bayt	http://www.bayt.com
Careerjunctionme.com	http://www.careerjunctionme.com
GulfJobSites.com	http://www.gulfjobsites.com
GulfJobsMarket.com	http://www.gulftalent.com/home/index.php
Gulf Talent	http://www.gulfjobsmarket.com
MonsterGulf.com	http://www.gulftalent.com
My Middle East Jobs	http://www.mymiddleeastjobs.com
NaukriGulf.com	http://www.naukrigulf.com

Montenegro

Bestjobs.rs	http://www.bestjobs.rs

Morocco

Rekrute	http://www.rekrute.com

Netherlands

CareerBuilder.nl	http://www.careerbuilder.nl
City Jobs	http://www.cityjobs.com
CV Market	http://www.cvmarket.nl
EEGA	http://www.eega.nl
GrapevineJobs.nl	http://www.mediajobsonline.nl/home.asp
Hospitality Net Virtual Job Exchange	http://www.hospitalitynet.org/index.html
Jobrapido.nl	http://www.jobrapido.nl
Jobs Netherland	http://www.jobs.nl
JobTrack.nl	http://www.jobtrack.nl/jobtrack
MonsterBoard.nl	http://www.monsterboard.nl
NationaleVacaturebank.nl	http://www.nationalevacaturebank.nl
StepStone	http://www.stepstone.com
TopLanguageJobs.nl	http://www.toplanguagejobs.nl

New Zealand

Executive Taskforce	http://executivetaskforce.org
Job.co.nz	http://www.job.co.nz
KiwiCareers	http://www.kiwicareers.govt.nz
RealContacts.com	http://jobs.realcontacts.com
SEEK	http://www.seek.co.nz
Trade Me	http://www.trademe.co.nz/Trade-me-jobs/index.htm
WineJobsOnline	http://www.winejobsonline.con
WorkingIn.com	http://www.workingin.com

Norway

CareerBuilder.no	http://www.careerbuilder.no
Finn.no	http://www.finn.no
Rubrikk.no	http://www.rubrikk.no
StepStone	http://www.stepstone.com

TopLanguageJobs.no — http://www.toplanguagejobs.no

Oman

Bayt — http://www.bayt.com

Gulf Talent — http://www.gulftalent.com

Pakistan

Bayt — http://www.bayt.com

Peru

Bumeran.com — http://www.bumeran.com

Empleate.com — http://www2.empleate.com

Laborum.com — http://www.laborum.com/laborum_com/Default.htm

TipTopJob.com — http://www.tiptopjob.com

Zeezo — http://peru.zeezo.com/jobs.htm

Philippines

JobStreet Philippines — http://www.jobstreet.com.ph

JobsDB — http://www.jobsdb.com

Jobs.NET — http://www.jobs.net

Philippines Jobs — http://www.philippinejobs.ph

Poland

CV-Online — http://www.cvonline.cz

Gazeta.pl — http://www.gazeta.pl/0,0.html

GazetaPraca.pl — http://gazetapraca.pl/gazetapraca/0,0.html

GrapevineJobs.pl — http://www.grapevinejobs.pl/glowna.asp

infoPraca.pl — http://www.infopraca.pl

JobPilot.pl — http://www.jobpilot.pl

Jobrapido.pl — http://www.jobrapido.pl

JobSpot.pl	http://www.jobspot.pl
MetroPlaca.pl	http://www.metroplaca.pl
MonsterPolska.pl	http://www.monsterpolska.pl
Pracownicy.it	http://pracownicy.it
Pracuj.pl	http://www.pracuj.pl
Targi24.pl	http://www.targi.pracuj.pl

Portugal

| StepStone | http://www.stepstone.com |
| Super Emprego | http://emprego.sapo.pt |

Qatar

Bayt	http://www.bayt.com
GulfJobsMarket.com	http://www.gulfjobsmarket.com
Gulf Talent	http://www.gulftalent.com

Romania

BestJobs	http://www.bestjobs.ro
CV-Online	http://www.cvonline.cz
JobsinRO.ro	http://www.jobsinro.ro
RomJob.ro	http://www.romjob.ro

Russia

Career.ru	http://www.career.ru
CV-Online	http://www.cvonline.cz
HeadHunter	http://hh.ru
Job.ru	http://www.job.ru
Joblist.ru	http://www.joblist.ru
100rabot.ru	http://www.100rabot.ru
Rabota.ru	http://www.rabota.ru
SuperJob.ru	http://www.superjob.ru

Saudi Arabia

All Saud Arabia Jobs	http://www.allsaudiarabiajobs.com
ArabiaHotJobs.com	http://www.arabiahotjobs.com
Bayt	http://www.bayt.com
GulfJobsMarket.com	http://www.gulfjobsmarket.com
Gulf Talent	http://www.gulftalent.com

Scotland

InternalAuditJobs.net	http://www.internalauditjobs.net
Jobsword	http://www.jobsword.co.uk/scotland.html
JobTonic.com	http://www.jobtonic.com
ScotCareers.co.uk	http://www.scotcareers.co.uk
Scot Ed Jobs	http://www.scotedjobs.com
ScotlandJobs.net	http://www.scotlandjobs.net
ScotRecruit.com	http://www.scotrecruit.com
ScottishHospitalityJobs.com	http://www.scottishhospitalityjobs.com
ScottishJobs.com	http://www.scottishjobs.com
ScottishLegalJobs.com	http://www.scottishlegaljobs.com
S1jobs.com	http://www.s1jobs.com
TechJobsScotland	http://www.techjobscotland.com
TotalJobs.com	http://www.totaljobs.com
WorkWithUs.org	http://www.workwithus.org/careers/Default.aspx

Serbia

BestJobs	http://www.bestjobs.rs
Infostud	http://www.infostud.com

Singapore

JobStreet.com	http://www.jobstreet.com.sg
Jobs Central.com.sg	http://jobscentral.com.sg
JobsDB	http://www.jobsdb.com

Singapore Jobs Directory	http://www.jobs.com.sg
SingaporeJobsOnline.com	http://www.singaporejobsonline.com
Singapore Press Holdings	http://www.st701.com

Slovakia

CV-Online	http://www.cvonline.cz
Profesia.sk	http://www.profesia.sk

Slovenia

Moje Delo	http://www.mojedelo.com

South Africa

Best Jobs South Africa	http://www.bestjobs.co.za
BioCareers.co.za	http://www.biocareers.co.za
CareerClassifieds South Africa	http://www.careerclassifieds.co.za
CareerJunction	http://www.careerjunction.co.za
Jobs.co.za	http://www.jobs.co.za

South Korea

Career	http://www.career.co.kr
Incruit.com	http://www.incruit.com

Spain

CareerBuilder.es	http://www.careerbuilder.es
InfoEmpleo.com	http://www.infoempleo.com
InfoJobs.net	http://www.infojobs.net
Jobrapido.es	http://www.jobrapido.es
Laboris.net	http://www.laboris.net
Miltrabajos.com	http://www.miltrabajos.com
Monster Espania	http://www.monster.es
Opcionempleo.com	http://www.opcionempleo.com

SmartCV.org	https://www.smartcv.org/smartcv2/Login.do
SmartEmployer.org	http://www.smartemployer.org
Spanish-Living.com	http://www.spanish-living.com/jobs_offers.php
TopLanguageJobs.es	http://www.toplanguagejobs.es
Trovit.es	http://www.trovit.es
Zeezo	http://spain.zeezo.com/jobs

Sweden

Dagens Industri	http://di.se
Jobb24.se	http://jobb24.se
Jobb.Eniro.se	http://jobb.eniro.se
Jobbguiden.se	http://www.careerbuilder.se
Jobbporten.se	http://jobbporten.se
JobSafari.se	http://www.jobbsafari.se
JobbSverige AB	http://www.jobbsverige.se
Jobrapido.se	http://www.jobrapido.se
Jobs.se	http://www.jobs.se
Lokus.se	http://lokus.se/Exp_SearchStart_all.asp?
Platsbanken	http://www.arbetsformedlingen.se/platsbanken
Shortcut	http://www.shortcut.nu
StepStone	http://www.stepstone.com
TopLanguageJobs.se	http://www.toplanguagejobs.se
Workey.se	http://www.workey.se
WorkShopping.com	http://www.workshopping.com

Switzerland

Common Switzerland	http://www.common.ch
JobPilot.ch	http://www.jobpilot.ch
Jobrapido.ch	http://www.jobrapido.ch
JobScout24.ch	http://www.jobscout24.ch
Jobs.ch	http://www.jobs.ch/en

LeTemps.ch	http://www.letemps.ch
Math-Jobs.ch	http://www.math-jobs.com
MBA Exchange	http://www.mba-exchange.com
Monster.ch	http://www.monster.ch
StepStone	http://www.stepstone.com
TopJobs.ch	http://www.topjobs.ch

Taiwan

DragonSurf.biz	http://dragonsurf.biz
JobsDB	http://www.jobsdb.com

Thailand

JobStreet.com Thailand	http://www.jobstreet.com.th
JobsDB	http://www.jobsdb.com
ThaiEngineeringJobs.com	http://www.thaiengineerjobs.com/en/index.asp
ThaiFinanceJobs.com	http://www.thaifinancejobs.com/en/index.asp
ThaiITJobs.com	http://\www.thaiitjobs.com/en/index.asp

Turkey

Kariyer.net	http://www.kariyer.net

Ukraine

Rabota.ua	http://rabota.ua

United Arab Emirates (See also Dubai)

Bayt.com	http://www.bayt.com
GulfJobsMarket.com	http://www.gulfjobsmarket.com
Gulf Talent	http://www.gulftalent.com
UAE Dubai Jobs	http://www.uaedubaijobs.com

United Kingdom

Access-Science Jobs	http://www.access-sciencejobs.co.uk
AccountancyAgeJobs.com	http://www.accountancyagejobs.com
AccountancyJobsboard	http://www.accountancyjobsboard.co.uk
AccountingWeb	http://www.accountingweb.co.uk
Activate.co.uk	http://www.activate.co.uk
Aeronautical Engineering Jobs	http://www.aeronauticalengineeringjobs.co.uk
Age Positive Jobs	http://www.agepositivejobs.com
Aged2Excel.co.uk	http://www.aged2excel.co.uk
AircraftEngineers.com [United Kingdom]	http://www.aircraftengineers.com
AllExecutiveJobs.com	http://www.allexecutivejobs.com
AllHospitality.co.uk	http://www.hospitalityonline.co.uk
AllHousingJobs.co.uk	http://www.allhousingjobs.co.uk
AllJobsUK.com	http://www.alljobsuk.com
Animal-Job.co.uk	http://www.animal-job.co.uk
Architecture Jobs	http://www.architecturejobs.co.uk
ArtsJobsOnline.com	http://www.artsjobsonline.com/home/home.asp
Association of Graduate Careers Advisory Service	http://www.agcas.org.uk
Association of Online Recruiters	http://www.rec.uk.com/home
Association of University Teachers	http://www.AUT4Jobs.com
Aston University	http://www1.aston.ac.uk
Balfour Betty Rail UK	http://www.bbrailjobs.co.uk
Barzone	http://www.barzone.co.uk
Bconstructive	http://www.bconstructive.co.uk
Beachwood Recruit	http://www.beechwoodrecruit.com
Belperjobs	http://www.belperjobs.co.uk
BigBlueDog.com	http://www.bigbluedog.com
Billington UK.com	http://www.billingtonuk.com
BlowSearch.com	http://www.blowsearch.com
Blue Line Jobs	http://www.bluelinejobs.co.uk
BookaChef.co.uk	http://www.bookachef.co.uk

British Jobs	http://www.britishjobs.net
B7 Appointments	http://www.business7.co.uk/b7-appointments
BUBL Employment Bulletin Board	http://bubl.ac.uk
Building Services Jobs	http://www.buildingservicesjobs.co.uk
ButternutJobs.com	http://www.butternutjobs.com
Cactussearch.co.uk	http://www.cactussearch.co.uk
Call Centres	http://www.searchconsultancy.co.uk
Canary Wharf Careers.co.uk	http://www.canarywharfcareers.co.uk
CanaryWharfJobs.com	http://www.canarywharfjobs.com
CancerJobs.net	http://www.cancerjobs.net
Career-Ahead	http://www.career-ahead.co.uk
CareerBuilder.co.uk	http://www.careerbuilder.co.uk
Careers4a.com	http://www.careers4a.com
CareersinLogistics	http://www.careersinlogistics.co.uk
CareersinRacing.com	http://www.careersinracing.com
CareersInRecruitment.com	http://www.careersinrecruitment.com
Caterer.com	http://www.caterer.com
CatererGlobal.com	http://www.catererglobal.com
Changeboard	http://www.changeboard.com
CharityJob.co.uk	http://www.charityjob.co.uk
Check4Jobs	http://www.check4jobs.com
Chef Jobs	http://www.chefjobs.co.uk
ChemPeople.com	http://www.chempeople.com
Citifocus	http://www.citifocus.co.uk/home
City Careers	http://citycareers.com
CityJobs	http://www.citijobs.co.uk
ClearedJobs.co.uk	http://www.clearedjobs.co.uk
CollegeJobs.co.uk	http://www.collegejobs.co.uk
Confidential IT	http://www.confidentialit.com
Construction4Professional.co.uk	http://www.construction4professionals.co.uk

ConstructionJobSearch	http://www.constructionjobsearch.co.uk
ConstructionJobsNow.co.uk	http://www.constructionjobsnow.co.uk
Constructor	http://www.constructor.co.uk
ConsultantsBoard.com	http://www.consultantsboard.com
Consultants on the Net	http://www.consultantsonthenet.com
Consultants United	http://www.consultantsunited.com
Cronecorkill.co.uk	http://www.hirethinking.com/redirect/cc.aspx
The CV Index Directory	http://www.cvindex.com
CV-Library	http://www.cv-library.co.uk
CVServices.net	http://cv-masterclass.com/cv.html
CVTrumpet.co.uk	http://www.cvtrumpet.co.uk
CWJobs.co.uk	http://www.cwjobs.co.uk
Datascope Recruitment	http://www.datascope.co.uk
Daxic.com	http://www.daxic.com
DERWeb	http://www.derweb.co.uk
DesignJobs.co.uk	http://www.designjobs.co.uk
DigitalMediaJobs.com	http://www.digitalmediajobs.com
DMjobs.co.uk	http://www.dmjobs.co.uk
Do-It	http://www.do-it.org.uk
dotJournalism	http://www.journalism.co.uk
DrapersOnline	http://www.drapersonline.com
Driving Jobs Board	http://www.drivingjobsboard.co.uk
Earthworks-Jobs	http://www.earthworks-jobs.com
EasyJobs.com	http://www.easyjobs.com
Edie's Environmental Job Centre	http://www.edie.net
Education-Jobs	http://www.education-jobs.co.uk
eFinancialCareers.com	http://www.efinancialcareers.com
EFL Web	http://www.eflweb.com
E-itsales.com	http://www.e-itsales.com
e-job	http://www.e-job.net

Emedcareers	http://www.emedcareers.com
ENDS	http://www.ends.co.uk/bs
The Engineer	http://www.theengineer.co.uk
Engineerboard.co.uk	http://www.engineerboard.co.uk
EngineeringJobs.co.uk	http://www.engineeringjobs.co.uk
EngineeringJobsnow.co.uk	http://www.engineeringjobsnow.co.uk
The Engineering Technology Site	http://www.engineers4engineers.co.uk
ERTonline.co.uk	http://www.ertonline.co.uk
Escape Artist	http://www.escapeartist.com
Eteach.com	http://www.eteach.com
Ethnicjobsite.co.uk	http://www.ethnicjobsite.co.uk
Euro London	http://www.eurolondon.com
Exec2Exec.com	http://www.exec2exec.com
TheExecutiveClub.com	http://www.theexecutiveclub.com
Executive-i.com	http://www.executive-i.com
ExecutiveOpenings.com	http://www.executiveopenings.com
ExecutivesOnline	http://www.executivesonline.co.uk
ExecutivesontheWeb.com	http://www.executivesontheweb.com
Experteer.co.uk	http://www.experteer.co.uk
FEcareers.co.uk	http://www.fecareers.co.uk
FEjobs.com	http://www.fejobs.com
50Connect.co.uk	http://www.50connect.co.uk
Findawork.co.uk	http://www.findawork.co.uk
First Choice Recruitment	http://www.first-choice-uk.co.uk
1st Job	http://www.1stjob.co.uk
1st 4 Jobs.com	http://www.1st4jobs.com
Fish4	http://www.fish4.co.uk
Fledglings	http://www.fledglings.net
Focus-Management	http://www.focusmanagement.co.uk
Football-jobs.com	http://www.football-jobs.com

FootieJobs.com	http://www.footiejobs.com
4 Weeks	http://www.4weeks.com
Freeads.co.uk	http://uk.freeads.net
FreeLancers Network	http://www.freelancers.net
Free-Recruitment.com	http://www.free-recruitment.com
Friday-Ad	http://www.friday-ad.co.uk
The Friday Pint	http://www.mediaweekjobs.co.uk
Front Recruitment	http://www.frontrecruitment.co.uk
Fss.co.uk	http://www.hirethinking.com
FuseJobs.co.uk	http://www.fusejobs.co.uk
FutureGate	http://www.futuregate.co.uk/internet.html
G2legal	http://www.g2legal.co.uk
GAAPWeb.com	http://www.gaapweb.com
GetMoreJobOffers.com	http://www.getmorejoboffers.com
GisaJob.com	http://www.gisajob.com
Glenrecruitment.co.uk	http://www.glenrecruitment.co.uk
GoJobSite	http://www.jobsite.co.uk
GoldJobs.com	http://www.goldjobs.com
Goldensquare.com	http://www.goldensquare.com
TheGraduate.co.uk	http://www.thegraduate.co.uk
Graduate-jobs.com	http://www.graduate-jobs.com
GraduatesYorkshire	http://www.graduatesyorkshire.co.uk
Grapevine Jobs	http://www.grapevinejobs.com/home.asp
GreenJobsOnline	http://www.greenjobsonline.co.uk
GrocerJobs.co.uk	http://jobs.thegrocer.co.uk
GTNews	http://www.gtnews.com
Guardian Jobs	http://www.guardianjobs.com
Guardian News and Media	http://jobs.guardian.co.uk
Gumtree.com	http://www.gumtree.com
GxPJobs.com	http://www.gxpjobs.com

Hcareers	http://www.hcareers.co.uk
HealthJobsUK.com	http://www.healthjobsuk.com/select_sector
Hedge Fund Intelligence LLC	http://www.hedgefundintelligence.com
HighTech Partners	http://www.hightechpartners.com
HospitalityRecruitment.co.uk	http://www.hospitalityrecruitment.co.uk
Hotcourses.com	http://www.givemeajob.co.uk
HotJobsandCareers	http://www.hotjobsandcareers.com
HotRecruit	http://www.hotrecruit.com
Hotel Jobs	http://www.hotel-jobs.co.uk
HR Staff	http://www.hrstaff.co.uk
Hy-phen	http://www.hy-phen.com
icNetwork.co.uk	http://www.icnetwork.co.uk
Ics Jobsboard	http://www.instituteofcustomerservicejobs.com
InAutomotive.com	http://www.inautomotive.com
In the Middle	http://www.inthemiddle.co.uk
Indeed.co.uk	http://www.indeed.co.uk
The Independent Consultants Network	http://www.inconet.com
Industry Appointments	http://www.industryappointments.com
InHR	http://www.inhr.co.uk
InRetail	http://www.inretail.co.uk
Intega Online	http://www.compucaregroup.com
InternalAuditJobs.net	http://www.internalauditjobs.net
ITCV	http://www.itcvrecruitment.co.uk/home.htm
TheITJobBoard.com	http://www.theitjobboard.com
ItJobs-online.com	http://www.itjobs-online.com
ITJobsPost.com	http://www.itjobspost.com
Itjobsvault.co.uk	http://www.itjobsvault.co.uk
ITVacancies.com	http://www.itvacancies.com
Jim Finder	http://www.jimfinder.com
Jobboard.IT	http://www.jobboardit.com

Jobcentre Plus	http://www.jobcentreplus.gov.uk
Jobcorner	http://www.jobcorner.com
JobChannel	http://www.jobchannel.cn
Job Finder	http://www.jobfinder.com
Job Force	http://www.jobforce.com
Job4me.com	http://www.job4me.com
Jobit	http://www.jobit.co.uk
Job Jobbed	http://www.jobjobbed.com
JobJourneyNorthWest.co.uk	http://northwest.jobjourney.co.uk
JobLux	http://www.joblux.co.uk
Job Magic	http://www.jobmagic.net
Job Magnet	http://www.jobmagnet.co.uk
JobMax.co.uk	http://www.jobmax.co.uk
JobPlant.co.uk	http://www.jobplant.co.uk
Job-Quest	http://www.job-quest.net
Jobrapido.co.uk	http://www.jobrapido.co.uk
JobSafari	http://www.jobsafari.co.uk
Job Search UK	http://www.jobsearch.co.uk
JobseekersAdvice.com	http://www.jobseekersadvice.com
Job Serve	http://www.jobserve.us
Job Shop	http://www.workweb.co.uk
JobSite UK	http://www.jobsite.co.uk
Job Store	http://www.jobstore.co.uk
Job-surf.com	http://www.job-surf.com
JobTonic.com	http://www.jobtonic.com
JobTrack Online	http://jobs.mirror.co.uk
Job Watch	http://www.jobwatch.org
Jobworld UK	http://www.computing.co.uk
Jobs.ac.uk	http://www.jobs.ac.uk
Jobs.brandrepublic.com	http://jobs.brandrepublic.com

Jobs.co.uk	http://www.jobs.co.uk
JobsCheshire.co.uk	http://www.jobscheshire.co.uk
JobsFinancial	http://www.jobsfinancial.com
Jobs4a.com	http://www.jobs4a.com
Jobsgopublic	http://www.jobsgopublic.com
JobsinCredit	http://www.jobsincredit.com
Jobsin.co.uk	http://www.jobsearch.co.uk
Jobs in Marketing	http://www.jobs-in-marketing.co.uk
JobsinCatering	http://www.jobsincatering.com
JobsinConstruction	http://www.jobsinconstruction.co.uk
JobsinContactCentres	http://www.jobsincontactcentres.com
JobsinEducation	http://www.jobsineducation.com
JobsinHealth	http://www.jobsinhealth.co.uk
JobsinHotels	http://www.jobsinhotels.com
JobsinLeisure	http://www.jobsinleisure.com
JobsinNHS	http://www.jobsinnhs.co.uk
JobsinPlymouth	http://www.jobsinplymouth.co.uk
JobsinPublicSector	http://www.jobsinpublicsector.co.uk
JobsinRetail	http://www.jobsinretail.com
JobsinRisk.com	http://www.jobsinrisk.com
JobsinSearch.com	http://www.jobsinsearch.com
JobsinSocialWork	http://www.jobsinsocialwork.com
JobsinSurveying	http://www.jobsinsurveying.co.uk
JobsinTravelandTourism	http://www.jobsintravelandtourism.com
JobsinWaste	http://www.jobsinwaste.co.uk
Jobs-Merseyside.co.uk	http://www.jobs-merseyside.co.uk
JobsMidlands.co.uk	http://www.jobsmidlands.co.uk
JobsNortheast.co.uk	http://www.jobsnortheast.co.uk
JobsNorthwest.co.uk	http://corporate.menmedia.co.uk
Job Souk	http://www.jobsouk.com

Jobs-Southeast.co.uk	http://www.jobs-southeast.co.uk
Jobs.telegraph.co.uk	http://http://jobs.telegraph.co.uk
Jobs.ThirdSector.co.uk	http://jobs.thirdsector.co.uk
Jobs2.com	http://www.jobs2.com
Jobs2seek.co.uk	http://www.jobsretail.co.uk
JobsWithBalls.com	http://www.jobswithballs.com
Johnston Vere	http://www.johnston-vere.co.uk
Journalism.co.uk	http://www.journalism.co.uk
JustClick.co.uk	http://www.justclick.co.uk
Just Construction	http://www.justconstruction.net
Just Engineers	http://www.justengineers.net
Just Go Contract!	http://www.gocontract.com
Just Graduates	http://www.justgraduates.net
JustIT	http://www.justit.co.uk
Just Rail	http://www.justrail.net
JustSalesandMarketing.net	http://www.justsalesandmarketing.net
JustTechnicalJobs	http://www.jobsgroup.net
KillerJobs.com	http://www.killerjobs.com
Labourstartjobs.org	http://www.labourstart.org
Laser Computer Recruitment	http://www.laserrec.co.uk
Law Gazette Jobs	http://www.lawgazettejobs.co.uk
Legal Jobs Board	http://www.legaljobsboard.co.uk
Legal Prospects	http://www.legalprospects.com
Leisure Jobs	http://www.leisurejobs.com
Leisure Jobs	http://www.leisurejobs.net
Leisure Jobs Now	http://www.leisurejobsnow.co.uk
Leisure Opportunities	http://www.leisureopportunities.co.uk
Leisure Recruit Ltd	http://www.thelrgroup.co.uk
LettingCareers	http://www.lettingcareers.com
Local Government Jobs	http://www.lgjobs.com

LocalJobSearch.co.uk	http://www.localjobsearch.co.uk
LocalRecruit.co.uk	http://www.localrecruit.co.uk
Locum Group Recruitment	http://www.locumgroup.co.uk/home.php
The London Biology Network	http://www.biolondon.org.uk
London Careers	http://www.londoncareers.net
London Jobs	http://www.londonjobs.co.uk
London Net	http://www.londonnet.co.uk
LondonOfficeJobs.co.uk	http://www.londonofficejobs.co.uk
TheLondonPaper.com	http://www.thelondonpaper.com
LondonSecretarialJobs.co.uk	http://www.londonsecretarialjobs.co.uk
LookTech.com	http://www.looktech.com
Mandy.com	http://www.mandy.com/1/filmtvjobs.cfm?jt=usa
Marine Recruitment Co.	http://www.marine-recruitment.co.uk
MarketingJobBoard.co.uk	http://www.marketingjobboard.co.uk
Maxim Recruitment	http://www.maximrecruitment.co.uk
MediaSalesJobs.co.uk	http://www.mediaweekjobs.co.uk
MedicSolve.com	http://www.medicsolve.com
Medjobsuk.com	http://www.medjobsuk.com
Milkround.com	http://www.milkround.com
Monster.com UK	http://www.monster.co.uk
MyAccountancyJobs	http://www.myaccountancyjobs.com
Mycvonline UK	http://www.mycv-online.com
MyHousingCareer	http://www.myhousingcareer.com
MyJobGroup.co.uk	http://www.myjobgroup.co.uk
My9to5.com	http://www.my9to5.com
My Oyster	http://www.myoyster.com
NannyJob.co.uk	http://www.nannyjob.co.uk
National Information Services and Systems	http://www.hero.ac.uk/uk/home/index.cfm
Net J	http://www.netjobs.co.uk
New Life Network	http://www.newlifenetwork.co.uk

NewMonday.co.uk	http://www.newmonday.co.uk
News International/The London Paper	http://www.thelondonpaper.com
NHS Jobs	http://www.jobs.nhs.uk
NHSjobs.com	http://www.nhsjobs.com/select_sector
Nixers.com	http://www.nixers.com
NMC4Jobs.com	http://www.nmc4jobs.com
Northwest Workplace	http://www.northwestworkplace.com
NurseryWorldJobs.co.uk	http://www.nurseryworldjobs.co.uk
Nurseserve	http://www.nurserve.co.uk
TheNursingJobSite.com	http://www.thenursingjobsite.com
Nursingnetuk	http://www.nursingnetuk.com/job_search/s1
Office Recruit	http://www.officerecruit.com
Offsite Jobs	http://www.offsitejobs.co.uk
Oil Careers	http://www.oilcareers.com/worldwide
1job.co.uk	http://www.1job.co.uk
Online Insurance Jobs	http://www.onlineinsurancejobs.co.uk
OnlineMarketingJobs.com	http://www.onlinemarketingjobs.com
OnrecJobs.com	http://www.onrecjobs.com
OutdoorStaff	http://www.outdoorstaff.co.uk
Oxygen	http://www.oxygenonline.co.uk
PersonnelTodayJobs.com	http://www.personneltoday.com
PFJobs	http://www.pfjobs.co.uk
Pharmacareers.co.uk	http://www.pharmacareers.co.uk
PharmaTalentPool.com	http://www.pharmatalentpool.com
Pharmiweb.com	http://www.pharmiweb.com
Phee Farrer Jones Consultancy	http://www.pfj.co.uk
PhoneAJob	http://www.phoneajob.com
PlanetAudit	http://www.planetaudit.net
PlanetRecruit	http://www.planetrecruit.com
PlatinumJobs.com	http://www.platinumjobs.com

Pr4a.com	http://www.pr4a.com
ProductionBase.co.uk	http://www.productionbase.co.uk
Prospects.ac.uk	http://www.prospects.ac.uk
PRWeek Jobs	http://www.prweekjobs.co.uk
The Publican	http://www.thepublican.com
PublicJobsDirect.com	http://www.publicjobsdirect.com
PurelyIT.co.uk	http://www.purelyit.co.uk
QUANTster.com	http://www.quantster.com
Qworx.com	http://www.qworx.com
Rail Job Search	http://www.railjobsearch.com/index.html
Ready People	http://www.readypeople.eu
Recruit Construction	http://wwww.recruitconstruction.com
RecruiterSite	http://www.recruitersite.co.uk
Recruitment	http://www.recruitment.com
Recruitmentcareers.co.uk	http://www.recruitmentcareers.co.uk
Recruitment Jobz	http://www.recruitmentjobz.com
Recruitment-Marketing	http://www.recruitment-marketing.co.uk
Recruit-TV.com	http://www.recruit-tv.com
Redadvertising	http://www.redadvertising.co.uk
Redgoldfish.co.uk	http://www.redgoldfish.co.uk
Reed.co.uk	http://www.reed.co.uk
RenewableEnergyJobs.com	http://www.renewableenergyjobs.com
Resourcing International Consulting	http://www.cyber-cv.com
Resortjobs.co.uk	http://www.resortjobs.co.uk
Resort Work	http://www.resortwork.co.uk
Restaurant Jobs	http://www.restaurantjobs.co.uk
RetailCareers.co.uk	http://www.retailcareers.co.uk
RetailChoice.com	http://www.retailchoice.com
RetailHomepage.co.uk	http://www.retailhomepage.co.uk
RetailJobsBoard.co.uk	http://www.retailjobsboard.co.uk

RetailMoves.com	http://www.retailmoves.com
RetailWeek.com	http://www.retailweek.com
Rugby-jobs	http://www.rugby-jobs.com
S1jobs.com	http://www.s1jobs.com
SalesTarget.co.uk	http://www.salestarget.co.uk
SalesVacancies.com	http://www.salesvacancies.com
SalesWise.co.uk	http://www.saleswise.co.uk
Sciencecareers.org	http://sciencecareers.sciencemag.org
ScientistWorld.com	http://www.scientistworld.com
Season Workers	http://www.seasonworkers.com
Seasonal-Jobs.com	http://www.seasonal-jobs.com
Secrecruit.co.uk	http://www.secrecruit.co.uk
SecretarialCareers.co.uk	http://www.secretarialcareers.co.uk
Secretarialjobsboard.co.uk	http://www.secretarialjobsboard.co.uk
Secsinthecity	http://www.secsinthecity.co.uk
SecurityClearedJobs.com	http://www.securityclearedjobs.com
SimplyHRJobs	http://www.simplyhrjobs.co.uk
SimplyITSalesJobs	http://www.simplyitsalesjobs.co.uk
SimplyLawJobs	http://www.simplylawjobs.com
SimplyMarketingJobs	http://www.simplymarketingjobs.co.uk
SimplyMediaSalesJobs	http://www.simplymediasalesjobs.co.uk
SimplyPRJobs	http://www.simplyprjobs.co.uk
SimplySalesJobs	http://www.simplysalesjobs.co.uk
SkillsArena.com	http://www.skillsarenacorporate.com
Smarter Work	http://www.smarterwork.com
SmugOne.com	http://www.smugone.com
Solar Jobs	http://www.solarjobs.com
SourceThatJob	http://www.sourcethatjob.com
SpaOpportunities	http://www.spaopportunities.com
StepStone	http://www.stepstone.com

SupplyChainOnline	http://www.supplychain.co.uk
SupplyChainRecruit.com	http://www.supplychainrecruit.com
Synergygroup.co.uk	http://www.synergygroup.co.uk
Teachnetwork.co.uk	http://www.teachnetwork.co.uk
Technojobs	http://www.technojobs.co.uk
Tefl-jobs.co.uk	http://www.tefl-jobs.co.uk
Temps Online	http://www.tempsonline.co.uk
TipTopJob.com	http://www.tiptopjob.com
Top-Consultant.com	http://www.top-consultant.com
Top Contracts	http://www.topcontacts.com
TopITconsultant	http://www.topitconsultant.co.uk
Top Jobs	http://www.topjobs.net
Top Jobs	http://www.topjobs.co.uk
Top Language Jobs	http://www.toplanguagejobs.co.uk
TotalJobs.com	http://www.totaljobs.com
Totally Legal	http://www.totallylegal.com
TrainingProviderJobs.co.uk	http://www.trainingproviderjobs.co.uk
TravelJobSearch.com	http://www.traveljobsearch.com
Trovit.co.uk	http://www.trovit.co.uk
247recruit.com	http://www.247recruit.com
UK Graduate Careers	http://www.gti.co.uk/home
UK Therapist.co.uk	http://www.uktherapist.co.uk
Utility Job Search	http://www.utilityjobsearch.com
Vault	http://www.vault.com/wps/portal/usa
Wirelessmobile-Jobsboard.com	http://www.wirelessmobile-jobsboard.com
Work4a.com	http://www.work4a.com
Workcircle.com	http://www.workcircle.com
Workhound.co.uk	http://www.workhound.co.uk
Workingmums.co.uk	http://www.workingmums.co.uk
WorksFM.com	http://www.worksfm.com

Workthing.co.uk   http://www.workthing.com

Worksfm.com   http://www.worksfm.com

Venezuela

Bumeran.com   http://www.bumeran.com

MeQuierolr.com   http://www.mequieroir.com

Vietnam

JobStreet.com   http://www.jobstreet.com

JobsAbroad   http://www.jobsabroad.com/search/vietnam

VietnamWorks.com   http://www.vietnamworks.com

Wales

JobsinWales.com   .   http://www.jobsinwales.com

JobsWales.co.uk   http://www.jobswales.co.uk

WelshJobs.com   http://www.welshjobs.com

Investment/Brokerage (See also Finance & Accounting)

Advocis   http://www.advocis.ca

Annuitiesnet.com   http://www.annuitiesnet.com

Association for Investment Management and Research   http://www.cfainstitute.org

Bond Buyer   http://www.bondbuyer.com

BrokerHunter.com   http://www.brokerhunter.com

CareerBank.com   http://www.careerbank.com

CommodityCareers   http://www.commoditycareers.com

eFinancialCareers.com   http://www.efinancialcareers.com

International Association for Registered   http://careers.iarfc.org
Financial Planners

Investment Management and Trust Exchange   http://www.antaeans.com

National Association of Securities Professionals Current Openings	http://www.nasphq.org/career.shtml
National Association of Securities Professionals (Atlanta) Current Openings	http://www.naspatlanta.org
National Association of Securities Professionals (New York) Underground Railroad	http://www.nasp-ny.org
National Venture Capital Association	http://www.nvca.org
New York Society of Security Analysts Career Resources	http://www.nyssa.org/AM/Template.cfm?Section=career_development
Securities Industry Association Career Resource Center	http://www.sifma.com/services/career_center/career_center.html
Society of Actuaries	http://www.soa.org
Society of Risk Analysis Opportunities	http://www.sra.org/opportunities.php

-J-

Job Fairs Online

BrazenCareerist	http://www.brazencareerist.com
Job Dex	http://www.jobdex.com
NAACP Job Fair	http://www.naacpjobfair.com
OilCareerFair	http://www.oilcareerfair.com
TargetedJobFairs.com	http://www.targetedjobfairs.com
Targi24.pl [Poland]	http://www.targi.pracuj.pl

Journalism & Media (See also Graphic Arts)

Airwaves Job Services	http://www.airwaves.com
American Society of Business Press Editors	http://www.asbpr.org
American Society of Journalists & Authors	http://www.freelancewritersearch.com
Animation Industry Database	http://www.aidb.com
Animation World Network	http://www.awn.com

Association of Electronic Journalists	http://www.rtnda.org
Association for Women in Communications	http://www.womcom.org
Association for Women in Communications WDC Chapter	http://www.awic-dc.org
Audience Development	http://www.audiencedevelopment.com
Communications Roundtable	http://www.roundtable.org
Copy Editor Newsletter	http://jobs.copyeditor.com/home/index.cfm?site_id=502
Coroflot	http://www.coroflot.com
Creative Freelancers	http://www.freelancers.com
CyberJournalist.net	http://www.cyberjournalist.net
DigitalMediaJobs.com [United Kingdom]	http://www.digitalmediajobs.com
dotJournalism [United Kingdom]	http://www.journalism.co.uk
Editor & Publisher	http://www.editorandpublisher.com
eFront.com	http://www.efront.com
eLance.com	http://www.elance.com
FolioMag.com	http://www.foliomag.com
FreeLanceWriting.com	http://www.freelancewriting.com
The Friday Pint [United Kingdom]	http://www.mediaweekjobs.co.uk
GamesPress.com	http://www.gamespress.com
GrapevineJobs.com [United Kingdom]	http://www.grapevinejobs.com/home.asp
Grist.org	http://jobs.grist.org
Guru.com	http://www.guru.com
HTML Writers Guild HWG-Jobs	http://www.hwg.org/lists/hwg-jobs
I-Advertising	http://internetadvertising.org
International Association of Business Communicators Career Centre	http://www.iabc.com
The Internet Advertising Bureau Job Board	http://www.iab.net/jobs
JobLink for Journalists	http://newslink.org/newjoblinksearch.html
JobsinSearch.com	http://www.jobsinsearch.com
Journalism.co.uk [United Kingdom]	http://www.journalism.co.uk
JournalismJob.com	http://www.journalismjob.com

Journalism Jobs	http://www.journalismjobs.com
JournalismNext.com	http://www.journalismnext.com
Journalism Now	http://www.journalismnow.com
Mandy.com	http://www.mandy.com/1/filmtvjobs.cfm?jt=usa
MassMediaJobs.com	http://www.massmediajobs.com
mediabistro	http://www.mediabistro.com
Media Communications Association International Job Hotline	http://www.mca-i.org
Media Human Resource Association	http://jobs.com
MediaJobMarket.com	http://www.mediajobmarket.com
Medialine	http://www.medialine.com
MediaRecruiter.com	http://www.mediarecruiter.com
National Alliance of State Broadcasters Associations CareerPage	http://www.careerpage.org
National Diversity Newspaper Job Bank	http://www.newsjobs.net
National Writers Union Job Hotline	https://nwu.org
NationJob Advertising and Media Jobs Page	http://www.nationjob.com/media
News Jobs	http://www.newsjobs.net
Newspaper Association of America Newspaper CareerBank	http://www.naa.org/classified/index.html
OnlineMarketingJobs.com [United Kingdom]	http://www.onlinemarketingjobs.com
PaidContent.org	http://jobs.paidcontent.org
Print Jobs	http://www.printjobs.com
ProductionBase.co.uk [United Kingdom]	http://www.productionbase.co.uk
Silicon Alley Connections	http://www.salley.com
Society for Technical Communications	http://www.stc.org
SourceThatJob [United Kingdom]	http://www.sourcethatjob.com
StaffWriters Plus, Inc.	http://www.staffwriters.com
Sun Oasis	http://www.sunoasis.com
Telecommuting Jobs	http://www.tjobs.com
TV Jobs	http://www.tvjobs.com
Ultimate TV	http://www.ultimatetv.com

VFXWorld	http://www.vfxworld.com
VideoGameJournalismJobs.com	http://www.videogamejournalismjobs.com
Voice123	http://www.voice123.com
Webmonkey Jobs	http://www.webmonkey.com
Workinpr.com	http://www.workinpr.com
The Write Jobs for The Writers Write	http://www.writejobs.com
WritersWeekly.com	http://www.writersweekly.com

-L-

Law/Legal

Alliance of Merger and Acquisition Advisors	http://www.amaaonline.com
AlternativeLawyerJobs.com	http://www.alternativelawyerjobs.com
American Association of Law Libraries Job Placement Hotline	http://www.aallnet.org/hotline/hotline.asp
American Bankruptcy Institute Career Center	http://www.abiworld.org
American Bar Association	http://www.abanet.org
American Corporate Counsel Association	http://www.acc.com
American Immigration Lawyers Association	http://www.aila.org
American Lawyer Magazine	http://www.americanlawyer.com
Attorney Jobs	http://www.attorneyjobs.com
Attorney Pages	http://attorneypages.com
Barry University of Orlando	http://www.barry.edu/law/default.aspx
Bench & Bar	http://www2.mnbar.org/classifieds/position-available.htm
Connecticut Law Tribune	http://www.ctlawtribune.com
Corporate Counsel	http://www.law.com/corporatecounsel
Corporate Legal Times	http://www.insidecounsel.com./Pages/default.aspx
Counsel.net	http://www.counsel.net

Daily Report - Atlanta, GA	http://www.dailyreportonline.com
Degree Hunter	http://degreehunter.net
eAttorney.com	http://www.martindale.com/Careers/Careers.aspx
Elite Consultants	http://www.eliteconsultants.com
Emplawyernet	http://www.emplawyernet.com
Find Law	http://careers.findlaw.com
FirmJobs.com	http://www.patentjobs.com
G2legal [United Kingdom]	http://www.g2legal.co.uk
HeadHunt.com [Canada]	http://www.thecounselnetwork.com
HG Legal Directories Legal Job Listings	http://www.hg.org/law-jobs.asp
Hieros Gamos Legal Employment Classified	http://www.hg.org/index.html
iHireLegal	http://www.ihirelegal.com
Intelproplaw	http://www.intelproplaw.com
International Association for Commercial and Contract Management	http://www.iaccm.com
The International Lawyers Network	http://www.iln.com
JobFox.com	http://www.jobfox.com
JobsLawInfo.com	http://jobs.lawinfo.com
TheLadders.com	http://www.theladders.com
Law.com	http://www.law.com/jsp/law/index.jsp
Law Bulletin	http://www.lawbulletin.com
LawCrossing	http://www.lawcrossing.com
Law Forum	http://www.lawforum.net
Law Gazette Jobs [United Kingdom]	http://www.lawgazettejobs.co.uk
Law Guru	http://www.lawguru.com
Law Info	http://www.lawinfo.com
Law Jobs	http://www.lawjobs.com
Law Match	http://www.lawmatch.com
Law Office	http://lp.findlaw.com
Law Source	http://lawsource.com

Law Technology News	http://www.law.com/lawtechnologynews
The Legal Career Center Network	http://www.legalcareernetwork.com
The Legal Employment Search Site	http://www.legalemploy.com
Legal Gate	http://www.legalgate.com
Legal Hire	http://www.legalhire.com
The Legal Intelligencer (Philadelphia)	http://www.law.com/jsp/pa/index.jsp
LegalJob.ca [Canada]	http://www.legaljob.ca/default_en.html
Legal Job Store	http://www.legaljobstore.com
Legal Jobs Board [United Kingdom]	http://www.legaljobsboard.co.uk
Legal Jobs in New York	http://www.legal-jobs-in-new-york.com
Legal Prospects [United Kingdom]	http://www.legalprospects.com
Legal Report	http://www.legalreport.com
Legal Serve	http://www.legalserve.com
Legal Staff	http://www.legalstaff.com
Legal Times (Washington, D.C.)	http://www.law.com/jsp/nlj/legaltimes/index.jsp
Massachusetts Lawyers Weekly Jobs	http://classifieds.lawyersweekly.com
National Association of Legal Assistants	http://www.nala.org
National Employment Lawyers Association	http://www.nela.org/NELA/
National Federation of Paralegal Associations	http://www.paralegals.org
National Law Journal	http://www.law.com/jsp/nlj/index.jsp
National Paralegal	http://www.nationalparalegal.org
Nationwide Process Servers Association	http://www.processserversassociation.com
New Hampshire Legal Assistance	http://www.nhla.org
New Jersey Law Journal	http://www.law.com/jsp/nj/index.jsp
New York Law Journal	http://www.newyorklawjournal.com
Paralegal City	http://www.paralegalcity.com
Paralegaljob.ca [Canada]	http://www.paralegaljob.ca
Paralegal Job Finder	http://www.paralegaljobfinder.com
Piper Pat	http://www.piperpat.co.nz
The Recorder	http://www.law.com/jsp/ca/index.jsp

RegulatoryCareers.com — http://www.regulatorycareers.com

ScottishLegalJobs.com [Scotland] — http://www.scottishlegaljobs.com

SimplyLawJobs.com [United Kingdom] — http://www.simplylawjobs.com

Texas Lawyer — http://www.law.com/jsp/tx/index.jsp

Totally Legal [United Kingdom] — http://www.totallylegal.com

TotallyLegal.com.au [Australia] — http://www.totallylegal.com/australia

Trial Lawyers for Public Justice — http://www.tlpj.net

Law Enforcement & Fire Departments

Academy of Correctional Health Professionals — http://careers.correctionalhealth.org

American Correctional Health Services Association — http://careers.achsa.org

American Society for Law Enforcement Training — http://www.aslet.org

Blue Line Jobs [United Kingdom] — http://www.bluelinejobs.co.uk

The Blue Line: Police Opportunity Monitor — http://www.theblueline.com

The Brass Key — http://www.thepoliceexecutive.com

DiscoverPolicing.org — http://www.discoverpolicing.org

EMSFireRescueJobs — http://www.emsfirerescuejobs.com

EMS World — http://www.emsresponder.com

FireandSecurityJobs.net — http://www.fireandsecurityjobs.net

FireJobs.com — http://www.firejobs.com

FireRecruit.com — http://www.firerecruit.com

FireRescue1 — http://www.firerescue1.com

FireRescueJobs — http://www.firerescuejobs.com

FireServiceEmployment.com — http://www.fireserviceemployment.com

Firefighter Nation — http://www.firefighternation.com

Firehouse.com — http://www.firehouse.com

FiremenJobs — http://www.firemenjobs.com

GoLawEnforcement.com — http://www.golawenforcement.com

High Technology Crime Investigation Association — http://www.htcia.org

Hispanic American Police Command Officers Association — http://www.hapcoa.org

iHireLawEnforcement.com	http://www.ihirelawenforcement.com
JobCop	http://www.jobcop.com
LawEnforcementJobs.com	http://www.lawenforcementjobs.com
LawOfficer	http://www.lawofficer.com
National Black Police Association	http://www.blackpolice.org
National Organization of Black Law Enforcement Executives	http://www.noblenational.org
National Latino Peace Officers Association	http://www.nlpoa.org
911 Hot Jobs	http://www.911hotjobs.com
Officer.com	http://www.officer.com
Police Employment	http://www.policeemployment.com
Police Jobs	http://www.policejobs.com
Police Link	http://www.policelink.com
PoliceOne.com	http://www.policeone.com
Public Safety Jobs	http://www.publicsafetyjobs.com
Public Safety Recruitment	http://www.publicsafetyrecruitment.com
TechLawAdvisor.com Job Postings	http://techlawadvisor.com/jobs
Wild Fire Jobs	http://www.wildfirejobs.com
Women in Federal Law Enforcement	http://www.wifle.org

Library & Information Science

American Association of Law Libraries Job Placement Hotline	http://www.aallnet.org/hotline/hotline.asp
American Library Association	http://www.ala.org/ala/educationcareers/index.cfm
American Society for Information Science & Technology	http://www.asis.org
Art Libraries Society of North America JobNet	http://www.arlisna.org/jobnet.html
Association of Research Libraries	http://www.arl.org
BUBL Employment Bulletin Board [United Kingdom]	http://bubl.ac.uk
Inside Higher Ed	http://www.insidehighered.com
Libjobs.com	http://www.libjobs.com

LibraryJobPostings.org	http://www.libraryjobpostings.org
Library Journal	http://www.libraryjournal.com
LisJobs.com	http://www.lisjobs.com
LYRASIS	http://www.lyrasis.org
Media Central	http://mediacentral.net
Music Library Association Job Placement	http://www.musiclibraryassoc.org
New Mexico Library Association	http://www.nmla.org
Special Libraries Association	http://www.sla.org

Linguistics

Jobs in Linguistics	http://linguistlist.org/jobs
Linguistic Enterprises	http://web.gc.cuny.edu/dept/lingu
The Linguist List	http://linguistlist.org/jobs/index.cfm

Logistics & Maintenance

All Port Jobs	http://www.allportjobs.com
The Association for Operations Management	http://www.apicscareercenter.org
Blue Collar Jobs	http://www.bluecollarjobs.com
CareersinLogistics [United Kingdom]	http://www.careersinlogistics.co.uk
Energy Careers	http://www.energycareers.com
FM Link-Facilities Management	http://www.fmlink.com
HVAC Agent	http://www.hvacagent.com
iHIreLogistics	http://www.ihirelogistics.com
iHireMaintenanceandInstallation	http://www.ihiremaintenanceandinstallation.com
Jobstor.com	http://www.jobstor.com/cgi-bin/index.cgi
Jobs4Logistics.com [United Kingdom]	http://www.jobs4logistics.com
Jobs4Trucking.com	http://www.jobs4trucking.com
JobsinTrucks.com	http://www.jobsintrucks.com
JobsinLogistics.com	http://www.jobsinlogistics.com

Journal of Commerce/Logistics Career Center	http://www.logisticscareercenter.joc.com
LogisticsJobShop.com [United Kingdom]	http://www.logisticsjobshop.com
Logistics World	http://www.logisticsworld.com
LogJobs.com	http://www.logjobs.com
MaintenanceEmployment.com	http://www.maintenanceemployment.com
RoadTechs.com	http://www.roadtechs.com
SupplyChainBrain.com	http://www.supplychainbrain.com
SupplyChainJobs.com	http://www.supplychainjobs.com
SupplyChainOnline.co.uk [United Kingdom]	http://www.supplychainonline.co.uk
SupplyChainRecruit.com [Europe]	http://www.supplychainrecruit.com
Truckdriver.com	http://www.truckdriver.com
Virtual Logistics Directory	http://www.logisticsdirectory.com
WarehouseJobs.com	http://www.warehousejobs.com

-M-

Military Personnel Transitioning into the Private Sector

Army Career & Alumni Program	http://www.acap.army.mil
Blue-to-Gray	http://www.corporategray.com
CareerBuilder.com	http://www.careerbuilder.com
Center for Employment Management	https://www.cfainstitute.org/pages/index.aspx
CivilianJobs.com	http://www.civilianjobs.com
ClearanceJobs.com	http://www.clearancejobs.com
Corporate Gray Online	http://www.corporategrayonline.com
The Defense Talent Network	http://www.defensetalent.com
G.I. Jobs	http://www.gijobs.com
Green-to-Gray	http://www.corporategray.com
HelmetstoHardhats.com	http://www.helmetstohardhats.com
HirePatriots.com	http://www.hirepatriots.com

Hire Quality	http://www.hire-quality.com
HireVeterans.com	http://www.hireveterans.com
HireVetsFirst.gov	http://www.dol.gov/vets
Jobs2Vets.com	http://www.jobs2vets.com
Jobs4Vets.com	http://www.jobs4vets.com
Landmark Destiny Group	https://www2.recruitmilitary.com
Marine Executive Association	http://www.marineea.org
Military.com	http://www.military.com
Military Careers	http://www.todaysmilitary.com/careers
Military Connection	http://www.militaryconnection.com
Military Connections	http://www.militaryconnections.com
MilitaryHire.com	http://www.militaryhire.com
MilitaryExits	http://www.militaryexits.com
MilitaryJobWorld.com	http://www.militaryjobworld.com
Military JobZone	http://www.militaryjobzone.com
Military Officers Association of America	http://www.moaa.org
Military Spouse Corporate Career Network	http://www.msccn.org
Military Spouse Job Search	http://jobsearch.spouse.military.com
MilitaryStars.com	http://www.militarystars.com
My Future	http://www.myfuture.com
National Defense Industrial Association	http://www.defensejobs.com
Operation Transition	http://www.dmdc.osd.mil/appj/dwp/index.jsp
RecruitAirForce.com	https://www2.recruitmilitary.com
RecruitMarines.com	https://www2.recruitmilitary.com
RecruitMilitary.com	https://www2.recruitmilitary.com
RecruitNavy.com	https://www2.recruitmilitary.com
Reserve Officers Association	http://www.roa.org/site/PageServer
Stripes.com	http://www.stripes.com
Transition Assistance Online	http://www.taonline.com
TransitionCareers.com	http://www.transtioncareers.com

VeteranEmployment.com	http://www.veteranemployment.com
VeteranJobs.com	http://www.veteranjobs.com
VetJobs	http://www.vetjobs.com

Mining

Jobs4Mining	http://www.jobs4mining.com
MineJobs.com	http://www.minejobs.com
Petroleum & Mining Portal	http://www.pmjobs.net

Modeling

ModelService.com	http://www.modelservice.com
ModelService.com	http://www.modelservice.com
OneModelPlace.com	http://www.onemodelplace.com
Supermodel.com	http://www.supermodel.com

Music

FilmMusic.net	http://www.filmmusic.net
The Internet Music Pages	http://www.musicpages.com
Key Signature [United Kingdom]	http://www.keysignature.co.uk
MusiciansBuyLine.com	http://www.musiciansbuyline.com/music_jobs_avail.html

-N-

Networking (See also Social Media)

Adholes.com	http://adholes.com
BusinessCard2.com	http://businesscard2.com

Eurekster	http://www.eurekster.com
LinkedIn	http://www.linkedin.com
LinkedMe [Australia]	http://www.linkme.com.au
Monster Networking	http://www.monster.com
RealContacts	http://jobs.realcontacts.com
ReferYes.com	http://www.referyes.com
Rypple.com	http://www.rypple.com
Ryze Business Networking	http://www.ryze.com
Spoke	http://www.spoke.com
Wink.com	http://www.wink.com
Xing [Germany]	http://www.xing.com

Non-Profit

AllHousingJobs.co.uk [United Kingdom]	http://www.allhousingjobs.co.uk
American Alliance of Museums jobHQ	http://www.aam-us.org/resources/careers
American Society of Association Executives Career HQ	http://www.asaecenter.org
boardnetUSA	http://www.boardnetusa.org/public/home.asp
Bridgestar	http://www.bridgestar.org
Career Action Center	http://www.careeraction.org
CharityJob.co.uk [United Kingdom]	http://www.charityjob.co.uk
Chronicle of Philanthropy	http://philanthropy.com/section/Home/172
Community Career Center	http://www.nonprofitjobs.org
DotOrgJobs.com	http://www.dotorgjobs.com
ExecSearches	http://www.execsearches.com
The Foundation Center	http://foundationcenter.org
Fundraising Jobs	http://www.fundraisingjobs.com
Georgia Center for Nonprofits	http://www.gcn.org
Good Works	http://goodworksfirst.org
Idealist	http://www.idealist.org
International Service Agencies	http://www.charity.org

JobsinPublicSector [United Kingdom]	http://www.jobsinpublicsector.co.uk
The National Assembly	http://www.nassembly.org
Non Profit Career Network	http://www.nonprofitcareer.com
Nonprofit Charitable Organizations	http://nonprofit.about.com
Non Profit Employment	http://www.nonprofitemployment.com
Non-Profit Marketing	http://www.cob.ohio-state.edu/fin/nonprofit.htm
Nonprofit Times	http://www.nptimes.com
NPO	http://www.npo.net
Opportunity Knocks	http://www.opportunityknocks.org
Philanthropy Journal	http://www.philanthropyjournal.org
Philanthropy News Network Online	http://www.pnnonline.org/jobs
Social Service	http://www.socialservice.com
Tripod	http://www.tripod.lycos.com
VolunteerMatch	http://www.volunteermatch.org

-O-

Outdoors/Recreation/Sports

The Amateur Coaching Connection	http://www.tazsports.com
American Medical Society for Sports Medicine	http://careers.amssm.org
AnyWorkAnywhere.com [United Kingdom]	http://www.anyworkanywhere.com
Association for Environmental and Outdoor Education	http://www.aeoe.org
Camp Nurse Jobs	http://www.campnursejobs.com
CareersinRacing.com [United Kingdom]	http://www.careersinracing.com
C.O.A.C.H.	http://www.coachhelp.com
CoachingJobs.com	http://www.coachingjobs.com
Coaching Staff	http://www.coachingstaff.com
CoachingTalent.com	http://www.coachingtalent.com
Cool Works	http://www.coolworks.com

Cruise Job Link	http://www.cruisejoblink.com
Equimax	http://equ.equimax.com:8080/index.htm
FitnessJobs.com	http://www.fitnessjobs.com
Football-jobs.com [United Kingdom]	http://www.football-jobs.com
FootieJobs.com [United Kingdom]	http://www.footiejobs.com
Great Summer Jobs	http://www.petersons.com
Horticultural Jobs	http://www.horticulturaljobs.com
JobsinLeisure [United Kingdom]	http://www.jobsinleisure.com
Jobs In Sports	http://www.jobsinsports.com
JobsWithBalls.com [United Kingdom]	http://www.jobswithballs.com
Leisure Jobs [United Kingdom]	http://www.leisurejobs.com
Leisure Jobs [United Kingdom]	http://www.leisurejobs.net
Leisure Jobs Now [United Kingdom]	http://www.leisurejobsnow.co.uk
Leisure Recruit Ltd [United Kingdom]	http://www.thelrgroup.co.uk
Leisure Opportunities [United Kingdom]	http://www.leisureopportunities.co.uk
Lifeguarding Jobs	http://www.lifeguardingjobs.com
Motor Sports Employment	http://www.motorsportsemployment.com
National Athletic Trainers Association	http://jobs.nata.org/
National Sporting Goods Association	http://www.nsga.org
Online Sports Career Center	http://www.onlinesports.com/careercenter.html
Outdoor Ed	http://www.outdoored.com/jobs/oe/Default.aspx
OutdoorIndustryJobs.com	http://www.outdoorindustryjobs.com
The Outdoor Job	http://www.theoutdoorjob.com
OutdoorStaff [United Kingdom]	http://www.outdoorstaff.co.uk
Pet-Sitters.biz	http://www.pet-sitters.biz
PGA.com	http://www.pga.com/home
Resort Jobs	http://www.resortjobs.com
Resortjobs.co.uk [United Kingdom]	http://www.resortjobs.co.uk
Rugby-jobs [United Kingdom]	http://ww.rugby-jobs.com
SeasonalEmployment.com	http://www.seasonalemployment.com

Skiing the Net	http://www.skiingthenet.com
SportLink	http://www.sportlink.com
Sportscasting Jobs	http://www.sportscastingjobs.com
SummerJobs.com	http://www.summerjobs.com
TAZsport.com	http://www.tazsport.com
Teamwork Online	http://www.teamworkonline.com
Tennis Jobs	http://www.tennisjobs.com
WomenSportsJobs.com	http://www.womensportjobs.com
Women's Sport Services	http://www.wiscnetwork.com
WorkinSports.com	http://www.workinsports.com

-P-

Packaging for Food & Drug

Association of Industrial Metalizers, Coaters & Laminators	http://www.aimcal.org
Composite Can & Tube Institute	http://www.cctiwdc.org
CPGjobs.com	http://www.cpgjobs.com
Foodservice.com	http://foodservice.com
Institute of Food Science & Technology	http://www.ifst.org
PackJobs.com	http://www.packjobs.com
Supermarket News	http://supermarketnews.com
Technical Association of the Pulp & Paper Industry Career Center	http://careers.tappi.org

Pharmaceutical

Academy of Managed Care Pharmacy	http://www.amcp.org/home
American Academy of Pharmaceutical Physicians & Investigators	http://www.appinet.org

American Association of Pharmaceutical Sales Professionals	http://www.pharmaceuticalsales.org
American Association of Pharmaceutical Scientists	http://www.aapspharmaceutica.com/index.asp
American Chemical Society	http://portal.acs.org/portal/acs/corg/content
American College of Clinical Pharmacology	http://www.accp1.org
American College of Clinical Pharmacy	http://www.accp.com
American Pharmaceutical Association	http://www.pharmacist.com
American Society of Clinical Pharmacology and Therapeutics	http://www.ascpt.org
American Society of Consultant Pharmacists	http://bt.myrxcareer.com
American Society of Health-System Pharmacists	http://www.ashp.org
American Society of Pharmacognosy	http://www.phcog.org
Association for Applied Human Pharmacology [Germany]	http://www.agah.info
The Biomedical Engineering Network	http://www.bmenet.org/BMEnet
BioPharm International	http://www.biopharminternational.com
BioSpace	http://pwww.biospace.com
Board of Pharmaceutical Specialties	http://www.bpsweb.org
CareerTopJobs	http://www.careertopjobs.com
Careers in Pharmaceutical	http://www.careersinpharmaceutical.com
CenterWatch.com	http://www.centerwatch.com
ChemJobs.net	http://www.chemjobs.net/chemjobs.html
ChemPharma	http://www.chempharma.net
Drug Discovery Online	http://www.drugdiscoveryonline.com
Drug Information Association Employment Opportunities	http://www.diahome.org
Drug Topics	http://www.drugtopics.modernmedicine.com
Elite Pharmacy Jobs	http://www.elitepharmacyjobs.com
FindPharma.com	http://www.findpharma.com
Formulary Journal	http://www.formularyjournal.modernmedicine.com
Georgia Pharmacy Association	http://www.gpha.org
HireLifeScience	http://www.hirelifescience.com
HireRX.com	http://www.hirerx.com

iHirePharmacy.com	http://www.ihirepharmacy.com
International Society for Pharmaceutical Engineering	http://www.ispe.org
International Society for Pharmacoepidemiology	http://careers.pharmacoepi.org
Jobs in Chemistry	http://www.jobsinchemistry.com
Lifesciencejobs.com	http://www.lifesciencejobs.com
MedReps	http://www.medreps.com
Medzilla	http://www.medzilla.com
Missouri Pharmacy Association	http://www.morx.com
National Association of Boards of Pharmacy	http://www.nabp.net
National Association of Pharmaceutical Sales Representatives	http://www.napsronline.org
Pharmacareers.co.uk [United Kingdom]	http://www.pharmacareers.co.uk
Pharmaceutical Executive	http://www.pharmexec.com
PharmaceuticalJobsUSA.com	http://pharmaceuticaljobsusa.ning.com
Pharmaceutical Rep Jobs	http://pharmaceuticalrepjobs.org
Pharmacy Benefit Management Institute	http://careers.pbmi.com
PharmacyChoice.com	http://www.pharmacychoice.com
PharmacyTimes	http://www.pharmacytimes.com
PharmacyWeek	http://www.pharmacyweek.com
PharmaDiversity	http://www.pharmadiversity.com
PharmaOpportunities	http://www.pharmaopportunites.com
Pharmasys	http://www.pharmweb.com
PharmaTalentPool.com [United Kingdom]	http://www.pharmatalentpool.com
Pharm-Chem.com	http://www.pharm-chem.com
PharmTech.com	http://www.pharmtech.com
RPh on the Go	http://www.rphonthego.com
RPhrecruiter.com	http://www.rphrecruiter.com
Rx Career Center	http://www.rxcareercenter.com
Rx Times Pharmacy Magazine	http://careers.rxtimes.com
RxWebportal	http://www.rxwebportal.com

Physics

American Association of Physics Teachers	http://www.aapt.org
American Institute of Physics	http://www.aip.org
American Physical Society	http://www.aps.org
Board of Physics & Astronomy	http://www7.nationalacademies.org/careers
Institute of Physics	http://www.iop.org
Optics.org	http://optics.org/cws/home
Physics & Astronomy Online	http://www.physlink.com
Physics Jobs Online	http://tiptop.iop.org
PhysicsToday.org	http://www.physicstoday.org/jobs
Plasma Gate [Israel]	http://plasma-gate.weizmann.ac.il
The Science Jobs	http://www.thesciencejobs.com

Printing & Bookbinding

Digital Printing and Imaging Association Employment Exchange (with the Screenprinting & Graphic Imaging Association International)	http://www.sgia.org/employment
National Association for Printing Leadership	http://www.napl.org
Printing Impressions	http://www.piworld.com
Semper International	http://www.semperllc.com

Public Sector/Government

American Public Health Association CareerMart	http://careers.apha.org
Arizona Public Health Association	http://healthcarecareers.azpha.org
Association of Clinicians for the Underserved	http://careers.clinicians.org
Association for Community Health Improvement	http://careers.communityhlth.org
Blue Line Jobs [United Kingdom]	http://www.bluelinejobs.co.uk
The Blue Line: Police Opportunity Monitor	http://www.theblueline.com
Careers.vic.gov.au [Australia]	http://www.careers.vic.gov.au

Careers in Government	http://www.careersingovernment.com
Centers for Disease Control	http://www.cdc.gov
Civil Jobs	http://www.civiljobs.com
ClearedJobs.co.uk [United Kingdom]	http://www.clearedjobs.co.uk
Defense Jobs	http://ndia.monster.com
DEM Job	http://www.demjob.com
EMS Fire Rescue Jobs	http://www.fedworld.gov
Fed World	http;//www.emsfirerescuejobs.com
FederalGovernmentJobs.us	http://www.federalgovernmentjobs.us
Federal Job Search	http://www.americajob.com/Default.asp
FederalJobs	http://www.federaljobs.net
Federal Jobs Digest	http://www.jobsfed.com
FRS	http://www.fedjobs.com
GetaGovJob.com	http://www.getagovjob.com
GOP Job	http://www.gopjob.com
Governmentjobs.com	http://www.governmentjobs.com
GovernmentSecurity.org	http://www.governmentsecurity.org/jobs.php
GovernmentSupportJobs.com	http://www.governmentsupportjobs.com
GovMedCareers.com	http://www.govmedcareers.com
GovtJob.net	http://jobs.grist.org
Grist.org	http://www.govtjob.net
High Technology Crime Investigation Association	http://www.htcia.org
HRS Federal Job Search	http://www.hrsjobs.com
Intelligence Careers	http://www.intelligencecareers.com
Internet Job Source	http://statejobs.com
Jobsearch.gov.au [Australia]	http://www.jobsearch.gov.au
Jobsgopublic [United Kingdom]	http://www.jobsgopublic.com
Jobs In Government	http://www.jobsingovernment.com
JobsinNHS [United Kingdom]	http://www.jobsinnhs.co.uk
JobsinPublicSector [United Kingdom]	http://www.jobsinpublicsector.co.uk

Military.com	http://www.military.com
MilitaryJobWorld.com	http://www.militaryjobworld.com
NASA Jobs	http://www.nasajobs.nasa.gov
National Association of County and City Health Officials	http://http://careers.naccho.org
National Association of Hispanic Publications Online Career Center	http://www.nahp.org
NavyJobs.com	http://www.navy.com/navy/careers.html
NHS Jobs [United Kingdom]	http://www.jobs.nhs.uk
911HotJobs	http://www.opajobs.com
Opportunities in Public Affairs	http://www.911hotjobs.com
Poli Temps	http://www.politemps.com
Police Employment	http://www.policeemployment.com
Political Resources	http://politicalresources.com
PoliticalStaffing.com	http://politicalstaff.com
Public Health Service Jobs	http://www.publicjobsdirect.com
PublicJobsDirect.com [United Kingdom]	http://www.usphs.gov
Public Safety Jobs	http://www.publicsafetyjobs.com
Public Service Employees	http://www.pse-net.com
Public Works Magazine	http://www.pwmag.com
PWJobZone	http://www.publishersmarketplace.com
Regulatory Affairs Professionals Society Regulatory Career Connections	http://regulatorycareers.raps.org
SecurityClearedJobs.com [United Kingdom]	http://www.securityclearedjobs.com
Security Job Zone	http://www.securityjobzone.com
Security Jobs Network	http://www.securityjobs.net
StudentJobs.gov	http://www.usajobs.gov/studentjobs
TenStepsforStudents.org	http://www.tenstepsforstudents.org
Transportation Security Administration	http://www.tsa.gov
United States Department of Labor	http://www.dol.gov
US Air Force Careers	http://www.af.mil/careers
USAJOBS/U.S. Office of Personnel Management	http://www.usajobs.opm.gov http://www.defense.gov

USA Jobs   http://www.usajobs.com

VetJobs   http://www.vetjobs.com

Publishing

Book Business   http://www.bookbusinessmag.com

Bookjobs.com   http://www.bookjobs.com

Council of Literary Magazines & Presses   http://www.clmp.org

Editorial Freelancers Association   http://www.the-efa.org

Folio Magazine   http://www.foliomag.com

Fulfillment Management Association, Inc.   http://www.fmanational.org

MediaJobMarket.com   http://www.mediajobmarket.com

National Writers Union Job Hotline   https://nwu.org

PrintWorkers.com   http://www.printworkers.com

PrioritySearch.com   http://www.prioritysearch.com

Purchasing

American Purchasing Society   http://www.american-purchasing.com

BuyingJobs.com   http://www.buyingjobs.com

Institute for Supply Management Career Center   http://www.ism.ws

PurchasingJobs.com   http://www.purchasingjobs.com

Responsible Purchasing Network   http://www.responsiblepurchasing.org

SupplyChainRecruit.com [Europe]   http://www.supplychainrecruit.com

-Q-

Quality/Quality Control

American College of Medical Quality	http://careers.acmq.org
The American Health Quality Association	http://careers.ahqa.org
devBistro QA Jobs	http://www.devbistro.com/qa-jobs
iHireQualityControl.com	http://www.ihirequalitycontrol.com
I Six Sigma	http://www.isixsigma.com
Just QA Jobs	http://www.justqajobs.com
National Association for Healthcare Quality	http://careercenter.nahq.org
QA Engineer Jobs	http://www.qaengineerjobs.com
QA-Jobs	http://www.qa-jobs.com
QCEmployMe.com	http://regionalhelpwanted.com/quad-cities-il-ia-jobs
Quality America	http://www.qualityamerica.com
QualityEngineerJobs.com	http://www.qualityengineerjobs.com
Software QA and Testing Resource Center	http://www.softwareqatest.com
Test & Measurement World	http://www.tmworld.com
The Working Group for Electronic Data Interchange	http://careers.wedi.org

-R-

Real Estate

American Real Estate Society	http://www.aresnet.org/Jobs.phtml
Apartment Association of Greater Dallas	http://www.aagdallas.org
Apartment Association of Tarrant County	http://www.aatcnet.org/subsite/CareerCenter/careercenterindex.htm
ApartmentCareerHQ.org	http://www.apartmentcareerHQ.org
Apartment Careers	http://www.apartmentcareers.com

BuilderJobs	http://www.builderjobs.com
California Mortgage Brokers Association Career Center	http://www.cambweb.org
Escrowboard.net	http://www.escrowboard.net
FacilitiesJobs.com	http://www.facilitiesjobs.com
iHireRealEstate.com	http://www.ihirerealestate.com
Institute of Real Estate Management Job Bulletin	http://www.irem.org
Job Directories	http://inrealty.com
Jobsite.co.uk [United Kingdom]	http://www.jobsite.co.uk
Leasing Jobs	http://www.leasingjobs.com
LettingCareers [United Kingdom]	http://www.lettingcareers.com
Loan Closer Jobs	http://www.loancloserjobs.com
Loan Originator Jobs	http://www.loanoriginatorjobs.com
Loop Net	http://www.loopnet.com
MFHJobs.com	http://www.mfhjobs.com
MortgageBoard.com	http://www.mortgageboard.com
MortgageCareers.org	http://www.mortgagecareers.org
Mortgage Job Market	http://www.jobmag.com
Mortgage Jobstore	http://www.mortgagejobstore.com
Multifamily Executive Magazine	http://www.multifamilyexecutive.com
MyHousingCareer [United Kingdom]	http://www.myhousingcareer.com
NACORE International	http://www.nacore.com
National Apartment Association	http://www.naahq.org/Pages/welcome.aspx
NewHomeSalesJobs.com	http://www.newhomesalesjobs.com
Pike Net	http://www.pikenet.com
Real Estate Best Jobs	http://www.realestatebestjobs.com
Real Estate Careers	http://www.realestateexpress.com
Real Estate Finance Jobs	http://www.realestatefinancejobs.com
Real Estate Job Store	http://www.realestatejobstore.com
Real Estate Jobs	http://www.realestatejobs.com
Real Estate Lenders Association	http://www.rela.org

Real Jobs	http://www.real-jobs.com
Rebuz	http://www.rebuz.com
SelectLeaders.com	http://www.selectleaders.com
SeniorHousingJobs.com	http://www.seniorhousingjobs.com
Texas Apartment Association	http://www.taa.org/sitemap
Titleboard.net	http://www.titleboard.net
TopBuildingJobs.com	http://www.topbuildingjobs.com
Washington Multi-Family Housing Association	http://careers.wmfha.org

Recruiters' Resources

Abso	http://abso.com
Academy of Healthcare Recruiters	http://www.academyofhealthcarerecruiters.com
AIRS Directory	http://www.airsdirectory.com
Alliance of Medical Recruiters	http://www.physicianrecruiters.com
American Staffing Association	http://www.staffingtoday.net
Arizona Technical Recruiters Association	http://www.atraaz.org
Association of Executive Search Consultants	http://www.aesc.org/eweb
Association of Financial Search Consultants	http://www.afsc-jobs.com
Association of Staff Physician Recruiters	http://www.aspr.org
BackgroundBureau.com	http://www.backgroundbureau.com
BrainHunter	http://www.brainhunter.com
The Breckenridge Group, Inc.	http://www.breckenridgegroup.com
California Staffing Professionals	http://www.catss.org
Canadian Technical Recruiters Network	http://www.ctrn.org
Career MetaSearch	http://www.careermetasearch.com
CareersinRecruitment [United Kingdom]	http://www.careersinrecruitment.com
Changeboard [United Kingdom]	http://www.changeboard.com
Click Performance Group	http://www.click-performance.com
Climber	http://www.climber.com
Colorado Technical Recruiters Network	http://www.ctrn.org

CyberEdit	http://www.cyberedit.com
DataFrenzy.com	http://www.datafrenzy.com
DBM Career Services	https://www.dbmcareerservices.com
Defense Outplacement Referral System	https://www.dmdc.osd.mil/appj/dwp/index.jsp
Delaware Valley Technical Recruiters Network	http://www.dvtrn.org
Employment Management Association	http://www.shrm.org
ERE.net	http://www.ere.net
eQuest	http://www.joblauncher.com
ExecutiveResumes.com	http://www.executiveresumes.com
4sct.com	http://www.4sct.com
Free-For-Recruiters	http://www.free-for-recruiters.com
FreeResumeSites.com	http://www.freeresumesites.com
Global Media	http://www.globalmediarecruitment.com
GotResumes.com	http://www.gotresumes.com
H3.com	http://www.h3.com
HarQen	http://www.harqen.com
Houston High Tech Recruiters Network	http://www.hhtrn.org
Human Resource Management Association of Western New England	http://www.hrmawne.org
Human Resource Management Center	http://www.hrmc.com
Illinois Association of Personnel Services	http://www.searchfirm.com
Interbiznet.com	http://www.interbiznet.com/hrstart.html
International Association of Corporate and Professional Recruitment	http://www.iacpr.org
Investment Positions	http://www.investmentpositions.com
Jobcast.net	http://www.jobcast.net
Job Rooster	http://www.jobrooster.com
Jobster.com	http://www.jobster.com
Jobvite	http://www.jobvite.com
KarmaOne	http://www.karmaone.com
Lead411.com	http://www.lead411.com

Lee Hecht Harrison	http://www.lhh.com/Pages/default.aspx
Minnesota Technical Recruiters Network	http://www.mntrn.com
MovingCenter.com	http://www.movingcenter.com
Nasscom.org	http://www.nasscom.in
National Association of Executive Recruiters	http://www.naer.org
National Association for Health Care Recruitment	http://www.nahcr.com
National Association of Legal Search Consultants	http://www.nalsc.org
National Association of Personnel Services	http://www.napsweb.org
National Association of Physician Recruiters	http://www.napr.org
National Insurance Recruiters Association Online Job Database	http://www.nirassn.com
New Jersey Metro Employment Management Association	http://www.njmetroema.org
New Jersey Staffing Association	http://www.njsa.com
New Jersey Technical Recruiters Alliance	http://www.njtra.org
Northeast Human Resource Association	http://www.nehra.com
Northwest Recruiters Association	http://www.nwrecruit.org/nwra
NowHiring.com	http://www.nowhiring.com
The Portland Human Resource Management Assn	http://www.pbcs.jp
Project S.A.M.E.	http://www.staffingadvisors.com
Project S.A.V.E.	http://www.cluffassociates.com/projectsave.htm
PubliPac.ca [Canada]	http://www.publipac.ca
RecruitUSA	http://www.recruitusa.com
Recruiters Alliance	http://www.recruitersalliance.com
Recruiters Café	http://www.recruiterscafe.com
Recruiters for Christ	http://www.edmondspersonnel.com
Recruiters Network	http://www.recruitersnetwork.com
Recruiters Online Network	http://www.recruitersonline.com
Recruitics	http://www.recruitics.com
Recruiting.com	http://www.recruiting.com
RecruitingJobs.com	http://www.recruitingjobs.com
RecruitingMastery.com	http://www.greatrecruitertraining.com

Recruitment-Marketing [United Kingdom]	http://www.recruitment-marketing.co.uk
ReferYes.com	http://www.referyes.com
The Regional Technical Recruiter's Association	http://www.rtra.com
ResumeBlaster	http://www.resumeblaster.com
ResumeXPRESS	http://www.resumexpress.com
Resume-Link	http://resume-link.com
Resume Network	http://www.resume-network.com
ResumeRabbit.com	http://www.resumerabbit.com
Resumes on the Web	http://www.resweb.com
Resume Workz	http://www.resumeworkz.com
Russoft.org	http://www.russoft.org
Sacramento Area Human Resources Association	http://www.sahra.org
San Francisco Bay Area ASA	http://www.sfasa.org/joblist.htm
Semco	http://www.semcoenterprises.com
SHRM Atlanta	http://www.shrmatlanta.org
SHRM Jacksonville	http://www.shrmjax.org
SkillsArena.com [United Kingdom]	http://www.skillsarenacorporate.com
The Smart POST Network	http://www.smartpost.com/home/index.asp
Society for Human Resource Management HRJobs	http://jobs/shrm.org
Southeast Employment Network Inc.	http://www.nonprofitdata.com
SplitIt.com	http://www.splitit.com
Taleo (iLogos)	http://new.taleo.com
Technical Recruiters Network	http://www.trnchicago.org
Texas Association of Staffing	http://www.texasstaffing.org
Top Echelon Recruiters	http://www.topechelon.com
Universe.jobs	http://www.universe.jobs
UpSeek	http://www.upseek.com
VacancyFinder.co.uk [United Kingdom]	http://www.vacancyfinder.info/login.php
Virtual-Edge	https://www.virtual-edge.net/login/index.cfm
WebHire Network	http://www.webhire.com

WEDDLE's Research & Publications	http://www.weddles.com
Work4Labs	http://www.work4labs.com
You Achieve	http://www.youachieve.com
ZillionResumes.com	http://www.zillionresumes.com

Recruitment Advertising-Non-Newspaper Print & Online

Advertising Age's Online Job Bank	http://adage.com
American Medical Association Journal of the AMA (JAMA) Physician Recruitment Ads	http://www.ama-assn.org
American Psychological Association	http://www.apa.org/careers/psyccareers
Association for Computing Machinery Career Resource Center	http://acpinternational.org
Bernard Hodes Group	http://www.hodes.com
Book Business	http://www.bookbusinessmag.com
BuilderJobs	http://www.builderjobs.com
Career MetaSearch	http://www.careermetasearch.com
Cell Press Online	http://www.cell.com/cellpress
The Chronicle of Higher Education	http://chronicle.com/section/Jobs/61
Chronicle of Philanthropy	http://philanthropy.com/section/Home/172
CMPnet	http://www.ubmtechnology.com
Contract Employment Weekly Jobs Online	http://www.ceweekly.com
Daxic.com [United Kingdom]	http://www.daxic.com
eCareer Connections	http://www.ecareerconnections.com
eMarketing & Commerce's Job Connection	http://jobs.emarketingandcommerce.com
Engineering News Record	http://www.enrconstruction.com
The ePages Classifieds	http://www.ep.com
ERTOnline.co.uk [United Kingdom]	http://www.ertonline.co.uk
FolioMag.com	http://www.foliomag.com
FSS.co.uk [United Kingdom]	http://www.hirethinking.com
Heart Advertising	http://www.career.com
InformationWeek Career	http://www.informationweek.com/career

ITWorld.com's IT Careers	http://itjobs.computerworld.com/a/all-jobs/list
E&P Classifieds	http://www.editorandpublisher.com/Jobs.aspx
Louisville Internet Business Directory	http://www.beyondbis.com/lsvdir.html
Main Street On-Line Classifieds Service	http://classifieds.maine.com/Catalog/classifieds.cgi/index.html
MEDopportunities.com	http://www.medopportunities.com
NAS Recruitment Communications	http://www.nasrecruitment.com
Oil Online	http://www.oilonline.com
Online Help Wanted	http://www.ohw.com
Prospect City	http://www.prospectcity.com
PRWeekjobs.com	http://www.prweekus.com/Jobs/section/257
Shaker Advertising	http://www.shaker.com
Star Recruiting	http://www.bjonesassociates.com
TMP Worldwide	http://www.tmp.com/home.aspx/home.aspx

Regional-USA

Alabama

AlabamaJobs.com	http://www.alabamajobs.com
Alabama's Job Bank	http://dir.alabama.gov
Al.com	http://www.al.com
AuburnOpelikaHelpWanted.com	http://regionalhelpwanted.com/auburn-opelika-jobs
BestMobileJobs.com	http://www.bestmobilejobs.com
BetterAuburnJobs.com	http://www.betterauburnjobs.com
BetterMontgomeryJobs.com	http://www.bettermontgomeryjobs.com
Biotechnology Association of Alabama	http://www.bioalabama.com
BirminghamHelpWanted.com	http://regionalhelpwanted.com/birmingham-jobs
Birmingham News	http://www.bhamnews.com
DothanHelpWanted.com	http://regionalhelpwanted.com/dothan-jobs
HuntsvilleHelpWanted.com	http://regionalhelpwanted.com/huntsville-jobs
Huntsville Times	http://www.htimes.com

MobileHelpWanted.com	http://regionalhelpwanted.com/mobile-jobs
Mobile Register Online	http://www.mobileregister.com
Montgomery Advertiser	http://www.montgomeryadvertiser.com
MontgomeryAreaHelpWanted.com	http://regionalhelpwanted.com/montgomery-jobs
MyLakeAreaJobs.com	http://www.mylakeareajobs.com
The Tuscaloosa News	http://www.tuscaloosanews.com

Alaska

Anchorage Daily News	http://www.adn.com
Anchorage Diversity	http://www.anchoragediversity.com
Alaska Fishing Jobs	http://www.fishingjobs.com
AlaskaJobs.com	http://www.alaskajobs.com
Alaska's Job Bank	http://jobs.alaska.gov
AlaskaJobFinder.com	http://www.alaskajobfinder.com
Anchorage Daily News	http://www.adn.com
AnchorageHelpWanted.com	http://regionalhelpwanted.com/anchorage-jobs
Fairbanks Daily News	http://fairbanks.abracat.com
FairbanksHelpWanted.com	http://regionalhelpwanted.com/fairbanks-jobs
Frontiersman	http://www.frontiersman.com
HelpWantedAlaska.com	http://www.helpwantedalaska.com
I Love Alaska	http://ilovealaska.com/taxonomy/term/11
Juneau Empire	http://www.juneauempire.com
KodiakHelpWanted.com	http://regionalhelpwanted.com/kodiak-island-jobs
Nome Nugget	http://www.nomenugget.com

Arizona

Arizona Daily Sun (Flagstaff)	http://www.azdailysun.com
Arizona Hospital and Healthcare Association AZHealthJobs	http://www.azhha.org
ArizonaJobs.com	http://www.arizonajobs.com

Arizona Orthopaedic Society	http://careers.azortho.org
Arizona Public Health Association	http://healthcarecareers.azpha.org
AZFamily.com	http://www.azfamily.com
AZ-Jobs	http://www.az-jobs.com
BetterPrescottJobs.com	http://www.betterprescottjobs.com
The Daily Courier (Prescott)	http://www.dcourier.com
East Valley Tribune (Mesa)	http://www.eastvalleytribune.com
Geebo	http://www.geebo.com
HelpWantedPhoenix.com	http://regionalhelpwanted.com/phoenix-jobs
JobDig	http://www.jobdig.com
Jobing.com	http://www.jobing.com
LocalCareers.com	http://www.localcareers.com
Phoenix Employment	http://phoenix.jobing.com/
Phoenix Jobs	http://www.phoenixjobs.com
Phoenix News Times	http://www.phoenixnewtimes.com
Phoenix One Stop Career Center	http://www.ci.phoenix.az.us
SierraVistaHelpWanted.com	http://regionalhelpwanted.com/sierra-vista-jobs
Today's News-Herald (Lake Havasu City)	http://www.havasunews.com
TucsonHelpWanted.com	http://regionalhelpwanted.com/tucson-jobs

Arkansas

ARHelpWanted.com	http://regionalhelpwanted.com/arkansas-jobs
Arkansas Human Resources Association	http://www.ahra.org
ArkansasJobs.com	http://www.arkansasjobs.com
Arkansas Jobs	http://www.arkansasjobs.com
Arkansas Online	http://www.arkansasonline.com
Benton Courier	http://www.bentoncourier.com
HotSpringsHelpWanted.com	http://regionalhelpwanted.com/hot-springs-jobs
Jobdig	http://www.jobdig.com
JonesboroHelpWanted.com	http://regionalhelpwanted.com/jonesboro-jobs
Jonesboro Sun	http://www.jonesborosun.com

LittleRockHelpWanted.com — http://regionalhelpwanted.com/little-rock-jobs

RiverValleyHelpWanted.com — http://regionalhelpwanted.com/river-valley-jobs

The Sentinel-Record (Hot Springs) — http://www.hotsr.com

TexarkanaHelpWanted.com — http://regionalhelpwanted.com/texarkana-jobs

University of Arkansas — http://www.uark.edu/home

What A Job — http://www.whatajob.com

California

680 Careers.com — http://www.680careers.com/index.php

Abag — http://www.abag.ca.gov

Association for Environmental and Outdoor Education — http://www.aeoe.org

BAJobs — http://www.bajobs.com

BakersfieldHelpWanted.com — http://regionalhelpwanted.com/bakersfield-jobs

Bay Area Careers — http://www.bayareacareers.com/bay_area.php

Bay Bio — http://www.baybio.org

BayAreaClassifieds.com — http://www.bayareaclassifieds.com

BayAreaHelpWanted.com — http://regionalhelpwanted.com/bay-area-jobs

BayAreaJobFinder.com — http://www.bayareajobfinder.com

California Academy of Family Physicians — http://www.fpjobsonline.org

California Agricultural Technical Institute ATI-Net AgJobs — http://www.atinet.org/jobs.asp

CaliforniaCoastHelpWanted.com — http://regionalhelpwanted.com/california-coast-jobs

California Dental Hygienists' Association Employment Opportunities — http://www.cdha.org/employment/index.html

CaliforniaJobs.com — http://www.californiajobs.com

California Mortgage Brokers Association Career Center — http://www.cambweb.org

California Primary Care Association — http://jobs.cliniccareers.org

California Psychological Association — http://careers.cpapsych.org

California Radiological Society — http://careers.calrad.org

California Separation Science Society — http://www.casss.org

California State University - Chico — http://www.csuchico.edu/careers

CentralCaliforniaHelpWanted.com	http://regionalhelpwanted.com/central-california-jobs/
CentralCoastHelpWanted.com	http://regionalhelpwanted.com/central-coast-ca-jobs
CentralValleyHelpWanted.com	http://regionalhelpwanted.com/central-valley-ca-jobs
ChicoHelpWanted.com	http://regionalhelpwanted.com/chico-jobs
ChicoJobs.com	http://www.chicojobs.com
Coastline	http://www.ventura.com
ContraCostaJobs.com	http://www.contracostajobs.com
craigslist	http://www.craigslist.org
DesertHelpWanted.com	http://regionalhelpwanted.com/desert-ca-jobs
FinancialJobs.com	http://www.financialjobs.com
Foothill-De Anza Community College	http://www.fhda.edu/jobs
Forty Plus	http://www.fortyplus.org
Geebo	http://www.geebo.com
Go Job Zone	http://www.gojobzone.com
Healthcaare Human Resources Management Association of California	http://careers.hhrmac.org
HelpWantedSanDiego.com	http://regionalhelpwanted.com/san-diego-jobs
HighDesertHelpWanted.com	http://regionalhelpwanted.com/high-desert-jobs
Hispanic-Jobs.com	http://www.hispanic-jobs.com
HireDiversity.com	http://www.hirediversity.com
Hospital Association of Sourthern California	http://careers.allhealthinc.com
Human Resource Independent Consultants (HRIC) On-Line Job Leads	http://www.hric.org
InlandEmpireHelpWanted.com	http://regionalhelpwanted.com/inland-empire-ca-jobs
JobConnect.org	http://www.jobconnections.org
Job Meister	http://www.jobmeister.com
LA Working World	http://www.workingworld.com
LocalCareers.com	http://www.localcareers.com
LosAngelesHelpWanted.com	http://regionalhelpwanted.com/los-angeles-jobs

Los Angeles Times	http://www.latimes.com
MercedHelpWanted.com	http://regionalhelpwanted.com/merced-jobs
Mercury Center	http://www.mercurynews.com
Mercury News (San Jose)	http://www.bayarea.com
ModestoJobFinder.com	http://www.modestojobfinder.com
MontereyBayHelpWanted.com	http://regionalhelpwanted.com/monterey-bay-jobs
MontereyBayJobs.com	http://www.montereybayjobs.com
NorthBayCareers.com	http://www.northbaycareers.com/index.php
NorthBayHelpWanted.com	http://regionalhelpwanted.com/north-bay-jobs
Orange County Register	http://www.ocregister.com
Palo Alto Weekly	http://www.paloaltoonline.com
Presidio Jobs	http://www.presidio.gov/trust/jobs
ReddingHelpWanted.com	http://regionalhelpwanted.com/redding-jobs
ReddingJobs.com	http://www.reddingjobs.com
Sacramento Bee	http://www.sacbee.com
SacramentoHelpWanted.com	http://regionalhelpwanted.com/sacramento-jobs
SacramentoJobFinder.com	http://www.sacramentojobfinder.com
Sacramento Recruiter	http://www.sacramentorecruiter.com
San Bernardino County Medical Society / Riverside County Medical Society	http://healthcarecareers.sbcms.org
San Diego Careers	http://www.sandiegocareers.com/index.php
San Diego Jobs	http://www.sandiegojobs.com
San Diego Software Industry Council	http://www.sdsic.org
San Francisco Chronicle	http://www.sfgate.com
San Francisco Bay Area ASA	http://www.sfasa.org/joblist.htm
San Francisco Bay Area Job Hub	http://www.jobhub.com
San Francisco State University Instructional Technologies	http://www.itec.sfsu.edu
SantaBarbaraJobs.net	http://www.santabarbarajobs.net
SantaCruzJobs.com	http://www.santacruzjobs.com
SantaMariaJobAlert.com	http://www.santamariajobalert.com
SantaRosaJobs.com	http://www.santarosajobs.com

SLOJobs.com	http://www.slojobs.com
Sonic Net	http://www.sonic.net/jobs/ent
SonomaCountyHelpWanted.com	http://regionalhelpwanted.com/sonoma-county-jobs
SouthBayHelpWanted.com	http://regionalhelpwanted.com/south-bay-jobs
Southern California Electronic Data Interchange Roundtable	http://www.scedir.org
StocktonJobFinder.com	http://www.stocktonjobfinder.com
SutterButtesHelpWanted.com	http://regionalhelpwanted.com/sutter-buttes-jobs
University of California- Berkeley Work-Study Programs	http://workstudy.berkeley.edu
The Valley Exchange	http://www.thevalleyexchange.com
Jobs.WestsideRentals.com	http://www.westsiderentals.com/jobs

Colorado

American Academy of Cardiology - Colorado Chapter	http://careers.coloradoacc.org
Aspen Daily News	http://www.aspendailynews.com
BetterColoradoSpringsJobs.com	http://www.bettercoloradospringsjobs.com
BetterPuebloJobs.com	http://www.betterpueblojobs.com
Colorado Academy of Family Physicians	http://www.fpjobsonline.org
Colorado Computerwork	http://colorado.computerwork.com
Colorado Health and Hospital Association	http://www.cha.com
Colorado Hospital Association	http://healthcarecareers.cha.com
Colorado Human Resource Association Online	http://www.chra.org
Colorado Jobs	http://colorado.jobing.com
ColoradoJobs.net	http://www.coloradojobs.net
Colorado Online Job Connection	http://www.peakweb.com
ColoradoSpringsHelpWanted.com	http://regionalhelpwanted.com/colorado-springs-jobs
Colorado Springs Independent	http://www.csindy.com
Colorado Springs Society for Human Resource Management	http://www.csshrm.org
Colorado Technical Recruiters Network	http://www.ctrn.org

The Daily Sentinel (Grand Junction)	http://www.gjsentinel.com
Denver Post	http://www.denverpost.com
Durango Herald	http://www.durangoherald.com
Emergency Medical Services Association of Colorado	http://jobs.emsac.org
HighCountryHelpWanted.com	http://regionalhelpwanted.com/high-country-co-jobs
NorthernColoradoHelpWanted.com	http://regionalhelpwanted.com/northern-colorado-jobs
RockyMountainHelpWanted.com	http://regionalhelpwanted.com/rocky-mountain-co-jobs
Rocky Mountain News	http://www.rockymountainnews.com/jobs
State of Colorado	http://www.state.co.us
WesternSlopeHelpWanted.com	http://regionalhelpwanted.com/western-slope-co-jobs

Connecticut

The Advocate (Stamford)	http://www.stamfordadvocate.com
AllCountyJobs.com	http://www.allcountyjobs.com
Connecticut's BioScience Cluster	http://www.curenet.org
Connecticut Hospital Association	http://www.chime.org
ConnecticutJobs.com	http://www.connecticutjobs.com
Connecticut Orthopaedic Society	http://careers.ctortho.org
Connecticut State Medical Society	http://careers.csms.org
CT High Tech	http://www.cthightech.com
CT Jobs	http://www.ctjobs.com
Danbury News-Times	http://www.newstimes.com
EasternCTHelpWanted.com	http://regionalhelpwanted.com/eastern-connecticut-jobs
Fairfield, CT Jewish Jobs	http://www.jewishjobs.com
FairfieldCountyHelpWanted.com	http://regionalhelpwanted.com/fairfield-county-jobs
FairfieldCountyJobs.com	http://www.fairfieldcountyjobs.com
GetCTJobs.com	http://www.getctjobs.com

HartfordCountyJobs.com	http://www.hartfordcountyjobs.com
Hartford Courant	http://www.courant.com
HartfordHelpWanted.com	http://regionalhelpwanted.com/hartford-jobs
New England Higher Education Recruitment Consortium	http://www.newenglandherc.org
New England Job	http://www.jobct.com
NewHavenCountyJobs.com	http://www.newhavencountyjobs.com
NewHavenHelpWanted.com	http://regionalhelpwanted.com/new-haven-jobs
New Haven Register	http://www.newhavenregister.com
NewLondonCountyJobs.com	http://www.newlondoncountyjobs.com
Tri-StateJobs.com	http://www.tristatejobs.com
Waterbury Republican American	http://www.rep-am.com

Delaware

DelawareJobs.com	http://www.delawarejobs.com
Delaware Online	http://www.delawareonline.com
Delaware Valley Technical Recruiters Network	http://www.dvtrn.org
Delaware's Employment	http://www.delmarweb.com
Delaware JobLink	https://joblink.delaware.gov/ada
Delaware Nurses Association	http://nursejobs.denurses.org
Dover Post	http://www.doverpost.com
HelpWantedDelaware.com	http://regionalhelpwanted.com/delaware-jobs
JobCircle.com	http://www.jobcircle.com
JobNet	http://jobcircle.com/jobnet
ServiceSource Network	http://www.ourpeoplework.org
Tri-State Human Resource Management Assn	http://wss3.tristatehr.org/default.aspx

District of Columbia

AllCountyJobs.com	http://www.allcountyjobs.com
Capital Communicator	http://www.capitalcommunicator.com
The Catholic University of America Career Services Office	http://careers.cua.edu
dcaccountingjobs.com	http://www.dcaccountingjobs.com

DC Job Source	http://dcjobsource.com
DC Registry	http://www.dcregistry.com
DCWebWomen	http://www.dcwebwomen.org
District of Columbia Health Care Association	http://careers.dchca.org
DistrictofColumbiaJobs.com	http://www.districtofcolumbiajobs.com
Geebo	http://www.geebo.com
HelpWantedDC.com	http://regionalhelpwanted.com/washington-dc-jobs
Human Resource Association of the National Capital Area Job Bank Listing	http://hra-nca.org/job_list.asp
JobFetch.com	http://www.jobfetch.com
WashingtonJobs.com	http://www.washingtonpost.com
The Washington Post	http://www.washingtonpost.com
Washington Times	http://www.washingtontimes.com

East Coast

East Bay Works	http://www.eastbayworks.org
East Coast Jobs	http://www.eastcoastjobs.net
Planet Tech	http://www.planet-tech.si

Florida

American College of Cardiology - Florida Chapter	http://careers.accfl.org
BioFlorida	http://www.bioflorida.com
Central Florida Human Resource Association	http://www.cfhra.org
CoastalHelpWanted.com	http://regionalhelpwanted.com/coastal-fl-jobs
DaytonaHelpWanted.com	http://regionalhelpwanted.com/daytona-jobs
EmeraldCoastHelpWanted.com	http://regionalhelpwanted.com/emerald-coast-jobs
EmeraldCoastJobAlert.com	http://www.emeraldcoastjobalert.com
Florida Academy of Family Physicians	http://www.fpjobsonline.org
Florida Association Directors of Nursing Administration	http://careers.fadona.org
Florida Banking Jobs Online	http://www.bankjobsflorida.com
Florida CareerLINK	http://regionalhelpwanted.com/florida-jobs

FloridaCareers.com	http://www.FloridaCareers.com
Florida Healthcare Social Workers Association	http://careers.fhcswa.net
Florida Jobs	http://www.floridajobs.com
Florida Jobs Online!	http://www.florida-jobs-online.com
Florida Medical Directors Association	http://careers.fmda.org
Florida Naturopathic Physicians Association	http://careers.fnpa.org
Florida Psychological Association	http://careercenter.flapsych.com
Florida Society of Ambulatory Surgery Centers	http://careers.fsasc.org
Florida Times Union (Jacksonville)	http://jacksonville.com
FloridianJobs.com	http://www.floridianjobs.com
GainesvilleOcalaHelpWanted.com	http://regionalhelpwanted.com/gainesville-ocala-jobs
Geebo	http://www.geebo.com
GulfCoastJobAlert.com	http://www.gulfcoastjobalert.com
Human Resource Association of Broward County	http://www.hrabc.org
JacksonvilleHelpWanted.com	http://regionalhelpwanted.com/jacksonville-recruitment
JobCrank.com	http://www.jobcrank.com
Miami Herald	http://www.miami.com
Miami Jobs	http://www.miami-jobs.net
NorthFloridaHelpWanted.com	http://regionalhelpwanted.com/north-florida-jobs
Nova Southeastern University	http://www.nova.edu
OrlandoHelpWanted.com	http://regionalhelpwanted.com/orlando-jobs
Orlando Jobs	http://www.orlando-jobs.com
Orlando Sentinel	http://www.orlandosentinel.com
PanamaCityHelpWanted.com	http://regionalhelpwanted.com/panama-city-jobs
PensacolaHelpWanted.com	http://regionalhelpwanted.com/pensacola-jobs
Pensacola News Journal	http://www.pnj.com
RhinoMite	http://www.jobing.com/?chang=local&welcome=rhinomite
SarasotaHelpWanted.com	http://regionalhelpwanted.com/sarasota-jobs
St. Petersburg Times	http://www.sptimes.com

SHRM Jacksonville	http://www.shrmjax.org
SouthFloridaHelpWanted.com	http://regionalhelpwanted.com/south-florida-jobs
SouthwestFloridaHelpWanted.com	http://regionalhelpwanted.com/southwest-florida-jobs
SpaceCoastHelpWanted.com	http://regionalhelpwanted.com/space-coast-fl-jobs
Sun-Sentinel Career Path	http://www.sun-sentinel.com/classified/jobs
TallahasseeHelpWanted.com	http://regionalhelpwanted.com/tallahassee-jobs
Tampa Bay Employment	http://www.tampabaywired.com
Tampa Jobs.com	http://www.tampa-jobs.com
WestPalmBeachBocaHelpWanted.com	http://regionalhelpwanted.com/west-palm-beach-boca-raton-jobs

Georgia

The Albany Herald	http://www.albanyherald.net/classbrowse.htm
AtlantaHelpWanted.com	http://regionalhelpwanted.com/atlanta-jobs
Atlanta Job Resource Center	http://www.ajrc.com
Atlanta JobZone	http://atlanta.jobing.com
Atlanta-Jobs	http://www.atlanta-jobs.com
Atlanta Journal and Constitution	http://www.ajc.com
Augusta Chronicle	http://chronicle.augusta.com
AugustaHelpWanted.com	http://regionalhelpwanted.com/augusta-jobs
ChattahoocheeHelpWanted.com	http://regionalhelpwanted.com/chattahoochee-jobs
Emory University Rollins School of Public Health	http://www.sph.emory.edu
Georgia Academy of Family Physicians	http://www.fpjobsonline.org
Georgia Association of Personnel Services	http://70.85.148.53:5574/JobBoard/tabid/53/Default.aspx
GeorgiaCareers.com	http://www.georgiacareers.com
Georgia Center for Nonprofits	http://www.gcn.org
Georgia Department of Human Resources	http://www.dhrjobs.com
Georgia Orthopaedic Society	http://careers.georgiaorthosociety.org
Georgia Pharmacy Association	http://www.gpha.org
Georgia Society of Ambulatory Surgery Center	http://jobboard.gsasc.org

Georgia State University Career Services	http://www.gsu.edu/career
Georgia Tech Career Services Office	http://www.career.gatech.edu
GreatColumbusJobs.com	http://www.greatcolumbusjobs.com
Job Net	http://www.westga.edu
Macon Telegraph	http://www.macon.com
MidGeorgiaHelpWanted.com	http://regionalhelpwanted.com/mid-georgia-jobs
MyMiddleGeorgiaJobs.com	http://www.mymiddlegeorgiajobs.com
National Association of Securities Professionals (Atlanta) Current Openings	http://www.naspatlanta.org
NW Georgia Careers	http://www.careerdepot.org
SavannahHelpWanted.com	http://regionalhelpwanted.com/savannah-jobs
SavannahJobs.com	http://www.savannahjobs.com
Savannah Morning News	http://www.savannahnow.com
SHRM Atlanta	http://www.shrmatlanta.org
SoutheastGeorgiaHelpWanted.com	http://regionalhelpwanted.com/southeast-georgia-jobs
Southeast Employment Network Inc.	http://www.nonprofitdata.com
SouthwestGeorgiaHelpWanted.com	http://regionalhelpwanted.com/southwest-georgia-jobs
SouthGeorgiaHelpWanted.com	http://regionalhelpwanted.com/south-georgia-jobs

Hawaii

HawaiiJobs.net	http://www.hawaiijobs.net
HawaiiJobsOnDemand.com	http://www.hawaiijobsondemand.com
Hawaii Tribune-Herald (Hilo)	http://www.hawaiitribune-herald.com/index.html
Honolulu Advertiser	http://www.honoluluadvertiser.com
HonoluluHelpWanted.com	http://regionalhelpwanted.com/honolulu-jobs
Honolulu Star-Bulletin	http://www.starbulletin.com
JobsOnKauai.com	http://regionalhelpwanted.com/kauai-jobs
KamaainaJobs.com	http://www.kamaainajobs.com
Maui.net	http://www.maui.net
Maui News	http://www.mauinews.com

| Starbulletin | http://www.starbulletin.com |
| West Hawaii Today (Kailua) | http://www.westhawaiitoday.com |

Idaho

BetterIdahoFallsJobs.com	http://www.betteridahofallsjobs.com
BetterPocatelloJobs.com	http://www.betterpocatellojobs.com
BetterTwinFallsJobs.com	http://www.bettertwinfallsjobs.com
BoiseHelpWanted.com	http://regionalhelpwanted.com/boise-jobs
BoiseIdahoJobs.com	http://www.boiseidahojobs.com
Cedar Rapids Gazette	http://www.gazetteonline.com
The Daily Nonpareil (Council Bluffs)	http://southwestiowanews.com/council_bluffs/front/
Des Moines Register	http://www.desmoinesregister.com
Idaho Department of Labor	http://labor.idaho.gov/dnn/Default.aspx?alias=labor.idaho.gov/dnn/idl
IdahoJobs.com	http://idaho.jobing.com
NorthIdahoHelpWanted.com	http://regionalhelpwanted.com/north-idaho-jobs
Quad City Times (Davenport)	http://qctimes.com
Sioux City Journal	http://www.siouxcityjournal.com
SouthernIdahoHelpWanted.com	http://regionalhelpwanted.com/southern-idaho-jobs

Illinois

Accountant Jobs Chicago	http://www.accountantjobschicago.com
American Academy of Pediatrics - Illinois Chapter	http://careers.illinoisaap.org
Audit Jobs Chicago	http://www.auditjobschicago.com
BloomingtonHelpWanted.com	http://regionalhelpwanted.com/bloomington-jobs
CentralIllinoisHelpWanted.com	http://regionalhelpwanted.com/central-illinois-jobs
Chicago AMA	http://chicagoama.org
ChicagoJobs.com	http://www.chicagojobs.com
ChicagoJobs.org	http://www.chicagojobs.org
Chicago Medical Society	http://www.cmsdocs.org

Chicago Software Newspaper	http://www.chisoft.com
Chicago Tribune	http://www.chicagotribune.com
Chicagoland's Virtual Job Resource	http://www.chicagojobresource.com
FetchMeAJob.com	http://www.fetchmeajob.com
Geebo	http://www.geebo.com
HelpWantedSpringfield.com	http://regionalhelpwanted.com/springfield-illinois-jobs
Herald & Review (Decatur)	http://www.herald-review.com
Human Resource Association of Greater Oak Brook	http://www.hraoakbrook.org
ILJobs.com	http://www.iljobs.com
IllianaHelpWanted.com	http://regionalhelpwanted.com/illiana-jobs
IlliniHelpWanted.com	http://regionalhelpwanted.com/illini-jobs
Illinois Academy of Family Physicians	http://www.fpjobsonline.org
IllinoisCareers.com	http://www.illinoiscareers.com
Illinois CPA Society Career Center	http://www.icpas.org
IllinoisJobs.com	http://www.illinoisjobs.com
IllinoisJobs.net	http://www.illinoisjobs.net
Illinois Nurses Association	http://careers.illinoisnurses.com
Illinois Psychological Assocation	http://careers.illinoispsychology.org
Illinois Recruiters Association	http://illinoisrecruiter.ning.com
Job Force Network	http://www.jobforce.net
Jobs in Chicago	http://www.jobsinchicago.com
Loyola College	http://www.loyola.edu/thecareercenter/index.html
Metropolitan Chicago Healthcare Council	http://careerboard.mchc.org
The News-Gazette (Champaigne)	http://www.news-gazette.com
NPO	http://www.npo.net
PeoriaHelpWanted.com	http://regionalhelpwanted.com/peoria-recruitment
The Regional Technical Recruiter's Association	http://www.rtra.com
Register-News (Mount Vernon)	http://register-news.com
The State Journal Register (Springfield)	http://www.sj-r.com
SuburbanChicagoHelpWanted.com	http://regionalhelpwanted.com/chicago-area-jobs

Tax Jobs Chicago   http://www.taxjobschicago.com

University of Chicago   http://www.uchicago.edu/alumni

Indiana

BloomingtonHelpWanted.com   http://regionalhelpwanted.com/bloomington-jobs

CentralIndianaHelpWanted.com   http://regionalhelpwanted.com/central-indiana-jobs

The Evansville Courier   http://ads.evansville.net/employment

FetchMeAJob.com   http://www.fetchmeajob.com

FortWayneHelpWanted.com   http://regionalhelpwanted.com/fort-wayne-jobs

The Herald-Times (Bloomington) http://www.heraldtimesonline.com

IndianaJobs.com   http://www.indianajobs.com

IndianapolisHelpWanted.com   http://regionalhelpwanted.com/indianapolis-jobs

Indianapolis Star News   http://www.indystar.com

Indy Mall   http://www.indymall.com

LafayetteHelpWanted.com   http://regionalhelpwanted.com/lafayette-recruitment

The News-Sentinel (Fort Wayne) http://www.fortwayne.com

Online Jobs Indiana   http://www2.indystar.com/webcat/classified

Purdue University Management Placement Office   http://www.krannert.purdue.edu/departments/gcs

Post-Tribune (Gary)   http://www.post-trib.com/index.html

SouthBendHelpWanted.com   http://regionalhelpwanted.com/south-bend-jobs

South Bend Tribune   http://www.sbinfo.com

TerreHauteHelpWanted.com   http://regionalhelpwanted.com/terre-haute-jobs

TriStateHelpWanted.com   http://regionalhelpwanted.com/tri-state-jobs

Iowa

Access Dubuque   http://jobs.accessdubuque.com

AGC Iowa Careers   http://www.agciajobs.com

BetterHawkeyeJobs.com   http://www.betterhawkeyejobs.com

BetterQCJobs.com   http://www.betterqcjobs.com

BetterSiouxlandJobs.com	http://www.bettersiouxlandjobs.com
CedarRapidsIowaCityHelpWanted.com	http://regionalhelpwanted.com/cedar-rapids-iowa-city-jobs
CentralIowaHelpWanted.com	http://regionalhelpwanted.com/central-iowa-jobs
Corridor Careers	http://www.corridorcareers.com
DesMoinesHelpWanted.com	http://regionalhelpwanted.com/des-moines-jobs
Des Moines Register	http://www.desmoinesregister.com
Drake University	http://www.drake.edu
DubuqueHelpWanted.com	http://regionalhelpwanted.com/dubuque-jobs
FortDodgeHelpWanted.com	http://regionalhelpwanted.com/fort-dodge-recruitment
Iowa Biotechnology Association	http://www.iowabiotech.org
Iowa Jobs	http://www.iowajobs.org
IowaJobs.net	http://www.iowajobs.net
Iowa Orthopaedic Society	http://careers.iowaorthopaedic.org
NorthernIowaHelpWanted.com	http://regionalhelpwanted.com/northern-iowa-jobs
SiouxLandHelpWanted.com	http://regionalhelpwanted.com/sioux-land-jobs
SouthernIowaHelpWanted.com	http://regionalhelpwanted.com/southern-iowa-jobs

Kansas

American Academy of Pediatrics - Kansas Chapter	http://jobboard.kansasaap.org
Daily Union (Junction City)	http://www.thedailyunion.net
Kansas City Kansan	http://www.kansascitykansan.com
Kansas Hospital Association	http://kshealthjobs.net
KansasJobs.net	http://www.kansasjobs.net
Kansas Psychological Association	http://careers.kspsych.org
Kansas Works	http://www.kansasworks.com
My Kansas	http://www.kansas.gov/index.php
Salina Journal	http://www.saljournal.com
The Topeka Capital Journal	http://www.cjonline.com
TopekaHelpWanted.com	http://regionalhelpwanted.com/topeka-jobs

Wichita Eagle	http://www.kansas.com
WichitaHelpWanted.com	http://regionalhelpwanted.com/wichita-jobs

Kentucky

American Academy of Pediatrics - Kentucky Chapter	http://careercenter.kyaap.org
BluegrassHelpWanted.com	http://regionalhelpwanted.com/bluegrass-ky-jobs
The Courier-Journal (Louisville)	http://www.courier-journal.com
The Daily News (Bowling Green)	http://www.bgdailynews.com
Grayson County News-Gazette (Leitchfield)	http://www.gcnewsgazette.com
HelpWantedLexington.com	http://regionalhelpwanted.com/lexington-jobs
HuntingtonAshlandHelpWanted.com	http://regionalhelpwanted.com/huntington-ashland-jobs
KentuckyJobs.com	http://www.kentuckyjobs.com
Lexington Herald Leader	http://www.kentucky.com
LouisvilleHelpWanted.com	http://regionalhelpwanted.com/louisville-jobs
Louisville Internet Business Directory	http://www.beyondbis.com/lsvdir.html
Sentinel News (Shelbyville)	http://www.sentinelnews.com

Louisiana

AcadianaHelpWanted.com	http://regionalhelpwanted.com/acadiana-jobs
The Advocate (Baton Rouge)	http://www.advocate.com
BatonRougeHelpWanted.com	http://regionalhelpwanted.com/baton-rouge-jobs
BetterAcadianaJobs.com	http://www.betteracadianajobs.com
BetterBatonRougeJobs.com	http://www.betterbatonrougejobs.com
BetterHammondJobs.com	http://www.betterhammondjobs.com
BetterNorthshoreJobs.com	http://www.betternorthshorejobs.com
CenLAHelpWanted.com	http://regionalhelpwanted.com/central-louisiana-jobs
Info Louisiana	http://www.state.la.us
Louisiana Assisted Living Association	http://careers.laassisted.org
LouisianaJobs.com	http://www.louisianajobs.com

Louisiana Occupational Therapy Association	http://www.lota.org
Louisiana State Medical Society	http://careers.lsms.org
Med Job Louisiana	http://www.medjoblouisiana.com
MonroeHelpWanted.com	http://regionalhelpwanted.com/monroe-recruitment
NewOrleansHelpWanted.com	http://regionalhelpwanted.com/new-orleans-jobs
Orleans Parish Medical Society	http://www.opms.org
ShreveportHelpWanted.com	http://regionalhelpwanted.com/shreveport-jobs
The Times (Shreveport)	http://www.shreveporttimes.com
The Times-Picayune (New Orleans)	http://www.nola.com

Maine

Bangor Daily News	http://www.bangordailynews.com
Biotechnology Association of Maine	http://www.mainebiotech.org
CentralMaineHelpWanted.com	http://regionalhelpwanted.com/central-maine-jobs
EasternMaineHelpWanted.com	http://regionalhelpwanted.com/eastern-maine-recruitment
Employment Times Online	http://www.myjobwave.com
JobsinME.com	http://www.jobsinme.com
Kennebec Journal (Augusta)	http://www.kjonline.com
Lewiston Sun Journal	http://www.sunjournal.com
Maine-Job.com	http://www.maine-job.com
MaineJobs.net	http://www.mainejobs.net
Maine Street On-Line Classifieds Service	http://classifieds.maine.com
New England Higher Education Recruitment Consortium	http://www.newenglandherc.org
Portland Press Herald	http://www.portland.com
SouthernMaineHelpWanted.com	http://regionalhelpwanted.com/southern-maine-jobs
The Times Record (Brunswick)	http://www.timesrecord.com

Maryland

AllCountyJobs.com	http://www.allcountyjobs.com

BaltimoreHelpWanted.com	http://regionalhelpwanted.com/baltimore-jobs
Baltimore Sun	http://www.baltimoresun.com
The Capital (Annapolis)	http://www.hometownannapolis.com
Chesapeake Human Resource Association	http://www.chra.com
EasternShoreHelpWanted.com	http://regionalhelpwanted.com/eastern-shore-de-md-jobs
FrederickHelpWanted.com	http://regionalhelpwanted.com/frederick-jobs
Health Facilities Association of Maryland	http://careers.hfam.org
The Herald-Mail (Hagerstown)	http://www.herald-mail.com
Howard County Human Resources Society	http://www.hocohrs.org
Human Resource Association of the National Capital Area Job Bank Listing	http://hra-nca.org/job_list.asp
JobFetch.com	http://www.jobfetch.com
Maryland Association of CPAs Job Connect	http://www.macpa.org
Maryland Hospital Association	http://healthcarecareers.mhaonline.org
MarylandJobs.com	http://www.marylandjobs.com
Maryland Orthopaedic Association	http://jobboard.mdortho.org
Maryland State Dental Association	http://careers.dentalcompany.com
The Maryland State Medical Society	http://careers.medchi.org
MdBio, Inc. (Maryland Bioscience)	http://techcouncilmd.com/mdbio
Sailor	http://www.sailor.lib.md.us
The Star Democrat (Easton)	http://www.stardem.com
WashingtonJobs.com	http://www.washingtonpost.com

Massachusetts

AllCountyJobs.com	http://www.allcountyjobs.com
The Boston Globe	http://www.boston.com/bostonglobe
Boston.com	http://www.boston.com/jobs
Boston Hire	http://www.bostonhireonline.com
Boston Job Bank	http://www.bostonjobs.com
BostonJobs.com	http://www.bostonjobs.com

Boston JobZone	http://www.bostonjobzone.com
BostonSearch.com	http://www.bostonsearch.com
CapeAndIslandsHelpWanted.com	http://regionalhelpwanted.com/ cape-and-islands-jobs
The Eagle-Tribune (Lawrence)	http://www.eagletribune.com
Geebo	http://www.geebo.com
HelpWantedBoston.com	http://regionalhelpwanted.com/boston-jobs
HireCulture	http://www.hireculture.org
JobsinMA.com	http://www.jobsinma.com
JVS Career Moves	http://www.jvs-boston.org
Massachusetts Biotechnology Council	http://www.massbio.org
Massachusetts Environmental Education Society	http://www.massmees.org
Massachusetts Healthcare Human Resources Association	http://www.mhhra.org
MassachusettsJobs.com	http://www.massachusettsjobs.com
Massachusetts Lawyers Weekly Jobs	http://classifieds.lawyersweekly.com
New England Higher Education Recruitment Consortium	www.newenglandherc.org
Personnel Management Association of Western New England	http://hrmawne.shrm.org/webmodules/ webarticlesnet/templates/?a=1&z=1
SpringfieldHelpWanted.com	http://regionalhelpwanted.com/springfield-jobs
The Sun (Lowell)	http://www.lowellsun.com
The Salem News	http://www.salemnews.com
Union-News & Sunday Republican (Springfield)	http://www.masslive.com
WesternMassWorks.com	http://www.westernmassworks.com
Wicked Local	http://www.wickedlocal.com
Worchester Polytechnic Institute	http://www.wpi.edu

Michigan

Ann Arbor News	http://www.mlive.com/annarbornews
BetterMichiganJobs.com	http://www.bettermichiganjobs.com
Detroit Free Press	http://www.freep.com
FetchMeAJob.com	http://www.fetchmeajob.com

FlintHelpWanted.com	http://regionalhelpwanted.com/flint-recruitment
Flint Journal	http://www.mlive.com/flintjournal
GrandRapidsHelpWanted.com	http://regionalhelpwanted.com/grand-rapids-jobs
Grand Rapids Press	http://www.mlive.com/grpress
Healthcare Association of Michigan	http://careers.hcam.org
Human Resource Management Association of Mid Michigan Job Postings	http://www.hrmamm.com/jobpostings/index.php
HudsonValleyHelp Wanted.com	http://regionalhelpwanted.com/hudson-valley-jobs
KalamazooHelpWanted.com	http://regionalhelpwanted.com/kalamazoo-jobs
Lansing State Journal	http://www.lansingstatejournal.com
MichBIO	http://www.michbio.org
Michigan Association of Ambulance Services	http://employment.miambulance.org
Michigan Association of Emergency Medical Technicians	http://employment.maemt.org
Michigan CareerSite	http://www.themedc.org/jobs
MichiganJobs.com	http://www.michiganjobs.com
Michigan-Online	http://www.michigan-online.com
Michigan Web	http://www.michiganweb.com/site.html
MidMichiganHelpWanted.com	http://regionalhelpwanted.com/mid-michigan-jobs
MotorCityHelpWanted.com	http://regionalhelpwanted.com/motor-city-jobs
MuskegonHelpWanted.com	http://regionalhelpwanted.com/muskegon-jobs
MyTriCityJobs.com	http://www.mytricityjobs.com
Oakland University	http://www.oakland.edu/careerservices
Pride Source	http://www.pridesource.com
SouthwestMichiganJobs.com	http://regionalhelpwanted.com/southwest-michigan-jobs
HudsonValleyHelp Wanted.com	http://regionalhelpwanted.com/hudson-valley-jobs

Midwest

JobsintheMidwest.com	http://www.jobsinthemidwest.com
MidWest Career Matrix	http://www.careermatrix.com

Minnesota

Duluth News-Tribune	http://www.duluthnewstribune.com
Elk River Star News	http://www.erstarnews.com
The Journal (New Ulm)	http://www.oweb.com
HelpWantedRochester.com	http://regionalhelpwanted.com/rochester-mn-jobs
Hennepin County Job Openings	http://www.co.hennepin.mn.us
MinJobs.com	http://www.minjobs.com
Minneapolis Jobs	http://www.minneapolis-jobs.com
Minneapolis Star Tribune	http://www.startribune.com
MinnesotaDiversity.com	http://www.minnesotadiversity.com
MinnesotaJobs.com	http://www.minnesotajobs.com
Minnesota Medical Association	http://careercenter.mnmed.org
NorthlandHelpWanted.com	http://regionalhelpwanted.com/northland-jobs
SouthernMinnesotaHelpWanted.com	http://regionalhelpwanted.com/southern-minnesota-jobs
StCloudHelpWanted.com	http://regionalhelpwanted.com/st-cloud-jobs
Saint Paul Pioneer Press	http://www.twincities.com
TwinCitiesHelpWanted.com	http://regionalhelpwanted.com/twin-cities-jobs

Mississippi

BetterGulfCoastJobs.com	http://www.bettergulfcoastjobs.com
CentralMississippiHelpWanted.com	http://regionalhelpwanted.com/central-mississippi-jobs
The Clarion Ledger (Jackson)	http://www.clarionledger.com
GulfCoastHelpWanted.com	http://regionalhelpwanted.com/gulf-coast-jobs
MeridianHelpWanted.com	http://regionalhelpwanted.com/meridian-jobs
Meridian Star	http://www.meridianstar.com
Mississippi Ambulatory Surgery Center Association	http://jobboard.masca-ms.org
MississippiJobs.net	http://www.mississippijobs.net
Mississippi Nurses Association	http://careers.msnurses.org
The Natchez Democrat	http://www.natchezdemocrat.com

The Sun Herald (Biloxi) — http://www.sunherald.com

TupeloHelpWanted.com — http://regionalhelpwanted.com/tupelo-jobs

The Vicksburg Post — http://www.vicksburgpost.com

Missouri

American Academy of Pediatrics - Missouri Chapter — http://careers.moapp.org

BetterBransonJobs.com — http://www.betterbransonjobs.com

BetterSpringfieldJobs.com — http://www.betterspringfieldjobs.com

The Examiner (Independence) — http://www.examiner.net

Hannibal Courier-Post — http://www.hannibal.net

HeartlandJobs.com — http://regionalhelpwanted.com/heartland-mo-jobs

Human Resource Management Association of Greater Kansas City — http://hrma-kc.org

Jefferson City News Tribune — http://www.newstribune.com

Joplin Globe — http://www.joplinglobe.com

JoplinHelpWanted.com — http://regionalhelpwanted.com/joplin-jobs

Kansas City.com — http://www.kansascity.com

KansasCityHelpWanted.com — http://regionalhelpwanted.com/kansas-city-jobs

KCJobs.com — http://www.kcjobs.com

MidMissouriHelpWanted.com — http://regionalhelpwanted.com/mid-missouri-jobs

Missouri Academy of Family Physicians — http://www.fpjobsonline.org

Missouri Association of Personnel Services — http://www.moaps.com

MissouriJobs.com — http://www.missourijobs.com

Missouri Pharmacy Association — http://www.morx.com

Missouri State Government — http://www.mo.gov/working-in-missouri/job-seekers-employers

Online Columbia — http://www.onlinecolumbia.com/jobsearch.asp

OzarksHelpWanted.com — http://regionalhelpwanted.com/ozarks-jobs

Riverfront Times Virtual Career Fair — http://www.riverfronttimes.com

Springfield News-Leader — http://www.news-leader.com

StLouisHelpWanted.com — http://regionalhelpwanted.com/st-louis-jobs

St. Louis Jobs   http://st.louis.jobs.com

SouthCentralMOHelpWanted.com   http://regionalhelpwanted.com/south-central-missouri-jobs

Montana

Billings Gazette   http://billingsgazette.com

BillingsHelpWanted.com   http://regionalhelpwanted.com/billings-jobs

Bozeman Daily Chronicle   http://www.bozemandailychronicle.com

Helena Independent Record   http://www.helenair.com

Missoulian   http://www.missoulian.com

MontanaHelpWanted.com   http://regionalhelpwanted.com/montana-jobs

Montana Job Service   http://wsd.dli.mt.gov

MontanaJobs.com   http://www.montanajobs.com

The Montana Standard (Butte)   http://www.mtstandard.com

SouthwestMontanaHelpWanted.com   http://regionalhelpwanted.com/southwest-montana-jobs

WesternMontanaHelpWanted.com   http://regionalhelpwanted.com/western-montana-jobs

Nebraska

Columbus Telegram   http://www.columbustelegram.com

CornhuskerHelpWanted.com   http://regionalhelpwanted.com/cornhusker-jobs

Greater Omaha Economic Development Partnership   http://www.selectgreateromaha.com

Lincoln Journal Star   http://www.journalstar.com

NebraskaJobs.com   http://www.nebraskajobs.com

North Platte Telegraph   http://www.nptelegraph.com

OmahaHelpWanted.com   http://regionalhelpwanted.com/omaha-jobs

Omaha World-Herald   http://www.omaha.com

Scotts Bluff Star-Herald   http://www.starherald.com

Nevada

CarsonValleyJobs.com	http://www.carsonvalleyjobs.com
Elko Daily Free Press	http://elkodaily.com
LasVegasHelpWanted.com	http://regionalhelpwanted.com/las-vegas-jobs
Las Vegas Review-Journal	http://www.lvrj.com
Las Vegas Sun	http://www.lasvegassun.com
Nevada Appeal (Carson City)	http://www.nevadaappeal.com
NevadaJobs.com	http://www.nevadajobs.com
Nevada Mining	http://www.nevadamining.org
NVNurses.com	http://www.nvnurses.com
NVPublicJobs.com	http://www.nvpublicjobs.com
NVTeacherJobs.com	http://www.nvteacherjobs.com
NVMedicalJobs.com	http://www.nvmedicaljobs.com
NVAccountingJobs.com	http://www.nvaccountingjobs.com
NVTechnologyJobs.com	http://www.nvtechnologyjobs.com
RenoHelpWanted.com	http://regionalhelpwanted.com/reno-jobs
Reno Gazette Journal	http://www.rgj.com
RenoTahoeJobs.com	http://www.renotahoejobs.com
Vegas.com	http://www.vegas.com
WorkReno	http://reno.jobing.com

New England

Jobfind.com	http://www.bostonherald.com/jobfind
New England Job	http://www.newenglandjob.com
New England Careers	http://www.newenglandcareers.com
Northeast Human Resource Association	http://www.nehra.com
New England Higher Education Recruitment Consortium	http://www.newenglandherc.org
New England Journal of Medicine Career Center	http://content.nejm.org
OceanStateHelpWanted.com	http://regionalhelpwanted.com/ocean-state-jobs
Opportunity Knocks	http://www.opportunityknocks.org

New Hampshire

AllCountyJobs.com	http://www.allcountyjobs.com
Across New Hampshire	http://www.across-nh.com
Concord Monitor	http://www.concordmonitor.com
Employment Times Online	http://www.myjobwave.com
JobsinNH.com	http://www.jobsinnh.com
Keene Sentinel	http://www.keenesentinel.com
New England Higher Education Recruitment Consortium	http://www.newenglandherc.org
NewHampshireHelpWanted.com	http://regionalhelpwanted.com/new-hampshire-jobs
NewHampshireJobs.net	http://www.newhampshirejobs.net
New Hampshire Legal Assistance	http://www.nhla.org
NH.com	http://www.nh.com
nhjobs.com	http://www.nhjobs.com
Portsmouth Herald	http://www.seacoastonline.com
The Telegraph (Nashua)	http://www.nashuatelegraph.com
The Union Leader (Manchester)	http://www.theunionleader.com

New Jersey

ACHelpWanted.com	http://regionalhelpwanted.com/atlantic-city-jobs
App.com	http://www.app.com
AllCountyJobs.com	http://www.allcountyjobs.com
Atlantic City Jobs	http://www.acjobs.com
Asbury Park Press	http://www.app.com
Biotechnology Council of New Jersey	http://www.newjerseybiotech.org
CareerLocal.net	http://www.careerlocal.net
Courier-Post (Cherry Hill)	http://www.courierpostonline.com
Employment Channel	http://www.employ.com
JobCircle.com	http://www.jobcircle.com
JobNet	http://jobcircle.com/jobnet
MonmouthOceanHelpWanted.com	http://regionalhelpwanted.com/monmouth-ocean-recruitment

The Montclair Times	http://www.northjersey.com/towns/montclair.html
NewJerseyHelpWanted.com	http://regionalhelpwanted.com/new-jersey-jobs
The New Jersey Higher Education Recruitment Consortium	http://www.njepadeherc.org
New Jersey Hospital Association	http://healthjobs.njha.com
New Jersey Human Resource Planning Group	http://www.njhrpg.org
NewJerseyJobs.com	http://www.newjerseyjobs.com
New Jersey Metro Employment Management Association	http://www.njmetroema.org
New Jersey Net Connections	http://www.netconnections.net/nj/nj.html
New Jersey Online	http://www.nj.com
New Jersey Psychological Association	http://careers.psychologynj.org
New Jersey Staffing Association	http://www.njsa.com
New Jersey Technical Recruiters Alliance	http://www.njtra.org
New Jersey Technology Council	http://www.njtc.org
NJ Careers	http://hus.parkingspa.com/hc3.asp
NJ Jobs	http://www.njjobs.com
NJPAHelpWanted.com	http://regionalhelpwanted.com/edison-trenton-allentown-nj-pa-jobs
NorthJerseyHelpWanted.com	http://regionalhelpwanted.com/north-jersey-jobs
Princeton Info	http://www.princetoninfo.com
The Star Ledger (Newark)	http://www.nj.com
The Trentonian	http://www.trentonian.com
Tri-StateJobs.com	http://www.tristatejobs.com

New Mexico

Albuquerque Journal	http://www.abqjournal.com
The Gallup Independent	http://www.gallupindependent.com
HelpWantedNewMexico.com	http://regionalhelpwanted.com/new-mexico-jobs
HighPlainsHelpWanted.com	http://regionalhelpwanted.com/high-plains-nm-tx-jobs
Los Alamos Monitor	http://www.lamonitor.com
New Mexico High Tech Job Forum	http://www.nmtechjobs.com

NewMexicoJobs.net http://www.newmexicojobs.netbs.net

New Mexico Center for Nursing Excellence http://healthcarecareers.nmnursingexcellence.org

New Mexico Healthcare Association http://careers.nmhca.org

New Mexico Hospital Association http://careers.nmhanet.org

New Mexico Library Association http://www.nmla.org

New Mexico Medical Society http://healthcarecareers.nmms.org

New Mexico Osteopathic Medical Association http://healthcarecareers.nmoma.org

Santa Fe New Mexican http://www.santafenewmexican.com

The Silver City Daily Press http://www.scdailypress.com

New York

Accounting Jobs in New York http://www.accounting-jobs-in-new-york.com

AdirondackHelpWanted.com http://regionalhelpwanted.com/adirondack-jobs

Albany Democrat Herald http://democratherald.com

AllCountyJobs.com http://www.allcountyjobs.com

BigAppleHelpWanted.com http://regionalhelpwanted.com/tri-state-ny-nj-jobs

BinghamtonHelpWanted.com http://regionalhelpwanted.com/binghamton-jobs

BuffaloHelpWanted.com http://regionalhelpwanted.com/buffalo-jobs

CapitalAreaHelpWanted.com http://regionalhelpwanted.com/capital-area-jobs

CentralNewYorkHelpWanted.com http://regionalhelpwanted.com/central-new-york-jobs

ColumbiaCountyJobs.com http://www.columbiacountyjobs.com

ColumbiaGreeneHelpWanted.com http://regionalhelpwanted.com/columbia-greene-jobs

Employment Weekly http://www.employment-weekly.com

FingerLakesHelpWanted.com http://regionalhelpwanted.com/finger-lakes-jobs

411 NYC Jobs http://allnewyorkcityjobs.com

Geebo http://www.geebo.com

HelpWantedLongIsland.com http://regionalhelpwanted.com/long-island-jobs

HudsonValleyHelpWanted.com http://regionalhelpwanted.com/hudson-valley-jobs

Human Resource Association of New York http://www.nyshrm.org

IthacaCortlandHelpWanted.com	http://regionalhelpwanted.com/ithaca-cortland-jobs
Ithaca Times	http://www.zwire.com/site/news.cfm?brd=1395&nr=1&nostat=1
JobCircle.com	http://www.jobcircle.com
TheJobWire.com	http://www.thejobwire.com
LI Jobs	http://www.lijobs.com
LocalCareers.com	http://www.localcareers.com
Medical Society of New York - Sixth District Branch	http://www.jobbank.medsocieties.org
National Association of Securities Professionals (New York) Underground Railroad	http://www.nasp-ny.org
New York American Markerting Association	http://www.nyama.org
The New York Biotechnology Association	http://www.nyba.org
New York Department of Labor	http://www.labor.ny.gov/home
New York Foundation for the Arts	http://www.nyfa.org
NewYorkJobs.com	http://www.newyorkjobs.com
New York Post	http://www.nypost.com
New York Society of Association Executives Career Center	http://www.nysaenet.org
New York Society of Security Analysts Career Resources	http://www.nyssa.org/AM/Template.cfm?Section=career_development
New York State Academy of Family Physicians	http://www.fpjobsonline.org
New York State Society of CPAs	http://www.nysscpa.org/classified/main.cfm
The New York Times	http://www.nytimes.com
New York's Preferred Jobs	http://www.nycityjobs.com
NYCareers.com	http://www.nycareers.com
NY Job Source	http://www.nyjobsource.com
NY Preferred Jobs	http://newyork.preferredjobs.com
NYC Job Bank	http://www.nycjobbank.com
NYPAHelpWanted.com	http://regionalhelpwanted.com/erie-warren-bradford-buffalo-ny-pa-jobs
OleanHelpWanted.com	http://regionalhelpwanted.com/olean-jobs
Rensselaer Polytechnic Institute Career Development Center	http://www.rpi.edu/dept/cdc

RochesterHelpWanted.com	http://regionalhelpwanted.com/rochester-jobs
Rochester, NY Careers	http://www.rochestercareers.com
SeawayHelpWanted.com	http://regionalhelpwanted.com/seaway-jobs
Silicon Alley Insider	http://jobs.businessinsider.com
SyracuseHelpWanted.com	http://regionalhelpwanted.com/syracuse-jobs
Syracuse New Times	http://www.newtimes.com
Syracuse Online	http://www.syracuse.com
1000IslandsHelpWanted.com	http://regionalhelpwanted.com/1000-islands-jobs
Tri-StateJobs.com	http://www.tristatejobs.com
TwinTiersHelpWanted.com	http://regionalhelpwanted.com/twin-tiers-jobs
WestchesterCountyJobs.com	http://www.westchestercountyjobs.com
Westchester Jobs	http://www.westchesterjobs.com
Western NY JOBS	http://www.wnyjobs.com

North Carolina

AshevilleHelpWanted.com	http://regionalhelpwanted.com/asheville-jobs
BetterGreenvilleJobs.com	http://www.bettergreenvillejobs.com
Career Women	http://www.careerwomen.com
Carolina Computer Jobs	http://www.carolinacomputerjobs.com
CharlotteHelpWanted.com	http://regionalhelpwanted.com/charlotte-jobs
Charlotte Observer	http://www.charlotteobserver.com
Duke University Job Resources	http://career.studentaffairs.duke.edu
EastCarolinaHelpWanted.com	http://regionalhelpwanted.com/east-carolina-jobs
Employment Security Commission Home Page	http://www.ncesc.com/default.aspx
FayettevilleHelpWanted.com	http://regionalhelpwanted.com/fayetteville-jobs
Greensboro News-Record	http://www.news-record.com
News & Observer (Raleigh)	http://www.newsobserver.com
North Carolina Biotechnology Center	http://www.ncbiotech.org
North Carolina Genomics & Bioinformatics Consortium	http://www.ncgbc.org
North Carolina JobLink Career Center	http://www.nccommerce.com
NorthCarolinaJobs.net	http://www.northcarolinajobs.net

North Carolina Medical Society	http://careers.ncmedsoc.org
The North Carolina Office of State Personnel	http://www.osp.state.nc.us
North Carolina Orthopaedic Association	http://careers.ncorthopaedics.org
North Carolina Pediatric Society	http://www.ncpeds.org/job-listings
PiedmontHelpWanted.com	http://regionalhelpwanted.com/piedmont-jobs
StarNewsOnline.com	http://www.starnewsonline.com
TriangleHelpWanted.com	http://regionalhelpwanted.com/triangle-nc-jobs
Welcome to North Carolina	http://www.ncgov.com
WilmingtonHelpWanted.com	http://regionalhelpwanted.com/wilmington-jobs
Winston-Salem Journal	http://www2.journalnow.com/home

North Dakota

BismarckMandanHelpWanted.com	http://regionalhelpwanted.com/bismarck-mandan-jobs
Bismarck Tribune	http://www.bismarcktribune.com
Dakota Oil Jobs	http://www.dakotaoiljobs.com
FargoJobs.com	http://regionalhelpwanted.com/fargo-jobs
Grand Forks Herald	http://www.grandforks.com
The Jamestown Sun	http://www.jamestownsun.com
Minot Daily News	http://www.minotdailynews.com
NorthDakotaJobs.com	http://www.northdakotajobs.com
NorthernPlainsHelpWanted.com	http://regionalhelpwanted.com/northern-plains-md-jobs

Ohio

BetterTriStateJobs.com	http://www.bettertristatejobs.com
CareerBoard	http://www.careerboard.com
Case Western Reserve University	http://www.cwru.edu
Cincinnati Enquirer	http://www.enquirer.com
Cincinnati/Jobs	http://careerfinder.cincinnati.com
Cleveland Careers	http://www.cleveland.com

ClevelandHelpWanted.com	http://regionalhelpwanted.com/cleveland-jobs
The Cleveland Nation	http://www.clnation.com
Columbus Dispatch	http://www.dispatch.com
ColumbusHelpWanted.com	http://regionalhelpwanted.com/columbus-jobs
Dayton Daily News	http://www.daytondailynews.com
DaytonHelpWanted.com	http://regionalhelpwanted.com/dayton-jobs
FetchMeAJob.com	http://www.fetchmeajob.com
HelpWantedCincinnati.com	http://regionalhelpwanted.com/cincinnati-jobs
LimalandHelpWanted.com	http://regionalhelpwanted.com/limaland-jobs
MahoningValleyHelpWanted.com	http://regionalhelpwanted.com/mahoning-valley-jobs
MansfieldAreaHelpWanted.com	http://regionalhelpwanted.com/mansfield-area-jobs
MidOhioValleyJobs.com	http://www.midohiovalleyjobs.com
Ohio Careers Resource Center	http://www.ohiocareers.com
Ohio Job Prospector	http://www.jobprospector.com
OhioJobs.com	http://www.ohiojobs.com
Ohio Nurses Association	http://jobs.ohiorncareers.com
Ohio Orthopaedic Society	http://careers.ohioorthosociety.org
Ohio Psychological Association	http://careers.ohpsych.org
Ohio State Council	http://www.ohioshrm.org
SanduskyHelpWanted.com	http://regionalhelpwanted.com/sandusky-jobs
SoutheasternOhioHelpWanted.com	http://regionalhelpwanted.com/southeastern-ohio-jobs
Springfield News Sun	http://www.springfieldnewssun.com
ToledoHelpWanted.com	http://regionalhelpwanted.com/toledo-jobs

Oklahoma

Altus Times	http://www.altustimes.com
Lawton Constitution	http://www.lawton-constitution.com
OKC.gov	http://www.okc.gov
OklahomaCityHelpWanted.com	http://regionalhelpwanted.com/oklahoma-city-jobs

OklahomaJobs.com	http://www.oklahomajobs.com
Oklahoma State Medical Association	http://www.osmaonline.org
The Oklahoman (Oklahoma City)	http://www.newsok.com
Ponca City News	http://www.poncacitynews.com
Tulsa Area Human Resources Association	http://www.tahra.org
TulsaHelpWanted.com	http://regionalhelpwanted.com/tulsa-jobs
Tulsa World	http://www.tulsaworld.com

Oregon

AshlandJobAlert.com	http://www.ashlandjobalert.com
CentralOregonJobs.com	http://regionalhelpwanted.com/central-oregon-jobs
Columbia-Willamette Compensation Group	http://www.cwcg.org
East Oregonian (Pendleton)	http://eastoregonian.com/index.asp
EugeneHelpWanted.com	http://regionalhelpwanted.com/eugene-jobs
EugeneJobs.net	http://www.eugenejobs.net
JobDango.com	http://www.jobdango.com
KlamathJobs.net	http://www.klamathjobs.net
Oregon Bioscience Association	http://www.oregon-bioscience.com
Oregon Education Jobs	http://www.cosa.k12.or.us
Oregon Employment Department	http://www.employment.oregon.gov
OregonJobs.com	http://oregon.jobing.com
The Oregonian (Portland)	http://www.oregonian.com
PortlandHelpWanted.com	http://regionalhelpwanted.com/portland-jobs
The Portland Human Resource Management Assn	http://www.pbcs.jp
PortlandJobFinder.com	http://www.portlandjobfinder.com
The Register-Guard (Eugene)	http://www.registerguard.com
RogueValleyJobs.net	http://www.roguevalleyjobs.net
SalemJobFinder.com	http://www.salemjobfinder.com
SouthernOregonHelpWanted.com	http://regionalhelpwanted.com/southern-oregon-jobs
SouthernOregonJobs.com	http://www.southernoregonjobs.com

Springfield News   http://www.hometownnews.com

Statesman Journal (Salem)   http://www.statesmanjournal.com

Pennsylvania

AllCountyJobs.com   http://www.allcountyjobs.com

Allegheny County Medical Society   http://www.acms.org

CentreCountyHelpWanted.com   http://regionalhelpwanted.com/centre-county-jobs

ClearfieldJeffersonHelpWanted.com   http://regionalhelpwanted.com/clearfield-jefferson-jobs

Drexel University   http://www.drexel.edu

Erie Daily Times-News   http://www.goerie.com

ErieHelpWanted.com   http://regionalhelpwanted.com/erie-jobs

Geebo   http://www.geebo.com

HarrisburgHelpWanted.com   http://regionalhelpwanted.com/harrisburg-jobs

HelpWantedCentralPA.com   http://regionalhelpwanted.com/central-pennsylvania-jobs

TriStateHelpWanted.com   http://regionalhelpwanted.com/tri-state-jobs

JobCircle.com   http://www.jobcircle.com

JobNet   http://jobcircle.com/jobnet

JohnstownHelpWanted.com   http://regionalhelpwanted.com/johnstown-jobs

KeystoneHelpWanted.com   http://regionalhelpwanted.com/keystone-jobs

LehighValleyHelpWanted.com   http://regionalhelpwanted.com/lehigh-valley-jobs

NEPAHelpWanted.com   http://regionalhelpwanted.com/northeast-pennsylvania-jobs

PAJobMatch.com   http://jobs.triblive.com

Pennsylvania Academy of Family Physicians   http://www.fpjobsonline.org

Pennsylvania Ambulatory Surgery Association   http://careers.pasa-asf.org

PennsylvaniaJobs.com   http://www.pennsylvaniajobs.com

PennsylvaniaJobs.net   http://www.pennsylvaniajobs.net

Pennsylvania Orthopaedic Society   http://careers.paorthosociety.org

Pennsylvania Psychological Association   http://careers.papsy.org

PhiladelphiaHelpWanted.com   http://regionalhelpwanted.com/philadelphia-jobs

The Philadelphia Inquirer	http://www.philly.com
Philadelphia-Jobs	http://philadelphia.jobs.com
Philly.com	http://www.philly.com
PhillyWorks	http://www.phillyworks.com
PittsburghHelpWanted.com	http://regionalhelpwanted.com/pittsburgh-jobs
PittsburghJobs.com	http://www.pittsburghjobs.com
Pittsburg Post-Gazette	http://www.post-gazette.com
Scranton Times Tribune	http://thetimes-tribune.com
Three Rivers	http://trfn.clpgh.org
The Times Leader (Wilkes-Barre)	http://www.timesleader.com
Tri-StateJobs.com	http://www.tristatejobs.com
WesternPAHelpWanted.com	http://regionalhelpwanted.com/western-pennsylvania-jobs
WilliamsportHelpWanted.com	http://regionalhelpwanted.com/williamsport-jobs

Rhode Island

AllCountyJobs.com	http://www.allcountyjobs.com
JobsinRI.com	http://www.jobsinri.com
The Narragansett Times (Wakefield)	http://www.narragansetttimes.com
OceanStateHelpWanted.com	http://regionalhelpwanted.com/ocean-state-jobs
Networkri.org	http://www.networkri.org
The Pawtucket Times	http://www.pawtuckettimes.com
Providence Journal Bulletin	http://www.projo.com
Rhode Island Department of Labor and Training	http://www.dlt.state.ri.us
RhodeIsland Jobs.com	http://www.rhodeislandjobs.com
Sakonnet Times (Portsmouth)	http://www.eastbayri.com

South Carolina

Camden Chronicle Independent	http://www.chronicle-independent.com
Career Women	http://www.careerwomen.com
Carolina Computer Jobs	http://www.carolinacomputerjobs.com

Clemson University	http://www.clemson.edu
ColumbiaHelpWanted.com	http://regionalhelpwanted.com/columbia-jobs
Free Times (Columbia)	http://www.free-times.com
The Greenville News	http://www.greenvilleonline.com
LowCountryHelpWanted.com	http://regionalhelpwanted.com/low-country-sc-jobs
MyrtleBeachHelpWanted.com	http://regionalhelpwanted.com/myrtle-beach-jobs
OrangeburgHelpWanted.com	http://regionalhelpwanted.com/orangeburg-jobs
PeeDeeHelpWanted.com	http://regionalhelpwanted.com/pee-dee-jobs
The Post and Courier (Charleston)	http://www.postandcourier.com
South Carolina Ambulatory Surgery Center	http://jobboard.scasc.org
South Carolina Medical Association	http://careers.scmedical.org
South Carolina Orthopaedic Association	http://www.scoanet.org
South Carolina State Jobs	http://www.ohr.sc.gov
SumterHelpWanted.com	http://regionalhelpwanted.com/sumter-jobs
The Sun Times (Myrtle Beach)	http://www.thesunnews.com/myrtlebeachonline
UpstateHelpWanted.com	http://regionalhelpwanted.com/upstate-sc-jobs

South Dakota

Argus Leader (Sioux Falls)	http://www.argusleader.com
BlackHillsHelpWanted.com	http://regionalhelpwanted.com/black-hills-sd-jobs
Brookings Daily Register	http://www.brookingsregister.com
The Capital Journal (Pierre)	http://www.capjournal.com
The Freeman Courier	http://www.freemansd.com
Huron Plainsman	http://www.plainsman.com
SiouxFallsHelpWanted.com	http://regionalhelpwanted.com/sioux-falls-jobs
SouthDakotaJobs.com	http://www.southdakotajobs.com

Southeast

MyGA.net	http://www.myga.net
Thinkjobs	http://www.thinkjobs.com

Tennessee

BetterChattanoogaJobs.com	http://www.betterchattanoogajobs.com
BetterJacksonJobs.com	http://www.betterjacksonjobs.com
BetterKnoxvilleJobs.com	http://www.betterknoxvillejobs.com
BetterTCJobs.com	http://www.bettertcjobs.com
ChattanoogaHelpWanted.com	http://regionalhelpwanted.com/chattanooga-jobs
Chattanooga Times Free Press	http://www.timesfreepress.com
ClarksvilleHelpWanted.com	http://regionalhelpwanted.com/clarksville-jobs
CookevilleHelpWanted.com	http://regionalhelpwanted.com/cookeville-jobs
Daily Post-Athenian	http://www.dpa.xtn.net
Freestanding Ambulatory Surgery Center Association of Tennessee	http://jobboard.fascatn.org
JobDig	http://www.jobdig.com
KnoxvilleHelpWanted.com	http://regionalhelpwanted.com/knoxville-jobs
Knoxville News Sentinel	http://www.knoxnews.com
Memphis Flyer	http://www.memphisflyer.com
MemphisHelpWanted.com	http://regionalhelpwanted.com/memphis-jobs
Memphis Jobs Today	http://www.memphisjobstoday.com
MiddleTennesseeHelpWanted.com	http://regionalhelpwanted.com/middle-tennessee-jobs
Middle Tennessee-SHRM Central	http://www.mtshrm.org
NashvilleHelpWanted.com	http://regionalhelpwanted.com/nashville-jobs
Nashvillejobslink.com	http://www.nashvillechamber.com
TennesseeJobs.com	http://www.tennesseejobs.com
Tennessee Society of CPA's	http://www.tscpa.com
The Tennessean (Nashville)	http://www.tennessean.com
WestTennesseeHelpWanted.com	http://regionalhelpwanted.com/west-tennessee-jobs

Texas

AmarilloHelpWanted.com	http://regionalhelpwanted.com/amarillo-jobs
Apartment Association of Greater Dallas	http://www.aagdallas.org

Apartment Association of Tarrant County	http://www.aatcnet.org/subsite/CareerCenter/careercenterindex.htm
Austin American-Statesman	http://www.austin360.com
AustinHelpWanted.com	http://regionalhelpwanted.com/austin-jobs
Austin Jobs	http://www.austin-jobs.com
Austin@Work	http://www.catf-austin.org
Austin Texas Jobs	http://www.search-beat.com/austinjobs.htm
Austin-City Jobs	http://www.ci.Austin.tx.us
BetterTexarkanaJobs.com	http://www.bettertexarkanajobs.com
BetterTexomaJobs.com	http://www.bettertexomajobs.com
BrownwoodHelpWanted.com	http://regionalhelpwanted.com/brownwood-jobs
CareersinHouston.com	http://www.careersinhouston.com
CoastalBendHelpWanted.com	http://regionalhelpwanted.com/coastal-bend-tx-jobs
Dallas Human Resource Management Association	http://www.dallashr.org
Dallas Jobs	http://dallas.jobs.net
Dallas Morning News	http://www.dallasnews.com
Dallas News	http://www.dallasnews.com/classifieds/jobcenter
DFWHelpWanted.com	http://regionalhelpwanted.com/dallas-fort-worth-jobs
EastTexasHelpWanted.com	http://regionalhelpwanted.com/east-texas-jobs
ElPasoHelpWanted.com	http://regionalhelpwanted.com/el-paso-jobs
El Paso Times	http://www.elpasotimes.com
FortBendJobs.com	http://www.fortbendjobs.com
Geebo	http://www.geebo.com
Harris County Medical Society	http://www.hcms.org
Houston Chronicle	http://www.chron.com
Houston Human Resource Management Association	http://www.hrhouston.org
Houston Jobs	http://www.houstonjobs.com
Institute for Sustainable Charities	http://www.iscvt.org/who_we_are/jobs
JobDig	http://www.jobdig.com
Jobing.com	http://houston.jobing.com

LeadingAge Texas	http://careers.leadingagetexas.org
LocalCareers.com	http://www.localcareers.com
LubbockHelpWanted.com	http://regionalhelpwanted.com/lubbock-jobs
Metroplex Association of Personnel Consultants	http://www.recruitingfirms.com
NACCB	http://www.techservealliance.org
National Association of Hispanic Nurses Houston Chapter	http://www.nahnhouston.org
North Central Texas Workforce Solutions	http://www.dfwjobs.com
San Antonio Express News	http://www.mysanantonio.com
SanAntonioHelpWanted.com	http://regionalhelpwanted.com/san-antonio-jobs
SoutheastTexasHelpWanted.com	http://regionalhelpwanted.com/southeast-texas-jobs
SouthTexasHelpWanted.com	http://regionalhelpwanted.com/south-texas-jobs
StephenvilleHelpWanted.com	http://regionalhelpwanted.com/stephenville-jobs
Texas Apartment Association	http://www.taa.org
Texas Association for Home Care & Hospice	http://careers.tahch.org
Texas Association of Staffing	http://www.texasstaffing.org
Texas Healthcare & Bioscience Institute	http://www.thbi.org
TxJobs.com	http://www.txjobs.com
TexasJobs.com	http://www.texasjobs.com
Texas Marketplace	http://www.texas-one.org
Texas Medical Association	http://www.texmed.org
Texas Psychological Association	http://careers.texaspsyc.org
Texas Workforce Commission	http://www.twc.state.tx.us
TexomaHelpWanted.com	http://regionalhelpwanted.com/texoma-jobs
ValleyHelpWanted.com	http://regionalhelpwanted.com/valley-tx-jobs
WichitaFallsHelpWanted.com	http://regionalhelpwanted.com/wichita-falls-jobs
WorkAustin	http://austin.jobing.com
WT.Net	http://www.wt.net

Utah

The Daily Herald (Provo)	http://www.heraldextra.com
Herald Journal (Logan)	http://www.hjnews.com
JobDig	http://www.jobdig.com
SaltLakeCityHelpWanted.com	http://regionalhelpwanted.com/salt-lake-city-jobs
Salt Lake Tribune	http://www.sltrib.com
SouthernUtahHelpWanted.com	http://regionalhelpwanted.com/southern-utah-jobs
Standard-Examiner (Ogden)	http://www.standard.net
Utah Job Store	http://www.utahjobstore.com
UtahJobs.net	http://utah.jobing.com
Utah Life Sciences Association	http://www.utahlifescience.com
Utah Medical Association	http://docjobs.utahmed.org

Vermont

Addison County Independent (Middlebury)	http://www.addisonindependent.com
AllCountyJobs.com	http://www.allcountyjobs.com
Burlington Free Press	http://www.burlingtonfreepress.com
Deerfield Valley News (West Dover)	http://www.dvalnews.com
JobsinVT.com	http://www.jobsinvt.com
New England Higher Education Recruitment Consortium	http://www.newenglandherc.org
NorthCountryHelpWanted.com	http://regionalhelpwanted.com/north-country-jobs
Stowe Reporter	http://www.stowetoday.com
Valley News (White River Junction)	http://www.vnews.com
VermontJobs.net	http://www.vermontjobs.net

Virginia

BlueRidgeHelpWanted.com	http://regionalhelpwanted.com/blue-ridge-jobs
Career Pro	http://www.career-pro.com
CharlottesvilleHelpWanted.com	http://regionalhelpwanted.com/charlottesville-jobs
The Daily Progress (Charlottesville)	http://www2.dailyprogress.com
Danville Register Bee	http://www2.godanriver.com

HamptonRoadsHelpWanted.com	http://regionalhelpwanted.com/hampton-roads-jobs
HarrisonburgHelpWanted.com	http://regionalhelpwanted.com/harrisonburg-jobs
HighlandsHelpWanted.com	http://regionalhelpwanted.com/highlands-virginia-jobs
Human Resource Association of the National Capital Area Job Bank Listing	http://www.hra-nca.org
JobFetch.com	http://www.jobfetch.com
LocalVirginiaJobs.com	http://www.localvirginiajobs.com
Miedical Society of Virginia	http://jobboard.msv.org
The News-Advance (Lynchburg)	http://www2.newsadvance.com
North Virginia Job Openings	http://www.northern-viriginia.jobopenings.net
NRVHelpWanted.com	http://regionalhelpwanted.com/new-river-valley-va-jobs
Pilot Online	http://pilotonline.com
RichmondHelpWanted.com	http://regionalhelpwanted.com/richmond-jobs
Richmond Preferred Jobs	http://richmond.preferredjobs.com
Richmond Times-Dispatch	http://www2.timesdispatch.com
Roanoke.com	http://www.roanoke.com
RoanokeValleyJobs.com	http://www.roanokevalleyjobs.com
ShenandoahValleyHelpWanted.com	http://regionalhelpwanted.com/shenandoah-valley-jobs
TriCitiesHelpWanted.com	http://regionalhelpwanted.com/tri-cities-jobs
University of Virginia Career Planning and Placement	http://www.hrs.virginia.edu
Virginia Biotechnology Association	http://vabio.org
Virginia-Jobs	http://www.virginia-jobs.com
Virginia Working 925	http://www.working925.com
Virginian-Pilot (Norfolk)	http://pilotonline.com
WashingtonJobs.com	http://www.washingtonpost.com
Washington and Lee University	http://www.wlu.edu

Washington

American Academy of Pediatrics - Washington Chapter	http://careers.wcaap.org
BetterTriCityJobs.com	http://www.bettertricityjobs.com
The Columbian (Vancouver)	http://www.columbian.com
Communicators & Marketers Jobline (Seattle & Puget Sound)	http://cmjobline.org
Geebo	http://www.geebo.com
JobDango.com	http://www.jobdango.com
LocalWashingtonJobs.com	http://washington.jobing.com
Navigator Online	http://www.lwhra.org
The News Tribune (Tacoma)	http://www.thenewstribune.com
NorthwestWashingtronHelpWanted.com	http://regionalhelpwanted.com/northwest-washington-jobs
The Olympian (Olympia)	http://www.theolympian.com
PugetSoundHelpWanted.com	http://regionalhelpwanted.com/puget-sound-jobs
SeattleJobs	http://www.seattlejobs.com
Seattle Post-Intelligencer	http://www.seattlepi.com
SeattleTacomaJobs.com	http://www.seattletacomajobs.com
Seattle Times	http://www.nwjobs.com
SoutheasternWashingtonHelpWanted.com	http://regionalhelpwanted.com/southeastern-washington-jobs
SpokaneHasJobs.com	http://spokane.careerlink.com
SpokaneHelpWanted.com	http://regionalhelpwanted.com/spokane-jobs
SpokaneJobFinder.com	http://www.spokanejobfinder.com
The Spokesman-Review (Spokane)	http://www.spokane.net
University of Washington	http://www.washington.edu
Washington Biotechnology & Biomedical Association	http://www.wabio.com
Washington Multi-Family Housing Association	http://careers.wmfha.org
Washington State Radiological Society	http://careers.wsrs.org
Washington Workforce	http://access.wa.gov/employment/index.aspx
WesternWashingtonHelpWanted.com	http://regionalhelpwanted.com/western-washington-jobs

YakimaHelpWanted.com   http://regionalhelpwanted.com/yakima-jobs

YakimaValleyJobs.com   http://www.yakimavalleyjobs.com

West Virginia

BetterCharlestonJobs.com   http://www.bettercharlestonjobs.com

BluefieldHelpWanted.com   http://regionalhelpwanted.com/bluefield-jobs

Charlestown Daily Mail   http://www.dailymail.com

CharlestonHelpWanted.com   http://regionalhelpwanted.com/charleston-jobs

Clarksburg Exponent Telegram   http://www.cpubco.com

The Dominion Post (Morgantown)   http://www.dominionpost.com

GreenBrierValleyHelpWanted.com   http://regionalhelpwanted.com/green-brier-valley-jobs

HuntingtonAshlandHelpWanted.com   http://regionalhelpwanted.com/huntington-ashland-jobs

OhioValleyHelpWanted.com   http://regionalhelpwanted.com/ohio-valley-jobs

SouthernWestVirginiaJobs.com   http://www.southernwestvirginiajobs.com

Times West Virginian (Fairmont)   http://timeswv.com

WestVaHelpWanted.com   http://regionalhelpwanted.com/west-virginia-jobs

WestVirginiaJobs.com   http://www.westvirginiajobs.com

West Virginia Orthopaedic Society   http://careers.wvos.org

Wheeling News-Register   http://www.news-register.com

Wisconsin

CareerBoard.com   http://www.careerboard.com

ChippewaValleyHelpWanted.com   http://regionalhelpwanted.com/chippewa-valley-jobs

FetchMeAJob.com   http://www.fetchmeajob.com

Green Bay Press Gazette   http://www.greenbaypressgazette.com

HelpWantedMadison.com   http://regionalhelpwanted.com/madison-jobs

HelpWantedMilwaukee.com   http://regionalhelpwanted.com/milwaukee-jobs

HelpWantedWisconsin.com   http://regionalhelpwanted.com/wisconsin-jobs

Jobing.com   http://wisconsin.jobing.com

The Journal Times (Racine)	http://www.journaltimes.com
La Crosse Tribune	http://www.lacrossetribune.com
LocalCareers.com	http://www.localcareers.com
Milwaukee Journal Sentinel	http://www.jsonline.com
NEWHelpWanted.com	http://regionalhelpwanted.com/northeast-wisconsin-jobs
SouthValleyHelpWanted.com	http://regionalhelpwanted.com/south-valley-wi-jobs
University of Wisconsin-Madison School of Business Career Center	http://www.bus.wisc.edu/career
Wisconsin.gov	http://www.wisconsin.gov/state
Wisconsin Academy of Family Physicians	http://www.fpjobsonline.org
Wisconsin Biotechnology Association	http://www.wisconsinbiotech.org
Wisconsin Dental Association	http://careers.wda.org
Wisconsin Department of Workforce Development	http://www.dwd.state.wi.us
WisconsinJobNetwork.com	http://www.wisconsinjobnetwork.com
Wisconsin Medical Society	http://www.wisconsinmedicalsociety.org
Wisconsin State Journal (Madison)	http://host.madison.com

Wyoming

Douglas Budget	http://www.douglas-budget.com
WyomingatWork.com	https://www.wyomingatwork.com
WyomingHelpWanted.com	http://regionalhelpwanted.com/wyoming-jobs
WyomingJobs.com	http://www.wyomingjobs.com
Wyoming News.com	http://www.wyomingnews.com
Wyoming Tribune-Eagle	http://www.wyomingnews.com

Religion

BaptistLife	http://www.baptistlife.com
CatholicJobs.com	http://www.catholicjobs.com
CatholicSource	http://www.catholicsource.org
Catho Online [Brazil]	http://www.catho.com.br

ChristiaNet	http://www.christianet.com
Christian Help	http://www.christianhelp.org
Christian Jobs	http://www.christianjobs.com
ChurchEmployment.com	http://www.churchemployment.com
ChurchJobs.net	http://www.churchjobs.net
Church Jobs Online	http://www.churchjobsonline.com
Church Music Jobs	http://www.churchmusicjobs.com
ChurchStaffing.com	http://www.churchstaffing.com
Crosswalk.com	http://www.crosswalk.com
Gospel Communications Network	http://www.gospel.com
Jewish Community Center	http://www.jccworks.com
JewishJobs.com	http://www.jewishjobs.com
Jewish Vocational Service Career Moves	http://www.jvs-boston.org
Ministry Connect	http://ministryconnect.org
MinistryJobs.com	http://www.ministryjobs.com
MinistryEmployment.com	http://www.ministryemployment.com
MinistrySearch.com	http://www.ministrysearch.com
Orthodox Union Job Board	http://www.ou.org/jobs
PastorFinder.com	http://www.pastorfinder.com
Southern Baptist Convention Job Search	http://sbc.net/jobs/default.asp

Retail

AllRetailJobs.com	http://www.allretailjobs.com
Be The 1	http://www.bethe1.com
Careers in Grocery	http://www.careersingrocery.com
Chain Store Age	http://www.chainstoreage.com
Drug Store News	http://www.drugstorenews.com
ERTOnline.co.uk [United Kingdom]	http://www.ertonline.co.uk
RetailChoice.com [United Kingdom]	http://www.retailchoice.com
EmploymentGuide.com	http://www.employmentguide.com

GroceryHire	http://www.groceryhire.com
Grocer Jobs [United Kingdom]	http://jobs.thegrocer.co.uk
Home Channel News	http://www.homechannelnews.com
iHireRetail.com	http://www.ihireretail.com
Inc.com	http://www.inc.com
In Retail [United Kingdom]	http://www.inretail.co.uk
JobLoft.com [Canada]	http://www.jobloft.com
Jobs Retail	http://www.nowjob.com
JobsinRetail [United Kingdom]	http://www.jobsinretail.com
RetailCareers.co.uk [United Kingdom]	http://www.retailcareers.co.uk
RetailCareersNow	http://www.retailcareersnow.com
RetailJobs.ca [Canada]	http://www.retailjobs.ca
RetailingJobs.com	http://www.retailingjobs.com
Retailing Today	http://www.retailingtoday.com
RetailMoves.com [United Kingdom]	http://www.retailmoves.com

-S-

Sales and Marketing

Sales & Marketing-General

Adholes.com	http://adholes.com
BizJobs	http://www.bizjobs.com
Career Marketplace.com	http://www.careermarketplace.com
eChannelLinecareers.com [Canada]	http://www.echannellinecareers.com
eMarketing & Commerce's Job Connection	http://jobs.emarketingandcommerce.com
Grist.org	http://jobs.grist.org
The Internet Advertising Bureau Job Board	http://www.iab.net/jobs
Just Sales and Marketing [United Kingdom]	http://www.justsalesandmarketing.net
TheLadders.com	http://www.theladders.com

NationJob Network: Marketing and Sales Job Page   http://www.nationjob.com/marketing

Sales & Marketing Executives International Career Center   http://www.smei.org

Sales-Specific

ACareerinSales.com	http://www.acareerinsales.com
CareerinSales.com	http://www.careerinsales.com
HotSalesJobs.com	http://www.hotsalesjobs.com
iHireSalesPeople.com	http://www.ihiresalespeople.com
Jobs4Sales.com	http://www.jobs4sales.com
National Association of Sales Professionals Career Center	http://www.nasp.com
SalesAnimals.com	http://www.salesanimals.com
SalesCareersOnline.com	http://www.salescareersonline.com
Sales Classifieds	http://www.salesclassifieds.com
SalesEngineer.com	http://www.SalesEngineer.com
SalesGenomix.com	http://www.salesgenomix.com
SalesGravy.com	http://www.salesgravy.com
SalesJob.com	http://www.salesjob.com
SalesJobs.com	http://www.salesjobs.com
SalesJobs.ie [Ireland]	http://www.salesjobs.ie
SalesRecruits.com	http://cardbrowser.com
SalesRep.ca [Canada]	http://www.salesrep.ca
SalesRoles	http://www.salesroles.com
SalesTarget.co.uk [United Kingdom]	http://www.salestarget.co.uk
Sales Trax	http://www.salestrax.com
SalesWise.co.uk [United Kingdom]	http://www.saleswise.co.uk
SellingJobs.com/BrandingJobs.com	http://www.sellingjobs.com
Tigerjobs.com, Inc.	http://www.tigerjobs.com
Top Sales Positions	http://www.topsalespositions.com

Marketing-Specific

American Marketing Association Career Center	http://www.marketingpower.com
Audience Development	http://www.audiencedevelopment.com
Careers in Marketing	http://www.careers-in-marketing.com
Direct Marketing Association	http://www.the-dma.org/careercenter
eMarketing Silo	http://www.emarketingsilo.com
Event Design Magazine	http://www.eventdesignmag.com
Event Marketer	http://www.eventmarketer.com
iHireMarketing.com	http://www.ihiremarketing.com
Jobs In Marketing [United Kingdom]	http://www.jobs-in-marketing.co.uk
Marketing Career Network	http://www.marketingcareernetwork.com
MarketingHire.com	http://www.marketinghire.com
MarketingJobs.com	http://www.marketingjobs.com
MarketingPilgrim	http://www.marketingpilgrim.com
MarketingProfs	http://www.marketingprofs.com
Marketing Sherpa	http://www.marketingsherpa.com
MyMarketingJobs.com.au [Australia]	http://mymarketingjobs.com.au
New York American Markerting Association	http://www.nyama.org
Promotion Marketing Association Job Bank	http://www.pmalink.org/?jobbank
TalentZoo.com	http://www.talentzoo.com

Industry-Specific

Advertising Age's Online Job Bank	http://adage.com
Aeroindustryjobs	http://www.aeroindustryjobs.com
AllRetailJobs.com	http://www.allretailjobs.com
American Association of Pharmaceutical Sales Professionals	http://www.pharmaceuticalsales.org
Autojobs.com, Inc.	http://www.autojobs.com
BrokerHunter.com	http://www.brokerhunter.com
CallCenterCareers.com	http://www.callcentercareers.com
CallCenterJobs.com	http://www.callcenterjobs.com

CRN	http://www.crn.com/cwb/careers
DMjobs.co.uk [United Kingdom]	http://www.dmjobs.co.uk
GxPJobs.com [United Kingdom]	http://www.gxpjobs.com
iHireRetail.com	http://www.ihireretail.com
Industry Sales Pros	http://www.industrysalespros.com
InfoPresseJobs.com [Canada]	http://www.infopressejobs.com
In Retail [United Kingdom]	http://www.inretail.co.uk
InsuranceSalesJobs.com	http://www.insurancesalesjobs.com
InsuranceSalesWeb.com	http://www.insurancesalesweb.com
Job.com Retail JobNet	http://www.job.com
Just Tech Sales Jobs	http://www.justtechsalesjobs.com
Medical Marketing Association	http://www.mmanet.org
MedicalReps.com	http://www.medicalreps.com
MedicalSalesJobs.com	http://www.mymedicalsalesjobs.com
MedReps.com	http://www.medreps.com
Motorstaff.com	http://www.motorstaff.com
MyMedicalSalesJobs.com	http://www.mymedicalsalesjobs.com
National Association of Pharmaceutical Sales Representatives	http://www.napsronline.org
National Field Selling Association	http://www.nfsa.com
OnlineMarketingJobs.com [United Kingdom]	http://www.onlinemarketingjobs.com
NewHomeSalesJobs.com	http://www.newhomesalesjobs.com
Pharmacareers.co.uk [United Kingdom]	http://www.pharmacareers.co.uk
Pharmaceuticalrepjobs.com	http://pharmaceuticalrepjobs.org
Retail-Recruiter	http://www.retail-recruiter.com
RetailingJobs.com	http://www.retailingjobs.com
Software & IT Sales Employment Review	http://cardbrowser.com
SoftwareSalesJobs.com	http://www.softwaresalesjobs.com
Television Bureau of Advertising	http://www.tvb.org/nav/build_frameset.aspx

Science/Scientists

Access-Science Jobs [United Kingdom]	www.access-sciencejobs.co.uk
American Association for the Advancement of Science	http://aas.org/career
American Association of Brewing Chemists	www.asbcnet.org
American Association of Cereal Chemists	www.aaccnet.org
American Association of Pharmaceutical Scientists	www.aapspharmaceutica.com
American Association of Physics Teachers	http://www.aapt.org
American Chemical Society	http://portal.acs.org/portal/acs/corg/content
American Institute of Biological Sciences	http://www.aibs.org
American Physical Society	http://www.aps.org
American Institute of Physics PhysicsToday Jobs	http://www.physicstoday.org/jobs
American Meteorological Society Employment Announcements	http://www.ametsoc.org
American Psychological Society	http://www.psychologicalscience.org/jobs
American Society of Agronomy	http://www.agronomy.org
American Society of Animal Science	http://www.fass.org/job.asp
American Society for Cell Biology	http://www.ascb.org
American Society for Clinical Laboratory Science	http://www.ascls.org
American Society for Clinical Pathology	http://www.ascp.org
American Society of Clinical Pharmacology and Therapeutics	http://www.ascpt.org
American Society for Microbiology	http://www.asm.org
American Society for Gravitational and Space Biology	http://asgsb.org/index.php
American Society of Horticultural Science HortOpportunities	http://www.ashs.org/db/hortopportunities/assist_listing.lasso
American Society of Plant Biologists	http://www.aspb.org
American Water Works Association Career Center (Water Jobs)	http://www.awwa.org
Animal-job.co.uk [United Kingdom]	http://www.animal-job.co.uk
Association for Applied Human Pharmacology [Germany]	http://www.agah.info
Bay Bio	http://www.baybio.org
Bermuda Institute of Ocean Sciences	http://www.bios.edu

BioCareers.co.za [South Africa]	http://www.biocareers.co.za
Biofind	http://www.biofind.com
BioOptics World	http://www.bioopticsowrld.com
Bio Research Online	http://www.bioresearchonline.com
BioSource Technical Service	http://manpowerprofessional.com/us/en/default.jsp
BioSpace	http://www.biospace.com
Biotechnology Calendar, Inc.	http://www.biotech-calendar.com
Bioview	http://www.bioview.co.il
Board of Physics and Astronomy	http://www7.nationalacademies.org/careers
California Agricultural Technical Institute ATI-Net	http://www.atinet.org
California Separation Science Society	http://www.casss.org
Cell Press Online	http://www.cell.com/cellpress
Center for Biological Computing	http://papa.indstate.edu
Chemistry & Industry	http://www.soci.org
ChemJobs.net	http://www.chemjobs.net
Citysearch.com-Biotech	http://www.biofind.com
Controlled Release Society	http://www.controlledrelease.org
DataScienceCentral.com	http://www.datasciencecentral.com
Earth Works	http://www.earthworks-jobs.com
Environmental Careers World	http://www.environmentaljobs.com
Environmental Careers Bulletin Online	http://www.eceajobs.com
Environmental Jobs & Careers	http://www.ejobs.org
Environmental Careers Organization	http://www.eco.org
FASEB Career Resources	http://www.faseb.org
GeoWebServices-RocketHire	http://www.geowebservices.com
GIS Jobs Clearinghouse	http://www.gjc.org
GxPJobs.com [United Kingdom]	http://www.gxpjobs.com
History of Science Society	http://www.hssonline.org
HUM-MOLGEN [Germany]	http://hum-molgen.org/positions
iHireChemists.com	http://www.ihirechemists.com

Institute of Physics	http://www.iop.org
International Society for Molecular Plant-Microbe Interactions	http://www.ismpminet.org/career
The Internet Pilot to Physics	http://physicsworld.com
Jobscience Network	http://jobs.jobscience.com
Jobs.ac.uk [United Kingdom]	http://www.jobs.ac.uk
Jobs in Chemistry	http://www.jobsinchemistry.com
LaboratoryNetwork.com	http://www.laboratorynetwork.com
Laser Focus World	http://www.laserfocusworld.com
The London Biology Network [United Kingdom]	http://www.biolondon.org.uk
MeteorologyJobs	http://www.meteorologyjobs.com
National Organization of Black Chemists and Chemical Engineers	http://www.engin.umich.edu/societies/nobcche
National Society of Black Physicists	http://www.nsbp.org
National Weather Association Job Corner	http://www.nwas.org
Naturejobs	http://www.nature.com
New Scientist	http://www.newscientist.com
NukeWorker.com	http://www.nukeworker.com
Oceanography Society	http://www.tos.org
OSU: College of Food, Agricultural and Environmental Sciences	http://cfaes.osu.edu/current-students/launch-your-career
Optics.org	http://optics.org/cws/home
Organic Chemistry Jobs Worldwide [Belgium]	http://www.organicworldwide.net/jobs
Physics & Astronomy Online	http://physlink.com
PhysicsToday.org	http://www.physicstoday.org
Plant Pathology Online APSnet	http://www.scisoc.org
Plasma Gate [Israel]	http://plasma-gate.weizmann.ac.il
Poly Sort	http://www.polysort.com
Royal Society of Chemistry	http://jobs.rsc.org/careers/jobsearch
RPh on the Go	http://www.rphonthego.com
RPhrecruiter.com	http://www.rphrecruiter.com
Sci Central	http://www.scicentral.com

Science Careers	http://sciencecareers.sciencemag.org
ScienceCareers.org [United Kingdom]	http://sciencecareers.sciencemag.org
Sciencejobs.com	http://www.newscientistjobs.com
The Science Jobs	http://www.thesciencejobs.com
Science Online	http://www.scienceonline.org
Science Professional Network	http://sciencecareers.sciencemag.org
ScientistWorld.com [United Kingdom]	http://www.scientistworld.com
Scijobs.org	http://sciencecareers.sciencemag.org
Society for Laboratory Automation and Screening	http://careers.slas.org
Society of Mexican American Engineers and Scientists	http://www.maes-natl.org
Society for Neuroscience	http://neurojobs.sfn.org
Space Jobs	http://www.spacejobs.com
Spectroscopy Magazine	http://www.spectroscopyonline.com
SPIE Web-International Society for Optical Engineering	http://spie.org/app/buyersguide/index.aspx
Student Conservation Association	http://www.thesca.org
Texas A&M Poultry Science Department	http://gallus.tamu.edu
Texas Healthcare & Bioscience Institute	http://www.thbi.org
Utah Life Sciences Association	http://www.utahlifescience.com
Vision Systems Design	http://www.vision-systems.com
Weed Science Society of America WeedJobs: Positions in Weed Science	http://www.wssa.net

Search Engines-Employment

Beyond	http://www.beyond.com
CareerJet	http://www.careerjet.com
Check4Jobs [United Kingdom]	http://www.check4jobs.com
Employment Crossing	http://www.employmentcrossing.com
Finn.no [Norway]	http://www.finn.no
FlipDog	http://www.flipdog.com
Fusejobs.co.uk [United Kingdom]	http://www.fusejobs.co.uk

Gad Ball	http://www.gadball.com
Getjob.de [Germany]	http://www.getjob.de
GetTheJob.com	http://www.getthejob.com
Google Base	http://www.google.com/base
Hound	http://www.hound.com
ICjobs.de [Germany]	http://www.icjobs.de
Indeed	http://www.indeed.com
Indeed.co.uk [United Kingdom]	http://www.indeed.co.uk
ItsMyCareer.com	http://www.itsmycareer.com
JobAhoy [United Kingdom]	http://www.jobahoy.com
Jobalot.com	http://www.jobalot.con
Jobbi	http://www.jobbi.com
Jobbporten.se [Sweden]	http://jobbporten.se
JobCentral.com	http://www.jobcentral.com
JobCrawler.it [Italy]	http://www.jobcrawler.it
JobIndex.dk [Denmark]	http://www.jobindex.dk
Jobrapido [Italy]	http://www.jobrapido.it
Jobrapido.es [Spain]	http://www.jobrapido.es
JobSafari.se [Sweden]	http://www.jobbsafari.se
JobsCareers24	http://www.jobscareers24.com
JobsOnline	http://www.jobsonline.com
Jobster	http://www.jobster.com
JobsTodayNetwork.com	http://www.jobstodaynetwork.com
Juju	http://www.juju.com
JumpToJobs [Ireland]	http://www.jumptojobs.co.uk
Keljob.com [France]	http://www.keljob.com
Kimeta.de [Germany]	http://www.kimeta.de
Lokus.se [Sweden]	http://lokus.se/Exp_SearchStart_all.asp?
Miltrabajos.com [Spain]	http://www.miltrabajos.com
NiceJob.ca [Canada]	http://www.nicejob.ca

1Job.co.uk [United Kingdom]	http://www.1job.co.uk
Oodle.com	http://www.oodle.com
Opcionempleo.com [Spain]	http://www.opcionempleo.com
Purjob.com [France]	http://www.purjob.com
Rubrikk.no [Norway]	http://www.rubrikk.no
SearchforJobs.com	http://www.searchforjobs.com
Second Life Jobfinder	http://www.SLJobFinder.com
SimplyHired	http://www.simplyhired.com
Srchnkd.com	http://www.srchnkd.com
TipTopJob	http://www.tiptopjob.com
TopUSAJob	http://www.topusajob.com
Trovit.it [Italy]	http://www.trovit.it
Trovit.co.uk [United Kingdom]	http://www.trovit.co.uk
Trovit.es [Spain]	http://www.trovit.es
Wink.com	http://www.wink.com
Workey.se [Sweden]	http://www.workey.se
Workhound.co.uk [United Kingdom]	http://www.workhound.co.uk
WorkShopping.com [Sweden]	http://www.workshopping.com
WorkTree.com	http://www.worktree.com
Worldcircle.com [United Kingdom]	http://www.worldcircle.com

Search Firms/Staffing Agencies/Recruiters

Accounting Position	http://www.taftsearch.com
AD&A Software Jobs Home Page	http://softwarejobs.4jobs.com
Adecco	http://www.adecco.com
All Advantage	http://www.alladvantage.com
Alpha Systems	http://www.jobbs.com
American Staffing Association	http://www.staffingtoday.net
Aquent Partners	http://aquent.us
Association of Executive Search Consultants	http://www.bluesteps.com

The Beardsley Group	http://www.beardsleygroup.com
Best Internet Recruiter	http://www.bestrecruit.com
J. Boragine & Associates	http://www.jboragine.com
BountyJobs.com	http://www.bountyjobs.com
Buck Systems Inc.	http://www.bisinc.com
The Caradyne Group	http://www.pcsjobs.com/jobs.htm
Career Image Associates	http://www.career-image.com
Champion Personnel System	http://www.championjobs.com
Chancellor & Chancellor's	http://www.chancellor.com
Comforce	http://www.comforce.com
Corporate Staffing Group, Inc.	http://www.corporatestaffing.com
Creative Focus	http://www.focusstaff.com
Daley Consulting & Search/Daley Technical Search	http://www.dpsearch.com.sg
Darwin Partners	http://www.seek-consulting.com
Datalake-IT.com	http://www.datalake-IT.com
Dawson & Dawson Consultants, Inc.	http://www.dawson-dawson.com
EPCglobal.com	http://www.epcglobal.com
Erickson & Associates, Inc.	http://www.nursesearch.com
Executive Placement Services	http://www.execplacement.com
Fogarty and Associates, Inc.	http://www.fogarty.com
Gables	http://www.gablessearch.com
Global Careers	http://www.globalcareers.com
Hamilton, Jones & Koller [Australia]	http://www.hjk.com.au
Headhunters 4u	http://www.headhunters.com
Healthcare Recruiters	http://www.hcrnetwork.com
The HEC Group	http://hec-group.com
HireMeNow.com	http://www.hiremenow.com
Hire Quality	http://www.hire-quality.com
HR Connections	http://www.hrconnections.com
Hyman Associates	http://www.hymanassociatesconsulting.com

Ian Martin Limited	http://www.iml.com
Insurance National Search, Inc.	http://www.insurancerecruiters.com
Insurance Overload Systems	http://www.iosstaffing.com
Inter-City Personnel Associates	http://www.ipaservices.com
Int-Exec.com	http://www.int-exec.com
Laser Computer Recruitment [United Kingdom]	http://www.laserrec.co.uk
Life Work, Inc.'s Military Recruiting Group	http://www.lifeworkinc.com
The Little Group	http://www.littlegroup.com
Made-In-China.com	http://www.made-in-china.com
Manpower	http://www.manpower.com
Manpower.com.au [Australia]	http://www.manpower.com.au
MarketPro	http://www.marketproinc.com
McGregor Boyall [United Kingdom]	http://www.mcgregor-boyall.com
Medical Sales Associates	http://www.msajobs.com
Metroplex Association of Personnel Consultants	http://www.recruitingfirms.com
Mindsource Software	http://www.mindsrc.com
National Banking Network	http://www.banking-financialjobs.com
On-Campus Resources, Inc.	http://www.on-campus.com
1to1media.com	http://www.1to1media.com
Pacific Coast Recruiting	http://www.pacificcoastrecruiting.com
People Connect Staffing	http://www.peopleconnectstaffing.com
Power Brokers	http://www.powerbrokersllc.com
Premier Staffing, Inc.	http://www.premier-staff.com
Priority Search.com	http://www.prioritysearch.com
Pro Match of Silicon Valley	http://www.promatch.org
ProQwest, Inc.	http://www.proqwest.com
Provident Search Group	http://www.dpjobs.com
RAI	http://www.raijobs.com
Recruit Employment Services	http://www.recruitemployment.co.uk
Recruiter Networks	http://www.recruiternetworks.com

Recruiters for Christ	http://www.edmondspersonnel.com
RecruitingOptions	http://www.recruitingoptions.net
Robert Half	http://www.roberthalffinance.com
Rollins Search Group	http://www.rollinssearch.com
Romac International	http://www.romacintl.com
Roz Goldfarb Associates	http://www.rgarecruiting.com
Sanford Rose Associates	http://www.sanfordrose.com
Self Opportunity	http://www.selfopportunity.com
Semper International	http://www.semperllc.com
Silverman McGovern Staffing	http://www.silvermanmcgovern.com
SnagAJob	http://www.snagajob.com
Solomon Page Executive Search	http://www.spges.com
Sonasearch	http://www.sonasearch.com
Spherion Corporation	http://www.spherion.com
Stanley, Barber & Associates	http://stanleyb.net
Student Search System, Inc.	http://www.studentsearch.com
TechNix Inc. [Canada]	http://www.technix.ca
TMP Worldwide	http://www.tmp.com
Volt Information Sciences	http://www.volt.com
Winter, Wyman & Co.	http://www.winterwyman.com
The Virtual Coach	http://www.virtual-coach.com
Yoh Company	http://www.yoh.com
Amy Zimmerman & Associates, Inc.	http://www.weemployyou.net

Security/Building & Business

Fire and Security Jobs	http://www.fireandsecurityjobs.net
iHireSecurity.com	http://www.ihiresecurity.com
Insecure.org	http://seclists.org
Just Security Jobs	http://www.justsecurityjobs.com

LPjobsFREE	http://www.lpjobsfree.com
Maritime Security Jobs	http://www.maritimesecurityjobs.com
Private Security Jobs	http://www.privatesecurityjobs.com
Public Safety Jobs	http://www.publicsafetyjobs.com
SecurityFocus.com	http://www.securityfocus.com
SecurityJobs.com	http://www.securityjobs.com
Security Jobs Network	http://www.securityjobs.net
SecurityJobsToday.com	http://www.securityjobstoday.com
Transportation Security Administration	http://www.tsa.gov

Senior Workers/Mature Workers/"Retired" Workers

AARP	http://www.aarp.org/work
BoomerCareer.com	http://www.boomercareer.com
Boomer Jobs	http://www.boomerjobs.com
50Connect.co.uk [United Kingdom]	http://www.50connect.co.uk
GeezerJobs.com	http://www.geezerjobs.com
National Older Worker Career Center	http://nowcc.org
PrimeCB.com	http://www.primecb.com
RetiredBrains	http://www.retiredbrains.com
TheRetiredWorker.com	http://www.theretiredworker.com
RetirementJobs.com	http://www.retirementjobs.com
SeniorJobBank.com	http://www.seniorjobbank.com
Seniors4Hire.org	http://www.seniors4hire.org
SeniorsforJobs.com	http://www.seniorsforjobs.com
Workforce50	http://www.workforce50.com

Social Media Sites (See also Associations)

Academia.edu	http://www.academia.edu
Bebo	http://www.bebo.com

Biznik	http://www.biznik.com
BraveNewTalent	http://www.bravenewtalent.com
Facebook	http://www.facebook.com
Google+	http://www.google.com
Ibibio [India]	http://www.ibio.com
Jobcast.net	http://www.jobcast.net
Jobster	http://www.jobster.com
LinkedIn	http://www.linkedin.com
MeetUp	http://www.meetup.com
MyWorkster	http://www.myworkster.com
Networking for Professioals	http://www.networkingforprofessionals.com
Perfect Business	http://www.perfectbusiness.com
Plaxo	http://www.plaxo.com
Qapacity [Spain]	http://www.qapacity.com
Ryze	http://www.ryze.com
ScienceStage	http://www.sciencestage.com
StartUpNation	http://www.startupnation.com
SunZu	http://www.sunzu.com
Talkbiznow	http://www.talkbiznow.com
TweetMyJobs	http://www.tweetmyjobs.com
Twitter	http://www.twitter.com
UpSwing	http://www.upswing.com
Work4Labs	http://www.work4labs.com
Xing [Germany]	http://www.xing.com
Yammer	http://www.yammer.com
Yelp, Inc.	http://www.yelp.com
Ziggs	http://www.ziggs.com

Social Service/Human Service

ExOffenderReentry.com	http://www.exoffenderreentry.com
Georgia Department of Human Resources	http://www.dhrjobs.com
HSCareers.com	http://www.hscareers.com
iHireSocialServices.com	http://www.ihiresocialservices.com
Human Services Career Network	http://www.hscareers.com
JobsinSocialWork [United Kingdom]	http://www.jobsinsocialwork.com
Jobs.ThirdSector.co.uk [United Kingdom]	http://jobs.thirdsector.co.uk
Louisiana Assisted Living Association	http://careers.laassisted.org
National Association of Social Workers Joblink	http://joblink.socialworkers.org
The New Social Worker's Online Career Center	http://www.socialworker.com
North American Association of Christians in Social Work	http://jobnet.nacsw.org
SocialService.com	http://www.socialservice.com
socialservicenetwork.com	http://www.socialservicenetwork.com
SocialWork.com	http://www.socialwork.com
SocialWorkJobBank.com	http://www.socialworkjobbank.com
Tripod	http://www.tripod.lycos.com
Worklife Solutions	http://www.worklifesolutions.com

Statistical & Math

American Statistical Association Statistics Career Center	http://www.amstat.org/careers
icrunchdata.com	http://www.icrunchdata.com
Mathematical Association of America	http://www.mathclassifieds.com
Math-Jobs.com	http://www.math-jobs.com
MathJobs.org	http://www.mathjobs.org
Phds.org	http://www.phds.org
San Francisco Bay Area ASA	http://www.sfasa.org/joblist.htm
StatisticsJobs.com	http://www.statisticsjobs.com
Statistics Jobs in Australia & New Zealand	http://www.statsci.org/jobs
StatsCareers	http://www.statscareers.com

-T-

Telecommunications

Active Wireless	http://www.activewireless.com
Alden Systems	http://www.telcorock.com
Anywhere You Go	http://www.anywhereyougo.com
BroadbandCareers.com	http://www.broadband-careers.com
Cellular-News.com	http://www.cellular-news.com
CTIA	http://www.ctia.org
Fierce Wireless	http://www.fiercewireless.com
MobileWirelessJobs.com	http://www.mobilewirelessjobs.com
PlanetRecruit [United Kingdom]	http://www.planetrecruit.com
RF Job Network	http://www.rfjn.com
Telecom Careers	http://www.telecomcareers.net
Telecom Jobs	http://www.telecomcareers.net
Telecom Jobsite	http://www.telecomjobsite.com
Telecommunication Industry Association Online	http://www.tiaonline.org
Telepeople	http://www.telepeople.net
Teletron	http://www.telecomcareers.com
Utility Jobs Online	http://www.utilityjobsonline.com
Wirelessmobile-Jobsboard.com [United Kingdom]	http://www.wirelessmobile-jobsboard.com
Workaholics4Hire.com	http://www.workaholics4hire.com

Telecommuting

FlexJobs	http://www.flexjobs.com
GenerationMom.com	http://www.generationmom.com
MommysPlace.net	http://www.mommysplace.net
NextJobAtHome	http://www.nextjobathome.com
Telecommuting Jobs	http://www.tjobs.com

Telecommuting Techies	http://www.telecommuting-techies.com
TeleworkRecruiting.com	http://www.teleworkrecruiting.com
VirtualAssistants.com	http://www.virtualassistants.com
VirtualVocations	http://www.virtualvocations.com
WhyDoWork	http://www.whydowork.com

Trade Organizations

Ambulatory Surgery Center Association	http://careercenter.ascassociation.org
America's Health Insurance Plans	http://careersource.ahiphiwire.org
American Association of Tissue Banks	http:jobcenter.aatb.org
American Hospital Association	http://careers.aha.org
American Industrial Hygiene Association	http://www.aiha.org
Arizona Hospital and Healthcare Association AZHealthJobs	http://www.azhha.org
Assisted Living Federation of America	http://www.alfa.org
Biotechnology Industry Organization	http://www.bio.org
Building Industry Exchange	http://www.building.org
California Primary Care Association	http://jobs.cliniccareers.org
Children's Hospital Association	http://careers.childrenshospitals.net
Colorado Hospital Association	http://healthcarecareers.cha.com
Drilling Research Institute	http://www.drillers.com
Drug Information Association Employment Opportunities	http://www.diahome.org
Equipment Leasing and Finance Association	http://www.elfaonline.org
Florida Society of Ambulatory Surgery Centers	http://careers.fsasc.org
Financial Executives Institute Career Center	http://www.financialexecutives.org
Freestanding Ambulatory Surgery Center Association of Tennessee	http://jobboard.fascatn.org
GamesIndustry.biz	http://www.gamesindustry.biz
Georgia Society of Ambulatory Surgery Center	http://jobboard.gsasc.org
Health Facilities Association of Maryland	http://careers.hfam.org
Hospital Association of Sourthern California	http://careers.allhealthinc.com

Institute of Food Science & Technology	http://www.ifst.org
Institute of Real Estate Management Jobs Bulletin	http://www.irem.org
International Association of Conference Centres	http://www.iacconline.org
International Association of Employment Web Sites	http://www.employmentwebistes.org
International Map Trade Association	http://www.maptrade.org
Maryland Hospital Association	http://healthcarecareers.mhaonline.org
Media Communications Association International Job Hotline	http://www.mca-i.org
Metropolitan Chicago Healthcare Council	http://careerboard.mchc.org
Michigan Health & Hospital Association	http://careers.mha.org
National Association of Rehabilitation Providers and Agencies	http://careers.naranet.org
National Association for Printing Leadership	http://www.napl.org
National Contract Management Association	http://www.ncmahq.org
National Defense Industrial Association	http://www.defensejobs.com
National Federation of Paralegal Associations Career Center	http://www.paralegals.org
National Field Selling Association	http://www.nfsa.com
National Fire Prevention Association Online Career Center	http://www.nfpa.org
National Sleep Foundation	http://jobs.sleepfoundation.org
National Weather Association	http://www.nwas.org
New Jersey Hospital Association	http://healthjobs.njha.com
New Mexico Hospital Association	http://careers.nmhanet.org
Petroleum Services Association of Canada Employment	http://www.psac.ca
Physicians Hospitals of America	http://www.physicianhospitals.org/?CareerOpportunities
Risk & Insurance Management Society Careers	http://www.rims.org
Securities Industry Association Career Resource Center	http://www.sifma.com
Sheet Metal and Air Conditioning Contractor's Association	http://www.smacna.org
Society of Automotive Engineers Job Board	http://www.careercenter.sae.org
Society of Risk Analysis Opportunities	http://www.sra.org/opportunities.php

South Carolina Ambulatory Surgery Center	http://jobboard.scasc.org
South Florida Hospital and Healthcare Association	http://healthcareers.sfhha.com
SteelontheNet.com	http://www.steelonthenet.com
Technical Association of the Pulp & Paper Industry Career Center	http://www.careers.tappi.org
Telecommunication Industry Association Online	http://www.tiaonline.org
West Virginia Health Care Association	http://careers.wvhca.org

Training

American Society for Law Enforcement Training	http://www.aslet.org
American Society for Training & Development Job Bank	http://www.jobs.astd.org
Instructional Systems Technology Jobs	http://www.indiana.edu
International Society for Performance Improvement Job Bank	http://www.ispi.org
OD Network	http://www.odnetwork.org
Saba	http://www.saba.com
San Francisco State University Instructional Technologies	http://www.itec.sfsu.edu
TrainingConsortium.com	http://www.trainingconsortium.com
Training Forum	http://www.trainingforum.com
Trainingjob.com	http://www.trainingjob.com

Transportation, Land & Maritime

The Airline Employment Assistance Corps	http://www.avjobs.com
All Port Jobs	http://www.allportjobs.com
All-Trucking-Jobs.com	http://www.all-trucking-jobs.com
AviaNation.com	http://www.avianation.com
Aviation Employee Placement Service	http://www.aeps.com
Aviation Employment.com	http://www.aviationemployment.com
BigRigJobs	http://www.bigrigjobs.com
Careers in Gear	http://www.careersingear.com

CDLjobs.com	http://www.cdljobs.com
Classatransport.com	http://www.classatransport.com
Climbto350.com	http://www.climbto350.com
DrivingJobsBoard.co.uk [United Kingdom]	http://www.drivingjobsboard.co.uk
FastLaneHIres	http://www.fastlanehires.com
Find a Pilot	http://www.findapilot.com
FindaTruckingJob.com	http://www.findatruckingjob.com
Get Maritime Jobs	http://www.getmaritimejobs.com
Get Taxi Limo Jobs	http://www.gettaxilimojobs.com
HotCDLJobs.com	http://www.hotcdljobs.com
International Seafarers Exchange JobXchange	http://www.jobxchange.com
Jobs4Trucking.com	http://www.jobs4trucking.com
JobsinLogistics.com	http://www.jobsinlogistics.com
JobsinTrucks.com	http://www.jobsintrucks.com
Just Rail [United Kingdom]	http://www.justrail.net
Layover.com	http://www.layover.com
Maritime Career	http://www.maritimecareer.com
Maritime Connector	http://www.maritime-connector.com
Maritime Employment	http://www.maritimeemployment.com
Maritime Job Search	http://www.maritimejobsearch.com
MaritimeJobs.com	http://www.maritimejobs.com
Maritime Security Jobs	http://www.maritimesecurityjobs.com
M-I-Link	http://www.m-i-link.com
National Parking Association	http://www.careers.npapark.org
National Truck Driving Jobs	http://www.nationaltruckdrivingjobs.com
Oil Offshore Marine	http://www.oil-offshore-marine.com
RailJobSearch.com [United Kingdom]	http://www.railjobsearch.com
RoadTechs.com	http://www.roadtechs.com
TransportationJobStore.com	http://www.transportationjobstore.com
TruckDriver.com	http://www.truckdriver.com
TruckerJobSearch.com	http://www.truckerjobsearch.com

Truck Net	http://www.truck.net
TruckingJobs	http://www.truckingjobs.com
Trucking Unlimited	http://www.truckingunlimited.com
TruckinJobs	http://www.truckinjobs.com

Travel & Tourism

Adventure Travel Trade Association	http://www.adventuretravel.biz
Hcareers	http://www.hcareers.com
Job.com	http://www.job.com
JobDango.com	http://www.jobdango.com
JobsinCatering [United Kingdom]	http://www.jobsincatering.com
Season Workers [United Kingdom]	http://www.seasonworkers.com
SeasonalEmployment.com	http://www.seasonalemployment.com
Seasonal-Jobs.com [United Kingdom]	http://www.seasonal-jobs.com
TravelJobSearch.com [United Kingdom]	http://www.traveljobsearch.com
Vault	http://www.vault.com
WomensJobList.com	http://www.womensjoblist.com

-V-

Video - Resume & Interview

Cuzie Corporation	http://www.cuzie.com
HireVue	http://www.hirevue.com
JobPlant.co.uk [United Kingdom]	http://www.jobplant.co.uk
MyPersonalBroadcast	http://www.mypersonalbroadcast.com
VideoJobShop	http://www.videojobshop.com
Workblast	http://www.workblast.com

Volunteer Positions

Do-It [United Kingdom]   http://www.do-it.org.uk

GlobalCrossroad.com   http://www.globalcrossroad.com

Jobs.ThirdSector.co.uk [United Kingdom]   http://www.jobs.thirdsector.co.uk

Monster.com   http://www.monster.com

Volunteer Match   http://www.volunteermatch.org

VSO Worldwide Vacancies [United Kingdom]   http://www.vso.org.uk

-Y-

Young Adult/Teen Positions

CanadaParttime.com   http://www.canadaparttime.com

CoolWorks.com   http://www.coolworks.com

GrooveJob.com   http://www.groovejob.com

HotRecruit [United Kingdom]   http://www.hotrecruit.com

InternsWanted   http://www.campusinternships.com

TheJobBox.com   http://www.thejobbox.com

JobDoggy.com   http://www.jobdoggy.com

MySpace   http://www.myspace.com/careers

Part-Time Jobs   http://www.gotajob.com

SnagaJob   http://www.snagajob.com

StudentJobs.gov   http://www.usajobs.gov/studentjobs

Summerjobs.com   http://www.summerjobs.com

Teens4Hire   http://www.teens4hire.org

TeenJobSection.com   http://www.teenjobsection.com